Industrial Organization In the
European Union

Industrial Organization In the European Union

Structure, Strategy, and the Competitive Mechanism

STEPHEN DAVIES and BRUCE LYONS

with
Catherine Matraves,
Laura Rondi,
Alessandro Sembenelli

and
Jordi Gual,
Leo Sleuwaegen,
Reinhilde Veugelers

CLARENDON PRESS · OXFORD
1996

Oxford University Press, Walton Street, Oxford OX2 6DP

Oxford New York
Athens Auckland Bangkok Bombay
Calcutta Cape Town Dar es Salaam Delhi
Florence Hong Kong Istanbul Karachi
Kuala Lumpur Madras Madrid Melbourne
Mexico City Nairobi Paris Singapore
Taipei Tokyo Toronto
and associated companies in
Berlin Ibadan

Oxford is a trade mark of Oxford University Press

Published in the United States
by Oxford University Press Inc., New York

British Library Cataloguing in Publication Data
Data available

Library of Congress Cataloguing in Publication Data
Data available
Davies, Stephen, 1948–
Industrial organization in the European Union : structure,
strategy, and the competitive mechanism / Stephen Davies and
Bruce Lyons ; with Catherine Matraves . . . [et al.].
Includes bibliographical references (p.   ).
1. Industrial organization—European Union countries.
2. European Union countries—Foreign economic relations.
3. European Union countries—Manufactures—Econometric models.
4. Competition, International. I. Lyons, Bruce. II. Title.
HD2844.D38 1996   338.6'094—dc20   96–570

ISBN 0–19–828973–1

1 3 5 7 9 10 8 6 4 2

Typeset by Alliance Phototypesetters
Printed in Great Britain
on acid-free paper by
Bookcraft, Bath Ltd.,
Midsomer Norton, Avon

CONTENTS

....

Part III: The Strategy of EU Firms

List of Authors

STEPHEN DAVIES, Economics Research Centre, School of Economic and Social Studies, University of East Anglia, Norwich

JORDI GUAL, IESE, University of Navarra, Barcelona; and Directorate General for Economic and Financial Affairs, European Commission

BRUCE LYONS, Economics Research Centre, School of Economic and Social Studies, University of East Anglia, Norwich.

CATHERINE MATRAVES, Economics Research Centre, School of Economic and Social Studies, University of East Anglia, Norwich

ELENOR RAGAZZI, CERIS-CNR, Torino

LAURA RONDI, CERIS-CNR, Torino

ALESSANDRO SEMBENELLI, CERIS-CNR, Torino

LEO SLEUWAEGEN, Departement Toegepaste Economische Wetenschappen, Katholieke Universiteit Leuven

REINHILDE VEUGELERS, Departement Toegepaste Economische Wetenschappen, Katholieke Universiteit Leuven

List of Figures

List of Tables

Preface

....

This book reports some of the results of a collaborative international project financed by the European Commission under its 'Stimulation Programme for Economic Science' (SPES) programme (project number CT900028). It was undertaken by research groups in the research centres at The University of East Anglia, Norwich (Davies and Lyons); CERIS, Torino (Rondi and Sembenelli); Katholieke Universiteit, Leuven (Sleuwaegen and Veugelers); IESE, Barcelona (Gual), GRASP, Rotterdam (Schenk), and The Free University Berlin (Schwalbach). The German Monopolies Commission, in the person of Rainer Feuerstack, also took a very keen interest and contributed generously in terms of both time and data. We offer sincere thanks to the Commission for its financial support, to the participating research centres for making their facilities available, and to the German Monopolies Commission. Needless to say, none of these organizations is responsible for what we have to say in this book.

This book has also been a collaborative effort, and most of the chapters have benefited, in some form or another, from inputs from most of the group as a whole. Nevertheless, it is possible to attribute the writing and initial ideas to individual authors, and their names can be found at the end of each chapter.

The two of us are responsible for the overall structure of the book, and for editing and sometimes applying gentle pressure on individual authors to 'toe the official line'. Laura Rondi and Alessandro Sembenelli have also contributed significantly in this respect.

As always in a large data-intensive project of this sort, the authors have benefited from the help of numerous research assistants in the various research centres. The large task of co-ordinating data entry, fielding numerous 'nitty gritty' enquiries on our classification policy, and training new assistants from across Europe was conducted with enormous energy, efficiency and (sometimes) charm, by Kate Matraves. We should also like to single out for special thanks Sue Clitheroe and Rita Sepelie—in the first two years of data collection, their contributions were outstanding in both quality and quantity. Others who have provided invaluable research assistance include: Henrik Abram, C. W. Chan, Anthony Dohr, Robert Hoffmann, Steven Humphrey, Melanie Lund, Abdelilah Kasem, Raf Koene, Dave Petts, Elena Ragazzi, Jeroen Schuiten, and Stefan Winter. Some day perhaps, they will look back with warmth and gratitude at the time spent ploughing through endless company reports and (even more excitingly) learning, by rote, the NACE industrial classification scheme. They can hold their heads high and cherish their expertise in knowing, for example, which 3-digit industry includes the manufacture of metal umbrella frames. Thanks are due to them all!

A final debt of gratitude is due to the fellow academics who have contributed their local knowledge, time and/or data at various points in the project. These include: Hans Schenk, Joachim Schwalbach, Jose Mata, Costas Bourlakis, Bruce Kogut, and various individuals in Eurostat.

We cannot leave this preface without briefly stepping aside from professional acknowledgements. For both of us, this research project has been immense fun. In spite of his limited accounting abilities, Bruce Lyons was responsible for the general administration and control of the project's finances. In drawing up the initial budget, he was sensible enough to allocate small sums for three working conferences at EIASM Brussels, IAE Barcelona, and CERIS Turin; and for junior research staff to visit other research centres. These activities turned out to be both academically stimulating and excellent bonding devices. We have fond memories of first-class (but still inexpensive!) menus, and of late nights spent in salubrious bars scattered around Europe discussing Economics (one in Barcelona is impossible to forget). More seriously, many personal friendships, as well as professional collaborations, have flourished as a result of this project. We hope that they will bear more academic fruit in future years as this research programme continues.

STEVE DAVIES
BRUCE LYONS

Norwich
July 1995

PART I

BACKGROUND

1

Introduction

....

1.1 Objectives

The subject of this book is the industrial organization of the manufacturing sector in the European Union (EU). Drawing on a research project which involved extensive data collection, it reports a wide range of new facts which, taken together, paint a far more detailed and comprehensive picture of firm and industry structure than anything previously available. For example, we look at concentration, integration, multinationality and diversification. However, the purpose of the book is not primarily descriptive. Underlying our efforts to describe structure is a theoretical thesis which owes much to recent developments in the academic industrial organization literature. This is that, by studying aspects of industrial structure, one can learn much about the nature of the competitive processes which have given rise to that structure. A key part of our story will be about the crucial influence of different competitive mechanisms: price, advertising, and R & D. Ultimately, therefore, the subject of our book is the analysis of competition in general, and in particular in the context of the European integration process.

A wide range of questions motivated our research. The academic and policy debates were moving from the national to the European stage, yet little was known about the workings of European industry as a whole. To what extent are particular industries in the EU concentrated in the hands of a few leading firms, and why? How has national government intervention affected the organization of industry? How dominant are the corporate giants of the EU, and how does European industry compare with its main competitor economies of the USA and Japan? Which industries cause the greatest potential concern for competition policy? To what extent do leading European firms diversify their production across a broad product range and/or geographically across member states? Is this diversification random or does it follow an industrial logic? What motivates firms to operate multinationally across the member states of the EU? To what extent is the EU a single economy, and are there fundamental national differences within it? Underpinning each of these questions is the view that, by understanding how the observed structure of industries and firms has come about, we learn much about the underlying competitive processes at work.

In other words, the book is driven by three broad objectives. The first is factual. In the very early stages of our research, we were struck by how little is known about the structure of individual industries and firms within manufacturing. In part, this is because there is still no unified Census of Production for the European Union as a whole. Thus, while the British or German or Italian economist may reach for her/his own census to discover the size distribution of firms producing, say, machine tools or chocolate in her own country, no comparable source records the share of the leading firms in that industry in the EU observed as a single entity[1]. However, the problem is not just the absence of a European Census. Even the traditional national production census is limited in the range and detail of information it provides: restrictions on disclosure of confidential firm-specific information have long thwarted industrial economists in their empirical analysis—even when confined to single countries.

Thus we started our research programme by posing ourselves a question. Would it be possible for us, as a group of academic economists, to assemble a database which would be capable of filling this void at the EU level? Ideally, it should: (i) treat the EU as a single entity, (ii) generate census-type statistics at the industry level on concentration and the size distribution of firms; and beyond this, (iii) include information on the corporate structures of individual, named firms. Obviously, it would be far beyond the reach of any single research project to conduct an EU-wide census, but we concluded that we could achieve most of what we wanted, within the budget of our project, by constructing a much more compact and targeted database. Initially, we set ourselves this task for a single year of observation, 1987. However, our ultimate sights were longer-term. Such a database would be much more valuable if it was amenable to replication for subsequent years, on an ongoing basis. At present, our database refers only to 1987, but it has been designed with future replication in mind.

Our second objective is more academic in its origins. We believe that the term 'structure' is often conceived of too narrowly. Indeed, in the early days of industrial organization (IO) as a sub-discipline of economics, structure was frequently used merely as a synonym for industrial concentration. This is much too restrictive. Not only does it remove from the agenda other elements of structure which are just as intrinsically interesting as concentration—for example, trade specialisation, multinationality, and diversification—but it also

---

[1] Throughout this volume, the European Union is defined as the twelve member states in 1987. Since then, of course, the number has expanded to fifteen and Germany has expanded due to reunification. It is possible to aggregate the censuses for individual member states (where they are available), and Eurostat has made important advances in recent years in harmonizing the statistics of the different member states in this area. But sheer aggregation is insufficient, as can be seen if we consider the time-honoured structural measure—the concentration ratio. Knowledge of just the five-firm concentration ratio in each of the twelve member states does not allow us to calculate this index for the EU as a whole. To do this, one would need information on the individual shares of each of the leaders in each of the countries, and knowledge of which firms have production in more than one country. This sort of information is not published, for reasons of confidentiality, in national statistics, and although this is a task which Eurostat might conceivably undertake, given access to the raw data collected for national production censuses, there is no prospect of this being imminent.

ignores potentially valuable information on the outcomes of competition. After all, if the nature of competition is a crucial formative influence on the size distribution of firms in a given industry, it is also likely to influence the nature of trade flows, and the ways that individual firms structure their operations. Thus our second objective is to pursue a broadly based concept of structure, which embraces theory and empirical traditions of international economics and corporate strategy, as well as industrial organization. However, this is not without its own pitfalls: by embracing a multi-dimensional definition of structure, we run the risk of losing internal analytical coherence. Therefore there is an imperative to model the various elements of structure in an interdependent way, within an integrated framework. We have attempted to avoid this danger by organizing our analysis (and the layout of the book itself) within a framework of three core decompositions. These are essentially accounting identities which connect the various structural dimensions.

Our third objective derives from the first two. As academics, we hope that much of what we have to say has an element of generality about it. So, in claiming that the book is about an 'analysis of competition', we imply that it is of wider relevance than just the particular case in hand—the EU in the late 1980s. Nevertheless, the European integration process is especially interesting to us, as a group of European economists, and the book is also intended specifically as a contribution to the contemporary debate on integration. We have already mentioned some of the particular questions which motivated our research— most of them touch on the effects of the integration process, and they often have a potential policy dimension. Therefore, we hope that our research will be seen as relevant to topical issues such as: the evaluation of the single market; the benefits from scale economies and the fears of monopolization by the giants of European industry; the role of non-EU multinationals; worries about German dominance; and so on.

Having set out our objectives, a note of justified modesty is undoubtedly called for! Nearly all of the data we have collected is confined to structure, and it is largely devoid of a dynamic dimension. Our justification for this is largely one of priorities—data requirements have been enormously time consuming. Necessarily however, this constrains the contribution we are able to make. With this stage of the work complete, performance measures (such as profitability, productivity and innovation) now move to the top of the agenda for future research; and the need to examine changes in structure, by replicating our work for at least a second year, is equally pressing. This is also on our research agenda.

The book is grouped into four parts. Part I is devoted to context setting for the EU in the late 1980s, Parts II and III explore the structure of EU industries and firms respectively. Thus, broadly speaking, Part II might be viewed as the traditional territory of international and industrial economics, whilst Part III is, superficially, more the domain of the corporate strategist. Needless to say, we view both as parts of the same integrated whole. Part IV points to a range of policy conclusions.

1.2. A Factual Background

The next chapter uses *published statistics* to put our study into context. We establish three perspectives: globally, by comparison of the EU with the USA and Japan; temporally, by tracing out the trends of the late 1980s and early 1990s in merger activity, foreign direct investment and trade; and disaggregating, by establishing the pattern of production and trading relationships between member states and across industries. This serves as a convenient stylization which helps to inform later chapters, but it also illustrates, by default, the limited scope of data currently in the public domain. In that sense, it points us to the gaps which we hope to fill with our own database. The chapter also introduces an important element in our methodology, by suggesting a typology for classifying industries. This entails distinguishing differences in the nature of the product according to the means by which firms differentiate their products. In turn, this has consequences for the nature of competition—do firms compete mainly on price/quantity, or are advertising and R&D expenditures important competitive weapons? We argue, on both theoretical and empirical grounds, that this distinction matters deeply to most of the elements of structure in which we are interested.

Chapter 3 turns to our own data collection activities. Its main function is to describe the database discussed above, which we refer to as the European *Market Share Matrix*[2]. This is based on a simple idea. Suppose we are able to identify the five market leaders in each of the one hundred or so 3-digit industries in the manufacturing sector. Suppose that we also collect information, for each of these firms, on their market shares in all of the industries in which they produce (i.e. not only those in which they are amongst the five leaders). Since the set of firms so identified will probably include nearly all firms of any substantial aggregate size, the database will reveal the aggregate share of the very largest European producers (i.e. aggregate concentration), as well as a comprehensive picture of concentration in each industry, and diversification of each firm. This will imply a database of no more than 500 firms, and significantly less, if many firms are leaders in more than one industry. Suppose finally, that we are also able to disaggregate each cell in this matrix into the firm's production in each member state, then we will have added an entirely novel source of information about the extent of multinational operations within the EU. This is the basis on which the matrix has been constructed, and we believe that it is probably the most compact and concise way of gathering and ordering the data on the industrial organization of a multi-state economy.

1.3 The Structure of EU Industries

Part II of the book is about the determinants of the structure of EU industries, focusing on the role of the nature of the product and of technology. Thus,

---

[2] This used as its prototype a similar exercise undertaken for the UK, see Davies et al. (1991).

economies of scale, R&D and advertising each play a central role in our story. We are primarily concerned with understanding how structure emerged and what implications this has for the nature of the competitive process in the EU. In addressing these issues, we are able to draw various conclusions about the extent of integration achieved so far. Our emphasis is on the EU as a whole, and we largely set aside issues of particular nationality (although some are picked up in Parts III and IV). Nevertheless, the general issues of geographical specialization of production, international ownership, and the extent to which the competitive process has been operating at the EU or the national levels, are each central to our concerns.

The logic of this part of the book is probably best understood as follows. Suppose you were to ask an international trade economist, an industrial economist, and a business economist: what is the most important dimension of industrial structure? Each would probably give you a different answer. The international trade economist would point to the geographical distribution of production and the consequent pattern of international trade. The industrial economist would highlight the extent to which an industry is dominated by a few firms, because industrial concentration facilitates the abuse of market power. And the business economist would claim the importance of the international ownership of production, which facilitates the spread of efficient new technologies and business practices.

International specialisation, industrial concentration and multinational enterprise are, of course, each of considerable importance; and it is unfortunate that research on their causes and consequences too frequently has been conducted independently from each other. The inappropriateness of this conceptual isolation is accentuated with the study of EU industrial structure. To see why, imagine, for the moment, that the EU is composed of five equal-sized countries; and in a particular industry, there are eight equal-sized firms operating in each country. If none of those firms is multinational (that is, each confines its production to its home country), then there will be forty firms in the EU as a whole. Alternatively, if each of the firms is multinational to the extent of operating in two countries; then the number of EU firms under separate ownership is reduced to twenty. EU concentration, national concentration, multinationality and the number of producing countries are fundamentally linked, and it may be misleading to look at only one dimension in isolation.

Chapter 4 formalizes this identity relationship between the dimensions of industry structure using our *first core decomposition*. In effect, it generalizes the symmetric example just described to allow for differences in the degree of specialization of production between EU member states, inequalities in the sizes of firms, and differences in the degree of intra-EU multinationality. This decomposition gives a natural structure to Part II of the book, in which subsequent chapters, in turn, each describe one dimension of structure, and attempt to model and explain some of the forces that have shaped it.

We begin, in Chapter 5, with an econometric investigation of the degree of *specialization of production* within the EU. What determines why production becomes internationally specialized in some industries but not in others? International trade theory suggests that greater specialization is more likely if there are powerful forces of comparative advantage, or strong regional external economies. Of course, transport costs are also likely to be a major influence on the geography of production, and this is what we find; but we also find, for example, that high technology industries are more specialized by location. The crucial role of R&D in forming industrial structure will be a continuing theme throughout the book. Competitive forces in price and technology, however, are not the only influences on the international pattern of specialization. Within the EU, this has been heavily influenced by government intervention and protection, the legacy of which for the integration process is pursued in Part IV.

The second dimension of industrial structure is *concentration*. There are two levels at which this can be measured with our new database: for the EU and for component member states. Given the aims of the book, we emphasize the former. In Chapter 6, applying the new theory of industrial structure (see Sutton, 1991), we find evidence that the nature of competition (and the types of competitive weapon—advertising, R&D and price) has a striking part to play in explaining differences in the determination of EU concentration. We also investigate the influence of trade integration on the competitive process and consequent concentration.

The third dimension of the industrial structure jigsaw is international ownership of production facilities in more than one country by *multinational enterprises* (MNEs). In Chapter seven, we analyse production by industry leaders in more than one EU member state (intra-EU MNEs), before looking specifically, in Chapter 8, at the EU operations of subsidiaries of firms originating from outside the EU (mainly North American, Swiss and Swedish). A main focus in Chapter 7 is on the relationship between concentration and multinationality, and how this is affected by the extent of trade flows. It also seeks to explain differences between industries in the extent of their multinationality. The chapter culminates in the suggestion that the notion of 'European integration' should be more widely defined than is usual, by taking account of how far firms pursue *integrated corporate strategies*. The implication is that large intra-EU trade flows are not a necessary condition for integration. Where multinational (that is, multi-member state) operations occur, certain parts of the oligopoly game may still be played on the European stage, even although the *markets* of the member states are unintegrated. The theoretical basis of these two chapters derives from the theory of MNEs based on firm-specific assets. Such assets include design, production, and marketing skills, which are more likely to be generated in industries characterized by high advertising and R&D expenditures. These are, of course, just the sort of industries highlighted in our earlier analysis of both international location and industrial concentration.

We devote an additional chapter specifically to the non-EU owned MNEs, because they raise certain extra questions—partly of a political nature. We again seek an explanation for inter-industry differences, but in this case with more emphasis on international revealed comparative advantages (RCA)—both for the host member states and for the foreign firms' home countries.

1.4 The Strategy of EU Firms

In Part III of the book, we switch focus away from industries, towards the firm as the unit of analysis, and investigate the business strategies of the EU's leading manufacturing firms. We define the word strategy rather more narrowly than is usual in the corporate strategy literature, by equating it with the structure of the firm's production. Thus, we look at the outcome of past decisions rather than the decisions themselves: for example, market share, diversification, and multinational production, rather than pricing, investment, acquisitions, disposals, marketing, and R&D.

We begin, in Chapter 9, with a look at the aggregate size of the leading EU manufacturing firms. As an interesting by-product, this allows us to estimate, for the first time, the *aggregate concentration* of EU manufacturing. However, aggregate size is unlikely to be an end in itself, but rather the consequence of other corporate objectives. Thus, the main questions that concern us in this part of the book are: what corporate strategies led to this level of size? why do strategies differ across firms? and does nationality make any difference to the answers? We begin, as we did in Part II, with decomposition analysis that helps to organize our thoughts on the various dimensions of corporate strategy. This time, however, we have two parallel ways of looking at the issues. The first identifies operations in multiple industries, and the second identifies production in multiple countries.

Suppose all industries were the same size, then larger firms must have either a larger market share in particular industries, or be diversified into multiple industries, or both. Given that industries also differ in size, a third way of being large is to operate in larger industries. For example, a firm with total production of 7,200m. ECUs might have an 8% market share in each of three industries, with each industry being of total size 30,000m. ECUs. In Chapter 9, we formalize this idea using the *second core decomposition*. Again, it generalizes the symmetric case to allow for firms having different market shares in different industries, for firms producing disproportionately in different industries, and for firms operating in industries of different sizes. Applying this decomposition to the firm-level data, it turns out that the EU's leading manufacturers display a rich diversity of structures, and have achieved their aggregate size in each of the above ways, as well as in combination.

In chapter 10, we investigate *diversification* in more detail. Our central focus is on what determines the pattern of diversification: into which industries is a particular firm most likely to diversify and why? Two types of diversification can be identified, each of which can be explained by the theory of transaction costs. Vertical integration into input or output industries may take place to secure reliable supplies or outlets, which are not subject to opportunistic behaviour by suppliers or customers. The theory of pure diversification views the firm as a collection of specific assets generated by R&D, the skills of its work-force and marketing expertise. Spillovers and spare capacity mean that diversification should take place into industries which are related in the sense of requiring similar expertise, and in Chapter 10, we test this related-industry theory. We also consider differences between the member states.

The second way of looking at corporate strategy is to make international production the focus. Roughly speaking, a firm can be big because it is based in a large country, or because it produces in several countries, or both. Chapter 11 investigates the relationship between firm size, multinationality, and national-ity—*the third core decomposition*. What determines the pattern and direction of within-EU multinational activity by firms? This will depend on national and firm-specific factors. Size of home base may be a push factor as firms from smaller member states become more rapidly constrained by home market activities than firms from the larger member states. Level of development and distance are other national factors. At the firm level, size, industrial base, R&D, and advertising will also exert an influence. These and other factors are examined econometrically in Chapter 11.

Chapter 12 brings the two ways of looking at corporate structure together, by considering multinationality alongside diversification. This is an under-researched subject, even within the corporate strategy literature. We take a few preliminary steps towards understanding the apparent complementarities and trade-offs involved.

1.5 Implications for EU Policy

The two chapters in Part IV begin to apply the findings from earlier in the book to some issues of direct policy relevance. The main thrust of the Single European Market programme, popularly known as '1992' after the date it was meant to have been completed, was to abolish all non-tariff barriers to trade in the EU. One of the most significant and visible measures was the abolition of *public procurement bias* by national government agencies in favour of firms from their own country. All significant government contracts now have to be advertised in the Official Journal of the EU, but that was not the case for the years that formed the industrial structure of 1987. If such a bias was import-ant, it should show up in the international structure of industries heavily in-volved in public procurement, and this is why we look in more depth at such industries in Chapter 13. We also take a preliminary look at what has happened more recently to these industries, with a view to seeing if the recent opening

up of government contracts has begun to have any structural effects. W
it has.

In the concluding chapter, we take a broader look at how our findings inform
some of the important policy issues of the day. In doing so, we draw extensively
on the fundamental differences we have found between different types of industry, particularly those due to their differential uses of advertising and R&D
as competitive weapons. Apart from further commenting on the Single Market
programme, we ask: What are the most important sources of economies of
scale in manufacturing industry and how does competition help to achieve
such cost savings? Which particular industries raise the greatest concern for
competition policy, and does a clear pattern emerge to aid in formulating rules
for intervention? Does nationality matter either in the location of production
or in the ownership of firms and, if so, are there discernible patterns of national
dominance? Although we cannot provide definitive answers to these questions,
we do believe that the findings in this book allow us to take the debate forward.

STEVE DAVIES and BRUCE LYONS

2

EU Manufacturing Industry in Context

2.1 Introduction

The primary purpose of this chapter is to provide a broad preliminary context for the more detailed statistical analysis which follows in later chapters. For reasons already given, much of the book is devoted to a snapshot view of EU manufacturing as it stood in 1987. This immediately raises at least three questions. How does the EU compare with the rest of the world in the production of manufactured goods? Was 1987 a representative (or peculiar) year? And to what extent is the EU a coherent economic entity, as opposed to a group of very different member states? Of course, these are big questions, for which we cannot provide comprehensive answers, but we can assemble a collection of facts, drawn from existing published sources, which at least provide a setting for our own work in terms of its global, temporal, and member state contexts. The chapter is deliberately confined to existing datasources in order to highlight the gaps in our knowledge which remain unanswered by the published statistics on industrial structure in the EU.

A second purpose for this chapter is to introduce a classificatory scheme for grouping industries together in different industry 'types'. A recurrent theme throughout the book is that 'progressive' industries, on the one hand, and 'marketing intensive' industries, on the other hand, exhibit certain common characteristics of particular significance for industry structure. Of course, it is now commonplace to separate out 'progressive' industries as being somehow more important, perhaps for long-run growth potential,[1] although it is much less common to group together industries which are typified by significant marketing expenditures. We begin to look at these industry types separately in this chapter, though a full justification for these groupings will have to wait until Chapters 5, 6, and 7, which develop the full rationale (derived from modern theories of international trade, industrial concentration and multinational enterprise). Broadly speaking, 'progressive' industries engaging in substantial R&D activity, and 'marketing' industries engaging in substantial advertising, are associated with particular types of product differentiation, competitive

---

[1] See, for example, Emerson (1988) for the importance of progressive industries in motivating the development of the Single European Market programme.

mechanism, and firm-specific advantage; and these characteristics turn out to have important implications for the pattern of international trade, the degree of industrial concentration, and the extent of multinational operations by firms.

The next three sections examine the dimensions of industrial context mentioned above. In Section 2.2, we locate the EU as a single entity in the global context of what has become known as the Triad: the EU, North America, and Japan.[2] We compare patterns of production, competitive advantage, and corporate size. Section 2.3 examines the temporal context of structural change in the late 1980s and early 1990s; in particular, three aspects of corporate strategy are discussed: mergers, foreign direct investment, and international trade. The member state context is developed in Section 2.4, focusing on national size, differences in trading patterns, and corporate size. Our classification of industry 'types' is presented in Section 2.5, which also highlights some differences in production and trading patterns across these types. Finally, Section 2.6 concludes and evaluates the gaps that published statistics leave in our knowledge of the industrial organization of the EU.

2.2 A Global Context: Production, Trade, and Corporate Size in the Triad

This section compares the EU with North America and Japan. Because the EU is defined as a single entity, extra-EU trade flows are included, but intra-EU trade flows are excluded from the figures. The same applies to North America, which includes the USA and Canada. Since different countries use different industrial classifications, only a very broad sectoral analysis is possible.

2.2.1 The structure of manufacturing

The pattern of production across broad sectors within manufacturing is fairly similar for each member of the Triad, but there are some significant differences. These are highlighted in Table 2.1, which groups sectors sharing similar characteristics. Thus, classifying chemicals, engineering and transport equipment as 'progressive' industries,[3] the EU lags behind in the share of its production devoted to these industries: in spite of a comparative strength in chemicals, this is more than outweighed by the North American advantage in transport equipment and the tremendous Japanese comparative strength in engineering. The table is based on the 2-digit level of industry aggregation used

---

[2] Of course, the world is changing fast, and new blocs of economic power are continually evolving. However, this Triad was undoubtedly the most important in global manufacturing industry in the late 1980s.

[3] As we demonstrate later, these sectors include a large proportion of industries which engage in R&D.

EU Manufacturing Industry in Context

Table 2.1 The comparative production structures of the Triad
(percentage shares)

	EU	North America	Japan
'Progressive' sectors, of which:	48.6	51.1	57.7
Chemicals	14.5	13.2	11.3
Engineering	21.4	22.6	32.0
Transport equipment	12.7	15.2	14.4
Food, drink, and tobacco	16.6	14.9	11.4
Minerals	3.9	2.6	3.6
Metals	12.9	11.0	11.7
Textiles	3.9	3.2	3.3
Clothing	3.1	2.3	1.5
Wood, paper, and printing	9.7	14.1	9.7
Rubber	1.1	1.0	1.1
TOTAL MANUFACTURING	100	100	100

Source: UNCTAD Handbook of International Trade and Development Statistics, 1991. All figures relate to 1988–9 unless stated otherwise. North America includes the USA and Canada.

in most published sources, and this is less helpful in separating out the 'marketing' sectors. Nevertheless, most marketing-intensive industries belong to either the food, drink and tobacco, or chemical sectors,[4] and, in both, the EU reveals a comparative strength and Japan shows a comparative weakness.

2.2.2 Absolute Size Differences in the Triad

Since Table 2.1 focused only on differences in the structural make-up of manufacturing, it tells us nothing about differences in absolute size between the members of the Triad. This is rectified by Table 2.2, in which various EU aggregates are expressed as shares of the Triad total. Thus EU GDP accounted for 37% of total Triad GDP in 1987, rising to 41% in 1992.

As can be seen, the EU is roughly the same size as North America but almost twice as large as Japan measured by GDP. (The EU is even larger, when measured by population.[5]) However, the size of Japanese manufacturing production is much closer to the other two Triad, who are again almost identical in size; and the size gap is further substantially closed when focusing solely on the progressive sectors.

[4] For the EU, about two-thirds of food, drink, and tobacco production, and a third of the chemicals sector, is in highly advertised industries.

[5] GDP figures are compared using average exchange rates, *not* purchasing power. In terms of geographic area, which might also be important for certain types of integration, the USA is four times as big as the EU (and including Canada would double the contrast with North America). On the other hand, Japan is very much more compact than the EU relative to our other measures of size.

Table 2.2 Relative size and competitive advantage of the EU, North America, and Japan (percentage shares of Triad total)

	EU	North America	Japan
Population 1992	46.0	36.5	16.5
GDP 1987	37.1	42.2	20.7
1992	40.7	38.0	21.3
Production of:			
All manufacturing	35.8	37.4	26.9
'Progressive' sectors	35.5	36.7	29.8
Production growth (1985–9):			
All manufacturing	43.5	20.9	35.6
'Progressive' sectors	40.3	20.1	39.6
Intra-Triad exports:			
All manufacturing	29.6	30.3	40.1
'Progressive' sectors	26.1	28.0	45.9
Balance of trade relative to total trade:			
Manufacturing	7.1	–22.3	41.9
'Progressive' sectors	13.1	–18.9	62.0
Share of imports from other Triad	38.6	54.4	54.5

Source: As for Table 2.1; population and *GDP* from Eurostat, *Basic Statistics of the Community (1993)*. Shares refer to 1988–9 unless stated otherwise. Figures for 1992 include the former East Germany (DDR). GDP comparisons use average exchange rates, *not* purchasing powers. Production growth is the change in the value of production, unadjusted for inflation.

The sixth and seventh rows of the Table show how the North American share of production was shrinking relative to the other two of the Triad, and the pattern of near equality of size in the progressive sectors was being reinforced in the late 1980s.

The relative strength of Japanese manufacturing comes sharply into focus in the lower part of the Table where we focus on trade performance. Japan accounts for 40% of all exports between members of the Triad—over a third higher than those originating from the EU; and this dominance is even more acute in the progressive sectors, in which Japan's share is three-quarters higher than the EU. The contrast with 'marketing' sectors (not reported in the table) is striking, with the EU having a 45.7% share of intra-Triad exports, compared with only 10.6% for Japan. For each grouping, the EU and North American shares are very similar.

Broadening the picture to include trade with the rest of the world, the Table confirms the (well-known) Japanese balance of trade surplus and North American deficit. More relevant for present purposes, it also shows that the EU has an overall surplus which is particularly strong in progressive sectors, although this surplus was earned outside the toughest Triad markets. Similarly, non-Triad countries are a more important source of manufactured imports for the EU, due largely to its significant integration with the EFTA countries.

2.2.3 The world's largest companies

Unsurprisingly, nearly 90% of the world's largest 200 industrial firms originate from the Triad. Table 2.3 shows that, in 1986, the USA was dominant, with 79 firms (40%), accounting for 44% of these giants' turnover. The EU share of the largest firms (35% of the Triad's contribution) almost exactly reflected its share of Triad production in manufacturing, leaving Japan as 'underrepresented' amongst the giants. Since 1986, the EU has consolidated its position, while the US share has been eroded by the Japanese. Thus, by 1992, the EU and USA stood all square in the global corporate giants' league. However, we must sound a note of caution in interpreting these figures, which are typical of those widely available in the specialized press and industrial directories. First, they refer to the total size of firms, and these figures will be heavily influenced by international differences in diversification outside the production sectors (e.g. integration into services). Second, they refer to global turnover by origin of ownership, and given that there is substantial multinationality of production by these firms, they provide no necessary link with the location of production.[6] Unlike our own figures presented later in the book, they are, therefore, not strictly comparable with the production figures discussed earlier.

Table 2.3 World's 200 largest firms by origin

	1986		1992	
	No.	Share of turnover	No.	Share of turnover
EU	61	31.5	62	34.5
USA	79	44.1	63	34.0
Japan	36	15.8	49	21.7
EFTA	12	4.0	14	4.8
Other	12	4.6	12	5.0

Source: DABLE in *Panorama of EC Industry (1994)*.

2.3 A Temporal Context: Structural Change in the Late 1980s and Early 1990s

The Single European Act was made law in 1987, beginning a process designed to create the Single European Market by the end of 1992. At the time, it was expected that there would be significant corporate realignments as industry adapted to the new competitive conditions (Emerson, 1988). As an extreme characterization then, inasmuch as the EU was not integrated before the Act

---

[6] Furthermore, there is always a worry with commercial directories that insufficient care has been taken in identifying cross-ownership patterns. This has certainly been the case for the published European figures (see Section 2.4.2 below).

and firms had not already anticipated its effects, 1987 might be defined as the last year of the 'old' industrial structure. A full evaluation of 1987 as a watershed in the history of EU corporate strategy must await further research, but the more limited purpose of this section is to summarize some of the general trends in corporate strategy which emerged in the late 1980s and early 1990s. Two key aspects of this are corporate mergers and foreign direct investment.

2.3.1 Merger Activity

Figure 2.1 shows the trend in merger activity by large firms.[7] While the series must be treated with some caution,[8] it points to a steady growth of total merger activity through the 1980s, with an acceleration from 1987–90, followed by a clear downturn in 1991 and 1992. Although this particular series was discontinued in 1992, the new replacement series suggests the downward trend continued for at least another year. There is, therefore, clear evidence of a surge in merger activity in the immediate post-1987 period.

If merger activity is to be interpreted as a sign of adjustment towards a new equilibrium for industrial organization, it is particularly interesting to note that the most active sectors have been chemicals, followed by food and drink, then metals, machinery, electricals, and wood, paper, and printing. In other words, the major changes have been taking place in the 'marketing' sectors, followed by the 'progressive' sectors. This is a possible indication of where the Single Market may have been having most effect.

Similarly, the geographical stretch of mergers may hold some clues to their interpretation: arguably, if they were predominantly within the borders of individual member states, they might be interpreted as being less aimed at integration than if they crossed national borders. In fact, as the figure shows, national mergers (i.e. between firms from the same member state) held fairly steady from 1987–90, having been responsible for most of the increase prior to that time.[9] This leaves the major source of the post-1987 increase as being EU mergers (i.e. between firms from different member states); with a substantial contribution also from international mergers (i.e. between firms from member

---

[7] The Merger data in this section are taken from CEC Reports on Competition Policy (various issues 1983–93). Data for each year relate to the twelve months ending 31 May of that year. From 1987, the dataset is based on mergers (acquisition of majority holdings) by the 1,000 largest EU firms and 500 largest industrial firms world-wide. Figures prior to 1987 were collected from a more restricted search and so may underestimate acquisitions. Manufacturing is defined to exclude construction and extractive industries. This series is known as the DOME database, and was replaced in 1993 with a new AMDATA series, which overlaps only back to 1988.

[8] First, the coverage was broadened in 1987, so pre-1987 activity may be underestimated; and second, it shows a simple count of the number of deals without recording the value of assets changing hands. A little comfort on the latter is provided by the fact that the series on mergers involving combined turnover in excess of 1b. ECUs closely mirrors the total figures; but, of course, this would still include small acquisitions by big firms which were already at or near the threshold.

[9] The new AMDATA series also suggests that national merger activity, though not EU mergers, continued on the plateau until 1992.

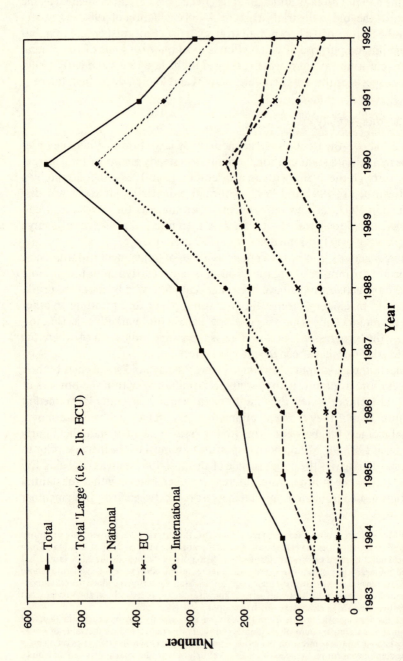

Fig. 2.1. Mergers and acquisitions
Source: CEC competition reports, various

states and third countries, with effects on the EU market).[10] Again then, the sparse evidence we have from official sources is consistent with international ownership changes in anticipation of the Single Market. Nevertheless, it is important to note that there was also a massive merger wave in the USA at the same time, much of it involving EU firms; so we cannot necessarily reject the hypothesis that acquisition activity in the EU may simply have been part of a global picture, due to the economic boom, or even simple fad.

Undoubtedly, we would have a better understanding if we knew what factors had influenced the corporate decision-making process. In this respect, a cautious insight can be gleaned from the CEC Competition Reports, which monitor motives for merger as reported in the specialist press. Such reports are notoriously dangerous to interpret: for example, the jargon changes over the years, and executives are likely to justify their actions in terms that they expect people, particularly regulators and shareholders, will want to hear. But, for what it is worth, there does appear to have been a distinct shift in the reported reasons given for merger after 1987. Before then, a quarter of the reasons cited were for 'rationalization' or 'restructuring', but this dropped to below 10% after 1987.[11] On the other hand, 'strengthening market position' rose from less than 10% to over a third. This might be interpreted as a change from production or supply side motives towards marketing or demand side reasons. Thus, the mergers may have been more to exploit sales opportunities than economies of scale. However, it may also simply be that firms became more open in their declared motives, as regulators, anticipating the Single Market, became less worried by motives which could be interpreted as enhancing monopoly.[12]

2.3.2 Foreign Direct Investment

The second way we attempt to track the evolving pattern of corporate ownership is by examining the data on foreign direct investment (FDI). Of course, there is some overlap between mergers and FDI (in particular, mergers between firms of different nationalities are included in both). Nevertheless, there are important differences: for example, the merger data allow a comparison with intra-national trends, while only FDI will include greenfield developments.

[10] France, Germany, and the UK have been the major centres for both acquiring and acquired firms since 1987, though the Netherlands and Belgium are active proportionate to size (and Germany rather less so). Spain is a significant source of acquired firms without Spanish firms undertaking many acquisitions themselves. In 1991, the USA was responsible for about half as many acquisitions as each of the leading three EU countries, while each of Switzerland, Sweden, and Japan acquired about a sixth as many.

[11] Multiple reasons are allowed, and 'no reason' is counted as a response, so the number of reasons given can be greater than or less than the number of mergers.

[12] At the same time, simple 'expansion' as a motive also rose from an average of 15% to over 20% of reasons given, while 'synergy' or 'complementarity' remained around 10%. Two minor reasons are worth recording, simply because they are so minor. 'R&D' never rose above the odd percentage point or two, and 'diversification' fell from an average of 6% pre-1988 to less than half that afterwards.

Figure 2.2 (taken from Davies, 1992, and derived from harmonized balance of payments statistics) plots total inflows and outflows of FDI into and by each member of the Triad. For instance, in 1989, Japan invested 40bn. ECUs abroad, while receiving essentially no inward investment. Points above the dotted line represent greater outflows than inflows, and the reverse is true for points below the line. The figure shows how investment from outside the EU into the EU grew from around 6bn. ECUs in 1984 to 28bn. ECUs in 1989, rising further in 1990 before dropping back.[13] Over the same period (1984–9), intra-EU direct investment (not shown in the figure) rose from 4bn. ECUs to around 34bn. ECUs. Thus, the levels of extra-EU inflows and intra-EU flows are similar, and both increased massively in the late 1980s, though the latter rose more rapidly. As with the merger wave, however, it is important to put this activity into a wider Triad context. FDI into the USA, much of which came from the EU, was on a very much larger scale, rising to 67bn. ECUs in 1989, and without any similar stimulus from the Single Market. This cautions us against drawing any simple conclusions about causation. Figure 2.2 also shows that outward direct investment from the EU was always greater than inward investment in the period, though it did begin to grow less fast than inward flows

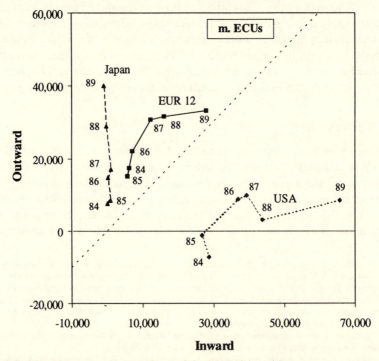

Fig. 2.2 Direct investment into and out of the EU, USA and Japan
Source: Davies 1992

---

[13] We focus on 1984–9 because there are more comparative data for this period.

after 1987. The broad balance of inflows and outflows for the EU is in sharp contrast to the USA, which had relatively tiny outflows and huge inflows in the period, and Japan, which was the complete opposite with negligible inflows and an enormous outflow of investment.

The sectoral pattern of direct investment in the second half of the 1980s was very similar to that for mergers. Chemicals, food and drink, and electricals were the major recipients of investment, with chemicals leading the intra-EU flows and electricals topping the extra-EU flows. Once again, these are the 'marketing' and 'progressive' sectors.[14]

2.3.3 Trends in EU Trade

The final aspect of structural change that can be investigated using published statistics is international trade. The conventional wisdom about the effects of the Single Market programme on EU trade is quite straightforward:

(a) trade in manufactured goods was expected to increase as a result of abolishing non-tariff barriers between member states;

(b) member states should be in the best position to take advantage of the new situation;

(c) a 'Fortress Europe' might develop to the disadvantage of third countries.

We first look at these propositions for manufacturing in the EU as a whole, returning to differences between member states and industry types in later sections.

Looking at the aggregate statistics, it is clear that trade did indeed increase throughout the period 1984–90. This is shown in the first row of Table 2.4, which shows significant increases in overall import penetration (measured by total intra-EU plus extra-EU imports relative to total EU production plus extra-EU imports). However, the share of those imports that were intra-EU trade appears to have reached a plateau of just over 60% around 1987. This ratio (also used by Jacquemin and Sapir, 1988, in their study of integration, 1975–85) is shown in the second row of the table. It appears that the continuing integration process was benefiting external partners equally with member states. A clearer view of trade creation (between member states) and trade diversion (away from non-members) is given in the third and fourth rows of the table, which report the separate trends in intra-EU and extra-EU imports relative to gross demand (as employed by Truman, 1975, and Neven and Roller, 1991). The increase in the former up to around 1987 suggests trade creation

---

[14] The source countries for extra-EU inflows also match the pattern of international mergers. However, some significant differences emerge in the host country pattern. The UK dominates as the main host for inflows, while Germany is a trivial recipient; contrasting this with the merger data, this suggests that the UK may be receiving particularly more greenfield foreign investment. In part, the host pattern might reflect the attractions of the English language to non-Europeans, but this is unlikely to be a complete explanation. Since intra-EU flows reveal a similar though rather less striking pattern of hosts, it is also likely that labour costs may have been playing an important role.

Table 2.4 Trade trends in EU manufacturing

	1984–5	1986–8	1989–90
Import share of gross demand (%)[a]	24.7	26.0	27.4
Intra-EU share of trade (%)	57.2	61.6	61.4
'Trade creation'[b]		+1.9	+0.9
'Trade diversion'[c]		–0.6	+0.5

[a] Total production (including exports) plus imports.
[b] Percentage point change in intra-EU imports relative to gross demand since the previous period.
[c] Percentage point change in extra-EU imports relative to gross demand since the previous period.

Source: Unpublished trade data provided by Eurostat; see Appendix 3 for the source of production data. Shares are calculated as two- or three-year averages.

was taking place, perhaps alongside a very little trade diversion; but after 1987, there was similar growth in both sources of imports. Neven and Roller suggest that, in the 1975– 85 period, non-tariff barriers hampered trade with the rest of the world more than trade between European partners, and the limited evidence in Table 2.4 is consistent with this view. Alternatively, given the stability of the extra-EU import ratio, it may simply be that such imports are not particularly close substitutes for EU produced goods, and so were impervious to the changes that were going on. But whatever the truth about extra-EU imports, there is no evidence of any extraordinary (i.e. above trend) increase in intra-EU trade integration in the late 1980s.

2.4 Member State Context: Production, Trade, and Corporate Size

Although most of this book treats the EU as a single entity, it would be misleading to overlook entirely the individual member states. A perspective on the member states—in particular, their relative sizes, trade performance, and size distribution of firms—provides additional insights on EU integration. The main thrust of this section is to identify any patterns of similarities or differences between member states, which might reflect on the cohesion of the EU as an economic unit. Inevitably, we find that national size significantly influences most measures of the degree of integration (smaller countries have more external trade), so countries in the following tables are ranked by the size of national manufacturing production.

2.4.1 Differences in Trade and Production

As is well known, the 'Big 4'—Germany, France, Italy, and the UK—quantitatively dominate the EU. Table 2.5 underlines this using four measures of

Table 2.5 Relative sizes of member states (percentages)

	Population (1993)	GDP (1987)	GDP (1992)	Manu-facturing
Germany	23.2	25.7	27.6	28.3
France	16.6	20.6	18.8	18.3
Italy	16.4	17.6	17.4	17.7
UK	16.7	16.0	14.9	14.7
Spain	11.3	6.8	8.2	8.6
Netherlands	4.4	5.0	4.6	4.6
Bel/Lux	3.0	3.4	3.3	3.6
Denmark	1.5	2.4	2.0	1.7
Portugal	2.8	0.8	1.6	1.0
Ireland	1.0	0.7	0.7	0.9
Greece	3.0	1.1	1.1	0.7
EU	100.0	100.0	100.0	100.0

Source: Population and GDP from Eurostat, *Basic Statistics of the Community (1993)*; figures for 1992 include East Germany (DDR); for share of manufacturing production (1987) see Appendix 3.

relative size; for example, these countries combine to produce 79% of manufacturing output, with Germany alone producing over 28%. But a more interesting issue is whether, beyond any straightforward relationship with size, there are national peculiarities to the pattern of trade within the EU.

Table 2.6 examines three dimensions of trade by member states. The first column shows that, in all member states, the share of imports that come from other member states always exceeds 50%.[15] But this ratio does vary significantly. It should be expected that smaller countries will naturally trade more (proportionately) with their larger neighbours, as industrial linkages spill over borders, and this is indeed the case. Controlling for this broad relationship, however, the most noticeable differences are that France is relatively more directed towards EU trade, and the UK and Denmark are rather less so.[16]

A different angle on trade integration, focusing more on comparative advantage, is given by export specialization, which reflects the degree to which a country concentrates its exports in a few industries. This is captured by the coefficient of variation in the share of production that is exported, shown in the second and third columns, and measured across the 100 3-digit manufacturing industries we use throughout the book. High variation means that a country's exports are more specialized in a few industries. Again, one would expect smaller countries to be more specialized, as larger countries have a greater ability to produce across the full range of industries, and again this is generally supported by the figures. The exceptions are the Benelux countries, which are less specialized than expected for intra-EU exports (but not for extra-EU

[15] In each country, the trend was the same as for the overall EU, rising to 1987, then stabilizing. This is why we have reported only the 1986–90 average.

[16] Denmark maintained strong Scandinavian links with EFTA countries.

Table 2.6 Trade by member states

	Intra-EU[a] imports (share)	Export specialization[b]		Intra-industry trade[c]			
		Intra-EU	Extra-EU	Intra-EU		Extra-EU	
				Level	Change	Level	Change
Germany	55	.42	.48	.80	3.0	.61	5.5
France	71	.55	.67	.81	3.4	.71	5.8
Italy	63	.86	.84	.62	5.2	.54	3.6
UK	52	.70	.69	.77	4.8	.69	3.0
Spain	68	1.04	1.13	.70	1.0	.58	11.6
Netherlands	67	.72	1.15	.80	7.4	.63	−1.5
Bel/Lux	71	.68	1.35	.71	−7.0	.67	2.1
Denmark	57	1.62	1.16	.61	8.0	.57	3.9
Portugal	78	2.40	2.96	.42	1.8	.41	−2.3
Ireland	71	1.23	2.10	.61	−1.2	.57	−1.5
Greece	69	3.56	3.21	.29	2.4	.34	−4.1

[a] Share of total imports that are intra-EU (average 1986–90).

[b] Measured by the coefficient of variation of export to production ratios across 100 3-digit manufacturing industries, averaged 1986–91.

[c] The Grubel–Lloyd index (i.e. 1 minus the absolute difference between imports and exports relative to imports plus exports for each industry, averaged across industries). The 'level' refers to 1989–91 and 'change' to the absolute change in the index over the previous six years. The change has been multiplied by 100.

Source: Unpublished Eurostat trade data.

trade), and perhaps the UK and Italy, which are less and more specialized respectively than might be expected. For most countries, export specialization is generally a little higher with respect to external trade. An examination of the time series data (not reported in the table), reveals no clear trend in intra-EU specialization, and only a slight increase up to 1987 for extra-EU specialization, followed by stability. Thus, there is no evidence of a continuing process of export specialization within the EU.

However, there is a significant trend in another aspect of the trade pattern: intra-industry trade. This refers to the percentage of trade that is matched by reciprocal flows within the same industry, and it is often interpreted as a consequence of trade in differentiated products between countries of similar levels of development and production structure.[17] This is investigated in the last four columns of Table 2.6, using the Grubel–Lloyd index. For a given industry in a given country the index will be zero if it either exclusively imports or exports; but if it exports and imports equal amounts, the index will be 1. The values in the table are averages of this index across 100 3-digit industries. For similar reasons to those given for the other measures, there is likely to be a national size effect here, with larger countries engaging in more intra-industry trade, and

[17] See Chapter 5 for the theory of intra-industry trade and an empirical examination of flows within the EU.

smaller countries having relatively more inter-industry trade. This is again borne out, with the exception that Italy has less intra-industry trade than might be expected given its size, and the Benelux countries have more (once again only for their intra-EU trade). This national pattern is similar to that of export specialization.

Comparing the intra-EU and extra-EU columns, in general, there is substantially more intra-industry trade within the EU than with external partners. This is to be expected given that member states are at more similar levels of development than they typically are with external countries, and it supports the view that the EU is a relatively homogeneous area with member states exchanging similar but differentiated products. Unlike our other indices of trade and integration, intra-industry trade exhibits a fairly consistent increasing trend. The change columns show the absolute change in the index (multiplied by 100) between 1984–5 and 1989–91. Only for a few small countries are there any decreases. Taken together with the relative stability of export specialization, this suggests that integration was mainly encouraging the exchange of differentiated products, rather than consolidating comparative advantage.

2.4.2 The Origin of the EU largest firms by member state

Our final piece of evidence on member state differences relates to the country of origin of Europe's 200 largest industrial firms, shown in Table 2.7. Note that

Table 2.7 Europe's 200 largest firms by country

	1986		1992	
	No.	Share of turnover(%)	No.	Share of turnover(%)
Germany	42	26.2	41	26.4
France	44	20.8	49	22.6
Italy	10	8.8	14	11.1
UK	59	24.4	44	18.2
Spain	4	0.7	8	3.1
Netherlands	9	7.5	11	6.7
Bel/Lux	5	1.6	7	1.9
Denmark	—	—	1	0.1
EU	173	90.0	175	90.1
Switzerland	11	4.6	10	4.9
Sweden	11	3.6	9	2.7
Finland	2	0.6	3	0.8
Norway	2	1.1	2	0.8
Austria	2	0.6	—	—
EFTA	28	10.5	24	9.2

Source: DABLE in *Panorama of EC Industry, 1994*. Note that the totals do not add up, but no explanation is given in the source.

the reservations we expressed in Sub-section 2.2.3 about the construction of published 'Top 200' lists continue to apply. In Chapter 9, we return to the nationality of the EU's largest firms using our own more precise measure of size. But taking this table at face value for the present, it shows that the EU accounts for about 90% of the European Top 200, with Sweden and Switzerland accounting for most of the rest. It is revealing to compare the shares in Table 2.7 with those in Table 2.5, though it should be noted that only the former includes the EFTA countries in the calculated shares.[18] In 1986, Germany's representation amongst the largest firms was almost exactly proportional to its size in manufacturing. However, according to this list, there were substantial differences for most other member states. The UK and Netherlands had almost twice as many giant firms as expected from their size alone, and Italy only half as many. Spain and the small countries are very much underrepresented. The 1992 figures suggest there has been a significant move towards a more representative distribution of the largest firms, though factors such as the UK recession will have affected some individual figures. However, great caution should be exercised in interpreting the figures. As will be seen in Chapter 9, our new work correcting for production outside the EU and for non-manufacturing production, significantly revises these simple conclusions based only on aggregate turnover.[19]

2.5 A Closer Look by Type of Industry

Earlier in the chapter we identified some broad differences in the patterns of production, trade, mergers, and foreign direct investment between 'progressive', 'marketing', and other industries. In fact, the distinction between different industry types anticipates an important theme which runs through the remainder of the book. In this section, we pave the way for the more detailed analysis of later chapters, which will use our own database, by formalizing our classification scheme more precisely. We first briefly review the theoretical foundations and explain our operational criteria for categorizing industries types, and then apply the classification to the published trade and production data at the 3-digit level. This serves as a bridge between the more aggregate work earlier in the chapter (which is typical of most previous studies of EU integration) and the more disaggregated analysis of the rest of the book.

[18] A simple adjustment to allow for this when making comparisons is to add 10% to the shares of member states in Table 2.7, to obtain their shares of the largest EU Firms.

[19] Furthermore, the prevailing organizational structure adopted by firms differs across countries (e.g. the *M*-form in the UK and the business group in Italy). It is, therefore, crucial to identify the appropriate unit of organization both to identify the largest firms and not to double count. One example illustrates this point. In the *1994 Panorama of EC Industry*, there are fourteen Italian firms among the largest 200. The problem is that four of them (STET, SIP, Finmeccanica and Alitalia) are controlled by IRI, which is also in the list, so four firms are counted twice. Even worse, since SIP is controlled by IRI indirectly through STET, one firm is counted three times! Our own work has been careful to identify the proper parentage of firms.

2.5.1 Type 1 and Type 2 industries: Theoretical rationale and measurement

In this book, we will draw on a number of theoretical contributions in the economics literature, derived from the typically separated sub-disciplines of international trade, industrial organization, and international business. Traditionally, these contributions have focused on different units of analysis (the nation, the industry, and the firm), though more recent theoretical developments have rightly led to a cross-fertilization of ideas.

One connecting theme in the newer literature is product differentiation,[20] which is a concept that includes two distinct dimensions. Horizontal product differentiation arises from a preference for diversity, while vertical product differentiation arises from the desire for quality. For example, a wide range of breakfast cereals caters for differences in consumer tastes, while Kellogg's cornflakes are perceived to be a better quality than a supermarket's own brand; similarly, shirts of different colour or design are horizontally differentiated, while personal computers with microprocessors of successive generations are vertically differentiated. It is sometimes quite possible to create either sort of product differentiation by simple design without any major investment, but more usually it is a costly activity. The two most important investments associated with vertical differentiation are R&D and advertising. For example, a great deal of R&D is directed at improving product quality;[21] and advertising is often used to signal quality, or directly to create a perception of quality. Of course, both types of expenditure may also be linked with horizontal differentiation. For example, firms engaging in R&D may follow alternative research paths and come up with different product ideas. Similarly, advertising can create different product images that are attractive to different potential customers.[22]

Product differentiation has become important in the international trade literature because much trade involves countries exchanging differentiated products that are produced by similar technologies and for which trading partner countries have no obvious comparative advantage.[23] Even if economies of scale are only modest, a single country cannot produce all possible variants of a horizontally differentiated product, so international trade can fill the niches in the market, providing goods that are closer to the ideal specifications of

---

[20] For example, Krugman, 1979, and Gabszewicz *et al.*, 1980, for international trade; Dixit and Stiglitz, 1977, and Shaked and Sutton, 1983, for industrial organization; Dunning, 1979, and Williamson, 1981, for international business.

[21] Although R&D can be directed at process innovation, embodied process innovations more often come from the supplying capital good industry (see, for example, Davies, 1979, ch. 3). In fact, the distinction between product and process innovation makes little difference to the theories we apply.

[22] Caves has argued that advertising with this purpose is more necessary for firms in search of higher mark-ups if they have fundamentally homogeneous products (e.g. washing powder, cigarettes). Genuinely different products, he claims, do not need to shout that they are. However, it is also possible to argue that it is more necessary to send messages about your product characteristics if they are, indeed, different from the next firm's (e.g. Grossman and Shapiro, 1984).

[23] Of course, Table 2.6 has already shown this to be so for the member states.

individual consumers and generally catering for a preference for variety (Krugman, 1979). Vertical product differentiation can also motivate trade to satisfy individuals with different incomes or preferences for quality (Linder, 1960; Gabszewicz *et al.*, 1981).

Product differentiation also has a pervasive influence in the industrial organization literature, and of prime relevance to this book is the role that expenditures used to create vertical differentiation have in the competitive process that determines the number and relative sizes of firms in an industry. Advertising and R&D are essentially overhead investments. The incentive to make such investments is greater the larger is the market over which the benefits can be spread (Sutton, 1991). Thus, the size of these expenditures, and so the extent of vertical differentiation created by them, will be sensitive to the degree of integration of the EU.

In the international business literature, the core idea is that successful firms have specific assets which are difficult to exploit fully other than by multinational production; and these assets are often associated with R&D activity or a particularly marketable product. The optimal choice of business strategy to exploit a firm's specific assets (e.g. exporting, licensing, joint venture, international production) will be sensitive to the size and integration of the market.

Thus, for a very wide range of reasons, there are expected to be significant differences in the industrial and international organization of industries, depending on whether or not they are characterized by product differentiation, R&D and/or advertising. Partly because it is almost impossible to measure product differentiation directly, but also because of the direct role they play in corporate strategy, we focus on R&D and advertising in developing our classification of industry types.

Unfortunately, even for these two expenditures, there are no published data at the disaggregated level using the European NACE industrial classification. Therefore, we have had to piece together advertising data from a UK commercial source and R&D data from UK and Italian government publications (see Appendix 3). Obviously, such narrow datasources will fail to take account of international differences. However, even if the precise magnitudes are subject to substantial error, we feel fairly confident that the data are sufficiently robust to identify industries according to an essentially binary classification scheme as follows:

A Type 2 industry is one in which typically or innately (i.e. in most countries and in most time periods) firms engage in advertising and/or R&D competition. Roughly speaking, this means industries which have an advertising to sales ratio and/or R&D to sales ratio in excess of 1%. A Type 1 industry is one in which firms engage in neither type of competition.

Then, within Type 2, we identify three sub-sets:

A Type 2*A* industry is one in which firms typically engage in advertising, but not R&D, competition.

A Type 2*R* industry is one in which firms typically engage in R&D, but not advertising, competition.

A Type 2*AR* industry is one in which firms typically engage in both advertising and R&D competition.[24]

A full list of the 100 3-digit industries and their classification by type is given in Appendix 2. Type 2*A* industries (thirteen in number, accounting for 12% of EU manufacturing production) mostly come from the food, drink, and tobacco sector; Type 2*R* industries (twenty-two accounting for 26% of production) include some chemicals, but mainly come from machinery, instruments, and transport equipment; Type 2*AR* industries (nine accounting for 14% of production) include some chemicals such as pharmaceuticals, and soaps and detergents, and consumer durables such as cars and domestic electrical appliances; and Type 1 industries (fifty-six accounting for 48% of production) are mainly associated with processing materials, including iron and steel, cement, foundries, grain-milling, and the textile and wood processing industries.

2.5.2 Trade and Production by Type 1 and Type 2 industries

We now briefly re-examine the published sources on EU trade and production at the 3-digit level of aggregation, applying this classification scheme.

It is clear from Table 2.8 that industries engaged in R&D tend to be the most trade-intensive and that those competing through advertising are the least trade-intensive. (The table uses import penetration as a measure of the extent of trade, but export ratios tell a similar story.) Interestingly, these forces balance out in Type 2*AR* industries which typically engage in similar levels of trade to Type 1 industries.

There are also important differences in the geographical nature of trade flows. The share of trade that is intra-EU is about 10 percentage points higher in industries that advertise compared with Type 1 and Type 2*R*. Thus advertising is associated with low trade, particularly low with countries outside the EU; whilst R&D is associated with high trade, and there is no real difference in the intra-/extra-EU split compared to Type 1.

An inspection of the trends over time, shows that each industry type has enjoyed some trade creation (measured, as in Section 2.3, by the growth in intra-EU imports relative to gross demand), though this was minimal in Type 2*A* and most pronounced in R&D intensive industries. The small amount of trade diversion in the earlier period had been eliminated by the late 1980s, particularly in Type 2*R* industries, which enjoyed positive growth in the extra-EU import share (even in excess of the intra-EU growth.) Overall, this evidence suggests a continuing increase in intra-EU trade integration across all industry

---

[24] Our terminology of Type 1 and Type 2 follows Schmalensee (1992) in his review of Sutton's (1991) work, in which industries are called homogeneous and differentiated respectively. Both focus on advertising only, and do not make the R&D distinction.

Table 2.8 Trade trends by type of industry

	1984–5	1986–8	1989–90
Import share in gross demand			
Type 1	23.8	24.9	25.8
Type 2*A*	15.2	15.3	15.7
Type 2*R*	30.2	31.8	34.3
Type 2*AR*	23.8	26.0	26.4
Intra-EU share of trade			
Type 1	54.9	58.9	59.7
Type 2*A*	63.0	68.7	69.3
Type 2*R*	56.5	61.1	59.2
Type 2*AR*	63.0	66.6	67.4
'Trade creation'			
Type 1		+1.5	+0.8
Type 2*A*		+0.9	+0.4
Type 2*R*		+2.4	+1.0
Type 2*AR*		+2.3	+0.6
'Trade diversion'			
Type 1		–0.5	+0.2
Type 2*A*		–0.8	0.0
Type 2*R*		–0.7	+1.5
Type 2*AR*		–0.1	–0.2

Source: As for Table 2.4. For industry types see Appendix 2.

types, but this was small post-1987 compared with the earlier period. Trade diversion effects were substantially eliminated after 1987.

Turning to the pattern of production across member states, the first four columns of Table 2.9 show each country's share by industry type. Here, we encounter a very striking result. EU production in R&D-intensive industries tends to be far more concentrated within the largest member states; in particular, Germany accounts for over a third of all R&D-intensive production and, together with France, it accounts for 56% of Type 2*AR* output. Type 1 and Type 2*A* industries are more uniformly distributed, and the Type 1 group in Italy is nearly as large as in Germany.[25] Including Spain as a large country, only the Netherlands among the smaller states supplies over 5% of EU output for any industry type (Type 2*A*).

The last four columns in Table 2.9 reorganize the data to show the comparative advantage each country reveals in its production pattern (i.e. its share of production by industry type, relative to the EU average). This confirms the relative strengths of Germany, France, and Italy, as already discussed, and shows that the UK and Bel/Lux each have a broadly representative industrial distribution. A relative strength in Type 2*A* industries is shown in Spain, the Netherlands, Denmark, Ireland, and Greece. The Type 1 pattern is similar to,

---

[25] In Chapter 5, we present a much more detailed and precise analysis of specialization within the EU.

Table 2.9 Production by industry type and member state

Member State	Industry type share of EU production(%)				Industry type comparative production advantage*			
	1	2A	2R	2AR	1	2A	2R	2AR
Germany	23.8	23.0	36.5	33.3	0.84	0.81	1.29	1.18
France	17.6	17.9	17.5	22.3	0.96	0.98	0.96	1.22
Italy	22.5	12.5	13.7	12.7	1.27	0.71	0.77	0.72
UK	13.4	16.7	16.7	13.7	0.91	1.14	1.14	0.93
Spain	9.7	12.1	5.0	8.5	1.13	1.41	0.58	0.99
Netherlands	4.2	7.4	4.9	2.9	0.92	1.62	1.06	0.64
Bel&sl.Lux	3.9	3.4	3.0	4.0	1.08	0.93	0.82	1.11
Denmark	2.0	2.8	1.0	0.9	1.20	1.64	0.58	0.55
Portugal	1.3	1.1	0.6	0.7	1.32	1.04	0.57	0.64
Ireland	0.7	2.0	0.9	0.7	0.78	2.22	1.00	0.74
Greece	0.9	1.1	0.4	0.3	1.25	1.59	0.54	0.48
EU	100	100	100	100	1.00	1.00	1.00	1.00

* The country share of the industry type relative to the aggregate EU share of production of that industry type.

Source: See Appendix 3 for production data (1987) and definition of industry types.

but much less systematic than, the Type 2A: Denmark, Portugal, and Greece join Italy in its bias towards Type 1 industries. Overall, the Type 2A results confirm a traditional advantage in the food, drink, and tobacco industries in the generally less advanced and smaller member states, while the most advanced and largest member states maintain a comparative advantage in the R&D industries. Type 1 industries display no clear pattern of specialization across member states.

2.6 Conclusion

Most of this book is devoted to an in-depth analysis of the 100 individual industries (and their leading firms) within the EU manufacturing sector in 1987, as revealed by a new database we have assembled specifically for this purpose; and a key feature of our research is that we treat the EU as a single entity, rather than just an aggregation of twelve different countries. Given this focus for the book as a whole, the present chapter has had a mainly preliminary, scene-setting function. It has relied exclusively on existing, mostly published, sources to assemble a series of 'facts' which place EU manufacturing industry in 1987 into its global, temporal and member state contexts. Very briefly, our main findings are as follows.

1. When treated as a single entity, the EU is clearly a major player in the global economy in terms of both the size of its economy and its firms. Although there are strong similarities in the pattern of industrial production

across the Triad, we have noted the EU's relative success in 'marketing' industries and relative lack of success in 'progressive' industries.

2. No clear verdict is yet possible concerning the precise state of European integration, or degree of disequilibrium in the industrial structure, as it stood in 1987. The late 1980s was indeed a time of corporate realignments, with substantial (particularly cross-border) merger and foreign direct investment activity, especially in the 'marketing' and 'progressive' sectors. However, this was part of a world-wide phenomenon and it is unclear how much of this activity was a response to the actual or anticipated removal of non-tariff barriers as the Single European Market project got under way. From the trade statistics, there is some evidence that integration led to strong trade creation during 1984–7, but this lessened for 1987–90; similarly, there was some trade diversion in the first period, but not in the latter. Thus, the picture is certainly interesting, but equivocal—more definite conclusions must await longer series of data post 1987.

3. We must also remain equivocal about the cohesion of the EU as a single entity. Although we have found some systematic patterns in the specialization and trade of member states, these alone are insufficient to seriously challenge the view that the EU may already have developed into a substantially integrated economy. On the other hand, nor do they confirm such a view.

This much we have been able to discern from the published statistics. The general lesson is that aggregated statistics and the absence of well-specified and tested behavioural models, inevitably leave too much room for alternative interpretations. The first necessary step in advancing our knowledge is to develop a disaggregated database on the structure of EU industry. For example, the published statistics on the EU's leading firms have nothing to say about their dominance in particular industries, nor is it known how diversified they are—published lists of industry leaders invariably allocate all of a firm's turnover to its primary industry. We are similarly ignorant about the stretch of ownership of production facilities across the EU—published lists do not distinguish either the country of production by firms or the multinationality of ownership within countries. In fact, until now, as well as being surprisingly ignorant about the pattern of corporate activity in both product and geographic spaces across the EU, we have had to be content with only very isolated evidence from a few high profile industries about the extent to which market leaders dominate EU production. The first purpose of this book is to fill those gaps. The second purpose is to begin to explain the evidence we find, with a view to developing a better understanding of why the industrial organization of the EU looks the way it does.

With those objectives in mind, the present chapter has laid down the first cornerstone. We have introduced a classificatory scheme which distinguishes different broad types of industry, deriving from recent theoretical developments in the areas of industrial organization, international trade, and international business. This helps to formalize and extend the notions of 'marketing' and 'progressive' industries. Applying this classification scheme to the published trade and production data, we have found important differences between types of industries. For example, trade tends to be noticeably higher where firms compete via R&D, but lower where advertising is more prominent; and what trade there is in more advertising-intensive industries tends to be confined to within the EU. It also appears that R&D-intensive industries are more heavily concentrated in the larger more developed member states—particularly Germany and France. The following chapters carry this classification scheme forward to the further analysis of industrial concentration, multinationality, and trade flows.

BRUCE LYONS and ALESSANDRO SEMBENELLI

3

The EU Market Share Matrix

3.1 Introduction

At the heart of the empirical work in this book is a database constructed specifically for this project: the *EU market share matrix*. This matrix provides a concise, yet disaggregated and comprehensive, description of the structure of the EU manufacturing sector, and it goes far beyond the sort of information available in the published statistics analysed in the previous chapter. It is the product of a collaborative data collection effort, stretching over a three-year period, to which all of the national research teams have contributed. This chapter is devoted to a description of the matrix: explaining how it was constructed, and exploring some of its properties. Section 3.2 explains the underlying principles and logic of the matrix; Section 3.3 briefly describes the methods of data collection and collation; Section 3.4 reports its broad dimensions; and Section 3.5 assesses its likely 'accuracy'. Section 3.6 summarizes.

3.2. The logic of a leading firms' market share matrix

The previous chapter illustrates the limited scope of published data sources on EU industrial structure. Very little is known about concentration—either at the aggregate level or within individual industries; FDI statistics are only published at a very aggregate level, and nothing is known about the extent of cross-border production; the corporate structures of even the very largest firms are uncharted; and so on. As much as anything, it was a shared recognition of this paucity of disaggregated data that first spawned the idea of the collaborative research programme described in this volume.

It was always clear to us that any systematic attempt to fill these gaps in knowledge would be a time-consuming and costly exercise. And so it proved.[1] We leave it to others to judge whether our resources were well spent, but the end result is a unified database for the EU which is, at the same time, both more comprehensive and disaggregated than anything currently available in any published (or unpublished) source. It is comprehensive in that it covers the

[1] In the event, this data collection was even more demanding than expected, and it is perhaps fortunate that the team had something less than perfect foresight when first assessing the probable effort that would be involved!

entire manufacturing sector, but disaggregated in that the unit of observation is the market share of individual firms within reasonably well defined industries.

In some respects, the task we set ourselves can be likened to constructing a unified census of production at the EU level, but not subject to the usual confidentiality restrictions concerning the identities and market shares of individual firms in specific industries. Of course, it goes without saying that a comprehensive census of all EU firms would far exceed the resources of this, or any other, research project; and to keep the exercise within manageable proportions, we focused on only the largest firms in each industry.

One way that we might have proceeded would have been to concentrate our efforts on an already identified list of the leading firms in Europe—say, the top 500, as published in a commercially produced directory. It might be expected that a thorough disaggregation of the sales of such firms both by industry and location of output would tell us most of what we needed to know about, for example, concentration in most parts of the manufacturing sector. After all, such a set of giant firms should occupy the leading positions in most industries. In the event however, this is *not* how we proceeded - partly because all of the listings we examined suffer from serious deficiencies from our point of view,[2] and partly because, contrary to expectation, the giants of European industry are heavily concentrated in only certain sectors of manufacturing. Thus, whilst the top 500 European industrial firms will include all significant players in chemicals, vehicles, metals, electrical engineering etc., many of the specialized market leaders in more moderately sized industries will not appear. In other words, large aggregate firm size is an insufficient criterion for locating the market leaders in all industries. For this reason, we employed an alternative procedure which is essentially an extension of one previously used for the UK for 1986 (Davies and Morris, 1991, and Davies *et al.*, 1991). It involves the concept of a leading firms' market share matrix based on the following principles:

1. Define a firm as 'leading' if it is *one of the five largest European producers in at least one 3-digit industry*.
2. For any such firm, the matrix should include estimates of its production in *all* industries in which it operates—not only those in which it is a 'leader'.
3. Each such estimate should be made for both the EU in aggregate, and, where appropriate, disaggregated across the different member states in which the output is produced.

Thus, the rows of the matrix identify the EU production of each leading firm in all industries in which it operates; and the columns identify the leading producers in each manufacturing industry.

---

[2] For instance, they often exclude firms which are non-EU-owned but which nevertheless produce on a large scale in the EU; commonly they do not distinguish firms' production in manufacturing from that in services, energy or extraction; and invariably rankings are based on the magnitude of world, rather than EU, production. (See also n. 19, Ch. 2.)

These principles and definitions require elaboration in four respects. First, a European producer is defined as *any firm producing in the EU*, and its size is measured by the value of its production in the EU. It is perfectly feasible therefore that the matrix will include some major US (and other non-EU) multinational firms—but only their European production. Second, the choice of *five* leaders and the *3-digit* industry level are partly arbitrary deriving from historical precedent, and partly a matter of practicalities. In fixing on five firms in each industry, it is assumed that in most industries this will include the major actors, so far as market power is concerned; and in using the 3-digit level, it is assumed that this is sufficiently disaggregated to provide an economically meaningful definition of industry. In fact, it is not difficult to think of examples where one or both of these assumptions are invalid—especially the latter. On the other hand, this has the virtue of confining the matrix to manageable proportions—since there are roughly 100 3-digit industries in the European NACE classification, this places an upper limit of roughly 500 firms for which data is required (and significantly less if, as is confirmed later, many firms are leaders in more than one industry).

A matrix built on this basis is arguably the most economical way of investigating a range of structural dimensions of industries and firms for any large country or entity such as the EU. It will exhibit the following properties:

1. For any individual industry, it includes information on the market shares of the five largest producers and for a number of other non-leading firms who are significant players in other industries. This should be sufficient to calculate meaningful measures of *industry concentration*.
2. For any individual firm, the matrix reports the full extent of its *diversification* across industries.
3. For any individual firm or industry, the matrix reports the full extent of *intra-EU multinational production*.
4. At the aggregate level, virtually all firms of any significant absolute size will be included because the vast majority of the big firms will be in a leading position in at least one of the industries in which they operate. Thus it should be possible to meaningfully estimate the extent of *aggregate concentration*.

It follows from point 4 that the set of firms appearing on such a matrix is unlikely to differ very much from a list of the largest European firms, where size is measured by aggregate production (regardless of industrial distribution). But, for reasons mentioned above, there will be some differences. On the one hand, the matrix will include some really quite small firms which have qualified either as a leader of a small industry, or as one of the smallest leaders in a medium-sized industry. On the other hand, it will undoubtedly exclude some firms of large aggregate size which, because they are highly diversified, never attain a top five position in any particular industry. It may also exclude the occasional large firm which lies just outside the top five in a very large industry such as steel, cars, or aircraft.

3.3 Definitions and Methodology

Given that the matrix is essentially industry-driven in its key criterion, a potential starting point might be standard published national census type sources.
Unfortunately, at present they are inadequate for this purpose. One reason is
that there is still considerable heterogeneity between member states in the details and conventions used in industrial censuses. But even if all national censuses were perfectly harmonized, meaningful aggregation would still be
impossible given that national census authorities are precluded, for reasons of
confidentiality, from publishing information about individual firms. It would
be impossible, for example, to deduce the total EU size of any firm which operates across member states. Therefore the only real option was to create our own
database from primary sources—mainly, company reports, supported by business and trade directories and previous industry case-studies.

3.3.1 Definitions

As already mentioned, for reasons of practicality, the industry is defined at the
3-digit level. Although the 4-digit level is closer to the theoretical notion of an
industry comprising firms with fairly high cross-price elasticities of demand
and/or supply, the greater degree of detail would have increased the data requirement far beyond the project's resources. 1987 was chosen as the year of
analysis because, at the time when most of the information were collected, it
was the latest year for which comprehensive data were available. As it happens,
1987 was also the first full year of the run-up to the Single European Market in
1992, and this will make the 1987 matrix an interesting comparator for planned
similar ventures for later years.[3]
    To avoid confusion, we must define our measure of size very precisely (if
pedantically). The size of firms and industries is measured by *the value of sales
of goods produced in the EU*.[4] This is consistent with typical practice in national
production censuses.[5] It differs from production only to the extent of changes
in stocks, and for that reason we often refer below to size as production. More
importantly, it differs from sales in the EU: (a) at the firm level, because it includes the firm's extra-EU exports and excludes any EU sales which are
sourced from outside the EU; (b) at the industry level for the same reasons, and
also because it excludes all imports from non-EU producers. Thus, our use of
the term *market share*, when we divide a firm's production by industry production, is somewhat loose, and must be excused on the grounds of convenience. It is arguable whether true sales measures would have been preferable on

---

[3] At the time of writing, an update for 1993 is under way.
[4] Primary data was collected initially in national currencies and was subsequently converted
into ECUs using the 1987 average exchange rates.
[5] It is also the case for our source of data for European industry size (Eurostat, *Structure and
Activity of Industry* (1987), but see also Appendix 3 for adjustments made to these data.)

theoretical grounds—this will vary depending on the different contexts in which size is used. But pragmatic reasons make sales-based measures almost impossible. While it is simple to adjust industry-level production data by subtracting extra-EU exports and adding extra-EU imports, there are two real problems in identifying the shares of the leading sellers by sales: company accounts do not always report the existence of non-EU sourcing, and there is no systematic source of information on the market shares of leading importers not producing in the EU.

Lastly, every attempt has been made to consolidate all firms under a common ultimate parentage, and any firm operating in more than one EU country was recorded as a single entity on the matrix.[6]

3.3.2 Broad design of data collection

Stylizing our procedure somewhat, it can be explained as a four stage process. First, an initial set of potential candidate firms was extracted from a published list of the 500 largest European industrial firms by turnover (ELC, 1989). Each participating research centre was then responsible, by using company reports and local directories,[7] for disaggregating the production data of firms from its own country across 3-digit industries. Each centre also used local knowledge to add further candidate firms to the list. The results were then consolidated centrally (at UEA), so as to generate an initial list of leading firms for each industry at the EU level. However, this was only a starting point—for many industries, we had not even identified five significantly sized firms. This only confirmed our expectation that the 500 largest European firms in aggregate would not occupy all the leading positions in all industries.

A second stage was devoted to identifying and filling the gaps. An important role in this stage was filled by an hypothetical 'predicted' matrix—nicknamed the 'spoof matrix'.[8] This was constructed using the results of a previous similar exercise for the UK (Davies *et al.*, 1991). For each industry in the spoof, hypothetical entries were calculated by assuming that the market shares of the five leaders in each country were the same as those for the UK. Applying these shares to each country's aggregate production figure yielded hypothetical estimates of the absolute sizes of the top five firms in each country. Using a second assumption, that none of these hypothetical firms operated in more

---

[6] In this respect, *Who Owns Whom in Europe* (1990), was taken as the ultimate authority. Subsidiaries were consolidated if they were consolidated in the parent's accounts, or where the firm held 50% or more of equity. Associate companies with less than 50% held were also consolidated if there was evidence of control by a minority shareholding. A joint venture was treated as a separate entity if none of its parents produced separately in the industry concerned, otherwise, its production was split equally between the parents.

[7] The main centres were in Belgium, Germany, Italy, the Netherlands, Spain, and the UK, but we also had invaluable help from colleagues in Greece, France, Ireland, and Portugal. Typical sources included: *Key British Enterprises* (1987); *Britain's Top 20,000 Companies*; *France 30000*; *Kompass*; and *Dun's Europa*.

[8] A term which was sometimes misunderstood by research assistants unfamiliar with English vernacular!

than one country, yielded fifty-five anonymous candidates for inclusion in the European top five. These were then ranked by absolute size, thus providing for each industry five hypothetical leading firms with hypothetical sizes and country of origin. The spoof was then matched with the actual leaders so far identified in stage 1. This provided pointers to the approximate sizes and countries of origin of the missing firms; and, on this basis, the national research teams were then delegated to search for actual firms which might match these hypothetical firms.

Following this more targeted search, a third stage involved an iterative process, of sifting and double-checking, before a penultimate list of five leaders at the European level emerged for each industry.[9]

Fourthly, as the matrix neared completion, each leading firm's EU production in each industry was disaggregated into separate estimates of its production in each member state. This entailed returning to the worksheets already collated for each firm and using company reports and national directories to identify the geographical disaggregation across the eleven member states.[10] This stage of the work yielded the data for the analysis of multinationality described in Chapters 7 and 11, but it also provided an important cross-check on the accuracy of estimates at the EU level, and some late deletions and additions were made to the matrix.[11]

3.4 Coverage and Dimensions

The manufacturing sector in the NACE classification scheme (Divisions 2–4) comprises 111 3-digit industries. In the construction of the matrix, we decided to exclude nine of these industries because they include groups of products which are too heterogeneous or miscellaneous to be considered as self-standing industries, or because they conduct activities which are not, in reality, manufacturing.[12] A further four pairs of industries were each amalgamated because

[9] The number of firms investigated and ultimately discarded at this stage was quite substantial. These firms play no part in the matrix proper, but the information gained helped in a variety of ways when estimating the magnitudes of the contribution of non-leading firms, for example, to concentration within each industry.

[10] Throughout this book, Belgium is consolidated with Luxemburg.

[11] Using poetic licence, we have described this stage of the data collection as a premeditated integral part of the research design. In fact, honesty dictates that we should admit that the matrix was originally conceived as only having an aggregate EU dimension. However, at a relatively late stage, we realized that, with only a relatively minor extra research input, the database could be substantially enriched by adding the geographical breakdowns. As explained in the text, this also had the unexpected benefit of identifying a few last minute revisions to the aggregate EU estimates for some firms.

[12] The extraction/mining industries are: 211, extraction and preparation of iron ore; 212, extraction and preparation of non-ferrous metal ores; 231, extraction of slate, stone, chalk, sand, clay, and gravel; 232, mining of potassium salt and natural phosphates; 233, salt mining; and 239, extraction of other minerals and peat mining. Industry 348 is an assembly and installation activity (of electrical equipment/apparatus). Industries 365, miscellaneous vehicles, and 435, jute and polypropylene yarn and fabrics comprise small very heterogeneous products which are not always reported separately in national censuses.

Table 3.1 A fragment of the matrix

Firm (i)	Industry (j) (mn. ECUs)					
	1 221	4 224	11 247	13 255	15 260	All Manu- facturing
1 ABF		14				2,218
2 ACEC Union		1,139				1,786
3 Addis						57
4 Adolph Wurth						250
5 Aerospatiale						4,526
6 Agnesi						65
7 AKZO				830	1,053	5,090
8 Alcan		1,614				1,797
9 Allied Lyons						2,165
10 Alno Mobel						221
11 American Brands						4,448
12 Amorim						73
13 Amylum						256
14 Ara Schuhfabriken						144
15 Arbed	1,679					2,932
....						
....						
....						
....						
....						
300 Varta						642
301 VDO						787
302 Vereinigte						336
303 Viag	1,398					1,896
304 Villeroy & Boch			80			590
305 Zucchi						173
306 Voith						707
307 Volkswagen						24,450
308 VSEL						538
309 Welle						353
310 Wellman						169
311 Western United						382
312 W. Schimmel						27
313 Zahnradfab						1,962
TOTAL MATRIX	25,178	12,431	8,013	6,393	7,743	708,545
TOTAL EU	52,628	32,059	18,988	13,716	8,278	2,181,340

Notes: x_{ij} denotes firm i's production in industry j. There are also separate matrices for member states which report x_{ijk}, firm i's production in industry j in member state k.

the products and/or processes concerned were so closely related as to make it impossible for us to distinguish them when reading company reports. Indeed, some of these industries are also sometimes amalgamated in official statistical publications.[13] This leaves the matrix with 100 separate industries, and since the excluded industries are only very minor, the 100 accounted for 2,181bn. ECUs, which was 98.9% of aggregate EU manufacturing production in 1987.

Table 3.1 shows an excerpt from the full matrix: each entry refers to the aggregate EU production of a given firm in a given industry. Thus, for example, ACEC Union Minière's production in industry 224 (non-ferrous metals) was 1139m. ECUs. For obvious reasons of space, the table does not include all the firms operating in the set of industries shown, or all the industries in which this sample of firms operate, or the breakdown of production across member states. The row totals in the table show each firm's total production across all industries (1,786 for ACEC), and the column totals show each industry's aggregate EU production (32.1bn. ECUs for non-ferrous metals.)

Table 3.2 shows the broad dimensions of the matrix, and *en passant* this also reveals, albeit crudely at this stage, some elementary dimensions of EU manufacturing.

1. Although, by definition, there are 500 (100 * 5) leading positions to be filled on the matrix, these are captured by just 313 separate firms. Thus, the average matrix firm is in a leading position in 500/313 = 1.6 industries. This gives a rough indication of the extent of *diversification with strong market power implications*.

2. The matrix firms account for 32.5% of total EU manufacturing production (excluding the omitted industries). This gives a broad indication of the extent of *aggregate concentration* in Europe: about 300 firms account for nearly one-third of EU production.[14]

Table 3.2 Dimensions of the matrix

		Sales (bn.ECU)	Share of total EU manufacturing(%)
Number of firms	313		
Total entries in matrix, of which:	1,549	708.5	32.5
Leading shares	500	520.0	23.9
Non-leading shares	1,049	188.5	8.6

[13] These industries are: motor vehicle manufacturing (351) and bodies, trailers and semi-trailers, caravans (352); wine (426) and cider and perry (425); printing (473) and publishing (474); rubber products (481) and retreading/repairing tyres (482).

[14] It should be recalled that the matrix firms do not map exactly onto the set of largest European firms measured by aggregate size—some very large firms will not appear on the matrix because they fail to occupy a top five position in any one industry. Therefore, this figure understates aggregate concentration—although not by very much (see Section 9.2.2).

3. The sum of the firms' leading shares account for 23.9% of total manu-facturing. In effect this is the sales-weighted *average five-firm concentra-tion ratio*—in the typical industry, the top 5 firms account for nearly one-quarter of EU production.
4. The matrix firms account for 1,549 separate entries. Thus, on average, the 313 firms operate in 4.92 industries, of which 3.3 are *not* leading entries. Since these non-leading entries account for 9% of total manufacturing, and 27% of the total sales of the 313 matrix firms, there appears to be sub-stantial *non-leading diversification* by market leaders.

Tables 3.3 and 3.4 report the coverage of the matrix by sectors and member states. The industrial sectors most heavily represented are man-made fibres, computers, cars and other vehicles, chemicals, and metals, whilst coverage is significantly lower in timber and furniture, leather and fur, clothing, and metal goods. This is as might be expected: from the criteria used to construct the mat-rix, it will tend to be more comprehensive in those sectors in which market leaders are more dominant (i.e. the most concentrated industries), and within which there is homogeneity of technologies (resulting in more narrow diversi-fication by leaders between adjacent industries).

Table 3.4 turns to the geographical coverage of the matrix by member state. Precisely because many matrix firms operate across member state borders, there

Table 3.3 Coverage of matrix firms by industrial sector

Industrial sector		Production (bn. ECU)		Coverage (%)
		Matrix	Total EU	
22	Metal manufacturing	47.9	109.6	43.7
24	Mineral products	22.9	92.5	24.8
25	Chemicals	110.2	230.1	47.9
26	Man-made fibres	7.7	8.3	93.5
31	Metal goods	16.8	157.0	10.7
32	Mechanical engineering	52.3	182.3	28.7
33	Office machinery & computers	25.4	30.6	82.9
34	Electrical engineering	78.4	189.6	41.4
35	Motor vehicles & parts	139.8	192.7	72.5
36	Other transport	33.7	57.2	58.8
37	Instrument engineering	8.7	21.8	40.2
41/42	Food, drink, & tobacco	97.9	397.0	24.7
43	Textiles	9.5	90.0	10.5
44	Leather	1.1	14.0	7.9
45	Footwear & clothing	5.1	78.5	6.4
46	Timber & furniture	5.0	81.3	6.1
47	Paper, printing, publishing	20.7	141.8	14.6
48	Rubber & plastics	22.5	85.5	26.3
49	Other manufacturing	3.0	21.5	14.0
TOTALS		708.4	2,181.3	32.5

Table 3.4 Coverage of matrix firms by member state

Country k	Matrix firms originating from k			Production share in k by all matrix firms
	Number	Share of matrix production		
		incl. non-EU	excl. non-EU	
Germany(28)	75	31	36	36
France(18)	58	20	23	21
Italy(18)	49	10	12	12
UK(15)	65	15	17	18
Netherlands(5)	11	7	8	4
Bel/Lux(4)	12	2	2	4
Spain(9)	5	1	1	3
Portugal(1)	2	0	0	0.3
Denmark(2)	0	0	0	0.2
Greece(1)	0	0	0	0.3
Ireland(1)	0	0	0	0.2
Non-EU	36	14	—	n.a.
TOTALS	313	100	100	100

Notes: Bracketed figures after country name indicate the size of that country's manufacturing sector as a share of the EU total, measured by production (see Table 2.5). Unilever and Shell have both been designated as Dutch firms throughout the book. In fact, they are of joint Dutch/UK origin. They account for 2.5% of the aggregate production of all matrix firms.

are two dimensions to this. For each country, we can estimate the importance of firms originating from that country, and also the importance of the country as a location of production. Thus there are seventy-five German firms on the matrix, and they account for 31% of the total production of all matrix firms. On the other hand, the last column shows that 36% of all matrix production is located in Germany. Note, however, that the difference between these two figures is entirely accounted for by the presence on the matrix of thirty-six firms who are subsidiaries of non-EU owned companies.[15] These firms account for 14% of total matrix output, and this can be likened to 'inward investment'; on the other hand, the matrix includes no equivalent to 'outward investment' in non-EU countries by EU firms. For this reason, the third column shows the share of firms from each member state as a percentage of the matrix total excluding the production of non-EU owned firms. As can be seen, once this asymmetry is removed, Germany's share is 36%, whether measured by the output of its firms or by production of matrix firms in Germany. Similarly, the UK's share is virtually identical by both measures when non-EU firms are excluded (UK production is boosted by the extensive operations by US firms in the UK).

As might be expected, on both measures the four largest member states are dominant: Germany, France, UK, and Italy account for just over three-quarters

[15] These originate from USA (25), Canada (3), Switzerland and Sweden (7), and Japan (1).

of the firms and 87–8% of production. Within the big 4, Germany, France and, to a lesser extent, the UK have a presence on the matrix that is disproportionately large relative to their manufacturing base, but the Italian presence is strikingly small. Outside the big 4, only the Benelux countries have a significant presence in the matrix. Dutch firms tend to be absolutely large with extensive multinational operations, whilst Belgium/Luxemburg has as many (but much smaller) firms. This leaves Spain and Portugal with only token representation and the smaller countries with no matrix firms and only limited production within their borders by leading 'foreign' multinationals. The multinational dimension of the matrix will receive far more detailed attention in later chapters (7,8, and 11), but these figures give a preliminary flavour of this aspect of the matrix.

3.5 An Assessment of Accuracy

Because this is the first-ever study to attempt to extract data of this sort, there is no totally convincing way of cross-checking the accuracy of the matrix. Nevertheless, there are three reasons for having some confidence in the quality of our estimates.

1. Data collection was allocated a singularly large proportion of our research time. The project was also deliberately organized so that the responsibility for collecting and checking primary information rested with national research teams, whilst reconciliation, consolidation, and harmonization was done centrally. We believe this combination of 'local knowledge' and central cross-checking minimized the chances of double counting or other straightforward computing or definitional errors.

2. The methodology itself was checked in the earlier project which constructed a UK market share matrix for 1986 using similar methods (Davies *et al.*, 1991). In that case they were able to conduct consistency checks on the top tail of the matrix size distribution, using the aggregate size distribution table for UK manufacturing, as published in the *Census of Production* (Davies and Morris, 1991). Not only were the two distributions very similar for individual size classes within the top tail, but the top 100 firms had very similar distributions of production across 2-digit sectors.

3. Similar checks are impossible here because there is no official published aggregate-size distribution for the EU. But it is possible to compare the top tail of the matrix firms with a semi-official listing for 1987 reported in the *Panorama of European Industry, 1990*: 51; see also our Table 2.7). This shows the identities of the top European-owned manufacturers in 1987 but unfortunately, it was restricted to only seventy firms. Sixty-three of these seventy firms also appear amongst the 100 largest matrix firms. Of the remaining seven, four were firms which derived most of their turnover outside manufacturing and/or outside Europe,[16] and three, Rover, Montedison, and L'Air Liquide, were very

large firms operating in very large industries—cars and chemicals. They were not included in the matrix because, in spite of their aggregate size, they were still smaller than the fifth largest firms in their respective industries. Interestingly, of the firms in the matrix top 100 but not in Panorama's top 70, 18 were non-EU owned firms who were excluded, by definition, from the Panorama listing. Obviously, this check falls far short of a rigorous test for the matrix, but it is reassuring that it fails to identify any instances of firms which have been incorrectly omitted.

3.6 Conclusion

Because most of the empirical work in this book draws heavily on the European market share matrix, it is important to understand the underlying concept, its properties and weaknesses.

It is a matrix which covers virtually all of the 3-digit industries within the manufacturing sector and all of the leading firms therein. For each firm, the matrix shows its share of industry production in each industry in which it operates; and this information is recorded at both the aggregate EU level, and for each member state. It has been confined to manageable proportions by defining a 'leading firm' as one which occupies a leading position (i.e. in the top five) in at least one 3-digit industry. Although 100 industries are included, the number of firms is only 313 because many of these firms hold leading positions in more than one industry.

Needless to say, with a database limited to just 313 firms, we cannot pretend that this provides a complete picture of the structure of the manufacturing sector in such a large entity as the European Union. Nevertheless, we do believe that it is a remarkably powerful and economical tool with which to tackle the subjects in the following chapters. To see this, visualize the matrix (in spreadsheet terms) as comprising a 'master matrix', in which the columns refer to industries and the rows to firms. Underlying the master matrix are eleven 'stacked' member state matrices, which show how each firm's aggregate EU entry in each industry can be disaggregated across the member states. Then, from the master matrix:

1. Read down the columns to examine EU concentration (and size inequalities) in individual industries.
2. Read across the rows to examine each firm's diversification across industries.

[16] The most extreme example of the difference between the two listings is Grand Metropolitan, recorded by *Panorama* as in twenty-third place with a turnover of 8075m. ECUs, but figuring only in seventy-fourth place on the matrix, with an EU manufacturing turnover of only 2352m. ECUs. An examination of this firm's company report reveals that most of its activities lie outside manufacturing, and it also has substantial operations outside the EU. This illustrates very vividly the problems with most 'Top 100' type listings that are currently published.

3. Sum the row totals to estimate aggregate concentration in the manufacturing sector as a whole.

Switching to the stacked, constituent member state matrices:

4. Read across matrices for any firm to observe its (intra-EU) multi-nationality, both in aggregate and within individual industries.
5. Read across matrices for any industry to observe its (intra-EU) multi-nationality.
6. Examine the matrix for any one member state to observe concentration, and diversification in that state. (Although, in this case, the information is far less complete—excluding many nationally important firms, especially in smaller member states—and is not investigated in this book.)

Each of the structural dimensions just mentioned is examined in detail in subsequent chapters, but from a fairly cursory look at the dimensions of the matrix, we have already established some crude facts of considerable interest. In the typical industry, the five largest firms account for about one-quarter of total EU output. Leading firms are often significantly diversified across industries: the typical firm considered here operates in five industries, in 1.6 of which it is in a leading position. The 313 firms in the matrix account for almost one-third of total European manufacturing output; and a significant proportion of this represents cross-border production activity.

However, we should close the chapter with a 'health warning'. Necessarily, we have placed an overriding reliance on company reports. In that companies are not compelled to publish their reports in standardized homogenous form, data collection has been not only an enormous task, but it has also required many judgements and informed guesses. Undoubtedly errors have been made (e.g in failing to always correctly identify the five leaders in each industry, and in disaggregating individual firms' outputs across industries and member states). Needless to say, both within and across the individual national teams contributing to this project, estimates have been subjected to scrutiny and double-checking, but undetected errors must remain.

STEVE DAVIES and CATHERINE MATRAVES

PART II

The Structure of EU Industries

4

The Dimensions of Industrial Structure

4.1 Introduction

The five chapters which make up this part of the book focus on the individual industry as the unit of observation. In turn, they examine different elements of industry structure: specialization, trade, and integration (Ch.5); concentration (Ch.6); intra-EU multinationality (Ch.7); and the role of non-EU multinational firms (Ch.8). On a factual level, they use the market share matrix to build up an integrated statistical mapping of various elements of the structure of manufacturing in the EU. But, running alongside this factual flow, there is also an underlying conceptual theme. This is that, by observing different facets of the structure of EU industry, we gain important insights into the nature of the competitive processes at work. This is of interest for both policy purposes and as a test of contemporary industrial organization theory. For example, is competition truly European, or does it remain partly localized within national boundaries? And, can we detect differences between industries which can be explained, as predicted by theory, in terms of the type of competitive weapons used by firms?

The present chapter starts the map-plotting task, in Section 4.2, by extracting estimates of EU industrial concentration from the matrix. This provides the first-ever assessment of prevailing levels of market dominance on the European stage. We are able to identify the types of industries in which the market leaders are most prominent, and to draw comparisons with the concentration levels typically observed in previous studies at the national level. The second purpose of the chapter is to introduce the conceptual framework within which EU concentration can be related to the other dimensions of structure: concentration in member states, the extent of trade specialization, and multinationality. This framework is derived in Section 4.3 in the form of an algebraic identity, and the components of the identity are estimated in Section 4.4. This identity (or decomposition) really holds the key to this part of the book, and it serves to introduce each of the following chapters as part of an integrated and interlocking whole. Indeed, we believe that it constitutes a significant methodological advance since it serves as a link which integrates three sub-disciplines of economics (industrial organization, international trade, and international business). Section 4.5 summarizes.

4.2. Industrial Concentration at the EU Level

4.2.1 Measuring Concentration

Industrial concentration is not a single dimensional concept and there is no one summary measure which is superior under all circumstances. In this book, we shall employ the two indices most widely used in the industrial organization literature and in anti-trust policy—the concentration ratio and the Herfindahl index.[1]

Since the market share matrix was constructed so as to include the market shares of at least the five largest producers in each industry, the five firm concentration ratio is an obvious point at which to start. This is defined as:

> *C5EU*: the five firm concentration ratio, measured as the combined production of the five largest producers in the industry as a share of total EU production

Estimates of *C5EU* for each of the 100 industries can be found in Appendix 2.1; but here we summarize using the frequency distribution shown in Figure 4.1 and Table 4.1 which lists the most and least concentrated industries. As can be seen, the distribution exhibits a definite positive skew, with most industries bunched at fairly moderate levels. The arithmetic mean value is 22.3%, and C5EU is less than 30% in three-quarters of the population. However, a few industries exhibit much higher values—in six cases concentration exceeds 50%—and Table 4.1 identifies the twenty most concentrated industries.

Viewed sectorally, the most concentrated industries come from a fairly diverse range, although chemicals, electrical engineering, and vehicles are especially well represented. Similarly, there is a rough balance between consumer- and producer-goods industries. However, a very strong connection emerges when we classify according to Type 1 or 2, as defined in Chapter 2. Sixteen of the twenty most concentrated industries produce differentiated products for which competition can be associated with high advertising or research and development, or both. There are only four exceptions, and two of these are from iron and steel (for which there was traditionally heavy state aid for national champions) and one other, glass, includes an important sub-sector for which R&D is important. This central role for product differentiation is reinforced in the second part of the table, which identifies the least concentrated industries. Not unexpectedly, this set of industries comes from a narrow range of traditional sectors such as clothing and textiles, wood and metal products, and none is Type 2.

Two additional preliminary observations can be drawn by looking at Table 4.2, which reports the descriptive statistics for *C5EU* alongside those for the four other concentration ratios (the four- firm ratio, and so on) which can be calculated from the matrix. First, the correlation coefficients between *C5EU* and the other ratios are extremely high: this suggests that any findings are

---

[1] See Section A1.2.1 of Appendix 1 for a fuller discussion of concentration indices.

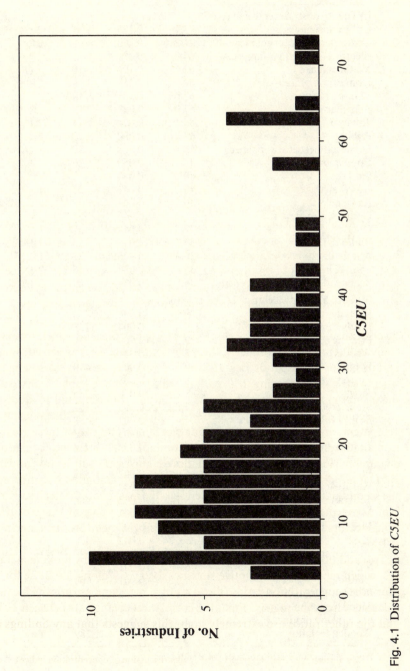

Fig. 4.1 Distribution of C5EU

Table 4.1 The most concentrated and least concentrated industries

Industry	C5EU	HEU	NEU	Type
(i) The 20 most concentrated (*C5EU* > 33.3%)				
Optical instruments	73.1	0.135	7	2AR
Computers/Office machinery	71.2	0.203	5	2R
Electric lamps & lighting, etc.	64.7	0.189	5	2R
Motor vehicles	62.9	0.104	10	2AR
Domestic & office chemicals	62.9	0.118	9	2R
Man-made fibres	62.6	0.105	10	2R
Aerospace	57.0	0.087	12	2R
Tobacco	56.1	0.074	14	2A
Rubber	48.7	0.080	12	2R
Domestic electrical appliances	46.4	0.060	17	2AR
Confectionery	43.7	0.050	20	2A
Steel tubes	40.5	0.044	23	1
Iron & steel	40.2	0.041	25	1
Rail stock	40.1	0.043	23	2R
Cycles & motorcycles	39.3	0.046	22	2R
Glass	37.8	0.048	21	1
Radio & TV	37.2	0.045	22	2AR
Abrasives	36.4	0.036	28	1
Paint & ink	35.8	0.038	26	2AR
Soaps & detergents	34.8	0.034	29	2AR
(ii) The 25 least concentrated (*C5EU* < 10%)				
Household textiles	9.6	0.004	276	1
Leather products	9.4	0.004	258	1
Printing & publishing	9.3	0.004	270	1
Wood-sawing	8.9	0.004	257	1
Forging	8.5	0.002	470	1
Cotton-weaving	8.2	0.003	375	1
Jewellery	8.1	0.004	255	1
Stone products	7.8	0.003	382	1
Boilers & containers	7.4	0.002	438	1
Wool	7.2	0.003	348	1
Leather-tanning	6.5	0.002	484	1
Knitting	6.4	0.002	544	1
Fur	5.9	0.002	582	1
Footwear	5.8	0.002	515	1
Tools and cans	5.7	0.002	588	1
Metal structures	5.7	0.002	589	1
Meat products	5.7	0.002	535	1
Plastics	5.6	0.002	479	1
Wooden structures	5.5	0.002	596	1
Silk	5.3	0.001	712	1
Clothing	4.3	0.001	1,000	1
Wooden containers	4.1	0.001	957	1
Metal treatment	3.8	0.001	1,111	1
Other wood products	3.2	0.001	1,390	1
Wooden furniture	3.1	0.001	1,289	1

Note: See Section 2.5.1 for definitions of industry types.

Table 4.2 Comparison of concentration indices

	Mean	S.Dev	Median	Max.	Min.	Correlation with *C5EU*
C5EU	22.3	16.7	17.2	73.1	3.1	n.a.
C4EU	19.8	15.0	15.2	66.3	2.7	0.996
C3EU	16.8	13.2	12.7	62.8	2.2	0.983
C2EU	13.1	10.9	10.4	56.7	1.7	0.956
C1EU	8.0	7.3	5.8	41.8	0.9	0.895
HEU	0.024	0.036	0.011	0.203	0.001	0.915
NEU	207	278	95	1,390	5	−0.601

unlikely to be sensitive to precisely which ratio is used. Second, a comparison of the mean values for the five ratios yields the typical market shares of the five top ranked firms across industries: $S1$ = 8%, $S2$ = 5.1%; $S3$ = 3.7%; $S4$ = 3%; and $S5$ = 2.5%. Again, these are only moderate compared to the typical values one might expect in a national study.[2] Of course, these are only mean values, and the magnitudes of the standard deviations and maximum values confirm that there are some industries in which only three, two, or even just one firm hold quite dominant positions on the European stage. The issue of individual market shares is pursued later in Chapter 9.

Although the concentration ratio is the most obvious index to use given the nature of the matrix, we have a preference for the other main concentration index used in the literature: the Herfindahl index (*HEU*) and its number-equivalent form (*NEU*). This is for two reasons: unlike C5, H ideally uses information on the shares of *all* firms in an industry (it therefore reflects inequalities amongst and outside the top); and it has more desirable decomposition properties, which is essential for the decomposition analysis which follows.[3] The indices are defined here in Table 4.4 and discussed in more detail in Appendix 1. In words:

> *HEU*, the Herfindahl index, is the summed squares of all firms' market shares and, *NEU*, the number equivalent, is the reciprocal of *H*. This expresses any given value of *H* (firm size distribution) as the number of hypothetical equal-sized firms which would be required to score that *H* value.

Intuitively, the *H* index can be thought of as the 'typical' market share of firms in a given industry: in effect it is the weighted average market share, with

[2] In fact, there are very few national studies which document the typical values of the top five ranked firms individually. But in one such study for the UK, Davies *et al.*, 1991:8, reports $S1$ = 18.5, $S2$ = 10.9, $S3$ = 6.8, $S4$ = 4.5, and $S5$ = 3.3. Apart from the obviously higher magnitudes, the pattern of shares is not dissimilar from that found here, with the proportionate difference between mean shares increasing as we move up through the ranks.

[3] Many other indices, including the Entropy (*E*) family, share these desirable properties and would have suited our purposes nearly as well as *H*. Our preference for *H* is not especially strong, although Davies (1979) has shown that *H* might be preferred to *E* because it represents the two dimensions to concentration—firm numbers and size inequalities—in a more balanced way than *E*.

the weight being simply the market share itself. Likewise, the number equivalent is the hypothetical number of firms there *would be* in the industry if all firms were identical, with market share = H. For example, suppose industry A has four equal-sized firms, then its H index is 0.25 (reflecting a typical market share of 25%) and $NH = 4$ (reflecting four equal-sized firms). In contrast, suppose industry B has one firm with 40% of the market and four other firms with 15% each. This configuration of shares also yields $H = 0.25$, reflecting a similar 'typical' market share to that in A; and, although B has five firms, because they are of unequal size, concentration is recorded as 'equivalent' to that in A. Quite generally, the number-equivalent measure will always be less than the *actual* firm number, and by more the greater are the size inequalities involved.

Strictly speaking, to estimate the H index, one requires information on the market shares of *all* firms in the industry; and, clearly, we cannot strictly fulfill this requirement with the data from the market share matrix since the typical European industry will include thousands of (unknown to us) firms. However, because the index is based on *squared* market shares, the contribution to H of smaller firms soon becomes negligible, once one goes beyond the leaders. Appendix 3 describes the methods we have used to allow for the effects of smaller non-matrix firms—it is easily confirmed that any errors involved will typically be of a very small order.

The summary statistics for HEU and NEU are reported in Table 4.2 (again, Appendix 2.1 reports the full set of estimates for all 100 industries): the average industry records $H = 2.4\%$, which has a number equivalent of nearly forty-two. As with any concentration index, these values really only assume much significance when used in a comparative way. But, superficially at least, one would not equate an industry with forty-two equal-sized firms, each with a market share of 2.4%, as tightly oligopolistic. The table also confirms that the correlation between HEU and $C5EU$ is very high, and the two measures give very similar rankings amongst the most highly and lowly concentrated industries shown in Table 4.1. This is in line with most previous empirical studies of concentration and suggests that the findings in the following chapters should be fairly robust to alternative concentration indices.[4] Figure 4.2 shows the distribution of HEU across the 100 industries: it displays an even more pronounced positive skew than $C5EU$—again, a result typical of previous comparative studies of concentration measures.

4.2.2 International comparisons

On the face of it, these estimates, both for $C5EU$ and HEU, suggest that typical levels of EU concentration are fairly moderate. Broadly speaking, the

[4] See Curry and George, 1983, Davies *et al.*, 1988:85–6; and Hay and Morris, 1991:215–16, for brief and clear surveys of the previous literature on the similarities and differences between H and $C5$ in practice.

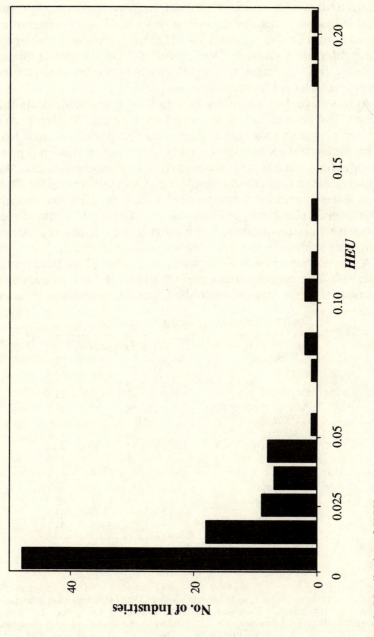

Fig. 4.2 Distribution of *HEU*

mean for $C5EU$ is little more than half the magnitude of typical values reported in previous national studies at the 3-digit level.[5] However, comparisons between the EU and individual nations need great care given that integration was incomplete in 1987 and that, anyway, the EU is larger than most individual nations by an order of magnitude. A more interesting perspective might be inter-temporal—is EU concentration increasing or decreasing as integration proceeds? While this is high on our agenda for ongoing research, it is impossible at present—precisely because these are the first known estimates of concentration at the EU level.

At this stage then, comparisons with individual countries are the only option. Two types of comparison afford some interest. The first is with concentration in the member states themselves: this provides a useful reference point for the next section, in which we derive a formal relationship between concentration in the EU and typical levels in the member states. Here, the facts are very clearcut (and unsurprising): taking a weighted average for $C4$, for the same 100 industries, in the four member states for which we have comparable estimates (Germany, Italy, UK, and Belgium), $C4EU$ is 14.5 points lower than national concentration levels. This is roughly as expected given the previous studies in the literature mentioned above.

A second comparison, with the other two members of the Triad (and, therefore, with different connotations) is reported in Table 4.3, again using $C4$ because this is the form in which the US and Japanese data are available.

Table 4.3 International comparisons of $C4$

	Sample means	
	I	II
$C4EU$	20.1	21.8
Average member state*	34.5	34.6
$C4USA$		
Minimum	24.0	30.9
Maximum	37.7	40.6
Average	31.4	35.7
$C4Japan$		
Minimum		48.1
Maximum		62.7
Average		55.4
Sample size	96	76

* Weighted average for Belgium, Germany, Italy, and UK.

Sources: See Appendix 3.

[5] In fact, previous studies reveal pronounced international differences, but it is usual to find typical 4 or 5 concentration ratios somewhere in the region of 30 to 60%. In the UK, for example, the typical value lies between 40 and 50%, depending on the sample and time period considered (Davies *et al.*, 1991; Davies *et al.*, 1988:88–90; or Clarke, 1987:22). Davies *et al.*, 1988, and George and Ward, 1975, also report various international comparisons.

The comparison is complicated for two reasons: (i) the US and Japanese data refer to 4-digit industries, which we have aggregated to the 3-digit level for comparability with our estimates, (ii) it is impossible to achieve a complete concordance for all 100 industries. Because of the latter, we are only able to match ninety-six industries for the USA, and seventy-six for Japan. But the former problem is more serious since accurate aggregation necessitates information on the diversification of firms across the 4-digit industries within each 3-digit industry. Unfortunately this is unknown and we have had to proceed by making two alternative, extreme assumptions on this question—reflected in the maximum and minimum estimates shown in the table.

From a bilateral comparison of means (column I), it appears that EU concentration is between 4 and 17 percentage points lower than in the USA, depending on the assumption made about diversification in the USA. A trilateral comparison (column II) on the subsample of seventy-six industries for which comparable data are available for both Japan and USA is even more conclusive. Whichever of the estimates is used, the ranking is robust, with Japan on average the most concentrated, followed by the USA and then the EU. Using the midpoint US and Japan estimates, EU market concentration is 14 points lower than the USA and 34 points lower than in Japan[6].

Obviously these comparisons merit deeper examination, especially as later and better data become available (see also Section 6.2). Nevertheless, as shown earlier in Table 2.2, the US and (to a lesser extent) Japanese manufacturing sectors are roughly equal in size to that in the EU. Perhaps their concentration levels *may* be indicative of what is to come for the EU as integration proceeds.

4.3. EU Concentration, National Concentration, International Specialization, and Multinationality: a Framework for Analysis

Having established these facts on EU concentration, we can now turn to the second purpose of the chapter—developing a framework within which EU concentration can be related to the other dimensions of industrial structure mentioned in the introduction: concentration within individual member states, international specialization (i.e. the extent to which EU production is spread equally or concentrated in a few of the member states), and multinational enterprise (i.e. the extent to which firms operate in more than one member state). Intuitively, it is likely that these elements of structure *are* interrelated; this section formalizes this intuition.

---

[6] Rather surprisingly, the simple correlation coefficients between $C4$ in the three 'countries' are low: 0.5 to 0.6 between EU and the USA, and only 0.25 to 0.35 between the EU and Japan (depending on the sample and which estimates are used.)

4.3.1. The symmetric case

To fix ideas, imagine for the moment that the EU is composed of eleven equal-sized member states.[7] Then, if in a particular industry there are ten equal-sized firms operating in each member state, and if each firm confines its production to its home base, there will be 110 firms in the EU as a whole. However, if firms produce in more than one member state (defined here as multinationality), then, for given national structures, there will be fewer separate firms at the EU level. For example, in the above case, if each firm operates equally in two countries, then the number of EU firms under separate ownership is reduced to fifty-five. More generally, with *NNAT* equal-sized firms in each of *K* equal-sized member states, with each firm producing in *NM* states, the total number of firms in the EU is:

$$NEU = NNAT * K / NM \qquad (4.1)$$

In this symmetric case, firm numbers are the obvious (inverse) measure of concentration, and (4.1) shows that EU and national concentration, multi-nationality and the number of countries are connected by a simple identity.

4.3.2. Allowing for size inequalities

In reality, firms are not equal-sized, nor are all member states; also, firms differ in the extent of their multinational operations. Therefore we need measures of concentration and multinationality which allow for size inequalities, and which are readily decomposable; and we also require a measure of the extent to which EU production is more or less specialized in the leading member states.

Given that we measure concentration by the *H* index, it is consistent and convenient to measure these other dimensions by similar *H* type indices.[8] These are defined in Table 4.4, and using straightforward algebra (see Appendix 1, Section A1.4.1) the relationship between them can be derived as:

$$HEU = HNAT * SPEC * (1 - M)^{-1} \qquad (4.2)$$

where:
HEU   = the *H* index of industry concentration in the EU as a whole
HNAT = the weighted average *H* index across the member states
SPEC = the specialization index of national productions over member states
M   = the weighted average of firms' multinationality over member states

Thus, in a given industry, EU concentration is related positively to the average concentration in member states; the extent to which production is specialized

---

[7] Recall that we treat Belgium and Luxemburg as one country.
[8] But similar decompositions can easily be derived for many other indices, for example, the Entropy.

Table 4.4 Indices of structure used in the decomposition

EU Herfindahl index	HEU	$= \Sigma(x_i/x)^2$
Number equivalent	NEU	$= 1/HEU$
National Herfindahl index	$HNAT$	$= \Sigma(u_k x_{ik}/x_k)^2$
Number equivalent	$NNAT$	$= 1/HNAT$
Multinationality	M	$= 1 - \Sigma(x_{ik}^2/x_i^2)$
Number equivalent	NM	$= 1/(1 - M)$
Specialization	$SPEC$	$= \Sigma(x_k/x)^2$
Number equivalent	$NSPEC$	$= 1/SPEC$

Notes: All magnitudes refer to a particular industry (j subscript dropped for clarity); all summations are over the $i = 1..N$ firms operating in the industry. x_i is firm i's (total) output; x_{ik} its output in country k; x_k is total industry output in country k; x is total EU output; and u_k is a weight reflecting (squared) national size. See Appendix 1 for a full discussion of all indices.

within the largest producing states; and the extent of multinational production by firms across member states. As always for an H index, HEU and $HNAT$ lie within the range $1/N$ to 1, with larger values indicating greater concentration. $SPEC$ is also a Herfindahl index, based on the member states' shares of total EU industry production. Its minimum value is $1/11$, if member states are equally-sized in the industry concerned. In most industries, the largest states will tend to account for disproportionately larger shares and $SPEC$ will comfortably exceed this minimum. M, the multinational index, is discussed in more detail in Chapter 7. Here, it is sufficient to note that, for a given industry, it is the average degree of multinationality *in that industry* across all firms. Its lower value is zero (when firms are uninational), rising to $1 - (1/11) = 0.909$, when all firms produce equally in all member states.

Alternatively, the decomposition can be expressed in number-equivalent form:

$$NEU = NNAT * NSPEC / NM \tag{4.3}$$

As can be seen, this is virtually identical to the symmetric case, with number equivalents substituted for the actual numbers in (4.1).

4.4 Estimation of the Decomposition

4.4.1 Deriving the estimates

We now turn to the task of estimating the three right-hand side components of the identity for each of the 100 industries. $SPEC$ is straightforward—it is easily computed from adjusted Eurostat data on the scale of production in the industry in each member state. However, in order to estimate *HNAT* and *M*, we strictly need information on all firms' outputs in each of the member states. Of course, we have this information only for the matrix firms, and we must make an allowance for the unknown contribution of non-matrix firms. Fortunately, because (4.2) is an identity, with the left-hand side already known, we need only directly estimate either *HNAT* or *M*, leaving the other to be recovered as a residual. We opt to estimate the *M* index—mainly because multinationality plays a more significant role than *HNAT* in the following chapters, but also because the adjustment for non-matrix firms is computationally much more simple.

The details of our estimation procedure for *M* are described in Chapter 7; but the broad idea can be explained briefly here as follows. First *M* is calculated for each industry simply as the weighted average *for the top five firms only* in that industry. We then make two alternative extreme assumptions about non-matrix firms—either they are equally as multinational as the top five, or they are not multinational at all. Since the truth will generally lie somewhere between, we label the estimates based on these assumptions 'Upper' and 'Lower', and generally use the midpoint of the two in most of the rest of the book. Since *HNAT* is computed as the residual, this also has an upper-lower range, and again we usually use the midpoint. However, in Section 4.3.3 we use both lower and upper estimates to demonstrate the relative insensitivity of the general picture to the non-top five assumptions.

Estimates of the decomposition for all 100 industries are reported in full in Appendix 2.1, and the following chapters focus in detail on the different components in turn. The rest of the present chapter is devoted to three summary devices which give an introductory overview.

4.4.2 A Graphical Depiction

It is clear from the decomposition that any given level of EU concentration may come about in a variety of ways. For example, high EU concentration may be largely associated with very high concentration in one or two dominant member states; alternatively, member state concentration may be less pronounced, but with the same (multinational) firms dominating in most of the individual states.

Figure 4.3 provides a simple graphical device for illustrating how this works out in practice. It plots *HNAT* against $\{SPEC * (1-M)^{-1}\}$, for each of the industries. For expositional convenience, we label the latter *MULTIPEN* since it can be interpreted as an indicator of *multinational penetration*: it measures the extent of actual multinational operations, relative to the maximum feasible, given the relative sizes of the member states. This can be seen more easily if *MULTIPEN* is re-expressed in number-equivalent form as *NM/NSPEC*: the number-equivalent countries firms actually produce in, relative to the number-equivalent

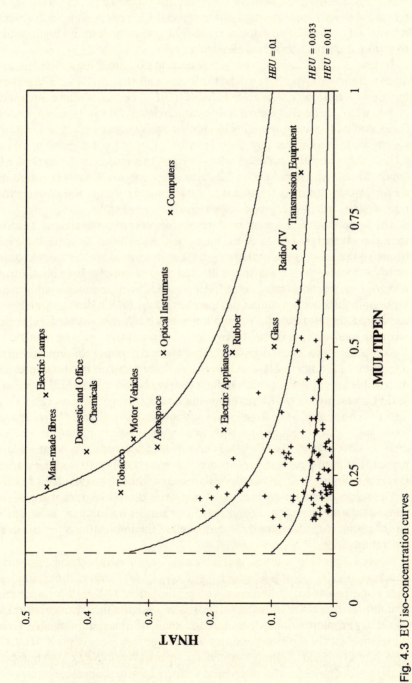

Fig. 4.3 EU iso-concentration curves

countries available. This will reach its theoretical maximum of 1 when all firms produce in all countries, with the proportions of their output in each country mirroring exactly that country's share of total EU production; and its minimum of 1/11 when all firms operate in only one country, despite a uniform distribution of production across all member states.

To interpret this diagram, we merely need to note from (eqn. 4.2) that any given rectangular hyperbola will be the locus of all *HNAT*, *MULTIPEN* combinations consistent with a given value of *HEU*. The figure shows three such curves, which we label as *EU iso-concentration curves*, for values of *HEU* = 0.1, 0.033, and 0.010—corresponding to number equivalents of 10, 30, and 100 respectively. It follows that any given industry's location is described by (i) the EU iso-concentration curve on which it lies—this indicates the level of EU concentration, and (ii) where on the curve it lies—south-easterly positions indicate relatively high multinational penetration and lower national concentration, whilst north-westerly positions indicate the reverse.

The diagram identifies some of the most concentrated industries. As can be seen, the six most concentrated EU industries, as identified earlier in Table 4.2, lie above the *H* = 0.1 curve. However, these industries are distributed quite widely across the space. Starting with man-made fibres, we have an industry which is highly concentrated at the EU level solely because concentration is exceptionally high within individual member states; multinational activity, on the other hand, is quite limited, and many much less concentrated industries record higher values for this. Moving down to computers, multinational penetration becomes the more dominant influence and national concentration less important (although still relatively high). An even more pronounced spread is discernible amongst the sixteen industries lying between the *HEU* = 0.1 and 0.033 curves: radio and TV and transmission equipment owe much of their high EU concentration to significant multinational operations, whilst tobacco scores high EU concentration largely as a result of high concentration within member states. Below the *H* = 0.033 curve, the scatter tends to become less dispersed, but even amongst these more moderately concentrated industries, there are still quite different structures consistent with any given value for *HEU*.

This suggests that the more detailed analysis in the following chapters of the constituents of the decomposition may be valuable not only for what it tells us about the constituents *per se*, but also for the implications for EU concentration.

4.4.3 A simple summary: descriptive statistics

The most obvious way of summarizing is to evaluate the decomposition at 'typical' (geometric mean[9]) values for each of the components of the

---

[9] Although the decomposition holds exactly for each of the 100 industries individually, because it is in mutiplicative form, it will only hold for average values if these are measured as geometric means.

decomposition. These are reported in part (i) Table 4.5 in both Herfindahl and number-equivalent forms; and the 'upper' and 'lower' estimates are both given to indicate sensitivity to the assumptions made about multinationality amongst non-top firms.

• It is 'as if' the typical EU manufacturing industry includes ninety-four equal-sized firms. This confirms what we already know from Table 4.2—the typical industry is not particularly concentrated at the EU level.[10]

• EU production is distributed as if across 4.8 equal-sized member states; this gives an idea of how far the leading member states dominate the EU in the typical industry.

• The typical firm operates geographically as if it had equal operations in between 1.27 (on the lower estimate) and 1.40 member states. This points to quite significant multinational penetration—between 26% and 29% of the upper limit (given by *NSPEC*). It also shows that the precise adjustment made for the unknown multinationality of non-top five firms is not too crucial.

Table 4.5 The decomposition of EU concentration

(i) Analysis of means

	HEU	=	*HNAT*	*	*SPEC*	/	(1–*M*)
UPPER	0.0105	=	0.036	*	0.208	/	0.715
LOWER	0.0105	=	0.040	*	0.208	/	0.789

	NEU	=	*NNAT*	*	*NSPEC*	/	*NM*
UPPER	94.4	=	27.45	*	4.81	/	1.399
LOWER	94.4	=	24.85	*	4.81	/	1.267

(ii) Analysis of variances
$$V(NEU) = V(NNAT) + V(NSPEC) + V(NM)$$
$$+ 2C(NNAT,NSPEC) + 2C(NNAT,NM)$$
$$+ 2C(NSPEC,NM)$$

	UPPER (%)	LOWER (%)
V(NEU)	1.757	1.757
V(NNAT)	1.478 (84)	1.450 (83)
V(NSPEC)	0.046 (3)	0.046 (3)
V(NM)	0.114 (6)	0.075 (4)
2C(*NNAT,NSPEC*)	–0.057 (–3)	–0.067 (–4)
2C(*NNAT,NM*)	0.188 (11)	0.256 (15)
2C(*NSPEC,NM*)	–0.012 (–1)	–0.002 (0)

Note: The analysis of variance is conducted in logarithms

---

[10] Mean EU concentration is lower here than in Table 4.2 because the geometric mean is less than the arithmetic mean—as is inevitable given the positive skew of the *HEU* distribution.

• Concentration in the typical member state in the typical industry is as if there are between twenty-five and twenty-seven equal-sized firms. This is less than the typical EU number equivalent by an order of three, and given that this is an average, it might suggest very high typical national concentration in some industries. This might, or might not, be a cause for concern, depending on whether competition occurs at the EU or member state levels.

A second order summary device is to conduct an analysis of the variances in the decomposition. To do this, the identity must first be transformed from multiplicative to additive form, by taking logarithms:

$$V(NEU) = V(NNAT) + V(NSPEC) + V(NM) + 2C(NNAT, NSPEC) \\ + 2C(NNAT, NM) + 2C(NSPEC, NM) \qquad (4.4)$$

where V and C refer, respectively, to variances and covariances.[11] The values and percentage contributions, *in purely statistical terms*, to the overall variance in *NEU*, shown in part (ii) of Table 4.5, reveal that typical national concentration (*NNAT*) makes by far the most important contribution—it accounts for roughly five-sixths of the sample variance in EU concentration. In comparison, the influences of *NM* and *NSPEC* are relatively minor, accounting for only between 4–6% and 3% respectively of the overall variance. The three covariance terms make trivial contributions, with the exception of the covariance of *NNAT* and *NM*. This indicates that there is a positive relationship between multinational operations and national concentration which accounts for most of the remaining variation in EU concentration.

In other words, most of the variance in EU concentration across industries is matched by a variance in national concentration of almost corresponding magnitude. Variability in multinational operations serves as an additional, if secondary, effect which is accentuated by a tendency for multinationality to be greater in industries with higher national concentration. (This is a theme we pursue in Chapter 7.) Whilst the extent of national specialization also clearly varies between industries, its differential impact on EU concentration is relatively minor. Finally, it should be emphasized that this analysis of variances investigates only statistical associations, and a discussion of causal relationships must await later chapters.

4.5 Conclusion

This chapter has reported a number of new 'facts' concerning the structure of EU manufacturing. It also serves a methodological purpose by establishing the framework within which the different dimensions of structure can be seen as part of an integrated whole.

---

[11] Because of the logarithmic transformation, the decomposition of variance in HEU form is identical.

According to our estimates, in the typical industry, the top five firms account for rather less than one-quarter of total EU production. This level of concentration is only moderate when compared against values typically reported in previous studies of concentration in individual countries. Indeed, this is confirmed by two new statistics we ourselves report: typically, the four-firm EU concentration ratio is 14.5 percentage points lower than it is on average in a group of four member states; similarly, the Herfindahl equivalent number of firms is three times larger at the EU level than it is in the typical member state. However, this is not altogether surprising, given that the EU is an aggregation of member states, and since it is almost impossible arithmetically for EU concentration to be higher than in individual member states. A rather more telling comparison is with the two other members of the Triad (which have roughly similar market sizes to the EU). Here, again, we find EU concentration to be comparatively low. However, as we show in Chapter 6, these averages hide important and revealing differences across industry types.

We have also introduced an identity which allows us to decompose concentration in the EU into three constituent parts: concentration in the member states, the extent of multinational production, and the specialization of production by member states within the Union. When evaluated at average values, this allows us to summarize succinctly as follows. It is 'as if' the typical EU industry includes ninety-four equal-sized firms, distributed over 4.8 equal-sized member states; and because the typical firm operates equally in 1.33 member states, each of those states has twenty-six (i.e. $94 = 4.8 * 26 / 1.33$) equal-sized firms.[12] However, the real value of the decomposition extends far beyond such simple calibration at mean values. More importantly, it provides the structure for this part of the book, allowing succeeding chapters to investigate the four components in turn, as part of an integrated whole. We have already seen, for example, that some industries with very similar levels of EU concentration differ quite significantly in the extent of their member state concentration on the one hand, and the multinationality of their firms on the other hand. The task of following chapters is to investigate the determinants of the various structural dimensions in a way which recognizes this underlying interdependence, and which takes us further in our understanding of the competitive process in the context of European integration.

STEVE DAVIES and BRUCE LYONS

[12] The numbers used here are the midpoints of those shown as 'upper' and 'lower' in Table 4.5.

5

Specialization, Trade, and Integration

5.1 Introduction

What determines the degree of specialization in production and trade across member states within the EU? And how integrated is EU industrial production? As the decomposition in the previous chapter made clear, there are two importantly different dimensions to integration: by trade and by international ownership. The integration of ownership is dealt with in later chapters on multinational enterprise. Here, our concern is with trade; and, given our focus on integration within the EU, this will be confined to intra-EU trade.[1]

A particular measure of intra-EU international specialization, *SPEC*, falls out of the Chapter 4 decomposition of European concentration, and this provides a convenient starting point for looking at the various dimensions of trade. In particular, we investigate the determinants of both inter-industry and intra-industry trade: both are aspects of trade integration, but they have different causes and different implications for the distribution of income (Krugman, 1981). For example, inter-industry trade, based on comparative advantage, reduces the real incomes of factors of production specialized in, or intensive in, the import-competing sector; but intra-industry trade, based on the exchange of products with similar manufacturing technologies (and factor intensities), has no such distributional problems. While both forms of trade improve the aggregate real income of the economy (or the variety of goods available), because of the distributional implications, they generate different political pressures.

In this chapter, we do not attempt to explain the precise patterns of bilateral comparative advantage or bilateral flows of trade between different member states. Our aim is rather more limited: to describe and explain the total volume of intra-EU trade, and the extent to which that trade is intra-industry. In Section 5.2, we examine the pattern of specialization of production across member states (*SPEC*) and show how this is related to the two dimensions of trade just mentioned. The relevant theory of international trade and specialization is then reviewed in Section 5.3, and an econometric model is estimated in Section 5.4. Section 5.5 concludes.

---

[1] Intra-EU trade (trade between member states) should not be confused with intra-industry trade (trade in which pairs of member states exchange products classified to the same industry).

5.2 The Relationship Between Trade and Production Specialization

In Chapter 4, we introduced a decomposition of EU concentration, which shows how an index of member state *specialization of production*, *SPEC*, is an important element in our understanding of EU market structure. This index measures the extent to which EU production in a given industry is concentrated in the largest member states. In principle, it can take a minimum value of 1/11—if all the member states produce equal amounts—but, in practice, we would expect a significantly larger value for most industries, reflecting the relative dominance of the Big 4 member states. This expectation is borne out by the descriptive statistics in Table 4.5: the typical (geometric mean) value of *SPEC* was 0.208, and it is *as if* the EU comprises just about five equal-sized member states for the average industry. This sort of value was to be expected given the underlying size inequalities between the economies of the eleven member states. Moreover, the relatively small variance across industries suggests that this was true for most industries. On the other hand, there are some significant inter-industry differences, and we now turn to a closer examination of the index itself for clues on what these reveal about trade integration.

5.2.1 An Appropriate Index of Trade Specialization

SPEC measures the concentration of production, and so it will depend, at least in part, on the magnitudes of intra-EU trade flows. *Ceteris paribus*, where these are large, those member states with a comparative advantage in a given industry will secure larger shares than implied by the size of their domestic markets. But if we are to pursue the connection much further, it is clear that we shall first need to normalize for two factors: international differences in consumption patterns; and the unequal sizes of member states.

The first factor is fairly straightforward. If there was no intra-EU trade and the Italians consumed more pasta than residents of other member states, then Italy would have a disproportionate share of pasta production. Since we shall have nothing to say about what determines the Italian preference for pasta, such international taste differences would introduce unnecessary noise into our investigation of trade specialization. The first adjustment to the index is, therefore, to look not directly at the specialization of production, but rather at that specialization relative to the specialization of consumption. This idea will be made precise shortly.

A second, potentially more confusing, effect on *SPEC* derives from the unequal sizes of member states. This means there will be no clearcut monotonic relationship between *SPEC* and trade specialization. Starting from a position of no trade, if we increase specialization in a larger country which then exports to smaller member states, this will accentuate the basic size inequalities between member states and *SPEC* will rise. However, if comparative advantage lies with a smaller state, then international specialization will cause *SPEC* to fall, as the size of production becomes more equal (in absolute terms) across the EU. Examples of the former include various types of machinery for which Germany has a comparative advantage, while Belgian carpets and Portuguese cork products provide examples of the latter. On its own, therefore, SPEC is a very imperfect measure of trade specialization.[2]

The first step in our analysis is to separate out these two influences on *SPEC*. Using the derivation shown in the Appendix to this chapter, *SPEC* can be decomposed for a given industry as follows:

$$SPEC = CONSPEC + SIZEADJ + (TRADESPEC)^2 \qquad (5.1)$$

where

CONSPEC   = the concentration of 'apparent consumption' within the EU,

SIZEADJ   = the extent to which comparative advantage lies with larger states,

TRADESPEC = the extent of trade specialization within the EU

CONSPEC is an *H* index, reflecting the distribution of member state sizes when measured by 'apparent consumption', rather than production. This captures the 'pasta effect' just mentioned, and accounts for the basic size inequalities or taste differences between member states. In fact, it also accounts for another effect. A member state's 'apparent consumption' is defined as its production plus its imports from elsewhere in the EU, minus its exports to other member states. Thus, extra-EU trade is ignored, and domestic consumption will be overestimated for any state with a balance of trade surplus with the rest of the world. Since we are uninterested here in either the scale of true domestic consumption or extra-EU trade, little is lost by grouping the two together in this way; but it does mean that 'apparent consumption' is a loose, albeit convenient, shorthand.

SIZEADJ is a measure of the covariance of 'apparent consumption' and the intra-EU trade balance, and this will be positive if larger member states are more likely to run intra-EU balance of trade surpluses, and negative if the smaller countries tend to be in surplus. In other words, this takes account of the second effect mentioned above.

Once these two effects are netted out from *SPEC*, we are left with the third term, *TRADESPEC*—this is our preferred measure of *trade specialization*. As shown in the Appendix, it is the standard deviation across member states of the net intra-EU trade balance in a given industry, normalized by the size of the industry. Since the mean trade balance is, of course, zero, its standard deviation will tend to be larger, the greater are trade flows in absolute terms, and the more pronounced are comparative advantages (and disadvantages) between states.

---

[2] A further problem with any specialization index based on national data is that geographic specialization need not respect national boundaries. This is likely to become an increasingly important issue as the European market becomes more integrated. For the purposes of this chapter, however, we are concerned with the member state as the relevant unit.

Table 5.1(a) The most trade-specialized industries*

NACE	Industry	SPEC	CONSPEC	SIZEADJ	TRADESPEC
451	Footwear	0.255	0.188	0.0266	0.202
438	Carpets	0.160	0.186	−0.0525	0.164
436	Knitting	0.244	0.201	0.0182	0.159
373	Optical instruments	0.243	0.208	0.0129	0.149
327	Paper machinery etc.	0.359	0.253	0.0874	0.137
374	Clocks & watches	0.317	0.242	0.0563	0.136
260	Man-made fibres	0.199	0.184	−0.0011	0.124
323	Textile machinery	0.301	0.288	0.0607	0.110
346	Domestic electrical appliances	0.200	0.173	0.0166	0.104
414	Fruit & vegetable products	0.154	0.181	−0.0373	0.102

  * Ranked by *TRADESPEC*

Table 5.1(b) The least trade-specialized industries*

NACE	Industry	SPEC	CONSPEC	SIZEADJ	TRADESPEC
314	Metal structures	0.179	0.177	0.0018	0.011
473	Printing & publishing	0.158	0.159	−0.0008	0.011
364	Aerospace	0.295	0.292	0.0037	0.009
419	Bread & biscuits	0.154	0.155	−0.0010	0.009
428	Soft drinks	0.162	0.163	−0.0010	0.009
311	Foundries	0.219	0.214	0.0050	0.008
463	Wooden structures	0.183	0.184	−0.0010	0.008
312	Forging	0.191	0.188	0.0027	0.008
243	Concrete	0.169	0.169	0.0000	0.007
464	Wooden containers	0.182	0.182	0.0005	0.003

  * Ranked by *TRADESPEC*

Table 5.1(c) Trade specialization by industry type

Arithmetic mean:		SPEC	CONSPEC	SIZEADJ	TRADESPEC
Full Sample	($n = 91$)	0.213	0.201	0.008	0.052
Type 1	($n = 48$)	0.199	0.191	0.004	0.046
Type 2A	($n = 13$)	0.190	0.189	−0.001	0.044
Type 2R	($n = 21$)	0.255	0.231	0.020	0.060
Type 2AR	($n = 9$)	0.219	0.197	0.015	0.073

Tables 5.1(a) and 5.1(b) show the Top ten and Bottom ten trade-specialized industries. Textiles figure prominently at the top of the list,[3] which also includes

[3] They might have been even more prominent but for the fact that the trade data are inconsistent with the NACE classification for many textiles, and we have lost six such industries from our initial 100. Three further industries (basic chemicals, jewellery, and miscellaneous manufacturing) also have abnormalities in the trade data, so this chapter is based on ninety-one manufacturing industries. The full set of observations is provided in Appendix 2.

some machinery and domestic electrical appliances. Notice that the high trade specialization in carpets and fruit and vegetable products is obscured in low *SPEC* values because of the second effect mentioned earlier—they are concentrated in small countries (*SIZEADJ* < 0). As might be expected, the least trade-specialized industries include many with substantial transport costs due to weight, bulk or perishability (e.g. concrete, wooden containers, bread and biscuits). More strangely and interestingly, aerospace also enters the list. This is because domestic purchases are very highly concentrated, reflecting the disproportionate defence and general aerospace spending by larger countries, and production is similarly concentrated due to public procurement bias. The net effect is that there is little trade specialization relative to consumption.

Although this index of trade specialization is novel, we can make some broad comparisons with US geographic specialization by state, drawing on the work of Krugman (1991). He shows that US industry is generally more geographically specialized than in the EU, but makes only anecdotal industry comparisons. However, he does calculate Gini coefficients of production by industry for the USA. Given the differences in the sizes of US states, the Gini coefficient may suffer from similar problems to *SPEC* as a measure of trade specialization, though any such problems may be diluted by the much larger number of US states compared with EU members. We are unable to make formal EU–USA comparisons, given that different measures and industrial classifications are being used, and because Krugman's list excludes food, drink, and tobacco and many mineral- and wood-based industries. Nevertheless, it is striking that in the USA, even more than in the EU, the textile industries are the most geographically specialized, and photographic equipment (like optical instruments in the EU) is high in the US list. Metal structures, some parts of printing and publishing, and foundries are geographically diffuse in the USA as well as in the EU, but there are significant differences in machinery. According to Krugman's calculations, several categories of machinery industry are low in geographic specialization, while in the EU they tend to be in the upper half of the list. This may be due to a technological lead in Germany. Aircraft and parts are a third of the way down the US specialization list, and other parts of aerospace are even more geographically specialized; this is consistent with our suggestion that the location of the European industry has been distorted by public procurement bias.

Table 5.1(c) examines the averages of the components in this decomposition by industry type. *SPEC* is lowest in Type 1 and 2*A* industries and highest in Type 2*R*, and there is a similar ranking for *TRADESPEC*. Also, *CONSPEC* tends to be noticeably higher in 2*R* industries. This may be for two reasons. First, as we argue below, these industries often provide important inputs into other industries and there are benefits to proximate location, so customers are more likely to be located in the same country. Second, remember that 'apparent consumption' also includes extra-EU trade balances. This suggests that the larger member states have favourable trade balances with the rest of the world in R&D-intensive industries. However, when we focus on those industries in which both advertising and R&D are high (Type $2AR$), a different picture emerges. *TRADESPEC* is the highest for this type, whilst *CONSPEC* is typically similar to the values observed in non-R&D-intensive industries. The former indicates that intra-EU trade flows are high in this type of industry; but the latter points to less pronounced differences in 'apparent consumption', probably reflecting the fact that advertising is aimed at final consumers, who are more widely distributed than are the customers of Type 2R industries. Finally, *SIZEADJ* shows that comparative advantage seems to lie with the larger countries for R&D-intensive industries, whilst the reverse is true for advertising.

5.2.2 Specialization, Total Trade, and Intra-Industry Trade

We do not attempt to explain either *CONSPEC* or *SIZEADJ* in the present book,[4] rather, the focus of our attention is on *TRADESPEC*. But before proceeding to an econometric analysis of this, we introduce a second level decomposition which introduces another important dimension of the integration process. This is intra-industry trade, which has become characteristic of trade within the EU (see Chapter 2). This type of trade is concealed by *TRADESPEC*; which will record a value of zero if trade is balanced between all member states (i.e. there is no geographic specialization), even if there are large trade flows between countries exchanging similar, but differentiated products.

So, rather than looking only at net trade (*TRADESPEC*), we wish to investigate both the forces that determine the total volume of trade, and the share of that trade that is intra-industry. The relationship between these types of trade is formalized in the Appendix to the chapter as follows:

$$TRADESPEC = TRADE * (1 - INTRA) * (HTRADE)^{1/2} \qquad (5.2)$$

where:

TRADE	= total intra-EU trade relative to EU production;
INTRA	= the share of intra-EU trade that is intra-industry;
HTRADE	= an *H* index of the concentration of total intra-EU trade.

TRADE offers an obvious and simple measure of trade integration in the EU: it is defined as the sum of intra-EU imports and exports relative to EU

---

[4] Theoretically, there are some interesting things to say about *SIZEADJ*. For example, as long as there are international trading costs (or there is inertia following a history of such trading costs) large countries can be expected to have an advantage in industries which have technologies with large economies of scale. However, empirically with only eleven countries, the pure effects of national size are likely to be swamped by institutional factors; such as the fact that the larger countries (e.g. Germany, France, Italy) are generally more advanced than the smaller countries (e.g. Portugal, Ireland, Greece). Similarly, and as already noted, *CONSPEC*, as defined, undoubtedly contains interesting information on the patterns of extra-EU trade across industries. Both issues remain on the agenda for future research.

production, and it picks up on both inter-industry and intra-industry trade. Note that if measured accurately, intra-EU imports and exports should be identical. Therefore, apart from measurement error, TRADE should equal exactly twice intra-EU imports, which is the measure of trade integration used elsewhere in this book. We deviate in this chapter from the general definition of *TRADE* used in this book merely for consistency with the decomposition of *TRADESPEC*.

INTRA is a straightforward indicator of the split between intra-industry trade (measured by an index with similar properties to the Grubel–Lloyd index) and inter-industry trade. *HTRADE* is probably best thought of as a technical adjustment to *TRADESPEC*—it reflects the extent to which total intra-EU trade is concentrated in a few member states. So, while *TRADESPEC* is sensitive to whether a given volume of trade is between, say, just two large member states or between six smaller ones, *INTRA* and *TRADE* are independent of the number of traders. This independence is attractive when looking at the overall pattern of intra-EU trade, because we need not be concerned about the size of countries which have a comparative advantage in a particular industry.

The identities of the most and least trade-integrated industries are reported in Tables 5.2(a) and 5.2(b). Some of the textile industries appear again as amongst the most trade-integrated (high *TRADE*) as well as being the most trade-specialized (high *TRADESPEC*). However, other industries which are geographically quite diffuse are also amongst the most heavily traded (e.g. computers, domestic and office chemicals, toys and sports, non-ferrous metals). The difference between these two groups is that the former trade is largely based on comparative advantage, while the latter engage in a huge amount of intra-industry trade. The least trade-integrated industries are familiar from the earlier low trade specialization list, and the reasons are the same—compared with most manufacturing industries, they are substantially non-traded goods.[5]

The influence of industry type is shown in Table 5.2(c).[6] Industries which engage in R&D are twice as trade-integrated as those which do not, and they also engage in more intra-industry trade. Perhaps surprisingly, advertising is associated with a lower *INTRA* than even Type 1 industries. Advertising in combination with R&D appears to raise *TRADE* a little, but reduce *INTRA*. We resist further commentary on this table as the next section develops a multiple regression model with a view to deepening our understanding of the forces at work. Finally, although we have little to say about *HTRADE*, there is one observation to be made. Following our earlier finding that both production and 'consumption' in Type 2R industries is concentrated in the larger countries, it is not surprising that trade in these industries is also concentrated (*HTRADE* is high).

[5] Aerospace, which is geographically dispersed relative to consumption, is an above average trader; but with *INTRA* = 0.951, it is the industry with the highest share of intra-industry trade.

[6] Because the decomposition in Equation 5.2 is multiplicative, geometric means have been calculated, and this accounts for the different 'average' *TRADESPEC* in Tables 5.1(c) and 5.2(c). The arithmetic means for the full sample are: *TRADESPEC* = 0.052; *TRADE* = 0.364; *INTRA* = 0.627; and *HTRADE* = 0.163.

Table 5.2(a) The most trade-integrated industries*

NACE	Industry	TRADESPEC	TRADE	INTRA	HTRADE
373	Optical instruments	0.149	1.373	0.737	0.171
330	Computers & office machinery	0.071	1.159	0.843	0.151
260	Man-made fibres	0.124	0.836	0.628	0.159
259	Domestic & office chemicals	0.062	0.820	0.806	0.152
438	Carpets	0.164	0.785	0.488	0.166
494	Toys & sports	0.087	0.700	0.676	0.146
224	Non-ferrous metals	0.043	0.693	0.845	0.160
436	Knitting	0.159	0.649	0.381	0.157
374	Clocks & watches	0.136	0.643	0.522	0.197
451	Footwear	0.202	0.616	0.208	0.172

* Ranked by *TRADE*.

Note: Because of the decomposition of *TRADESPEC*, *TRADE* is defined in this chapter only as the total of intra-EU imports and exports. Since these flows should be equal, apart from measurement error, this should equal exactly twice intra-EU imports (which is the measure of *TRADE* used elsewhere in this book).

Table 5.2(b) The least trade-integrated industries*

NACE	Industry	TRADESPEC	TRADE	INTRA	HTRADE
416	Grain milling	0.014	0.095	0.615	0.140
473	Printing & publishing	0.011	0.086	0.673	0.148
428	Soft drinks	0.009	0.082	0.758	0.186
427	Beer	0.012	0.078	0.571	0.139
419	Bread & biscuits	0.009	0.069	0.679	0.155
242	Cement	0.017	0.067	0.422	0.200
463	Wooden structures	0.008	0.056	0.625	0.140
312	Forging	0.008	0.054	0.647	0.171
464	Wooden containers	0.003	0.041	0.787	0.137
243	Concrete	0.007	0.040	0.566	0.163

* Ranked by *TRADE*.

Table 5.2(c) Trade integration by industry type

Geometric mean		TRADESPEC	TRADE	INTRA*	HTRADE
Full Sample	($n = 91$)	0.038	0.283	0.661	0.161
Type 1	($n = 48$)	0.031	0.220	0.643	0.152
Type 2A	($n = 13$)	0.035	0.218	0.596	0.157
Type 2R	($n = 21$)	0.049	0.446	0.731	0.170
Type 2AR	($n = 9$)	0.057	0.458	0.691	0.162

* Complement of the geometric mean of 1–*INTER*.

5.3 The Theory of Trade and Specialization

This section provides a theoretical framework for our econometric specification of the determinants of the two dimensions of trade and specialization in Equation 5.2: *TRADE* and *INTRA*.

Most of the received theory of international trade has been aimed at explaining the pattern of comparative advantage between pairs of countries. The purpose of this chapter is rather different. We want to understand why some industries are more geographically specialized and trade within the EU more than others; and what proportion of that trade is reciprocated with the exchange of similar types of product. Individual member states do not explicitly enter the story. Implicitly, of course, anything that determines trade between a country pair also contributes to the overall total. However, we are constrained by the lack of comparable data across member states and so we concentrate on aggregate EU variables only. For example, if natural resources are unequally distributed across the EU, then a measure of that inequality might help explain the international specialization of production and consequent trade. In the absence of data on the inequality of natural resource distribution, and its importance by industry, we are left with a more limited search for testable hypotheses. Thus, we cannot expect to explain more than a relatively small part of the pattern of intra-EU trade.

In what follows, we review the relevant theory and present our empirically operational variables; more detailed definitions and data sources are given in Appendix 3 at the end of the book.

5.3.1 Determinants of Total Trade (*TRADE*)

Transport costs

Transport costs are probably the most straightforward influence on the volume of trade, generally eroding the benefits of geographical specialization.

TRS = transport costs relative to the value of sales

Comparative advantage

Following the famous work of Heckscher and Ohlin, a major source of comparative advantage trade is relative factor abundance:[7] the greater the difference in relative endowments across member states, the greater will be the volume of all trade (see, for example, Helpman and Krugman, 1985, ch. 8). However, in general equilibrium, this does not necessarily say anything about why particular industries should be more heavily traded than others; for example, in a two-industry world, even if factor intensity is 'important' in only one industry's

---

[7] Technology-based comparative advantage is discussed separately below.

technology, the need to keep a trade balance means that both must be equally traded. Nevertheless, given some trading costs and in a multi-industry world, it seems likely that the greater incentive to trade will reside in industries with technologies requiring more extreme factor intensities (e.g. very labour intensive). The argument is clearer if there is no factor price equalization, so small differences in relative factor prices become magnified by large differences in factor requirements. Roughly speaking, then, extreme requirements of capital, labour, skills, raw materials, etc, should raise trade. It is not obvious how best to measure this. But if we assume that intra-EU differences in capital costs will tend to be small relative to differences in labour costs (because capital is much more mobile than labour), we would expect a negative relationship between trade and the capital–labour ratio.

KL = the capital–labour ratio

Internal economies of scale

Large economies of scale internal to the firm encourage trade as a means of achieving lower costs.[8] However, the minimum efficient scale for a production unit is relevant only relative to the size of the market; otherwise, economies of scale could be achieved in the national market.

MES = an estimate of the minimum efficient scale of production
$EUSIZE$ = the size of EU industry production

Regional external economies

The idea that external economies of scale are important dates back to Marshall (1920), but only much more recently has their true importance for trade become widely acknowledged, largely due to the work of Krugman (1991). Marshall gave three reasons why firms in the same industry may benefit from agglomerating in the same region: the emergence of a pooled market for workers with specialist skills; the development of local specialist input manufacturers and services; and local technological spillovers as firms can observe and communicate easily. In fact, it is likely that the appropriate unit of geographical analysis is not the nation, but a smaller region—and such regions may even cross national borders. Nevertheless, the general effect of localization should still be observable using national data, albeit diluted by national aggregation with other regions.

So which types of industry are most likely to benefit from external economies? Engineering industries require complex assembly and skilled workers,

---

[8] Transport costs in the presence of scale economies can also have an important and complex effect on the location of production at the core or periphery of the EU (see Krugman and Venables, 1990). Very high transport costs may prohibit trade. As they fall, initially this favours the specialization of production at the core of the EU, close to the market. However, as transport costs become small, location at the low wage cost periphery becomes attractive.

both of which favour agglomeration. For example, if their products incur significant transport costs, then specialist subcontractors may be happier to set up where there are several potential customers so they are not over-reliant on just one. In effect, this is a transaction cost argument, founded in the fear of opportunism if over reliant on a single customer (Williamson, 1985), and it does not apply to very standard inputs which can easily be sold to a wide range of potential customers. If proximity of location is important for such inputs, two corollaries follow. First, agglomeration in downstream assembly industries will increase their propensity to trade. But second, industries will not be heavily traded if they are comprised of large numbers of subcontractors making intermediate goods for local sale. The importance of proximity will be most important when semi-manufactured goods are processed by a specialist before being returned for assembly. Examples extend beyond the engineering sector, and might include tanning for the leather product industry, printing and publishing, textile finishing, and some plastics. A broad, and very imperfect, way to capture the specialist input effect is to argue that upstream industries, selling their output to other firms as intermediate goods (but not as capital goods), should trade less than downstream industries further down the production chain and selling to final consumers, governments, etc. A more direct way to capture the subcontractor effect is to identify industries which undertake subcontracted work as a service for other industries. As to Marshall's two other sources of external economies, we do not have a direct measure to capture the value of a local market in specialist labour, and technology spillovers will be discussed next.

INT = the share of the industry's output sold to other firms as intermediate inputs

$SUBCON$ = a dummy variable equal to one if the industry is associated with undertaking subcontracted work[9]

Technology

The speed with which technology is developing affects geographic dispersion in two ways: external to the firm, and internal to the firm. First, rapid technological development generates agglomeration economies including a technologically proficient labour market and spillovers of knowledge across firms. Technological development also benefits from regional pockets of scientific knowledge supplied by research institutes and university strengths, so there is a two-way interaction between technology and location. This can lead to regional agglomeration that translates into national comparative advantage. Second, for a particular firm, product and process development is often most

[9] Based on industries with over 50% of work rendered for other firms; source: UK Census of Production, 1989.

efficiently carried out in a single locality.[10] Also, given that feedback between production and development is important, this is facilitated by the local proximity of the R&D function and factories. Taken together, these arguments suggest that industries populated by firms which engage in R&D may become more internationally specialized.

$TYPE2R$ = dummy variable equal to 1 if firms in the industry engage in significant R&D (and equal to 0 otherwise).

$TYPE2AR$ = dummy variable equal to 1 if firms in the industry engage in significant R&D and advertising.

Product differentiation

In general, we expect product differentiation to increase the volume of international trade. In order to be more precise, it is helpful to distinguish vertical from horizontal differentiation. Vertical differentiation refers to products of different perceived quality, while horizontal differentiation refers to products of different perceived characteristics. In their pure forms, everyone would agree that vertically differentiated product A is of higher quality than product B, but consumers would differ in preference according to personal taste for horizontally differentiated products.

Vertical differentiation can result from better design, better quality inputs, R&D, or advertising (either signalling or promoting perceived quality). We concentrate on the latter two as being measurable at the industry level. R&D has already been discussed in relation to technology. In addition, R&D is likely to generate different product specifications because firms follow different research paths and discover different results. The resulting product differentiation will promote trade to satisfy different income groups and tastes for variety and quality.[11] While R&D is typically internationally exploitable, and so can be concentrated in one location, advertising must generally be repeated in each country because each member state has a different language, media, and marketing tradition (though there may still be economies of international scope in developing and exploiting a brand). With advertising intensive industries, therefore, there is no reason to specialize location and increase trade. Quite to the contrary, inasmuch as there are reasons to produce close to the market to benefit from marketing feedback and to fine-tune products to national tastes, this may encourage the dispersion of production to reflect the international pattern of demand.

---

[10] Though some specialist R&D by global firms may be carried out at separate laboratories located in countries with a particular technological competence. External economies are also important if technological spillovers and highly skilled local labour markets encourage the agglomeration of independent research laboratories.

[11] This passes over a point that will be crucial in the next chapter. The discussion of technology in the previous paragraph applies whether R&D is an exogenous cost to firms or an endogenous decision variable. When it comes to the competitive consequences of R&D as an element in vertical product differentiation, however, it will be crucial not to suppress the idea of R&D as an endogenous strategy.

Horizontal differentiation, combined with even quite limited economies of scale, results in more trade to satisfy the demand for variety (Krugman and Helpman, 1985, ch. 8). Thus, particular varieties made in one country meet niche demands in another country, and vice versa. Unfortunately, it is almost impossible to measure the potential for horizontal differentiation at the industry level, but for reasons already given, this is naturally created as a by-product of R&D activity. The same cannot be said to apply internationally to advertising which has been carried out in national markets.

$TYPE2A$ = dummy variable equal to 1 if firms in the industry engage in significant advertising

$TYPE2R$ = as defined above

$TYPE2AR$ = as defined above; note that the advertising and R&D effects are expected to work against each other

Government intervention

In 1987, there was a common external tariff round the EU, but no internal tariffs except some transitional arrangements with the newer members (Spain, Portugal, and Greece). This does not mean that there were no internal barriers to trade—indeed, this was the year that the programme for a Single European Market was launched with a view to eliminating non-tariff barriers to trade. Some non-tariff barriers (e.g. border controls) have widespread effects, while others are industry specific. We focus on three types of national-government-induced non-tariff barrier which vary importantly across industries: specific subsidies; public procurement bias; and regulatory standards. If a member state has a comparative disadvantage that puts pressure on a domestic industry, this often results in political pressure to subsidize that industry. On this view, subsidies are often designed to neutralize a comparative disadvantage, particularly if the disadvantage has recently worsened. The effect on intra-EU trade depends on who is the main competitor country. If the competition comes from within the EU then trade is suppressed, but if it is with a third country, then trade may be diverted, in which case intra-EU trade rises. It is, therefore, dangerous to make generalizations about the effect of subsidies. The other two types of intervention, however, are clearly trade-suppressing. Public procurement bias means that national governments will buy from their home producers even when a better or cheaper product could be imported. Unnecessarily complex national regulatory standards (e.g. French tiles, German beer) meant that, prior to the implementation of the Single Market legislation, firms geared up for domestic regulations had to incur multiple certification and product adjustment costs if they were to be able to export.

GOV = the share of the industry's output sold to government departments

REG = dummy variable equal to one for industries which have strong national regulatory standards

These various hypotheses can be summarized by the following estimating equation, where expected signs of regression coefficients are shown below each variable. Given the complexity of the theoretical effects and the simplicity of our proxy variables, however, great caution will be necessory in interpreting our empirical results.

$$TRADE = f(TRS, KL, MES, EUSIZE, INT, SUBCON,$$
$$\quad\quad\quad [-] \;\; [-] \;\; [+] \quad\quad [-] \quad\;\; [-] \quad\;\; [-]$$

$$TYPE2R, \; TYPE2AR, \; TYPE2A, \; GOV, \; REG) \quad\quad (5.3)$$
$$\;\;\; [+] \quad\quad\quad [?] \quad\quad\quad [-] \quad\quad [-] \;\;\; [-]$$

5.3.2 Determinants of Intra-Industry Trade (*INTRA*)[12]

We now turn to the factors which may influence the proportion of total trade which is intra-industry. Many of the above arguments in relation to total trade are also directly relevant to understanding the share of that trade which is intra-industry. Some factors, such as horizontal product differentiation, directly raise both total trade and intra-industry trade; while other factors, which raise trade based on comparative advantage, may reduce the share of total trade that is intra-industry. A third group of factors, such as transport costs, which reduce all types of trade fairly equally, should not affect the share that is intra-industry.

Categorical aggregation

Elsewhere in this book, we have already explained some of the limitations of working at the 3-digit level of the NACE industrial classification. Industries defined at this level inevitably include a range of product categories, and the number of such categories may influence *INTRA* in a purely statistical way by aggregating trade flows between countries with different comparative advantages in different categories. The following variable is included as a correction for the heterogeneity of the industrial classification.

HET = a measure of the number of product categories included in the 3-digit NACE industry definition.

Comparative advantage

Trade which flows from comparative advantage will not be intra-industry. Therefore, we would expect *INTRA* to be positively related to our earlier (very imperfect) proxy, *KL*.

---

[12] Grubel and Lloyd (1975) were the first to systematically study intra-industry trade, though pioneering earlier work is in Linder (1961). An important theoretical contribution is in a series of papers by Krugman (1979, 1980, 1981). A good example of empirical work is Loertscher and Wolter (1980) and Greenaway and Milner (1989) provide an empirical review.

Internal economies of scale

Here, there are two forces that tend to work against each other. On the one hand, substantial economies of scale may result in international specialization generating relatively more inter-industry trade. But, on the other hand, the absence of significant scale economies will allow more product variety to be produced domestically, therefore reducing the motive for intra-industry trade. Thus, the net effects of our two scale measures, *MES* and *EUSIZE*, are ambiguous.

Local production

We have already argued that intermediate goods industries have less tendency to agglomeration, and are likely to be regionally dispersed. Nevertheless, assembly firms will want to buy the most appropriate input specification for their products, and this may involve an international search. This will generate intra-industry trade (and may offset the trade suppressing effect discussed in the previous subsection). Thus, we expect our *INT* proxy to have a positive influence on *INTRA*.

Technology

Inasmuch as the technology argument developed earlier relates to a source of national advantage, *TYPE2R* should be expected to have a negative influence on *INTRA*. However, such industries are also associated with product differentiation, to which we now turn.

Product differentiation

Horizontal product differentiation directly raises intra-industry trade, and we have already developed the link with R&D which generates new products. Our earlier discussion of the effects of advertising suggested an association with low regional specialization (i.e. little inter-industry trade). This could mean that any residual trade would be intra-industry. However, Caves has argued that goods which are advertised tend to have little inherent horizontal differentiation—that is one reason why advertising is deemed necessary to achieve a competitive edge. This leads us to expect a positive influence for *TYPE2R* and probably also *TYPE2AR*, but the expectations for *TYPE2A* are ambiguous.

Government intervention

If government intervention is aimed at reducing imports based on comparative disadvantage, then the suppression of such trade should raise the share of intra-industry trade. Governments find it politically difficult not to discriminate in favour of home producers when the home industry is under severe pressure of international competition. In contrast, industries with more balanced trade will generate less political lobbying for interference. Thus, we expect a positive influence for *GOV*. While public procurement bias may be responsive to the net trade position in this way, national regulations are likely to suppress all forms of trade, so the sign on *REG* is ambiguous.

Putting these hypotheses together, we form the second estimating equation:

$$INTRA = f(HET, KL, MES, EUSIZE, INT, TYPE2R,$$
$$[+] \quad [+] \quad [?] \quad [?] \quad [+] \quad [+]$$

$$TYPE2AR, TYPE2A, GOV, REG) \qquad (5.4)$$
$$[?] \qquad [?] \qquad [+] \quad [?]$$

5.3.3 Determinants of Geographic Specialization (*TRADESPEC*)

Given Equation 5.2, *TRADESPEC* is 'determined' by *TRADE*, *INTRA* and *HTRADE*. Of course, the word 'determined' should be treated with care since 5.2 is an identity without causal connotations. However, if we are able to explain the right-hand side variables, *TRADESPEC* naturally follows. Since we have interpreted *HTRADE* as essentially a technical adjustment, there is nothing to add to the theoretical discussion in the previous two sections. Geographic specialization is determined by whatever determines total trade, modified to exclude that part of trade which is intra-industry.

5.4 Econometric Results

We proceed by estimating the determinants of *TRADE* and *INTRA*, before combining the two sets of variables to look at *TRADESPEC*. Table 5.3 presents the results of our econometric analysis, having eliminated the capital intensity and economies of scale variables which do not significantly influence the regression results in any of the three equations.[13] Given the complexity and delicacy of the theoretical justification for these variables, this lack of significance should not be too surprising.

In the *TRADE* equation, all the remaining variables attract coefficients with the expected sign, mostly significantly so. Thus we find that transport costs strongly reduce trade intensity. *SUBCON* has a similar effect, which shows

---

[13] Because there are two outliers in the measurement of *TRADE*, with optical instruments and computers being around 50% more trade intensive than the next highest industries, the *TRADE* equation was also estimated excluding the two trade-intensive outliers. The significance of the variables was unaltered and, as expected with sample reduction, the R^2 improved. The *INTRA* equation was also estimated over a subsample to include only observations for which *TRADE* > 20%. This was because the size of *INTRA* may be subject to measurement error when trade flows are small. Once again the basic results were unaltered. The reported results are based on linear dependent variables, but they are not sensitive to functional form (e.g. logarithmic dependent variables).

Specialization, Trade, and Integration

Table 5.3 Regression analysis of measures of trade specialization

	TRADE	INTRA	TRADESPEC
Constant	0.475	0.169	0.101
	$(7.08)^a$	$(1.68)^c$	$(3.54)^a$
Type 2A	−0.019	0.102	−0.016
	(−0.266)	$(1.97)^c$	(−1.20)
Type 2R	0.144	0.095	0.006
	$(2.37)^b$	$(2.81)^a$	(0.51)
Type 2AR	0.186	0.123	0.012
	$(1.66)^c$	$(2.63)^a$	(0.75)
TRS	−0.30		−0.004
	$(-3.87)^a$		$(-2.45)^b$
HET		0.067	−0.001
		$(3.56)^a$	(−0.12)
SUBCON	−0.199		−0.020
	$(-3.29)^a$		(−1.53)
INT	−0.080	0.238	−0.050
	(−0.93)	$(4.49)^a$	$(-2.90)^a$
GOV	−0.351	0.519	−0.138
	$(-2.58)^b$	$(4.52)^a$	$(-5.25)^a$
REG	−0.136	0.020	−0.020
	$(-1.80)^c$	(0.25)	(−1.57)
R-squared	0.327	0.407	0.312
Corrected R-squared	0.261	0.357	0.236
F-statistic	4.98	8.15	4.09

Notes: t values in parentheses (standard errors are heteroscedastically consistent); ^{a} indicates significance at the 1% level, ^{b} at the 5% level and ^{c} at the 10% level. *INT* and *GOV* are expressed as proportions, not percentages, to bring them in line with the dependent variables.

that industries geared to processing materials for incorporation into the products of downstream, often assembly, industries trade less, even taking account of transport costs. In fact, such industries engage in a very substantial 20% points less trade. Turning to technology and product differentiation, R&D intensive industries clearly engage in substantially more trade than others. On its own, this result could be due to either international specialization or trade in differentiated products. Anticipating the results on INTRA, however, it is apparent that the product differentiation effect is dominant. There is no trade-stimulating effect, however, for advertising intensive industries—the Type 2A dummy variable is completely without significance in the *TRADE* equation. This produces a tension for Type 2AR industries: whilst the quantitative effect of *TYPE2AR* is similar to that of *TYPE2R*, it is statistically less significant. Finally, government intervention is revealed to have a substantial impact. An industry selling 30% of its output to government departments, *ceteris paribus*, has about 10 percentage points less *TRADE* than an industry selling no output to government. The effect of national regulatory standards is somewhat less significant, but regulations also appear to suppress trade.

The results for *INTRA* are, if anything a little stronger, though this is partly due to the variable measuring heterogeneity in the industrial classification, *HET*, which is an important standardization for the measurement of intra-industry trade. The importance of the international exchange of differentiated products is shown by all Type 2 industries engaging in an intra-industry trade share which is roughly 10 percentage points higher than Type 1. A larger share of output sold as intermediate goods to other firms (*INT*) also promotes intra-industry trade as firms search for optimal input combinations. The strong, positive coefficient on *GOV* confirms that governments act to suppress comparative disadvantage, but are less domestically biased against balanced intra-industry trade. On the other hand, the insignificant coefficient on *REG* suggests that, unlike procurement bias, national regulations suppress all forms of trade equally.

Putting together our results on total trade and intra-industry trade, the final regression in Table 5.3 estimates the combined impact on international specialization within the EU. Transport costs suppress specialization, as expected. However, the most interesting results are to be found in the net effects of the industry type and government intervention variables. Most strikingly, R&D-intensive industries do not have a greater tendency to national specialization *once the other factors in the regression have been taken into account*. Thus, the increase in *TRADE* is due entirely to the intra-industry component and not to a stronger association with comparative advantage or whatever motivates inter-industry trade. In contrast, public procurement strongly suppresses national specialization, reducing both trade and particularly the inter-industry component. National regulations have a similar, but statistically weaker effect.

5.5 Conclusion

This chapter has investigated the causes of national specialization within the EU. The most specialized sectors include the textile industries, but on average, R&D intensive industries are the most geographically specialized of our industry types. This is reflected in their much greater propensity to trade, though a large part of this is intra-industry. However, our econometric analysis suggests that once other factors have been taken into account, R&D-intensive industries are *not* noticeably more specialized, though they *are* substantially more trade-integrated than other industry types. Their greater national trade specialization may, therefore, be due to their association with low transport costs, the fact that they are not intermediate goods, or that fewer sales are made to government buyers (rather than to technological economies of local agglomeration). Finally, the strongest conclusion of this chapter must be that government purchasing policies have substantially distorted the natural pattern of international specialization.

BRUCE LYONS and JORDI GUAL

APPENDIX to Chapter 5

....

This appendix formally derives the two decompositions used in the main text of the chapter. For notational convenience, we take as given that all summations are over $k = 1....11$ EU member states, including Bel/Lux as one state, and all variables refer to a particular industry, j. Thus, x_k = production (of industry j) in country k, and $x = \Sigma x_k$ = total EU production (in industry j).

Following Chapter 4, the index of intra-EU specialization is defined as

$$SPEC = \Sigma(x_k/x)^2 \tag{A5.1}$$

In addition, let

e_k = intra-EU exports from k, and $e = \Sigma e_k$ = total intra-EU exports;
m_k = intra-EU imports into k, and $m = \Sigma m_k$ = total intra-EU imports;
and c_k = 'apparent consumption' of EU produced goods in k.

Note that $e = m$ (in the absence of measurement error), and

$$c_k = x_k - e_k + m_k \tag{A5.2}$$

Thus,

$$c = \Sigma c_k = \Sigma x_k - \Sigma e_k + \Sigma m_k = x - e + m = x \tag{A5.3}$$

Define:

CONSPEC $= \Sigma(c_k/c)^2$ = Herfindahl index of apparent EU consumption

SIZEADJ $= 2\Sigma\left(\dfrac{e_k - m_k}{c}\right)\dfrac{c_k}{c}$

$\quad\quad\quad\quad$ = covariability of the trade surplus and country size

TRADESPEC $= [\Sigma(e_k - m_k)^2]^{1/2}/x$ = the 'standard deviation' of intra-EU trade balances, relative to production.[14]

Thus, from A5.1 - A5.3,

$$\frac{\Sigma x_k^2}{x^2} = \frac{\Sigma(c_k + e_k - m_k)^2}{c^2} = \frac{\Sigma c_k^2}{c^2} + \frac{2\Sigma c_k(e_k - m_k)}{c^2} + \frac{\Sigma(e_k - m_k)^2}{c^2}$$

$$\text{or } SPEC = CONSPEC + SIZEADJ + (TRADESPEC)^2 \tag{5.1}$$

Next define:

$TRADE$ $= (e + m)/x$ = total intra-EU trade as a share of production
$INTER$ $= [\Sigma(e_k - m_k)^2 / \Sigma(e_k + m_k)^2]^{1/2}$ = inter-industry trade
$INTRA$ $= 1 - INTER$ = intra-industry trade
$HTRADE$ $= \Sigma[(e_k + m_k)^2 / (e + m)^2]$ = Herfindahl index of trade

Then, rewrite

---

[14] Of course, a true standard deviation of trade balances would require the summation to be divided by $11^{1/2}$. Hence, the inverted commas. Note also that calculated $SIZEADJ$ is not the true covariance of the trade balance and apparent consumption (relative to total consumption) because measured e is empirically less than measured m. This measurement error biases $SIZEADJ$ upwards and explains the generally positive values in Table 5.1.

$$(TRADESPEC)^2 = \left(\frac{e+m}{x}\right)^2 \frac{\Sigma(e_k - m_k)^2}{\Sigma(e_k + m_k)^2} \frac{\Sigma(e_k + m_k)^2}{(e+m)^2}$$

so $TRADESPEC = TRADE * INTER * (HTRADE)^{1/2}$ (A5.5)

or, $TRADESPEC = TRADE * (1\text{-}INTRA) * (HTRADE)^{1/2}$ (5.2)

Of these terms, *TRADE* is self-explanatory, but *INTRA* and *HTRADE* deserve some comment. If either $\{e_k = 0 \text{ or } m_k = 0\}$ for all k, then *INTRA* = 0; and if $e_k = m_k$ for all k, then *INTRA* = 1. The former represents complete specialization in trade (countries either import or export, but not both) and the latter represents completely matched intra-industry trade flows. Between these two bounds, holding total trade constant and looking at symmetric countries, *INTRA* decreases proportionately with the absolute trade balance (e.g. for $e_k + m_k = 10$: e_k [or m_k] = 4 implies *INTRA* = 0.8; e_k [or m_k] = 3 implies *INTRA* = 0.6; e_k [or m_k] = 2 implies *INTRA* = 0.4 and e_k [or m_k] = 1 implies *INTRA* = 0.2).

INTRA differs from the standard Grubel–Lloyd index in that we eliminate the sign of the trade balance by squaring, and then take the square root after aggregation across countries; while they take absolute values. For a single country (or aggregated over symmetric countries), *INTRA* records identical values to the Grubel–Lloyd index; but the aggregation properties differ when countries are not symmetric. In general, there seems little to choose between the two measures, but ours is preferred here because it fits neatly into our decomposition.

HTRADE is best understood by looking at its reciprocal, which is the number of equivalent-sized trading partners. The range of this number-equivalent is between 2 (when all trade is between just two member states) and 11 (when all eleven trade equal volumes). The lower bound of 2 rather than 1 results because there have to be at least two partners to trade.

6

Industrial Concentration

6.1 Introduction

Why are some EU industries dominated by a few firms while others are very fragmented? And does the evidence on concentration reveal anything about the competitive process in the EU? These two apparently separate questions turn out to be intimately linked. A central theme in this chapter will be that, by looking carefully at market structure, we can draw inferences about how firms in the industry compete. For example, for a given degree of economies of scale, fiercer price competition leaves room for fewer firms; so the observation of a more concentrated industry, *ceteris paribus*, tells us about the severity of price competition. This idea will be developed more fully in section 6.3.

Part of the reason why some industries are so much more concentrated than others may lie in the degree of trade integration in the EU at the time. For example, in the last chapter we found that Type $2A$ industries were much less trade integrated than Type $2R$. One consequence might be that firms in Type $2A$ industries were typically competing in a large number of small markets, while those in Type $2R$ industries were competing across the EU. If true, this would certainly affect the EU market structure. One purpose of this chapter is to investigate the relationship between concentration and trade integration.

In Chapter 4, we presented a statistically exact (identity) relationship between EU concentration, national concentration, specialization, and multinationality. In Chapter 5, we provided an econometric explanation of geographic specialization, and in the next we shall provide an econometric study of multinational operations. Given the identity, this leaves *either* EU concentration *or* national concentration to be explained. We cannot independently explain both. Either competition operates at the national level, in which case EU concentration is the product of national concentration, geographic specialization, and international production by firms; or concentration is determined at the EU level, leaving average national concentration as the residual consequence of the geographic location of industry and ownership by multinational firms. More formally, we cannot provide separate explanations of both EU and national concentration because the system would be over-identified. Given that our empirical data collection has been very much at the EU level, it is on EU concentration that we focus our attention, while using measures of trade integration to adjust for the appropriate geographical level of competition and to reveal the importance of trade in integrating the market.

The remainder of this chapter is structured as follows. In Section 6.2, we provide some more detail on international comparisons of concentration, and on how the components of the concentration identity differ between industry types. Section 6.3 develops the theory of industrial concentration, and econometric tests are given in Section 6.4. Section 6.5 concludes.

6.2 Concentration By Industry Type

Advertising and, in particular, R&D will be central to our understanding of industrial concentration. This suggests it is fruitful to look at concentration according to the industry typology we developed earlier in the book (see Section 2.5). In this section we answer two questions about relative concentration. First, to what extent does our earlier finding, that EU concentration is much less than that in the USA, differ across industry types? Second, how does the statistical decomposition of EU concentration in terms of national concentration, geographic specialization, and intra-EU multinationality, differ across industry types? The answers are suggestive of the competitive forces at work, and the behavioural explanation is taken up in the next section.

Table 6.1 Relative EU and US concentration ratio by industry type

	Type 1	Type 2*A*	Type 2*R*	Type 2*AR*
C4US/C4EU	2.08	1.67	1.15	1.27
C4US–C4EU	13.5	14.7	4.8	9.6

Sources: See Appendix 3 and Section 4.2.2.

Although most of this chapter measures concentration by the Herfindahl index (or its reciprocal—the number equivalent), US comparisons are only possible using the four-firm concentration ratio. A discussion of our US data is given in Secton 4.2.2. Table 6.1 measures the gap between US and EU concentration using both the ratio and the simple difference. As we have already reported in Chapter 4, US concentration is typically much higher than in the EU (see Table 4.3). However, we can now see that the gap is smaller for Type 2 industries than for Type 1, and particularly so for industries which engage in significant R&D. In fact, there is only a modest concentration gap in Type 2*R* industries, whilst, for Type 2*A*, the gap is no smaller in absolute terms than in Type 1 industries. Inasmuch as the USA has an industrial structure appropriate to an integrated domestic market, these descriptive statistics are suggestive that R&D-intensive industries are the most integrated in the EU.

Table 6.2 Number equivalent decomposition of
concentration by industry type

	NEU	=	NNAT	*	NSPEC	/	NM
Type 1	180	=	44	*	5.0	/	1.24
Type 2A	64	=	19	*	5.4	/	1.55
Type 2R	32	=	12	*	4.0	/	1.49
Type 2AR	26	=	10	*	4.7	/	1.77

Notes: Figures shown are geometric means for each Type.
Estimates of *NM* and *NNAT* are based on the midpoints of the
upper and lower estimates of multinationality (see Section 4.4).
For full definitions of the variables, see Table 4.4.

In Table 6.2, we return to the decomposition of EU concentration using the
number-equivalent measure, in order to focus on differences across industry
types in the levels of EU and typical member state concentration (*NEU* and
NNAT respectively). A striking pattern is immediately apparent. Moving down
the *NEU* column, we find that EU concentration is very much higher (i.e. the
number-equivalent is lower) in Type 2 than in Type 1 industries, and R&D is
more strongly associated with high concentration than is advertising. A similar, but less strong, pattern is also apparent for *NNAT*—the ratio of *NEU* to
NNAT falls as we move down the columns, showing that the Type 2 effects are
relatively stronger at the EU level than at the national level.

Thus, comparing Type 2 and Type 1, Type 2 industries are:

1. more concentrated at the EU level;
2. more concentrated at the national level;
3. relatively more concentrated at the EU than at the national level; and
4. closer to US concentration levels.

Furthermore, comparing R&D-intensive and advertising-intensive Type 2
industries, the above four findings are:

(a) stronger for R&D-intensive industries; and
(b) strongest for industries which combine R&D and advertising in-
    tensity.

Additionally, the *NSPEC* column of Table 6.2 repeats our finding from
Chapter 5 that Type 2*R* industries are more geographically specialized within
the EU, and Type 2*A* are less geographically specialized, than are other industries. A proper discussion of multinationality is postponed until the next chapter, but for now we note that the last column reveals Type 2 industries to be
more multinational than Type 1, this time with advertising having the stronger
apparent effect.

Overall, R&D and advertising clearly have a strong association with industrial concentration. In the next section, we investigate the theoretical foundations for such a relationship.

6.3 Theory of Industrial Concentration

6.3.1 Background

Until the last fifteen years, most economists tended to treat industrial concentration as an important determinant of the way firms set price and other competitive weapons, but they gave relatively little thought to the fundamental determinants of concentration itself. Market structure was somehow assumed to be the consequence of a few basic conditions, such as economies of scale relative to the size of the market, and exogenous consumer tastes. However, this was not thought to be fundamentally important, except that if economies of scale were relatively large, then this would result in few firms and this, in turn, might confer a degree of monopoly power. Only the last line in this causal link was seen as crucial for economic policy. This broad approach was known as the structure-conduct-performance (SCP) model.[1]

More recently, economists have come to appreciate the importance of viewing industrial concentration as the outcome of the competitive process rather than only as an exogenously given determinant of competition. The way firms compete, and the competitive weapons they use, together forge the industrial structure in which firms operate, as well as determining the final product prices and other decision variables. This new approach encompasses the key insights of the SCP model, for instance, that as a market becomes more concentrated, this confers extra monopoly power. However, it embeds them in a richer understanding of why different industries have different structures. Even more intriguingly, it is sometimes possible to work back from the observed market structure to draw conclusions about how the competitive process must have worked in order to generate that structure.

Game theory is a crucial part of the tool-kit that has been used to develop this new approach to understanding industrial organization. This has provided some fascinating insights, but they have not come without a cost. Previously, economists working in the SCP paradigm could hold onto the fixed concept of exogenous firm numbers and/or dominance, then investigate a range of types of behaviour by firms. But once we move to viewing firm numbers and firm size as endogenous to the competitive process, the analyst need another fixed concept from which to work. Game theory fulfils that function, giving the economist an idealized concept of rational behaviour with which to examine the consequences of different technological and historical conditions.

An important lesson learned from this approach is that market structure is likely to be very sensitive to slight changes in these conditions. This does not mean that anything can happen, but it does mean that if we want to draw broad generalizations that might be applicable to a broad range of industries, then we are restricted to a relatively limited set of general results that are robust to small

---

[1] This brief summary does little more than caricature the SCP approach, which is definitively set out in Scherer (1980).

changes in conditions. The object of this chapter is to examine one set of such results, focusing on the relationship between industrial concentration and market size. It turns out that even this deceptively simple relationship reveals crucial information about the underlying competitive process in European industry.

6.3.2 Concentration and market size: Type 1 theory[2]

We begin by considering Type 1 industries, in which the predominant form of competition is through price, and advertising and R&D are not significant competitive weapons. The new approach to the theory of concentration, as developed most fully by Sutton (1991), begins with an analysis of pricing behaviour. Although there is no single, widely accepted model of oligopoly pricing, most theories support a negative relationship between the number of firms and the price–cost margin they can achieve. This relationship is most clearly brought out in the Cournot model, which generates a very precise relationship for N firms with the same costs selling a homogeneous product: in that case the price-cost margin equals the reciprocal of the number of firms times the industry elasticity of demand. Although the spirit of a negative relationship is much broader, there are two extreme cases in which the negative relation does not hold: perfect collusion and Bertrand pricing with homogeneous products. With perfect collusion, the monopoly price is insensitive to the number of competitors; and in the Bertrand case, two firms are sufficient for perfectly competitive pricing. Neither extreme case is particularly plausible in most industrial markets,[3] but they do set the theoretical limiting bounds on feasible behaviour.

Within these extremes, we can express the practical limiting bounds for empirically observable industries: $\hat{P} = f(N)$ is the most collusive price given the number of firms (applicable, for example, to industries in which cartelization is possible, where collusion is easy because prices are observable by rival firms and retaliation to price cutting is swift, or where products are very differentiated); and $\underline{P} = g(N)$ is the most competitive price given the number of firms (applicable, for example, to industries characterized by infrequent transactions, a history of non-co-operation, and highly substitutable products). These relationships are drawn in Figure 6.1. In each case, there is a negative relationship between price and N; and following Sutton, we call this function the

---

[2] This section is closely based on the work of Sutton (1991, 1995*a* and 1995*b*), though we have substantially developed the diagrammatic analysis, and played down Sutton's sequential game formulation with its emphasis on sunk costs. Schmalensee (1992) and Dasgupta and Stiglitz (1980) demonstrate the generality of the key ideas to a simultaneous choice, fixed (not sunk) cost framework.

[3] Perfect collusion may be achievable when there are just a few firms, but inevitably breaks down if the number of firms is sufficiently large. The extreme Bertrand result of price equalling the marginal cost of the second lowest cost firm, regardless of firm numbers, breaks down if even a small amount of product differentiation is present.

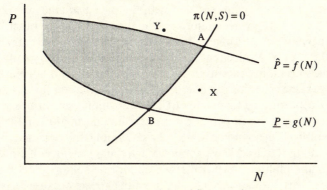

Fig. 6.1 The set of feasible outcomes: price and firm numbers

toughness of price competition. Thus, $g(N)$ represents tougher price competition than $f(N)$.

Next consider what determines the number of firms in an industry, given the technology of production and the above relationship between pricing and firm numbers. Formally, this can be characterized as the first stage of a two-stage game, in which firms decide whether or not to enter in anticipation of the second-stage price competition. Once again, the extreme cases illustrate the limits to what might happen. If barriers to entry are sufficiently high, or the first firm in the market can credibly act to fill all the profitable opportunities, then the industry may remain a monopoly. At the other pole, entry may be free in the sense that incumbent firms have no advantage over new entrants, in which case entry will continue until the marginal potential entrant makes zero profits. With symmetric firms, this means that incumbent firms will also make only sufficient profits to keep them in the market (i.e. zero economic profits).[4] Given that there are economies of scale, for any given size of market, then the more firms there are in the market, the higher will be average costs. Thus, the more firms there are in the market, the higher must be the price in order for firms to just break even. The line $\pi(N, S) = 0$, also drawn on Figure 6.1, expresses this relationship. Points above and to the left of this line result in firms making positive profits, and points below and to the right mean firms make losses. S is a measure of the industry size relative to economies of scale in production; and if either market size rises or economies of scale fall, the break-even line shifts to the right.

We are now in a position to ask what price and firm number outcomes we might observe in an industry of size S. If we knew that the industry acted as

[4] Strictly speaking, this result is approximate because there may be 'integer effects'; which is to say that if there are N firms in the market, each may make strictly positive profits, while if another entered, the $N + 1$ firms would each make a loss. Thus, even with free entry, only N firms will enter. This integer effect is ignored in this chapter, on the grounds that it is likely to be small in the broadly defined industries we use in this book.

collusively as was feasible, then the equilibrium would be along the $\hat{P} = f(N)$
line; and if firms were symmetric and without any advantage over potential
entrants, then the long-run equilibrium would be at A. On the other hand, if
pricing behaviour was very competitive, then the symmetric free-entry equilibrium would be at B. Notice that the more competitive industry can support
fewer firms, so is more concentrated. Given that the EU and US markets are
roughly the same size, this provides a possible explanation for US industry
being more concentrated than in the EU: they are more competitive in setting
price. Leaving aside this possibility, if we have no information on the pricing
behaviour of firms in an industry, then the set of potential outcomes includes
all points along AB; and if we acknowledge the possibility of first mover
advantages and multi-product firms, we cannot rule out any outcome in the
shaded area. This is not to say that anything can happen, because certain possibilities are ruled out. For example, a point such as X suggests a feasible price
given the number of firms, but we cannot expect to observe such an outcome in
the long-run because firms would be making losses; and a point such as Y is not
feasible because price is unsustainably high. The fact that we cannot predict a
precise outcome, but instead accept a set of possibilities, should not be seen as
a weakness as long as this broad-based theory generates testable predictions. It
is to these that we now turn.

In Figure 6.2, we show how the set of feasible outcomes is extended as the
size of the market increases. With market size S_0, any outcome in the light-
shaded area is feasible with the maximum number of firms being N_0; and with
market size S_1, the feasible set of outcomes is extended to include the darker
area with the maximum number of firms being N_1. The dashed line in Figure
6.3 traces out the relationship between market size and this maximum feasible
number of firms. The vertical axis plots the Herfindahl measure of industrial
concentration, which with symmetric firms is simply the reciprocal of the number of firms. There are three important features of this relationship:

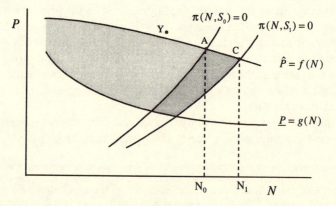

Fig. 6.2 Market size and the number of firms

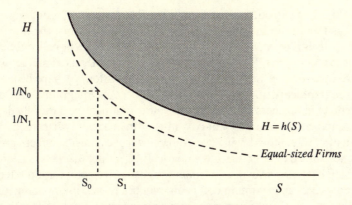

Fig. 6.3 Concentration and market size in Type I industries

1. As market size relative to economies of scale (S) rises, the theoretical min-imum level of concentration falls. In the limit as S becomes very large, this level of concentration will approach zero.

2. The dotted line refers to an industry with identical firms and no incumb-ent advantages. In practice, firms are never identical: either by accident (e.g. stochastic demand) or design (e.g. history leaving firms with different capac-ities), there are always inequalities in firm sizes. Because even the smallest firms in the industry must not make losses if they are to survive, then if some firms are larger, this reduces the maximum number of sustainable firms and raises concentration. Even a minimum amount of chance will push the minimum level of concentration at any S up to the solid line $H = h(S)$.[5]

3. $H = h(S)$ is a minimum, or lower bound, relationship. Higher levels of concentration are feasible, depending on: the degree of price competition, first-mover advantages (including barriers to entry), the credibility of market pre-emption strategies, and multi-product firms in differentiated product mar-kets. This feasible set is shown by the shaded area in Figure 6.3.

6.3.3 Concentration and Integration

Suppose a single country of size S_0 can sustain a maximum number of firms, N_0. If two such countries are empirically observed as a single market, despite the fact that they operate entirely separately from each other, the measured 'concentration' would appear to be $2N_0$, despite the fact that the competitively relevant 'concentration' is only N_0 in each integrated market. This is illustrated by points A and B in Fig. 6.4. Price in each market is P_A, and the maximum number of firms sustainable in each country is N_0, so the maximum for the so-called single market is $2N_0$. Next, suppose the two countries do indeed operate as a single market, but integration does not affect the toughness of price

---

[5] This idea is fully developed in Sutton (1995*b*).

competition. Then an outcome at B is not feasible because P_A is no longer sustainable as there is an increased number of competing firms: the maximum number of firms is only N_1, which is less than $2N_0$. This can be called the *direct market expansion effect*. Finally, suppose that a truly integrated market would also introduce tougher (less collusive) price competition, perhaps because of greater geographical distance between firms or because integration introduces heterogeneity in business cultures and the more competitive naturally dominates, or simply because a history of cosy inter-firm relations is disrupted. While any form of market growth will have a direct market expansion effect, 'growth' due to the joining of existing, but previously separate, markets is therefore much more likely to have an additional tougher-price-competition effect. In the extreme case, as maximum collusion switches to maximum competition, the maximum number of firms in the integrated market is reduced to $\underline{N}_1$.

Taking account of the minimum amount of firm size inequality, the lower bound relationship between concentration and the size of the single market is shown in Figure 6.5. $H = h_0(S)$ is the lower bound for an unintegrated market; $H = h_1(S)$ is the lower bound for an integrated market with no change in the toughness of price competition (i.e. no change in pricing behaviour other than due to the increase in firm numbers); and $H = h_1(S)$ is the lower bound for an integrated market which is also fundamentally more competitive. Note that each of these curves is strictly downward sloping and the lower bound for H gets close to zero as market size becomes very large. However, the important result is that integration shifts the lower bound upwards when industries are observed at the EU level.

The analysis so far considers only equilibrium outcomes. However, it is also of interest to consider the dynamics of market integration. If we start with two independent markets, each pricing with maximum collusion and with no incumbent advantages or size asymmetries, then observation of the two countries as a single entity would result in the price and firm number combination at B in Figure 6.4. Joining the two markets puts immediate downward pressure

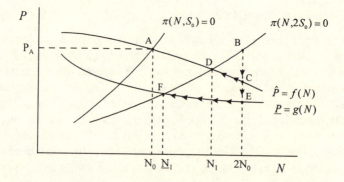

Fig. 6.4 Integration and the maximum number of firms

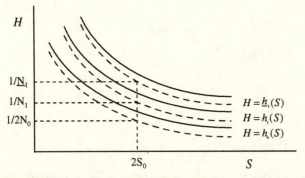

Fig. 6.5 Integration and market structure: shifting the lower bound

on price as more firms compete with each other (point C), and this results in negative net profits. In the long-run, firms will exit the market and as they do, price will edge up again, until the new equilibrium at D is reached. If integration also introduces qualitatively more competitive (tougher) pricing behaviour, then the price and market structure effects will be much stronger, in the extreme moving the industry initially from B to E, then gradually back to F.

6.3.4 Concentration and market size: Type 2 theory

Type 2 industries are not restricted to price as the only competitive weapon. They also compete in the 'endogenous fixed costs' (E) of advertising and/or R&D. Formally we can characterize this as an extra stage in the competitive process, with firms choosing E as a medium-run variable between the long-run entry decision and short-run pricing. We shall return to the differences between advertising and R&D a little later, but for now we emphasize two general properties they share: (i) they raise the perceived quality of the product being sold, and so also the consumer willingness to pay for it;[6] and (ii) while E is endogenous (i.e. within the control of firms in the industry), it is also a fixed cost in that it does not increase with output. These two effects are shown in Figure 6.6 for the case of symmetric firms each spending similar amounts on some fixed cost, E (i.e. advertising and/or R&D per firm). For clarity, the figure is drawn with only one type of pricing behaviour. Begin by supposing that E is exogenous, and consider the consequences of raising E from E_0 to E_1:

1. Price no longer depends only on the number of competitors, but also on E: higher E increases consumer willingness to pay for the product and so shifts up the price line ($E_1 > E_0$).

---

[6] Of course, R&D can be used to reduce production costs. The analysis in the text focuses on product enhancement for two reasons. First, while small scale process development typically takes place within the firm, most industries recognized as being R&D-intensive are primarily concerned with product development. Second, as Dasgupta and Stiglitz (1980) have shown, the central ideas in the theory of market structure and endogenous fixed costs carry through to process innovation.

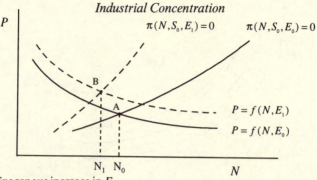

$\pi(N,S_0,E_1)=0$ $\pi(N,S_0,E_0)=0$

$P = f(N,E_1)$

$P = f(N,E_0)$

N_1 N_0

N

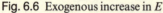

Fig. 6.6 Exogenous increase in E

2. Higher fixed costs raise average costs and so also the break-even price for any given market size and number of firms.

This exogenous increase in E shifts the equilibrium from A to B. Price definitely rises, but the effect on N depends on the strength of the marginal influence of E on willingness to pay. Figure 6.6 is drawn on the assumption that this is small relative to its cost.

However, advertising and R&D are not exogenous: they are endogenously determined by firms. A key determinant of how much firms will wish to spend is the size of the market over which the increased consumer willingness to pay can be reaped. Expectations as to the response of rivals will also be important and, together with the sensitivity of consumers, these forces will combine to determine equilibrium spending on E, as well as price and the number of firms. One intermediate conclusion follows. Since $E > 0$ in Type 2 industries, *ceteris paribus*, they will tend to be more concentrated than Type 1 industries.[7]

What happens as the size of the market increases? As for Type 1 industries, this creates a tendency to push the break-even line down and to the right; but at the same time it encourages higher spending on E, which works in the opposite direction. Sutton (1991) shows for a significant class of circumstances and very large market sizes, that the net effect is likely to be neutral on N, as firms escalate their spending on E. In particular, as market size increases, the maximum number of firms does not continually increase, but approaches some finite maximum, N_M. This case is depicted in Figure 6.7.

For less extreme market sizes, an increase in market size may be associated with either an increase or a decrease in the number of firms. The possibilities are illustrated in Figure 6.8. The solid line depicts an industry which does not find it profitable to engage in advertising or R&D until market size reaches S_1. Above that size, the escalation process results in no change in concentration. The relationship between size and concentration for other industries, with different economies of scale, sensitivities of consumers, etc., are given by the dashed and dotted lines. In the former case, once advertising or R&D become profitable, at market size S_0, increases in size still attract new entrants into the

---

[7] This assumes that the shift in the price line is small relative to the shift in the break-even line.

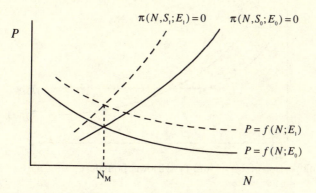
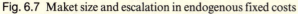

$\pi(N, S_1; E_1) = 0$ $\pi(N, S_0; E_0) = 0$

P

$P = f(N; E_1)$

$P = f(N; E_0)$

N_M N

Fig. 6.7 Maket size and escalation in endogenous fixed costs

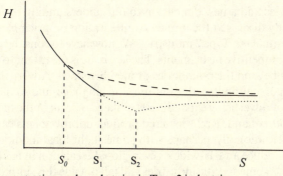
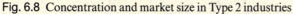

H

S_0 S_1 S_2 S

Fig. 6.8 Concentration and market size in Type 2 industries

industry, but at a lesser rate than in Type 1 industries. The dotted line illustrates the case where, once this type of quality competition sets in at size S_2, the competitive incentive to spend heavily is so great that fewer firms can survive.

To summarize, the key difference as compared with Type 1 industries is that the slope of the concentration-size relationship will be less steep, and may even be positive. Note that these predictions would not hold if advertising and R&D were exogenous fixed costs, like production overheads. If that were the case, then the lower bound would be shifted upwards, but the slope effects would not be present. Thus, the existence of a shallower slope in Type 2 industries would constitute evidence that these expenditures are active competitive weapons subject to escalation, and not simply a fixed cost of competing. Of course, the higher fixed costs in Type 2 industries will still shift the lower bound upwards. However, inasmuch as Type 2 industries are associated with greater product differentiation, this may also shift the type 2 lower bound to the left because such markets have more niches for small, specialist firms to fill. The net effect could be as depicted in Figure 6.9. Finally, for both Type 1 and Type 2 industries, these *are* lower bound relationships, and industries with a history of first mover or other advantages may be more concentrated.

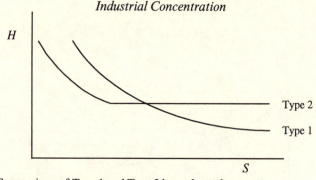

Fig. 6.9 Comparison of Type 1 and Type 2 lower bounds

6.3.5 Advertising, R&D and Integration

Type 2 industries add a new dimension to our understanding of integration. We have already discussed the impact of integration on pricing, and similar factors apply equally to Type 2 industries. We now have to consider advertising and R&D as competitive instruments. The key issue is the extent to which they can be applied beyond the boundaries of member states. Advertising is typically dependent on national media, culture, and language, and so the competitive escalation of advertising expenditures is likely to occur at the member state level. On the other hand, R&D-inspired product improvements can generally be applied internationally, perhaps with some slight local modification, and this is likely to induce an EU-wide or even global escalation in R&D expenditures. Of course, some specific industries will fall outside this simple characterization, but it stands as a working proposition.

How does the geographic range of endogenous fixed costs affect the relationship between EU concentration and EU market size? Begin by supposing that trade allows for the complete integration of production. For Type $2R$ industries, this means that the EU is the relevant market for analysis; or if the true market is global, at least it is closer to the relevant market than is the member state. For Type $2A$ industries, the high costs of multiple advertising expenditures combined with the production cost savings of integrated production would potentially provide a very strong concentrating force. Next consider the relationship when production remains local. For Type $2R$ industries, this raises the importance of production costs relative to R&D, and so makes them less different from Type 1 industries. For Type $2A$ industries, the relevant market becomes the member state, so concentration measured at the EU level will be lower due to the effect of market aggregation (see Section 6.3.3). Which of these characterizations is appropriate? As we have already seen in Chapter 5, Type $2R$ industries are much more trade integrated than are Type $2A$ industries. Thus, an analysis of EU concentration is more likely to produce a clear and strong Type 2 relationship in R&D-intensive industries than it is for advertising-intensive industries. Finally, Type $2AR$ industries have two endogenous fixed costs with which to compete. This should exacerbate Type 2 effects as escalation takes place on two fronts.

6.3.6 Summary of hypotheses relating concentration and market size

This analysis has revealed the complexity and richness of what has tradition-ally been thought of as a relatively straightforward and unimportant relation-ship between concentration and market size. By exploring this relation, we are able to understand a considerable amount about how firms compete. The main theoretical results are summarized in the following hypotheses:

H1: For Type 1 industries, the lower bound to concentration approaches zero as market size increases; while for Type 2 industries, the limiting level of concentration (approached at very large market sizes) is strictly positive and independent of market size. Furthermore, the slope of the concentration-size relationship is less steep in Type 2 industries.

H2: For Type 2 industries, the lower bound to concentration as a function of market size need not be monotonically decreasing, and may even increase.

H3: The effects of advertising and R&D are cumulative, with industries en-gaged in both having the highest limiting level of concentration, the shallowest slope to the concentration-size relationship, and the greatest likelihood for concentration to increase with market size.

H4: International economies of scope suggest a shallower, more clearly de-termined relationship at the EU level for R&D-intensive industries than for advertising-intensive industries.[8]

H5: Trade integration shifts the lower bound relationship estimated at the EU level upwards for all industry types.

6.4 Econometric Results

6.4.1 Estimation procedure

The econometric problem is to estimate the lower bound to the concentration-size relation. There are two main issues: choice of functional form and choice of estimator. The chosen functional form (also used by Sutton, 1991) is sufficiently flexible to pick up the broad shapes in Fig. 6.9, and for industry Type t is given by:

$$LH_j = a_t + b_t\, SIZE_j + c_t\, INTEGRATION_j \qquad (6.1)$$

where

---

[8] This hypothesis does not claim there is no potential for international economies of scope in advertising (e.g. tradenames, reputation, marketing skills, etc.); the claim is simply that the scope is less than for R&D.

LH_i is a logistic transform of the Herfindahl index of EU concentration in industry j; $LH_j = ln(HEU_j / [1 - HEU_j])$

$SIZE_j$ is a transform of EU industry size adjusted for production economies of scale: $SIZE_j = 1/ln(MES/EUSIZE)_j$ (see Appendix for data sources).

$INTEGRATION_j$ is a measure of the extent of trade integration, based on the indices introduced in the previous chapter. Initially, it is measured by $TRADE$, i.e. total intra-EU trade relative to production; but we also experiment by separating this into the two components: $INTRATR$, intra-industry trade relative to production ($INTRA * TRADE$) and $INTERTR$, inter-industry trade relative to production ($[1-INTRA] * TRADE$);

and,

a_t, b_t and c_t are parameters specific to industry Type t, where $t = 1, 2A, 2R, 2AR$.

Turning to the choice of estimator, ordinary least squares is not appropriate because the theory suggests a minimum level of concentration associated with each market size and industry type, not an average relationship. We could proceed by fitting a curve which envelops all observations as does Sutton (1991) in his work on national markets in the food and drink industries. However, this deterministic approach does not allow for disequilibrium low levels of concentration, and it is not possible to claim that European industrial structure was in long-run equilibrium in 1987. We proceed by estimating a stochastic lower bound to the data, allowing for a two-sided (normal) error as well as for a (one-sided) distribution of observations above the lower bound. Unfortunately, there is little theory to guide on the choice of appropriate one-sided distribution,[9] but we tried the standard exponential, half-normal, and truncated normal estimators, and they each gave similar results.[10] We report the exponential results.

Assuming a similar error structure for each industry type, the final estimating equation is:

$$LH_i = a_1 + \Sigma_{t \neq 1} \alpha_t TYPE_{ti} + \Sigma_t b_t SIZE_{ti} + \Sigma_t c_t INTEGRATION_{ti} + v_i + u_i \qquad (6.2)$$

where:

$\alpha_t = a_t - a_1$
$f(u) = \theta \exp(-\theta u)$

and

$v \sim N(0, \sigma_v^2)$.

In other words, the equation is estimated with intercept and slope dummy variables, corresponding to the three sorts of Type 2 industries. Type 1 is set as the default, in order to preserve a constant in the estimation procedure. Thus,

---

[9] Though Sutton (1991) makes an interesting case for the Weibull.
[10] For some model specifications, the half-normal and truncated normal failed to converge. Estimation was carried out using *LIMDEP*.

coefficients on the intercept dummies show the effects for Type 2 industries relative to Type 1.

6.4.2 Results

Table 6.3 reports the results from the estimation of Equation (6.2) for various measures of trade integration. As a preliminary, *R1* and *R2* present base line results for the full 100 industry sample (*R2*) and for the ninety-one industries for which we have trade data (*R1*). There is very little difference between the two, which suggests that the omission of the nine industries does not create a bias. The coefficients on the Type 2 intercept dummies suggest that the limiting level of concentration as industry size becomes very large rises as we move from Type 1 (*NEU* = 5000) to Type 2*A* (*NEU* = 950) to Type 2*R* (*NEU* = 400) and to Type 2*AR* (*NEU* = 32) industries.[11] In terms of the slopes of these relationships (shown by the coefficients on *SIZEt*), there is a similar ranking, with Type 1 industries exhibiting the steepest relationship and Type 2*AR* the shallowest. In fact, we find the striking result that the Type 2*AR* slope is (insignificantly) positive. However, the difference between Type 1 and Type 2*A* industries is not statistically significant either for the slope or the intercept effects. This suggests that the escalation in endogenous costs is greatest in R&D intensive industries, and the combined effect of advertising and R&D as competitive weapons results in a very powerful effect. However, advertising is not as systematic as is R&D as a concentrating effect at the EU level. Thus, with only minor reservations in relation to Type 2*A* industries, the first four of our hypotheses in Section 6.3.6 receive strong support from the data.

Incorporating the trade variables in the regression analysis, the marginal effect of increasing trade integration is strongest in Type 2*R* industries, and there is also a significant effect in Type 1 industries. *R3* reports the results first using total intra-EU *TRADE* as a measure, and *R4* separates out that part which is intra-industry trade from that based on comparative advantage (or whatever has caused unbalanced trade). The evidence suggests that *INTERTR* has no significant effect, so *R5* focuses on INTRATR. The fact that *R5* has a slightly better log-likelihood than *R3* suggests intra-industry trade contributes a little more to the explanatory power of the model than does *TRADE* in total. This in turn suggests that intra-industry trade might be the better measure of the extent of trade integration.[12]

---

[11] The NEU figures (shown in brackets) are derived, in rounded form, from the estimated coefficients using the limit property of (6.1) that as $EUSIZE/MES \rightarrow \infty$, $H \rightarrow \exp(a_t)/[1 + \exp(a_t)]$.

[12] An alternative explanation might be that *INTRATR* is picking up horizontal product differentiation, and this allows firms to credibly fill more market niches and so dominate the market. In order to try to test this, we introduced *HET*, our measure of product category heterogeneity (used in Chapter 5 and defined in Appendix 3), into the above regressions. However, it was never significant, nor did it alter the significance of the other variables.

Table 6.3 Estimates of lower bound concentration-market size relation

	R1	R2	R3	R4	R5
Constant	−8.65	−8.42	−8.56	−8.61	−8.44
	(−25.88)[a]	(−23.57)[a]	(−25.29)[a]	(29.67)[a]	(−27.54)[a]
TYPE2A	1.73	1.64	1.90	1.07	1.31
	(1.32)	(1.19)	(1.20)	(0.61)	(0.63)
TYPE2R	2.61	2.50	1.45	1.68	1.61
	(5.17)[a]	(4.60)[a]	(2.31)[b]	(2.35)[b]	(2.51)[b]
TYPE2AR	5.20	5.01	4.27	3.53	3.79
	(4.41)[a]	(4.42)[a]	(2.67)[a]	(3.02)[a]	(2.77)[a]
SIZE1	−16.76	−15.48	−15.80	−15.42	−15.05
	(−8.79)[a]	(−7.45)[a]	(−8.33)[a]	(−9.16)[a]	(−7.91)[a]
SIZE2A	−10.58	−10.15	−9.96	−14.07	−11.46
	(−1.62)	(−1.47)	(−1.39)	(−1.60)	(−1.21)
SIZE2R	−8.14	−8.01	−8.33	−7.41	−7.61
	(−4.90)[a]	(−4.47)[a]	(−4.28)[a]	(−4.32)[a]	(−4.62)[a]
SIZE2AR	1.97	1.80	0.39	−3.03	−0.96
	(0.43)	(0.42)	(0.09)	(−0.87)	(−0.24)
TRADE1			0.92		
			(1.73)[c]		
TRADE2A			0.18		
			(0.16)		
TRADE2R			2.72		
			(3.70)[a]		
TRADE2AR			−1.49		
			(−0.77)		
INTRATR1				1.39	1.65
				(2.01)[b]	(2.34)[b]
INTRATR2A				4.84	1.41
				(1.26)	(0.78)
INTRATR2R				3.80	3.58
				(2.52)[b]	(2.43)[b]
INTRATR2AR				3.71	2.24
				(1.41)	(0.80)
INTERTR1				0.28	
				(0.24)	
INTERTR2A				−6.59	
				(−0.88)	
INTERTR2R				−0.26	
				(−0.08)	
INTERTR2AR				−4.17	
				(−1.43)	
θ	1.48	1.63	2.33	1.91	2.40
	(3.85)[a]	(3.52)[a]	(2.30)[b]	(3.35)[a]	(2.35)[b]
σ_v	0.46	0.52	0.55	0.43	0.53
	(3.70)[a]	(4.46)[a]	(3.98)[a]	(3.96)[a]	(4.32)[a]
Log-Likelihood	−103.4	−115.1	−94.6	−88.1	−91.1
No. of obs.	91	100	91	91	91

Notes: Figures in parentheses denote t values; [a] indicates significance at the 1% level; [b] at the 5% level; and [c] at the 10% level.

In any event, both measures of trade integration present the same picture. Type 2R industries are the most sensitive to trade. Thus low-trade Type 2R industries have more firms than in a fully integrated market. In turn, this is consistent with each firm doing less R&D than would be achieved in a fully integrated market; and this suggests that some such industries may well be prevented from achieving their full, research potential because of government or other impediments to trade. With Type 1 industries, also, low-trade integration is associated with lower EU concentration (see Figure 6.5). Although this may superficially appear to be good for competition, it is not, because low-trade industries face only national, not EU-wide competition. A stylization of what we are observing can be seen by referring back to Figure 6.4. The evidence suggests low trade industries are at a point such as *B*, while more integrated industries are at *D* or *F*. Unfortunately, we cannot distinguish the market expansion effect from any fundamental change in the toughness of price competition.

This leaves open the question of why the trade variables appear to have no significant effect in Type 2A and Type 2AR industries. Although this comprises the full set of advertising-intensive industries, advertising alone does not provide the complete explanation. As can be seen from Table 5.2(c), Type 2AR industries are among the most trade integrated, and it may be that they are sufficiently close to full integration that a little more or less trade makes no difference. On the other hand, Type 2A industries are amongst the lowest trade integrated and, added to the localized effectiveness of advertising, this locks them into national markets so that marginal increments in trade again have no great effect. These interpretations are supported by the fact that Type 2AR industries, like Type 2R are close to US concentration levels, while Type 2A industries are substantially less concentrated than in the USA (see Table 6.1).

6.5 Conclusion

In this chapter, we have shown that EU concentration is much lower than in the USA, particularly for non-R&D-intensive industries. The gap in concentration between US and even high-trade EU industries is consistent with greater price competition in the USA. There are also striking differences in the levels of EU concentration depending on their advertising and R&D intensities. The new theory of industrial concentration suggests high concentration in Type 2 industries is due to the competitive escalation of these expenditures as competitive weapons. Applying this theory, we have derived five testable propositions concerned with the relationship between concentration and market size, and the impact of market integration. The strong econometric support for these hypotheses suggests that there was already, in 1987, substantial integration in high-trade R&D-intensive industries. The evidence is suggestive that competition in Type 2AR industries was already operating at the EU level, regardless of the actual amount of trade. On the other hand, low-trade R&D industries did not compete at the EU level and this may have significantly dampened their R&D efforts. There is also room for further integration in low-trade Type 1 industries that compete predominantly through price.

Concentration in advertising-intensive industries is unrelated to trade, and this seems to suggest they may be competing only at the national level. However, that might be a misleading conclusion because trade is not the only avenue by which industries can be integrated. In the next chapter, we investigate the intra-EU multinationality of firms. As Table 6.2 shows, Type 2 industries tend to be populated by firms which are more integrated in their corporate strategies (i.e. multinationality), and this is a way in which industries which are not trade integrated may become more concentrated at the EU level.

BRUCE LYONS and CATHERINE MATRAVES

7

Intra-EU Multinationality of Industries

7.1 Introduction

What determines whether leading EU firms spread their production *across* member states, as opposed to concentrating production in their home bases? How is the scale of such intra-EU multinational operations related to the structure of industries—in particular, concentration? And what is the role of multinational operations in the European integration process? These are the questions motivating this chapter, which turns to the third dimension of structure identified in the core decomposition of Chapter 4.

Our estimates on the degree of industry multinationality provide the first-ever evidence of cross-member-state production observed at the relatively disaggregated 3-digit level. This opens up a wider range of questions than those usually explored in previous literature on multinational enterprises (MNEs), especially in the EU context. Very often, empirical studies have had to focus on the determinants of foreign direct investment flows, in the absence of production statistics; and they have often used aggregate national data (derived from balance of payments accounts). Alternatively, where firm-level studies have been attempted, they have usually been confined to only the very largest conglomerate firms, using only crude and over-aggregate industrial breakdowns. Inevitably therefore, industry-level characteristics have tended to play relatively minor roles in the analysis.

Because our database is organized by industry, and is for production, we are able to develop the analysis within an explicit Industrial Organization perspective, and in a way which is consistent with the two previous chapters. We explore the relationship between multinationality and concentration; and since multinational production is only one mode for serving foreign markets, this is inextricably linked with intra-EU trade. Indeed, the nexus of trade and multinationality also returns us to the question of EU integration; but here, we widen the notion of trade integration to encompass the integration of firms' corporate strategies as well as international trade. Thus, these three elements of structure—multinationality, trade, and concentration—figure continuously throughout the chapter.

Section 7.2 defines our index of multinationality. Section 7.3 sets out the key 'facts' on the extent of multinational production by 3-digit industry, and these are used in the following sections to answer the three questions raised above. Sections 7.4 considers the relationship between multinational production and EU concentration; building on this, Section 7.5 investigates the industry-level determinants of multinationality; and Section 7.6 explores the role of multinationality in the integration of the EU. Section 7.7 concludes. As explained, the main focus of the chapter is on industry aggregates, but in an appendix we also examine differences between firms *within* individual industries to see how far our emphasis on industries has concealed important heterogeneities.

At the outset, we should underline two deliberate limitations to the analysis. First and foremost, our canvas is confined exclusively to multinational production *within the EU*. Thus, 'multinational' is used henceforward to mean a firm producing in more than one member state—regardless of its operations outside the EU. This is a direct consequence of the objectives of the book as a whole. For the purposes of this chapter therefore, no distinction is made between firms originating from outside or within the European Union. Of course, the operations of non-EU-owned firms do raise certain additional questions, and these are the subject of the next chapter. Second, by emphasizing industry-level data, we side-step certain questions which have been central in much of the previous multinational literature: 'Why do some *firms* choose to go multinational' and 'Why do some *countries* have a greater propensity to produce MNEs, while others are more likely to be their hosts?'. Such questions are postponed to Chapter 11, which focuses explicitly on the firm as the unit of observation.

7.2 Measuring the Multinationality of Industries

There is a wide range of indices that could be used to measure the extent of firms' multinational operations. Two simple candidates would be to count the number of countries in which they operate, or to measure the share of their output produced outside their home bases. Alternatively, many of the traditional indices of concentration or product diversification could be applied, subject only to trivial reinterpretation. In fact, we choose the latter option by using a Herfindahl-based index, defined earlier in Table 4.4, which is identical to Berry's diversification index (1974), merely substituting spatial for product diversification. This has the obvious attraction of being compatible with the key decompositions of the book (see Appendix 1).

We define the degree of multinationality for industry j as the (weighted) sum of the multinationality of constituent firms across member states *in that industry*. Thus we start by defining the individual firm i's multinationality in industry j: this entails summing the squared shares of its output in the different member states ($k = 1\ldots11$) and then taking the complement,

$$M_{ij} = 1 - \Sigma(x_{ijk}^2 / x_{ij}^2) \tag{7.1}$$

This statistic increases with greater geographical dispersion of the firm's output, rising from zero when it produces only in a single country, to $1 - 11^{-1}$ if it has equal-sized operations in each of the eleven countries. This is then aggregated up to the industry level as follows:

$$M_j = \sum (M_{ij} * v_{ij}) \quad \text{where } v_{ij} = x_{ij}^2 / \sum x_{ij}^2 \, (i = 1 \ldots N) \qquad (7.2)$$

Note that the weighting structure involves using each firm's squared output as a share of the summed squared outputs of all firms; this unusual structure is chosen for compatibility with the decompositions. It is also important to note that all outputs refer only to firms' production in industry j. As such, M_j measures the degree of firms' multinationality in industry j: it is therefore not a measure of the aggregate multinationality of the constituent firms; for example, an industry will score a zero M_j value if none of the constituent firms is multinational in j, even if they are multinational in other industries.

For reasons of data availability, this index can be accurately only calculated for each industry's top five firms, and so we adopt a two-stage estimation procedure. The index is first estimated and aggregated solely across the top five firms (i.e. weighting by the squared share of each firm's output in the total sum of squared outputs of the top five), and, in a second stage, an adjustment is made for all non-top five firms. Since we have only very patchy information on multinationality of the latter, an exact adjustment is impossible, but the range of plausible adjustments can be considerably narrowed using two alternative extreme assumptions, which give rise to an upper and lower estimate for each industry:

Upper estimate assumes that multinationality within non-top five firms is identical to that within the top five. In general, this will be an overestimate since we would expect non-top five firms to be *less* multinational than the market leaders. This will be true if there is a positive correlation between firm size and multinationality (and Section A.7.2 certainly confirms such a correlation *amongst* market leaders).

Lower estimate assumes that no non-top five firm is multinational. Of course, this will always underestimate aggregate industry multinationality if any non-top five firms are multinational.

The two estimates are easily derived—the upper estimate is identical to that for the top five, and the lower estimate is formed by scaling down the figure for the top five by a factor which depends on the relative market shares of top five and non-top five firms.[1] We have no way of knowing which of these estimates is the more accurate, but we can be fairly certain that the 'true' industry value will lie somewhere between. Fortunately, the range is small for most industries, and all results discussed below are qualitatively robust to whichever set of

---

[1] It is easily shown that this factor depends on the relative contribution of non-top five firms to the industry's EU Herfindahl index. This is precisely the correction factor used to convert each industry's Herfindahl concentration index, based only on the market shares of matrix firms, into an estimate allowing for the contribution of non-matrix firms (see Appendix 3).

estimates is used. For that reason, hereafter, we generally employ the arithmetic midpoint of the two.

Finally, we shall usually employ the estimates in their number-equivalent form:

$$NM_j = (1 - M_j)^{-1} \qquad (7.3)$$

This will lie in the range 1, where no firms are multinational in j, to 11, where, hypothetically, all firms spread their operations equally across the equal-sized member states. In fact, the member states are never equal-sized, and the effective upper limit then depends on the value of *NSPEC*—typically in the range 4 to 6 (see Chapter 5).

7.3 Differences in Multinationality across Industries

NM_j has been estimated for all 100 3-digit NACE industries, and the distribution is shown in Figure 7.1. The arithmetic mean is 1.40, which implies that, while the typical EU leader concentrates most of its output in a main (usually its home) location, it does have significant operations in the other member states. For example, such an *NM* value would arise for a firm producing five-sixths of its output at home and one-sixth in a single 'foreign' country. The standard deviation of the estimate is 0.52; and, remembering that *NM* is bounded from below by 1, this reveals quite considerable divergence around the average.[2]

Our prior expectation was that the distribution would be positively skewed, with most industries relatively non-multinational, but with a small number considerably multinational. This is broadly true—for example, the median (1.2) is less than the mean—but the distribution is also discernibly bimodal, with the break somewhere in the region of *NM* = 1.4 to 1.8.

Table 7.1 exploits this breakpoint by identifying a set of 'highly multinational' industries as those having *NM* > 1.8. This particular value also has a convenient intuitive interpretation: 1.8 is the number which would be recorded by a firm producing two-thirds of its output at home and one-third in a single foreign location. As can be seen from the table, there is a preponderance of Type 2 industries amongst this set—glass[3] and concrete are the only exceptions; of the other thirteen, six are Type 2*A*, four are Type 2*R* and three are Type 2*AR*.

The table also lists the fifteen industries in which none of the market leaders is multinational and a further set of twelve which record trivially low values of NM < 1.05. They are concentrated heavily amongst the primary sectors—timber products (6); clothing and textiles (6), metals and manufactured metal

---

[2] These statistics refer to midpoint estimates; the arithmetic means of the upper and lower estimates are 1.492 and 1.323, and their standard deviations are 0.610 and 0.459 respectively.
[3] In fact, specialist parts of the glass industry are definitely of a 2*R* nature.

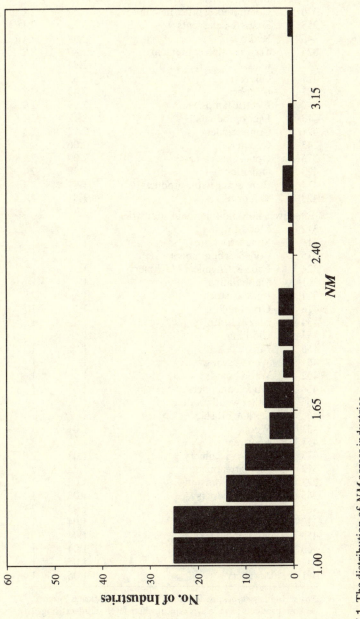

Fig. 7.1 The distribution of *NM* across industries

Table 7.1 The most and least multinational industries

NACE	Industry	*NM*	Type
'Highly multinational' industries			
330	Computers & office machinery	3.52	2R
258	Soaps & detergents	3.13	2AR
345	Radio & TV	2.98	2AR
326	Transmission equipment	2.80	2R
247	Glass	2.74	1
411	Oils & fats	2.61	2A
481	uRubber	2.49	2R
347	Electric lamps, etc.	2.19	2R
413	Dairy products	2.12	2A
421	Confectionery	2.12	2A
243	Concrete	2.06	1
373	Optical instruments	2.00	2AR
423	Other foods	1.98	2A
414	Fruit & vegetable products	1.89	2A
428	Soft drinks	1.81	2A
'Effectively non-multinational' industries			
312	Metal-forging	1	1
314	Metal structures	1	1
315	Boilers & containers	1	1
324	Food & Chemical Machinery	1	1
361	Shipbuilding	1	1
362	Railway stock	1	2R
416	Grain-milling	1	1
434	Flax & hemp	1	1
453	Clothing	1	1
456	Furs	1	1
461	Wood-sawing	1	1
462	Wood boards	1	1
464	Wood containers	1	1
465	Other wood products	1	1
466	Cork & brushes	1	1
431	Wool	1.01	1
451	Footwear	1.02	1
323	Textile machinery	1.02	2R
313	Metal treatment	1.03	1
223	Cold steel-forming	1.03	1
245	Stone products	1.03	1
364	Aerospace	1.03	2R
222	Steel tubes	1.04	1
455	Household textiles	1.04	1
463	Wood structures	1.04	1
242	Cement	1.05	1
491	Jewellery	1.05	1

Notes: Industry types are defined in Chapter 2.1 indicates 'homogeneous products'; 2 indicates typically high levels of advertising (2*A*), R&D (2*R*), or both (2*AR*).

articles (6), grain milling, cement, stone products, and some textile industries (3). Only three of these twenty-seven industries are Type 2, and in each case on the R&D criterion only; and two of these are vehicle industries which rely heavily on public procurement (aerospace, and rail stock). This central role for industry Type could have been forecast, of course, from Table 6.2 of the previous chapter, which reported typically higher *NM* values amongst Type 2 industries.

7.4 Multinationality and Concentration

Industrial concentration has occupied a key position in the Industrial Organization literature on MNEs.[4] In general, concentration and multinationality are found to be positively correlated, although it is unclear whether this results from the concentrating influence of MNEs or whether it is because MNEs are attracted to concentrated industries (Caves, 1982: 97–103). In the present context, the relationship assumes added significance because multinationality links concentration at the aggregate EU level to concentration within member states. This is shown by the core decomposition in Chapter 4:

$$NEU = NNAT * NSPEC / NM \qquad \text{(4.3 repeated as (7.4))}$$

Thus higher values of multinationality (*NM*) should be positively related to higher levels of EU concentration (i.e. lower *NEU*) *ceteris paribus*. One way of illustrating this is to recall the sample mean values reported in Table 4.5.[5] We found that the typical EU industry comprises 4.8 equal-sized member states, in each of which there are twenty-six equal-sized firms. In the absence of multinational firms, this would mean 4.8 * 26 = 125 equal-sized firms in the EU as a whole. In fact, many firms are multinational—the typical firm operates as if it produces equally in 1.33 of the member states—and the number of independent EU firms is therefore only 125/1.33 = 94. In this limited arithmetic sense then, we might say that aggregate equivalent firm numbers in the EU are 25% lower than they would be in the absence of multinational firms. However, the analysis of variances, also shown in Table 4.5, reveals a relatively minor role for multinationality as a contributor to the overall variance in *NEU*. It accounts for only 5% of the overall variance, being completely overshadowed by *NNAT* (typical concentration in the member states), which contributes 84%. Of course, analysis of variance is a purely descriptive device which may well underplay the concentrating role of multinational production in certain types of industry within the sample, especially if it has a contributory role in determining national concentration.[6]

[4] By this, we mean the tradition running through, for example, Hymer (1976), Caves (1982), Helpman and Krugman (1985), Lyons (1989).

[5] The numbers cited in this paragraph refer to the midpoints of the estimates of NM and NNAT reported in Table 4.5.

[6] Table 4.6(b) records a positive covariance between national concentration and multinationality.

This suggests that the specification of the formal econometric model might benefit from a preliminary examination of some of the individual industries. We start by posing a question.

7.4.1 Is Multinationality Necessary or Sufficient for High Concentration?

It is easily confirmed that the answer is 'no' to both parts of this question. This can be seen quite clearly in the graphical depiction of the decomposition used in Figure 4.3 of Chapter 4. Focusing on the twenty-three most concentrated industries, i.e. those lying above the iso-concentration curve for $HEU = 0.033$, the figure reveals that by no means all of these industries are very multinational. A number lie in the north-westerly area, indicating that high EU concentration is associated with high typical member state concentration but low multinational penetration. Similarly, a number of very multinational industries lie well within this curve, indicating low EU concentration.

This visual impression is confirmed more formally by Table 7.2, which compares the set of highly multinational industries from Table 7.1 with the set of highly concentrated industries just defined. Only nine of the fifteen highly multinational industries are also highly concentrated (List 1), and all but one of the other six have very moderate EU concentration (List 2)—in fact, most lie in the lower half of the NEU distribution. Evidently, high multinationality is *not sufficient* to secure high EU concentration. Similarly, fourteen of the twenty-three most highly concentrated industries are not highly multinational (List 3)—indeed, most of these industries are scarcely multinational at all. Thus high multinationality is *not necessary* for high concentration.

The table also records, for each industry, its 'Type', intra-EU trade position (*TRADE*), and the extent of its scale economies (*MES/EUSIZE*). A comparison of the three lists yields some striking differences.

First, combine Lists 1 and 2, the highly multinational industries. As noted earlier, with only two exceptions, they are all of Type 2. But now contrast lists 1 and 2: within the group, concentration is always high if the industry has typically high R&D outlays, but never high where advertising is intensive, unless this is combined with high R&D. It also apparent that high concentration tends to be associated with greater intra-EU trade flows: *TRADE* exceeds 20% in seven of the nine List 1 industries, but only for one List 2 industry.

Next, combine Lists 1 and 3, the highly concentrated industries. Here, an industry type effect is still apparent, if less pronounced—three-quarters of the twenty-three industries are of Type 2, and only two of these are Type 2*A*. But just as pronounced is a trade effect: three-quarters of the industries have *TRADE* > 20%. The main *difference* between these two lists involves the extent of scale economies. Where *MES/EUSIZE* is large, multinationality is less

Table 7.2 The most multinational and most concentrated industries

Industry	NM	NEU	Type	MES/ EUSIZE	TRADE
List 1: Highly multinational and concentrated					
Computers & office machinery	3.52	5	2R	8	47
Soaps & detergents	3.13	30	2AR	10	11
Radio & TV	2.98	22	2AR	7	25
Transmission equipment	2.80	22	2R	5	32
Glass	2.74	21	1	5	22
Rubber	2.49	13	2R	11	25
Electric lamps, etc.	2.19	5	2R	38	29
Confectionery	2.12	20	2A	6	15
Optical instruments	2.00	7	2AR	5	58
Average	2.66	16		10	29
List 2: Highly multinational but unconcentrated					
Oils & fats	2.61	53	2A	15	10
Dairy products	2.12	111	2A	6	15
Concrete	2.06	165	1	4	2
Other foods	1.98	96	2A	4	11
Fruit & vegetable products	1.89	145	2A	7	26
Soft drinks	1.81	42	2A	9	4
Average	2.08	102		7	11
List 3: Concentrated but not highly multinational					
Domestic electrical appliances	1.69	17	2AR	16	29
Abrasives	1.61	28	1	16	28
Sugar	1.33	30	1	8	6
Motor vehicles	1.28	10	2AR	53	33
Domestic & office chemicals	1.24	9	2R	22	40
Cycles & motorcycles	1.22	22	2R	27	20
Paint & ink	1.15	26	2AR	18	14
Man-made fibres	1.13	10	2R	43	60
Iron & steel	1.12	25	1	38	27
Tobacco	1.07	14	2A	63	6
Steel tubes	1.04	23	1	24	28
Aerospace	1.03	12	2R	122	19
Steel cold-forming	1.03	27	1	2	22
Railway stock	1.00	23	2R	47	6
Average	1.21	20		37	23

Notes: *MES/EUSIZE* refers to minimum efficient scale relative to total EU production (scaled up by 1000 for expositional clarity); *TRADE* measures the ratio of intra-EU trade to total EU apparent consumption.

Sources: see Appendix 3.

likely to be high: only two list 1 industries have *MES/EUSIZE* > 10, whilst only two List 3 industries have *MES/EUSIZE* < 10.[7]

This reveals a complex, and intriguing, three-way relationship between multinationality, trade, and concentration. Some highly concentrated industries are highly multinational, but others are not. They are usually integrated by trade and often involve high R&D. However, where scale economies are relatively large, multinationality is less likely. Equally, some highly multinational industries are concentrated whilst others are not. Either way, they are invariably of Type 2, but concentration only seems to accompany multinationality if endogenous sunk costs are due to R&D, and if there is trade integration.

7.4.2 The Decomposition by Trade Integration and Industry Type

Pursuing this line of enquiry, but now for all 100 industries, Table 7.3 returns to the decomposition analysis, distinguishing between industries classified by the extent of trade integration. We define an industry as trade integrated if intra-EU trade is at least 25% of EU apparent consumption. The first part of the table shows that EU concentration is typically three times as high in integrated industries, and part of the reason is that they tend to be more geographically specialized in the leading countries. This is consistent with results from the previous two chapters. However, a new result concerns multinationality. It appears that there is only a very slight tendency for trade-integrated industries to

Table 7.3 The decomposition by trade integration and industry type

	NEU	*NNAT*	*NSPEC*	*NM*
Geometric mean values				
Trade Integrated	44	13	4.5	1.4
Trade Unintegrated	129	34	4.9	1.3
Within unintegrated industries				
Type 1	220	51	5.1	1.2
Type 2	51	18	4.5	1.6
Within integrated industries				
Type 1	115	27	4.85	1.2
Type 2	24	8	4.5	1.6

Notes: 'integrated' industries have TRADE > 25%; 'type 2' industries have 'high' R&D and/or advertising.

[7] Standard tests of significance on the differences between the sample means and proportions of the three lists confirm these conclusions in the text. They show that *MES/EUSIZE* is significantly greater in List 3 than in Lists 1 and 2 and amongst the seventy-one other (i.e. 'unconcentrated' and 'not highly multinational') industries not shown in the table. *TRADE* is significantly higher in Lists 1 and 3 than in List 2. Industries in Lists 1 and 2 are significantly more likely to be Type 2; and List 1 industries are significantly more likely to be *2R/2AR*, whilst List 2 are significantly more likely to be Type *2A*.

be more multinational than trade-unintegrated industries; and the main 'reason' for higher EU concentration in the former is much higher member state concentration.

The second part of the table cross-tabulates by trade integration and industry type. As can be seen, concentration is highest (at both EU and national levels) in integrated Type 2 industries. But the most interesting result here concerns the differences in multinationality between groups. In both integrated and unintegrated industries, Type 2 industries are more multinational, and *the mean values of* NM *appear to be not at all sensitive to integration.* In other words, the fact that a market is unintegrated seems not to discourage multinational production, which may still be relatively high so long as the product is differentiated. However, where a Type 2 market is unintegrated, multinationality is associated with more moderate levels of EU concentration. Moreover, given the results of the previous subsection, we know that the integrated multinational Type 2 industries will tend to involve high R&D, whilst the unintegrated ones will not.[8]

7.5 Econometric Analysis of Inter-industry differences in Multinationality

Section 7.4 takes us about as far as is possible in interpreting the descriptive statistics. In order to take things further, we need a behavioural, i.e. causal, explanation of the differences in multinationality between industries. Our econometric modelling builds on the above discussion, whilst also providing a point

---

[8] The relative magnitudes of national and EU concentration in integrated and unintegrated industries provoke us to indulge in some 'back of the envelope' speculation. Suppose we have correctly identified 'integrated' and 'unintegrated' industries. If so, the economically appropriate measure of industry structure is EU concentration (NEU) in the former, and national concentration ($NNAT$) in the latter. The benefits of integration can then be interpreted as 'raising' the number of equivalent firms from fifty-one to 115 in Type 1 industries, and from eighteen to twenty-four in Type 2. In both cases then, integration has a deconcentrating effect; but the overall effect can be partitioned into two constituent parts. First, there is a direct 'market aggregation' effect (see also Figure 6.4 of the previous chapter): separate member states are aggregated and the number of firms in the newly expanded market-place increases (from eighteen to fifty-one for Type 2 and from fifty-one to 220 for Type 1). But second, an 'indirect rationalizing' process subsequently takes place, i.e. as a result of integration, there is exit of the inefficient, and perhaps mergers, which reduce firm numbers (from fifty-one to twenty-four for Type 2 and from 220 to 115 for Type 1). This interpretation of these numbers is, of course, mere speculation, since it employs static differences, observed in 1987, to tell a dynamic story about what might have happened over time with the integration process. Nevertheless, it highlights a fundamental question concerning European integration. It is almost inevitable that the 'market aggregation' effect will be softened by subsequent 'rationalization', involving exit of the inefficient and/or mergers. Indeed, this was anticipated in the Cecchini (1988) calculus of welfare improvements resulting from the Single Market (see Emerson *et al.*, 1992). The central issue, so far as competition is concerned, is whether the second phase effects are sufficiently strong to wipe out the numbers-enhancing direct effects. Time, and future research, will provide some of the answers; but, if our back of the envelope turns out to be accurate, it suggests that, in Type 2 industries at least, the effective number of competitors may not have increased very much (from eighteen to twenty-four in the table).

of contact with the wider empirical tradition of cross-industry regression studies on the determinants of multinationality.[9]

7.5.1 Hypotheses and Model

A firm wishing to sell in a foreign market faces a choice between different options, including exporting or setting up a production base in that market. (Buckley and Casson, 1976, 1981). This choice forms the basis of a number of theoretical models which generate some well known and robust predictions. The key point is that the production (multinational) option is likely to result in lower marginal costs, because of the avoidance of transport costs and/or tariffs, but higher fixed costs, associated with setting up additional plants. This suggests that multinationality is more probable in industries in which (a) the minimum efficient scale of production is smaller compared to the size of the market, and (b) where transport costs and trade barriers are higher. For example, these predictions flow from Smith's model (1987) of a duopoly industry producing an homogeneous good (see also Hirsch, 1976). Davies and Lyons (1989) generalize his model to N firms with differential efficiency and show that the multinational option is also more likely to be preferred where the market is more concentrated and protected by entry barriers. This follows if higher mark-ups allow the firm to more easily recoup the fixed outlay of setting up the new plant(s). However, Davies and Lyons also show that the theoretical relationship to concentration is two-way because, by going multinational and achieving lower marginal costs, the firm may well secure a larger, possibly dominant, market share.[10]

These models are usually formalized for homogeneous product industries, but similar arguments will also apply to differentiated product industries. In these cases, we also confront the other dominant hypothesis in the literature. As Caves argues, multinational production is more likely in industries in which the leaders have acquired/built up a 'specific asset'. This asset is often embodied in superior product differentiation, either 'real' or from a successful brand image, and it is argued that the asset is best exploited (and transaction costs are minimized) by local production in factories owned by the parent firm, rather than exporting or licensing.[11]. Empirical studies have confirmed this hypothesis, albeit imprecisely, by using the industry's advertising to sales and R&D to sales ratios as proxies for the incidence of such assets.[12] Given the earlier findings in this chapter, we might also anticipate a similar result here.

In addition to these general factors, we need also to acknowledge that our data refer to 1987, and they will still reflect an EU some way from full

---

[9] Caves (1982) remains the classic summary on this literature, but see also Martin (1991), Caves (1974 and 1979), Saunders (1982), Owen (1982).

[10] Note, however, that this simultaneous strategic effect should not affect the lower bound estimates of Chapter 6, which are based on symmetric firms, i.e. abstracting from certain firms having some sort of special advantage.

[11] See also the discussion in Section 13.3.   [12] See n. 9 for some such studies.

integration. In particular, non-tariff barriers, including some types of public procurement bias, may have been an important impediment to trade which could only be circumvented by local production.[13] On the other hand, industries subject to regulation may have been less likely to attract cross border operations—either through multinationality or trade.

These hypotheses are reflected in the following estimating equation:

$$NM = F(TYPE1, TYPE2A, TYPE2R, TYPE2AR,$$
$$MES/EUSIZE, HEU, NTB, TRS, PUB, REG) \qquad (7.5)$$

The *TYPE* variables are included to capture the effects of specific assets and differentiation; *MES/EUSIZE* measures the ratio of minimum efficient scale to total EU production, *HEU* is EU concentration, *REG* and *PUB* are dummy variables, taking values of unity for industries which are typically subject to regulation and public procurement respectively; *TRS* is a measure of relative transport costs and *NTB* measures the extent of non-tariff barriers. Appendix 3 reports fuller descriptions and data sources.

Although we focus on this single equation, throughout the chapter we have emphasized that there is a three-way relationship involving multinationality, concentration, and trade, and there are a number of ways this could be modelled econometrically. In this instance, our preference is for a fairly simple specification involving a two-way causal relationship between *NM* and concentration in which the parameters may vary depending on the extent of trade integration.[14] This confines the scale of the experiments to manageable proportions whilst retaining sufficient flexibility to capture some of the effects identified in the earlier sections. The model is estimated first using ordinary least squares (*OLS*), and then instrumental variables (*IV*), to allow for the simultaneous relationship between *NM* and *HEU*. The instruments used for *HEU* are the other explanatory variables in Equation (7.5) and the US concentration ratio for the comparable industry. The latter is used as a control for other unidentified concentration determinants, but because this is unavailable for four small industries, all regressions are estimated on ninety-six observations.[15] The dependent variable is logged to remove the pronounced positive skew revealed in Figure 7.1, and this is more likely to generate well-behaved residuals.

---

[13] See Chapter 13 for a more extended analysis of this particular issue.

[14] One might also argue that R&D and Advertising are simultaneously related to *NM*, if a greater incidence of multinationals increases an industry's advertising and research outlays. However, this is unlikely to pose a serious problem given the specification used here. Differentiation is captured by the inclusion of the type variables. These merely distinguish whether industries are intrinsically associated with high advertising and/or R&D, and are not continuous variables. Moreover, they are based on data for the UK and Italy only, and are meant to represent the innate nature of the industries/products concerned, rather than accurate observations on the magnitudes of R&D and Advertising in the EU as a whole.

[15] The US concentration data are those used earlier in Sections 4.2.2 and 6.2; see also Appendix 3. The four excluded industries are wine, silk, flax, and photolabs.

7.5.2 Results

Table 7.4(a) reports the results of estimating the model on the full sample—Equation (1) using *OLS* and (2) and (3) using *IV*; Equation (3*a*) should be ignored for the moment. The *OLS* result offers strong support for conventional theory: relative scale economies, concentration and the three *TYPE* variables are all significant at the 5% level (*TYPE* 1 is the omitted default), with coefficients with expected signs. It appears that industries are more likely to be multinational where production scale economies are relatively smaller, and if they produce differentiated goods (with endogenous sunk costs); moreover, concentrated industries tend to be more conducive to multinationality. Perhaps surprisingly, none of the four market imperfection variables is significant (although *TRS* and *REG* have the expected signs[16]). Nevertheless, the overall fit is reasonably high for this sort of cross-industry analysis; although the Jarque–Bera statistic, which indicates some deviation from normality of the residuals, is a cause for concern. An inspection of the residuals shows that this is due to four outliers, which are noticeably more multinational than predicted; and we return to this problem later.

When the model is re-estimated using instrumental variables, most of these results are robust, but, importantly, the Type 2*R* variable loses significance and the significance of *HEU* diminishes, although it still remains significant at the 5% level. Equation (3) in Table 7.4(a) represents the parsimonious form of the *IV* equation (i.e. excluding those variables which do not add to the overall explanatory power—*NTB* and *REG*), and it confirms the above conclusions.

One other noteworthy feature of all three equations concerns the differences *within* Type 2 industries: Type 2*R* consistently attracts a lower coefficient than do Types 2*A* and 2*AR*, and, as mentioned, is insignificant in the *IV* form. It appears that, unless accompanied by high advertising, R&D intensity has rather less effect on multinationality.

In Table 7.4(b), the model is re-estimated splitting the sample into two subsamples, according to the extent of intra-EU trade: as above, a critical value of *TRADE* = 25% is used to distinguish 'trade-integrated' and 'trade-unintegrated' industries.

For the *unintegrated* sample, the *OLS* result (4) largely replicates that for the full sample; but there are some differences. The Jarque–Bera test suggests a better behaved set of residuals, and the *REG* variable attracts a coefficient which is very nearly significant at the 5% level. More important however, EU concentration is now only significant at the 10% level. This latter result is underlined more dramatically when the equation is re-estimated using *IV*: in the parsimonious form of the model (5), the significance of *HEU* collapses, and we must conclude that, once reverse causality is allowed for, concentration has no discernible influence on multinationality.

---

[16] *PUB* is consistently and especially insignificant in all experiments and is omitted from all equations reported in the text. An explanation for this result is explored in Chapter 13.

Table 7.4a Regression analysis of inter-industry differences in *NM* using full sample

Explanatory variable	(1) OLS	(2) IV	(3) IV	(3a) OLS
Constant	0.055	0.051	0.098(^{a})	0.005
	(0.87)	(0.66)	(1.85)	(0.96)
Type 2A	0.284^a	0.277^a	0.256^a	0.259^a
	(2.91)	(3.32)	(3.17)	(3.39)
Type 2R	0.148^b	0.121	0.151	0.114^c
	(1.99)	(1.19)	(1.53)	(1.84)
Type 2AR	0.340^a	0.315^a	0.337^a	0.345^b
	(2.70)	(2.75)	(2.99)	(2.58)
MES/EUSIZE	−5.24^a	−5.79^a	−6.30^a	−3.98^a
	(3.92)	(2.71)	(3.01)	(3.23)
HEU	3.787^a	4.608^b	4.609^b	2.718^a
	(4.42)	(2.09)	(2.10)	(3.67)
NTB	0.036	0.034		0.058^c
	(1.18)	(0.89)		(1.92)
TRS	0.009	0.017	0.019	0.014
	(0.65)	(1.27)	(1.41)	(1.41)
REG	−0.224	−0.169		−0.144^c
	(1.37)	(1.06)		(1.76)
DUM				0.345^a
				(5.46)
R^2	0.427	n.a.	n.a.	0.571
Corrected R^2	0.375	n.a.	n.a.	0.520
Jarque–Bera	8.55	7.22	7.10	24.12
F	8.12	6.13	7.95	11.31
Observations	96	96	96	96

Notes: *t* values in parentheses; ^{a} indicates significance at the 1% level; ^{b} indicates significance at 5% level; ^{c} indicates significance at 10% level.

Equations (6) and (7) re-estimate the model for the set of trade-integrated industries (both reported only in their most parsimonious form). Here, there is an almost complete reversal of findings—with the exception of the scale economies variable (*MES/EUSIZE*), which remains significant. For this sub-set, there is strong evidence of a significant two-way relationship between *NM* and *HEU*, but product differentiation has no significant influence.

Taking these results together with those of earlier subsections, an intriguing, but complex, picture has emerged.

1. The most robust finding is that multinational operations are less likely the larger are production scale economies, relative to the size of the market. Since this is also an important concentrating influence in many industries (see the previous chapter), it accounts for our earlier finding that high concentration and high multinationality do not always coincide.

2. In general, the market imperfection variables appear to have little explanatory power. There is some weak evidence that regulated industries are less

Intra-EU Multinationality of Industries

Table 7.4b Regression analysis of inter-industry differences in *NM* splitting the sample by trade integration

Explanatory variable	Trade-unintegrated		Trade integrated	
	(*Trade* < 25%)		(*Trade* > 25%)	
	(4)	(5)	(6)	(7)
	OLS	IV	OLS	IV
Constant	0.079	0.134^b	0.202(^{a})	0.177^b
	(1.26)	(2.04)	(3.50)	(2.37)
Type 2A	0.272^b	0.224		0.197
	(2.21)	(1.56)		(1.08)
Type 2R	0.118	0.162		
	(1.10)	(1.25)		
Type 2AR	0.400^b	0.418^a		
	(2.60)	(2.92)		
MES/EUSIZE	−6.975^a	−8.631	−7.74^a	−7.57^b
	(2.95)	(1.58)	(3.45)	(2.01)
HEU	6.906^c	8.346	4.955^a	5.149^a
	(1.90)	(0.90)	(6.76)	(3.32)
NTB	0.043			
	(1.11)			
REG	−0.23^c			
	(1.92)			
R^2	0.416	n.a.	0.513	n.a.
Corrected R^2	0.347	n.a.	0.475	n.a.
Jarque–Bera	3.07	2.06	4.82	4.51
F	6.01	6.58	13.68	3.75
Observations	67	67	31	31

Notes: *t* values in parentheses; ^{a} indicates significance at the 1% level; ^{b} indicates significance at 5% level; ^{c} indicates significance at 10% level.

likely to attract multinational activities, especially where trade is low, but the overriding impression is that market imperfections play a less important role than was detected in Chapter 5 for intra-EU trade flows.[17]

3. The most interesting results concern the influence of product differentiation. Type 2 industries are clearly more likely to be multinational, especially if associated with high advertising and if trade flows are small. However, within the set of highly traded industries, the picture is more confused for two reasons. First, in these industries, R&D tends to be the dominant form of differentiation and this specific asset seems to be easier than marketing/advertising to exploit internationally through exports rather than international production. Second, it is difficult to disentangle the separate influences of R&D and concentration in these industries. Thus, although we know that a number of Type 2R high-trade industries are highly multinational, these industries also tend to

[17] However, see Chapter 13 where we present descriptive evidence that public procurement raises multinationality in Type 2R industries and reduces it in Type 1 industries.

be highly concentrated (see List 1 in Table 7.2). The regression results suggest that it is concentration, rather than research intensity, which is the main cause of the multinationality. Having said this, a high cross-correlation between *HEU* and *TYPE2R* and the necessity that we use the latter as an instrument for the former should caution us against over-confidence in this finding at this stage.

4. The effects of concentration itself are as might be expected, but subject to the qualification just mentioned. Absent trade integration, EU concentration has little influence on multinationality. This is quite plausible if competition in these industries tends to occur at the national level. If so, the level of EU concentration is largely irrelevant to firms' international production decisions. On the other hand, where trade integration has occurred, the evidence is suggestive of a significant two-way relationship. High EU concentration tends to attract multinational production, which is, itself, a significant concentrating influence.

Finally, we should acknowledge the limitations of our results. This partly reflects the range of special problems which is entailed in econometric modelling in this area. Undoubtedly, the determination of industry multinationality at the EU level belongs to a complex system of equations which also involve concentration and trade. However, given the incomplete state of EU integration, the structure of the relationship between multinationality and concentration varies between industries. A dynamic dataset would help in some of the modelling implications of this, and this is an important item on the research agenda. But some of the problems (e.g. the overall fit of the equations and the distributions of residuals) probably also reflect the inherent limitations of the industry-based approach we have adopted. The appendix to the chapter shows that, in a significant minority of industries, there are important differences between market leaders in the extent of their multinationality. This calls into question the notion that our estimated industry *NM* values reflect representative behaviour dictated by the nature of the industry. It may be instead that our 'industry' estimates reflect more the idiosyncratic behaviour of one or two leaders in a given industry; if so, firm-specific influences should be investigated. As a crude test of this, we have re-estimated the model on the full sample using OLS, adding a dummy variable for six industries in which we suspect this possibility to be the most real. This is shown as Equation (3*a*) in Table 7.4(a). Comparing it with Equation (1), the overall fit rises by a full 15% points, the dummy is strongly positively significant, and two of the market imperfection variables (*NTB* and *REG*) achieve significance at the 10% level. Apart from improving the general specification of the equation, this also suggests that, in these industries, observed *NM* is greater than predicted by the characteristics of the industries involved. Apparently, there are important firm-specific factors at work. This implies that future work, with access to a time dimension, might also involve a pooled firm-level dimension.

7.6 Multinationality and Integration

7.6.1 Defining the integrated industry

The conventional notion of an integrated European market is one in which there is unimpaired trade across the frontiers of member states. We have, ourselves, identified integrated industries as those with larger intra-EU trade flows—both earlier in this chapter, and in Chapter 5. However, we now want to argue that multinational operations within the EU is an additional form of integration. While multinationality may not always be associated with commensurate trade flows, it does suggest that the firms concerned are pursuing *integrated corporate strategies*, i.e. viewing the EU as an interrelated sphere of operations.

This can be formalized theoretically in terms of a two-stage oligopoly game, in which firms choose their endogenous sunk costs (advertising and/or R&D) in stage 1, and output or price in stage 2. Clearly, if the pricing/quantity decisions are taken at the single EU level, then both the market and the firms' strategies can be defined as integrated. This will probably, although not necessarily, result in cross member-state flows of trade. But what if the market is segmented? Prohibitively high transport costs or very different national (i.e. horizontal) tastes will dictate that the price/quantity decision remains member-state specific; but the stage 1 decision on endogenous sunk costs may still be taken on an integrated European basis, i.e. bearing in mind their effects on the willingness to pay of consumers throughout the EU, and/or economies of scope. Whether or not this is the case will depend, in turn, on whether the results of advertising and R&D are transferable across member states and whether marketing/design/research expertise is transferable. Following this line of thought, we now define the *integrated industry* as one in which corporate strategies are integrated. This is a wider concept than that of the *integrated market*— integrated markets necessarily imply integrated industries, but the reverse is not necessarily true.

In this section we employ the estimates of industry multinationality, alongside the intra-EU trade data, to plot the incidence of *industry* integration.[18] In particular, we are interested in whether this wider notion significantly changes the observed pattern of integration across broad sectors of manufacturing and between different types of industry. It also draws together the conclusions of the econometric analysis of trade in Chapter 5 and those of the previous section on multinationality.

---

[18] The implication of the following is that a high degree of multinational activity is suggestive of an integrated corporate strategy—in exactly the same way that high trade flows are indicative of an integrated market. This seems reasonable as a first approximation, although detailed case-studies of the strategies of individual firms are clearly called for in the future.

7.6.2 Distinguishing the Integrated and Unintegrated Industries

We use two critical values for *TRADE* and *NM* to split the full sample of industries into those which are trade integrated and unintegrated and those in which firms are significantly and insignificantly multinational. For consistency with what has gone before, we define an industry as integrated if *TRADE* > 25% and/or *NM* > 1.4. Roughly one-third of industries have values in excess of each of these critical levels (thirty-two for *NM*, and twenty-nine for *TRADE*.) Combining the two sets, and allowing for twelve industries which are integrated on both criteria, yields a group of forty-nine 'integrated' industries— almost exactly half the population.

Table 7.5(a) ranks the broad sectors of manufacturing by the proportion of their constituent industries which qualify as integrated using this broader definition; it also shows the separate numbers for trade and multinational integrated industries. Broadly speaking, the sectors fall into four groups:

1. Electrical and instrument engineering and chemicals each have a reasonably high incidence of trade-integrated markets: in total, nine out of nineteen. This rises even higher once the wider criterion is employed: seventeen of the industries can now be defined as integrated.

2. Metal manufacturing, mechanical engineering, other manufacturing, rubber and plastics, and clothing and footwear are also each reasonably integrated markets: thirteen out of twenty-three industries have high intra-EU trade. But, here, the wider criterion changes the picture only very marginally— switching only two additional industries into the integrated set.

3. Food, drink, and tobacco, and mineral products include virtually no trade-integrated markets (only two out of twenty-six), but significant numbers emerge as integrated industries once the wider definition is used: ten out of twenty-six.

4. In none of the remaining five sectors is integration very pronounced, either by trade or multinationality.

Table 7.5(b) repeats the exercise for the Type 1/2 classification. Type 2 markets are twice as likely to be trade-integrated as Type 1 and the proportional differential is even higher for the wider concept of industry integration. Thus, whilst three out of every four Type 2 industries are integrated, only one in three Type 1 industries is. *Within* the Type 2 group, the introduction of the wider definition narrows the gap between advertising and R&D-intensive industries. Using the narrow concept of trade-integration, over half of 2*R* markets are integrated, as opposed to a third of 2*AR* and only one-sixth of 2*A* industries. But, once multinationality is taken into account, 2*AR* industries are just as integrated as 2*R*, and over half of 2*A* industries are integrated. This is partly because of the tendency for 2*A* industries to involve high multinationality but low trade, and partly because seven 2*R* industries are integrated according to both criteria.

Table 7.5 Incidence of integrated industries

2-digit sector	Number of 3-digit industries			
	Total	integrated		
		Total	by *TRADE*	by *NM*
(a) By industrial sector				
Electrical & computers	8	8	4	8
Chemicals, man-made fibres	7	6	4	3
Instrument engineering	4	3	1	3
Metal manufacturing	4	3	3	1
Mechanical engineering	8	6	5	2
Other manufacturing	5	3	2	1
Rubber & plastics	2	1	1	1
Footwear & clothing	4	2	2	0
Food, drink, & tobacco	18	7	1	7
Mineral products	8	3	1	3
Paper, printing, publishing	3	1	0	1
Vehicles	6	2	2	1
Textiles & leather	10	3	3	0
Metal goods	6	1	0	1
Timber & furniture	7	0	0	0
All manufacturing	100	49	29	32
(b) By industry type				
Type 1	56	17	11	8
Type 2, of which:	44	32	18	24
Type 2A	13	7	2	6
Type 2R	22	18	13	12
Type 2AR	9	‚7	3	6
All Manufacturing	100	49	29	32

Notes: The total number of integrated industries refers to the numbers having *TRADE* > 25 and/or *NM* > 1.4. The number integrated by *TRADE* refers to integrated markets, i.e. those with *TRADE* > 25. The number integrated by *NM* refers to the numbers having *NM* > 1.4.

In other experiments, we have investigated the influence of a range of industry characteristics on this wider concept of integration. Since the results are dominated by the industry type variables, with otherwise predictable conclusions, a short summary will suffice. We first estimated a simple logit model (with a binary dependent variable for whether or not an industry is integrated) and then a regression analysis of the integrated set using 'mode of integration' as the dependent variable (measured by the ratio of *NM* to *TRADE*, in logged form). These confirm that Type 2 industries are more likely to be integrated, with multinationality relatively more important for advertising than R&D-intensive industries. Turning to other industry characteristics, integrated industries are more likely to be concentrated at the EU level, and to be larger (measured by industry production); but there are no significant differences between integrated and unintegrated industries in the extent of transport costs, non-tariff barriers, *MES*, or capital intensity. On the other hand, high transport costs and low scale economies do significantly influence the mode of integration: making integration more likely through multinationality than through trade.

7.7 Conclusion

This chapter has presented new evidence on the extent of multinational production *within* the EU. This has allowed us to investigate the connection between multinationality, concentration, intra-EU trade, and integration in a variety of ways. Here, we attempt to pull together the threads to give a brief synthesis.

The previous literature on multinational firms has stressed the importance of product differentiation, economies of scale, and industrial concentration. Our results have confirmed that these factors also play a significant role in the EU context. The effects of the first two are straightforward: multinational operations are more prevalent in industries with product differentiation and relatively low production scale economies. This is as one would expect given the relative attractiveness of international production over exports in such industries. However, there is an important difference between advertising- and R&D-intensive industries: in the former, multinationality occurs in place of trade, whilst in the latter, it is more likely to be accompanied by high trade. We have also found evidence for a simultaneous relationship between concentration and multinationality, but this is really only significant amongst trade-intensive industries. Because of this, it is not always the case that multinationality and concentration go hand-in-hand: some (especially 2*A*) industries are very multinational but unconcentrated, whilst some (scale-intensive) concentrated industries are not at all multinational.

Following on from these results, we have suggested that a wider interpretation of the word 'integration' may be called for. Whilst a *market* may only be integrated given significant trade flows within the EU, the *industry* may be integrated by either trade or multinational production—the latter being taken as evidence of integrated corporate strategies. When this wider concept is applied, we find evidence of much wider integration than is apparent from trade flows—especially for Type 2 industries. Of particular interest are advertising-intensive industries, in which multinationality appears to substitute for trade integration.

STEVE DAVIES and LAURA RONDI

A.7 APPENDIX to Chapter 7:
Within Industry Differences

This appendix briefly explores the extent of intra-industry differences in multinationality. In particular, it examines whether the aggregate industry NM values are representative of typical firm-level values within the industry, or whether they conceal a wide divergence between firms. Where the former applies (i.e. 'common behaviour'), industry-level analysis is probably justified; but where an industry aggregate conceals major differences between the market leaders, this poses some doubts about the meaning of the industry aggregate. For example, if an industry's NM value is heavily reliant on just one or two firms, we should query whether that value is really indicative of causal industry-level factors, or whether it merely reflects an idiosyncratic firm-specific structure. To put it another way, what should we make of an industry in which some market leaders have achieved a leading position via multinational production, whilst others have been able to achieve a leading position by concentrating production in their home country?

A.7.1 Analysis of Variance of Firm-level estimates

As a preliminary, we use a traditional analysis of variance to identify the relative magnitudes of inter- and intra-industry variations. Defining V as the variance of NM_{ij} across the pooled sample of 500 firms, V_m as the variance of the industry mean values of NM and V_j as the variance of NM within industry j, we can write:

$$V = V_m + (\Sigma V_j)/100 \qquad (A.7.1)$$
$$0.76 = 0.24 + 0.52$$

Thus, the overall variance can be re-expressed as the sum of between-industry variance in mean multinationality and the mean within-industry variance. The sample estimates, shown below the equation, reveal that the latter dominates the former in roughly the proportion 2 : 1. Since V_m is equivalent to the variance of our industry-level NM variable,[19] this cautions against a blind emphasis on merely inter-industry differences: it conceals potentially important differences within individual industries.

A.7.2 The Role of Firm Size

Of course, one might expect that some of these intra-industry differences can be accounted for by size differences between market leaders. For instance, multinational production should be more attractive relative to exporting for larger firms since the fixed costs of setting up a new plant can be spread over higher sales volumes; similarly, larger firms may have resulted from, and should be more able to develop the specific assets (technological and differentiation) which often motivate multinationality. Reversing

---

[19] Strictly speaking, V_m is the variance of the industry *unweighted* means, while NM is the *weighted* average industry mean.

the direction of causality, it is also likely that multinational production is the *means* by which firms achieve larger size: perhaps because of limited domestic market size, or perhaps because multinationality proffers some strategic advantage.

Again, a simple statistical device confirms a positive association with (relative) size. Calculating the average NM_{ij} values for each of number 1 to 5 ranked firms over the 100 industries, we find a simple positive relation between multinationality and size rank. Thus, the average number 1-ranked firm records $NM = 1.79$, as opposed to 1.60 for number 2, 1.425 for number 3, 1.33 for number 4, and 1.29 for the average fifth-ranked firm. Apparently, typical multinationality *does* increase with market share, and this accounts for a proportion of intra-industry differences.

A.7.3 Locating Intra-Industry Differences

Bearing in mind these two results, we next attempt to identify those industries in which aggregate multinationality is high, but in which 'common behaviour' does not exist. It is in such cases that the industry aggregate figure is most likely to reflect the behaviour of one or two firms rather than any general industry factors making for high multinationality across the board.

Narrowing the field to the thirty-two industries with $NM > 1.4$, there are eighteen in which either four or all five leaders are MNEs. These we define as displaying 'common behaviour', and we concentrate on only the remaining fourteen. Examining the NM values for individual market leaders in these industries, it is obvious that there is a strong size effect at work. In every case the number 1-ranked firm is highly multinational (with NM at least > 1.8), whilst only half of the second- and third-ranked firms, and a quarter of fourth- and fifth-ranked firms are at all multinational. Perhaps the three most striking instances are: measuring and medical instruments (where only the number 1 firm, Schlumberger, is MNE), and transmission equipment and oils and fats (in both of which only the two leaders, SKF and FAG, and Unilever and Saint Louis respectively are *MNEs*). One plausible hypothesis here is that multinationality only becomes a viable proposition in such industries once firm scale exceeds some threshold market size, and that only the very largest of firms exceed that threshold.

On the other hand, there are six industries in which the number 2-ranked firm is not multinational, even although one or two of its smaller competitors are. In such cases, it would appear that being multinational is not necessarily a natural strategy, even if some threshold is exceeded.

At present, it is unclear whether these six industries are qualitatively different from other very multinational industries in which common behaviour is more the norm. One possibility is that they may have been in some state of disequilibrium in 1987: either the non-MNEs amongst the leaders would be forced into becoming MNEs or those who were MNEs need not have been (given the characteristics of the industries concerned). This may become more clear when we are able to roll the database forward to a later year. In the meantime, however, there are two pieces of evidence which might be taken to support the disequilibrium hypothesis. First, three of the industries amongst the set feature amongst list 2 in Table 7.2 as 'highly multinational' but unconcentrated. Second, and more significant, is the evidence of regression (3a) of Table 7.4(a). When a dummy variable for these industries is inserted in the basic *OLS* estimating equation, it is found to be positively significant. This is consistent with an interpretation that observed multinationality in these industries was greater than it 'need' be, given the characteristics of the industries concerned. In other words, their high *NM* values may reflect 'unnecessary' multinationality by some leading firms. It will be interesting to see whether these firms change the structure of their international production in the years following 1987.

8

Non-EU Multinationals in the EU

8.1 Introduction

This chapter deviates from the book's general treatment of the EU as a single entity by singling out for special attention a subset of firms identified explicitly by their national origin. These are the subsidiaries of firms originating from countries outside of the European Union—'the non-EU-owned multinationals (MNEs)'. In one sense, these firms are no different from any others on the market share matrix: given they produce, in a leading way, within the EU, they are just as much leading European producers as all other matrix firms. Nevertheless, in terms of ultimate ownership, they are 'foreign', and, arguably, geographical origin does matter. Certainly, in popular discussion, they are the subject of special attention, and they do raise additional issues which are qualitatively different, both to the economic theorist and the policymaker. More pragmatically, our database provides the first-ever evidence at this level of disaggregation on the incidence of these firms, and this chapter provides an ideal opportunity for placing that evidence in the public domain—even if it fits less snugly than most within the book's overall structure.

Indeed, investment by foreign companies into the European market has always attracted considerable academic and popular attention, with its consequences for the EU's economic, political, and social objectives being hotly contested. Actually, the life cycle of papers on this issue has correlated closely with the various stages of European integration. In the 1950s and 1960s, US companies rushed into Europe, creating a fear of economic and political dependence throughout the continent.[1] Nowadays, the different structure of world FDI has created a more subtle atmosphere. The global trends have changed. The EU now plays a strong role as a source (home) country and, with the advent of the Single Market, as a powerful magnet host for FDI. Meanwhile, Japanese FDI into both the US and the EU has grown exponentially, though from initially very low levels. Within this setting, foreign investment flows into European industry are now evaluated more in terms of their employment and competitive consequences than of any implied economic or political dependency. In order to assess the impact of foreign companies on the

---

[1] Econometric tests yielded inconclusive results concerning the effects of integration on inward investment flows and the impact of such investment on economic growth in this period.

competitiveness and long-term performance of the EU, more in-depth studies of their motives and industrial location are required.

There are some important differences between traditional investment measures of foreign presence and our 'stock' measure of their production taken from the EU matrix. Investment flow data may give a reasonably clear picture of recent trends in multinational operations, but they offer only a rough indication of the scale of foreign penetration. Moreover, the nature of FDI data makes it inappropriate for disaggregation—both across the member states and down to an adequately disaggregated industry level. In contrast, the distribution of foreign affiliates across industries, supplemented with information on trade flows and alliances as alternative forms of foreign involvement, serves as a more useful measure of the impact of a foreign presence on the structure of EU industries. This chapter offers a first attempt to investigate foreign presence using the EU matrix.

The next two sections are of a preliminary nature. Section 8.2 returns to the published data on Foreign Direct Investment (FDI) discussed in Chapter 2, to sketch out what is already known about the sources and geographical and industrial distributions of inward FDI into the EU. Section 8.3 draws together in concise form the various information on non-EU matrix firms which appears in a more piecemeal way in other chapters. This 'potted summary' helps to set the scene for the main part of the chapter, which is directed towards explaining the pattern of inter-industry differences in the penetration of EU industry by non-EU multinationals. Section 8.4 presents and describes that pattern, Section 8.5 investigates the impact of industry characteristics, and Section 8.6 examines the effects of international comparative advantages. Section 8.7 concludes. In a short Appendix to the chapter, we show how the matrix's more accurate depiction of diversification by non-EU MNEs can be used to gauge the inaccuracies implicit in existing datasources (often on FDI), which tend to allocate all of a firm's production (or investment) to its primary industry.

8.2 The EU's inward flows of FDI

As shown earlier in Figure 2.2, the USA has long lost its position as the major source country of foreign investment flows; indeed, most US outward FDI flows are now reinvested earnings within the EU. In 1987, the year of the matrix, the world's main geographical source of outward investment was the EU itself, although it was displaced in the following years by Japan. In the meantime the USA has become the major host country. But, equally, the middle and late 1980s was a period in which a major development was the surge of inward investment into a EU stimulated by the 1992 integration programme.

Table 8.1 shows that aggregating all sources of FDI, the UK is easily the most important host member state for these investment flows, while the structure of the German capital market probably accounts for the negligible inward

Table 8.1 Inward FDI by member state and by industrial sector

Member state		Industrial sector	
UK	40	Chemicals	13
France	16	Agriculture & food	10
Italy	14	Electrical	5
Spain	11	Finance & banking	39
Netherlands	7	Real estate	12
Bel/Lux	6		
Germany	6		

Source: *European Communities Direct Investment, 1984–1989*, Eurostat, 1992.

FDI flows into that country. The published industry distribution of FDI is rather too aggregated for serious analysis, but it is at least apparent that inward flows were greatest in services, notably the finance and banking sector. Of the industrial sectors, chemicals was one of the major destinations in 1987.

In fact, about half of these flows were intra-EU, leaving just over half as genuinely 'foreign'. Of these, the EFTA countries accounted for 30%, USA for 15%, and Japan for 12%. Of course, the close economic linkages between the neighbouring EFTA and EU blocks is a primary reason for the strength of EFTA investment in the EU. In particular, Sweden and Switzerland have been traditionally very outward oriented, especially into the EU and in manufacturing; and recent FDI patterns have strengthened this orientation. US MNEs have traditionally been the most active investors in the EU, with a preference for the UK. Although manufacturing takes up the majority of US flows, banking, finance, and insurance are now also important sectors. While Japanese direct investment into the Community is increasing rapidly, it was still smaller in 1987 than that from the USA. Again the UK is the main beneficiary of Japanese inflows. Extra-EU inward inflows are dominated by finance and insurance representing almost one half of the total. In manufacturing, the electronics sector is the most important, followed by chemicals, machinery, and transport equipment (Eurostat, 1992).

8.3 The origins and structures of non-EU companies in the market share matrix

Various facts on the non-EU owned matrix firms are reported in other chapters, alongside analysis of the EU-owned firms by member state. A brief collation here provides a useful background for the rest of this chapter.

In Chapter 3, Table 3.4 reports that the matrix includes thirty-six firms which are subsidiaries of non-EU-owned parents. This is 12% of the total number of matrix firms. Since, on average, they tend to be somewhat larger than the EU-owned firms, they account for 14% of the total production of all matrix firms. The overwhelming majority (twenty-five) are US, reflecting the long-established presence of some American companies in Europe, seven are from the EFTA countries (i.e. Sweden and Switzerland), three are Canadian, and there is only one Japanese firm (reflecting the only recent nature of most Japanese investment).

Foreign companies are often characterized as constituting a distinct strategic group within an industry. Part three of the book contains a detailed structural analysis of all the matrix firms, considering firm size, market shares, diversification, and geographical spread. Since we only investigate the structures of firms within the EU, it should be remembered that the following facts refer only to the EU operations of 'foreign' firms.

(i) In Chapter 9 (Table 9.10), we find that EFTA firms are typically four times larger than the average matrix firm. North American owned subsidiaries are also larger on average, but by 'only' 66%. (Of course, these firms are not typical of all firms from their countries—the matrix was never designed to be a random sample).

(ii) From a decomposition of firm size in product space, we find that EFTA firms are larger for three reasons: they tend to locate in larger industries, have larger market shares, and be more diversified than the average matrix firm. For North American firms, the sole reason for their larger average size is that they tend to have larger market shares.

(iii) In Chapter 11 (Table 11.6), from an alternative decomposition of firm size in geographic space, we can attribute the larger size of EFTA firms both to a much wider spread across member states (over twice the average) and to a larger typical aggregate share of production in the states in which they operate. The North American firms are equally multinational, but their typical aggregate share within countries is similar to indigenous EU firms on average.

In short then, the small number of EFTA firms on the matrix (Nestlé, ABB, etc,) are typically very conglomerate, both by multinationality and diversification, with large shares in the member states and industries in which they operate.[2] The American firms tend to be more specialized (e.g. IBM, Ford, Procter and Gamble), typically achieving dominant market positions by producing in a number of member states, rather than by concentrating on any one particular location.

8.4 The industrial distribution of non-EU-owned firms

Given the small numbers of non-EU firms involved in the final version of the matrix, the rest of this chapter deviates from the general practice of the book

---

[2] This is as might be expected from the standard theory of very large MNEs. The intangible asset advantage, on which they build their international expansion, makes them less sensitive to the classical barriers to entry that characterize large-scale sectors. Moreover, given that they can always export in those industries where they would be unable to achieve minimum efficient scale, we only observe them actually producing in the EU where they are sufficiently large.

by drawing on a previous version of the matrix which contained ninety-four more firms in total. Although these extra firms marginally failed to qualify for inclusion on the final version of the matrix, they are all significant players in their respective industries. Table 8.2 shows the national breakdown of this 'extended' matrix, which is almost identical in proportionate terms to the final version. As can be seen, nine of the additional firms were non-EU subsidiaries.

Table 8.2 The extended market share matrix

	Number of firms	Production (m. ECU)	Average firm size (m. ECU)
TOTAL	407 (100%)	797,939 (100%)	1,960
EU	362 (89%)	681,056 (85%)	1,881
Non-EU	45 (11%)	116,583 (15%)	2,591
EFTA	8 (18%)	25,976 (22%)	3,247
USA	32 (71%)	85,516 (73%)	2,759
Canada	3 (7%)	4,360 (4%)	1,453
Japan	2 (4%)	730 (1%)	365

Even with these extra firms added, there are still only limited numbers of firms in some industries, and so we also switch to an industry classification which is more aggregated than the NACE 3-digit level used in the rest of the book. Figure 8.1 shows the non-EU MNE matrix share in terms of production and firm numbers for each of these industries. So as to heighten the MNE emphasis, industries are grouped in the figure according to the share of EU-owned MNEs in the industry.

Computers and office equipment is the industry in which the non-EU presence is greatest (54% by production), largely an IBM effect. Other industries with notably high non-EU shares of production are tobacco (34%), soap and cosmetics (31%), scientific and photographic equipment (28%), toys and sporting goods (27%), food (20%), motor vehicles (19%), and industrial and farm equipment (18%). Interestingly, in all these cases, the non-EU share is larger than that of EU-owned MNEs. Industries in which non-EU companies hold a negligible share are iron and steel (5%), non-metallic mineral products (3%), metal products (7%), other transport equipment (2%), aerospace (1%), textiles (4.5%), clothing (1%), and wood (0.5%). Most of these also have low EU MNE activities, indicating that it is probably industry characteristics, rather than home or host country characteristics, that explain this low penetration. On the other hand, in electrical engineering and electronics, non-EU firms hold a modest 8%, and in telecommunications only 4%, which contrasts with the much higher shares of EU MNE penetration in these industries.

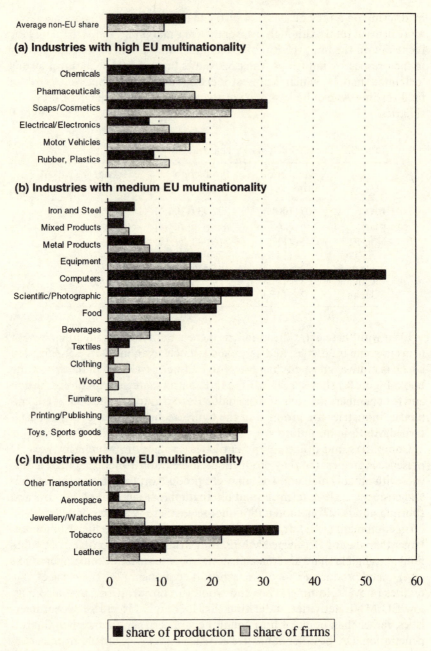

Fig. 8.1 The share of non-EU firms by broad industry

8.5. Explaining foreign penetration in terms of industry characteristics

In this section we investigate how far this pattern of non-EU penetration can be explained in terms of the characteristics of the industries concerned. Necessarily, some of the variables considered have already featured in the analysis of the previous chapter which modelled the determinants of total (i.e. EU and non-EU firms) multinationality at the industry level. But here, the limited size of the sample renders regression analysis inappropriate, and we merely examine the bivariate relationships on a one-by-one basis. Although this has its drawbacks, particularly when industry characteristics are correlated, we are able to introduce some global characteristics not used before.

As found in Chapter 7, intangible assets, such as technological know-how and/or brandnames, are a prime cause of the MNE phenomenon. Hence, we would expect non-EU MNEs to achieve greater penetration in Type 2 industries. This is indeed borne out by Table 8.3, in which non-EU MNEs are seen to have a greater presence—measured by both share of matrix output and firm numbers. Only for the latter are the differences in means significant, but, as we shall see, the small number of industries in the sample, militates against finding many statistically significant differences.

Besides exploiting intangible asset advantages, the international expansion of MNEs may also be driven by strategic motives. Follow-the-leader, pre-emption and footholds in rivals' home markets are all examples of strategic incentives for multinational operations; mutual forbearance on the other hand is a strategic motive that restricts international operations. These strategic incentives are more likely to prevail in industries where concentration on a global scale is high, and the table confirms that this is indeed the case; in fact, with the exception of chemicals, all non-EU-intensive industries have a high global concentration. The presence of important EU rivals, whose ownership specific advantages foreign firms may want to tap, or in whose home markets foreign firms may want to establish a foothold, seems to restrict foreign penetration: amongst other things, this might reflect mutual forbearance. Strategic considerations *vis-à-vis* EU rivals are more likely in chemicals, machinery, automobiles, food, and rubber and plastics, in which the EU global companies hold a comparative advantage.

Irrespective of intangible assets or strategic considerations, in some industries, a physical presence in the market-place may be necessary. Government intervention may be one reason requiring such a local presence (see Chapter 13). The table shows that industries in which public procurement, regulation, or other non-tariff barriers prevail (e.g. pharmaceuticals, computers, electrical and electronic equipment) are indeed more intensively penetrated by non-EU affiliates, as is also true for industries characterized by important scale advantages. No clear effect emerges for transport costs.

Table 8.3 The non-EU share by industry characteristics

		Non-EU shares (%) by	
		Production	Firm numbers
Intangible Assets			
R&D	HIGH	16.3	14.5*
	LOW	10.4	8.6*
Advertising	HIGH	20.0	17.0*
	LOW	10.6	9.4*
Strategic motives			
Global concentration	HIGH	14.1	11.5
	LOW	6.4	10.7
Strong EU rivals	HIGH	11.6	11.2
	LOW	14.0	11.5
Local presence			
Procurement/regulation	HIGH	16.9	12.7
	LOW	11.8	10.9
Non-tariff barriers	HIGH	14.5	12.2
	LOW	11.0	10.0
Transport costs	HIGH	11.4	10.8
	LOW	14.9	11.9
Scale economies	HIGH	16.8	13.4
	LOW	8.8	8.8
Alternatives to foreign production			
Global trade	HIGH	12.7	11.0
	LOW	14.2	12.1
EU–Non-EU trade	HIGH	12.6	10.2
	LOW	13.9	12.7
Global alliances	HIGH	14.6	12.4*
	LOW	6.0	6.0*
EU–Non-EU alliances	HIGH	12.8	13.3
	LOW	15.6	10.5

* Significantly different means at the 5% level.
Variable definitions and data sources: Unless otherwise shown, all variables are as defined in Appendix 3, which also provides the data sources. R&D-intensive sectors are Type $2R$ and Type $2AR$; and advertising intensive industries are Type $2A$ and Type $2AR$. Global concentration is measured by the share of the 4 largest firms in the total Fortune Global 500 sales: high is defined as $C4 > 30\%$. Strong EU rivals is measured by the revealed comparative advantage measure for the EU by global sales, see the next section. Procurement/regulation is measured by PUB and REG; non-tariff barriers and transport costs by NTB and TRS; and scale economies by MES. High global trade is defined as trade-intensity > 50% (source: European Economy). Alliance intensive industries are obtained from Veugelers (1994); high for EU-NON EU alliances reflects an above average percentage of alliances between a EU and a non-EU partner.

Of course, companies wanting to serve foreign markets may have other viable alternatives besides direct investment: exports avoid costly fixed investment in the host economy; alliances or joint ventures with local companies may provide access to the specific advantages of local partners, while exploiting complementarities and providing access to local distribution networks. The table confirms that high-trade industries tend to be less penetrated by foreign affiliates. Examples are transport equipment, aerospace, watches, and (to a lesser extent) clothing. However, trade is no viable alternative for non-EU companies looking towards the EU market in industries like pharmaceuticals, soap and cosmetics, food, tobacco, and rubber and plastics. Of these, only in pharmaceuticals can government intervention be pinpointed as a cause for this low export orientedness; in the other industries, local presence is more driven by the need for customer responsiveness. More specifically, industries in which there is an intense trade flow between EU and non-EU countries are less characterized by the presence of non-EU companies. Globally, alliance-intensive industries are typically more inhabited by multinational companies, a difference that is significant in terms of number of companies, indicating that alliances complement rather than substitute for multinational operations. However, in industries characterized by important alliances *between* EU and non-EU companies, non-EU companies have a larger share in terms of firm numbers but not in terms of production. A lack of alliances with EU companies, as an alternative mode of access to European markets, may explain the high non-EU presence in industries like soap and cosmetics, computers, food, and toys and sporting goods. On the other hand, alliances between EU and non-EU companies are actively being used, possibly as alternatives to local production, in drink, furniture, and printing and publishing.

8.6. Host and home market comparative advantages

We now re-examine the cross-industry pattern in terms of international comparative advantage. Since entrepreneurial advantages are most often derived from superior know-how or brand-names, it follows that the propensity of a company to invest abroad is directly based on its technological competitiveness *vis-à-vis* rival firms. The entrepreneurial advantages of MNEs are intrinsically linked to the specific characteristics of their home countries, stimulating and sustaining the technological advantages of companies located within their boundaries. Among these factors are the availability of educational facilities, efficient capital markets, and R&D incentives. If these advantages are internalized within companies, who exploit them through foreign direct investment, this will establish a positive link between a home country's competitive position and its outward direct investment or overseas production.

But equally these firms will look for internationally competitive countries in which to locate their production facilities. Target countries are those with favourable location conditions. To the extent that locational advantages establish a competitive advantage, there should also be a positive link between a host country's locational competitiveness and its inward direct investment. In addition, MNEs may also be attracted by the entrepreneurial competitiveness of host countries, being able to tap into the (technological) advantages of local companies. Simultaneously, the presence of foreign affiliates may boost the entrepreneurial competitiveness of local companies through spillovers, thereby reinforcing the positive link between host countries' comparative advantages and foreign involvement.

A profile of comparative advantages of the major home markets, as well as the EU host market, should therefore provide further insight into the motives behind the industrial distribution of non-EU firms. Such a profile is also important when evaluating the positive or negative impact of non-EU presence on the EU economy, requiring an assessment of the strength or competitive position of these non-EU firms, as well as the strength and weaknesses of EU firms. For example, it can be argued that the EU industry stands to gain more when foreign companies originate from stronger countries, but less where EU companies already prevail within the industry, and where the foreign presence merely attempts to tap into this advantage. In the latter case, the EU's competitive position may be endangered, unless, of course, this position has been built through the presence of those non-EU companies in the first place.

This section investigates these propositions using three indices:

1. Foreign penetration by firms from 'country' k in industry j is measured by their share of the EU market for j relative to their share in total manufacturing:

$$FP_{kj} = (X_{kj} / X_j) / (X_k / X)$$

where X_{kj} = the production of matrix firms from 'country' k in industry j; X_j = the production of all matrix firms in industry j; X_k = the production of matrix firms from 'country' k in all industries; and X = the total production of all matrix firms. Given the small numbers of firms in our database, the index is computed only for k = USA and EFTA.[3]

2. Global revealed comparative advantage of home market for firms from 'country' k in industry j is measured by the share of country k firms in total world sales of industry j relative to their world share in all industries:

$$GRCA_{kj} = (GX_{kj} / GX_j) / (GX_k / GX)$$

where GX = global sales (source: *Fortune*). We interpret $GRCA_{kj} > 1$ as indicative that country k holds a comparative advantage in industry j. This index is computed for the EU as well as USA and EFTA. In addition, for the EU we also calculate an extra index:

3. Export-revealed comparative advantage of EU firms in industry j is measured by the EU's share of the world market in j relative to its export share in all industries:

$$ERCA_{EUj} = (E_{EUj} / E_j) / (E_{EU} / E)$$

where E denotes exports (source: OECD).[4]

---

[3] Because of small numbers, we have had to group Switzerland and Sweden together under the EFTA category; of course, this will obscure any differences there may be between the two countries.

[4] Thus we measure the comparative advantage of EU industry using two alternative indices. *GRCA* should reflect entrepreneurial as well as locational advantages, whilst *ERCA* is more narrow, being more relevant to locational advantages. In fact, the data reveal that $ERCA_{EU} > 1$ in all industries for which $GRCA_{EU} > 1$.

Although these are admittedly crude and imperfect proxies, they yield a number of interesting observations. First, a simple comparison of *GRCA* with *FP* reveals that, with one exception, all industries in which the USA and EFTA have $FP > 1$, also display a $GRCA > 1$.[5] This indicates that their strong EU penetration is built on home country comparative advantages. The notable exception is car manufacturing: a sector in which the USA holds an above-average EU share, despite its current lack of a global competitive advantage ($GRCA_{USA} = .93$). Of course, firms like Ford and General Motors have been long-established in Europe, dating back to the time of the dominant US world position in this industry. In this industry, the EU has a strong competitive position in terms of global sales as well as exports. Undoubtedly, the US companies have contributed to this, whilst at the same time using the EU entrepreneurial and locational advantages.

Table 8.4 lists the industries in which US and EFTA companies hold a global comparative advantage, but separates them into two groups, depending on whether their EU penetration is relatively high or low. It also stars those industries in which the EU itself has a comparative advantage (as reflected by the $GRCA_{EU}$ and/or $ERCA_{EU}$ indices).

Table 8.4 Comparative advantage and foreign presence

(i) Industries in which strong foriegn presence is based on home country comparative advantage ($GRCA_{kj} > 1$ and $FP_{kj} > 1$)	
USA	**EFTA**
Soap & Cosmetics**	Machinery*
Computers	Food*
Scientific & Photographic equipment	Phamaceuticals**
Tobacco	Electronics
(i) Industries in which there is low foriegn presencedespite home country comparative advantage ($GRCA_{kj} > 1$ and $FP_{kj} < 1$)	
USA	**EFTA**
Food*	Minerals*
Phamaceuticals**	Metal products**
Drink**	Wood
Aerospace	Other transport
Wood	
Clothing	

* Also a global revealed comparative advantage for the EU ($GRCA_{EU} > 1$).
** Also an export revealed comparative advantage for the EU ($ERCA_{EU} > 1$).

[5] We can also compare $GRCA_{EU}$ with the penetration of EU multinationals in the EU. However, the latter measures their sales in their home market and is not an obvious proxy for multinationality. Nevertheless, the exercise reveals that the high share of EU multinationals in chemicals, machinery, cars, and rubber and plastics is built on a comparative advantage of the EU in these industries. However for industries like office equipment, electronics, scientific and photographic equipment, textiles, pharmaceuticals, and cosmetics, the high share of EU multinationals does not relate to a revealed comparative advantage for the EU ($GRCA_{EU} < 1$). Note that all these industries are characterized by non-tariff barriers, indicating that a protected EU market, rather than global entrepreneurial advantages, may be behind the high share of EU multinationals in the EU.

Thus, the first group shows that high US penetration in soap and cosmetics, computers, scientific and photographic equipment, and tobacco, is built on that country's strong world competitive position. Similarly building on a strong competitive position, EFTA companies are 'overrepresented' in the EU in pharmaceuticals, machinery, electrical and electronic equipment, and food. Interestingly, in six of the eight industries in this group, the EU has no global comparative advantage, and this suggests that home country advantage is the dominant factor. Machinery and food are the two exceptions, and here it may be that EFTA companies are attracted to the EU market not only by locational advantages, but also by EU entrepreneurial advantages. There may also be a strategic motive of reciprocal entry, establishing footholds in rivals' home markets, in these two cases. In two other industries, pharmaceuticals and soaps and cosmetics, the EU, despite a lack of global comparative advantage, does display a comparative advantage in exports, indicating locational advantages. Attracted by these EU locational advantages, the EFTA presence in pharmaceuticals, and the US pervasiveness in soaps and cosmetics, may itself contribute to the superior export performance in these industries.

The second part of the table shows those industries in which the non-EU multinationals have not secured a strong foreign presence within the EU, even though their home countries hold a strong global comparative advantage. In these cases, alternative strategies, like exports or alliances, as well as host-market characteristics may offer part of the explanation. In pharmaceuticals, aerospace, and wood, US companies do indeed often exploit their global comparative advantages through exports and alliances. But in food, drink, and clothing, neither exports nor alliances are used intensively. The fact the EU market offers no entrepreneurial or locational advantages on which to tap may also explain low US penetration in aerospace, wood, and clothing; whereas the locational advantages that the EU offers ($ERCA_{EU} > 1$) in pharmaceuticals and drink are not strong enough to compensate for the lack of entrepreneurial advantages. In food, the strong comparative advantage of the EU in terms of global production as well as exports may create a mutual forbearance effect which deters US companies from large-scale entry. Turning to the low presence of EFTA MNEs in four other industries, the low locational advantages of the EU may be the explanation for wood and other transportation equipment; in minerals, the presence of strong EU rivals may have acted as a deterrent; and in metal products, exports and alliances may be more attractive alternative modes. Finally, the lack of comparative advantage of the host country, may explain the lower penetration of foreign firms in industries like chemicals, rubber and plastics, jewellery and watches, iron and steel, and leather, despite the entrepreneurial and locational advantages the EU offers in these industries.[6]

---

[6] The Japanese presence in the EU matrix is too small to allow any thorough analysis. A quick overview of the sectors in which Japanese companies are present—mineral products (glass), machinery, automobiles and other transport equipment—reveals that only in machinery and automobiles do the Japanese have a comparative advantage (on the basis of their share in global

8.7 Conclusion

Subsidiaries of non-EU companies constitute what is most accurately referred to as a significant minority of the leading firms in the EU—about one-eighth of the total. They are mostly of US origin, although some of the largest foreign firms are from the EFTA countries, especially Switzerland; in 1987, the Japanese presence was minimal. Typically, these firms tended to be larger than their indigenous EU rivals—mainly because of a tendency to have larger market shares, but also, for the Swiss firms, because of their greater diversification and presence in large scale sectors. Foreign penetration of the EU is highest in computer and office equipment, food and tobacco, soap and cosmetics, scientific and photographic equipment, and toys and sporting goods. All of these industries display a strong intangible asset intensity—fitting into the Type 2 category used throughout this book. Nevertheless, it is also shown that global competitive considerations and, in a few instances government intervention, may drive this high foreign penetration. As ever, the welfare consequences are difficult to evaluate. However, we speculate that where there is a high non-EU presence in industries where the home country enjoys a comparative advantage, but where the EU scores mostly low on entrepreneurial as well as locational advantages, the EU is likely to benefit—cases such as computers, scientific equipment, and electronics. In other circumstances, this beneficial impact may be less obvious. The presence of strong EU rivals sometimes attracts their non-EU rivals, establishing footholds in industries like machinery, food, and automobiles. But a full assessment of the impact of foreign affiliates on the comparative advantage of the EU must await further more in-depth research.

REINHILDE VEUGELERS

A.8 APPENDIX to Chapter 8

....

Using the Matrix to 'Correct' a Misleading Picture from Traditional Sources

The detailed information provided by the matrix on the diversification strategies of non-EU MNEs provides a unique opportunity to 'correct' the picture given in many traditional data sources about foreign involvement within individual industries. Very often, traditional sources of information on foreign involvement (especially foreign

production as well as exports). More importantly, in all of these industries, the EU has a comparative advantage on the basis of share in global production, indicating that an apparent motive for Japanese foreign presence is to tap into specific advantages of the host market; locational—as well as entrepreneurial—advantages.

direct investment) ignore diversification, classifying all of a firm's activities entirely to the industry in which it has the most production, i.e. its primary industry. In contrast, the matrix allows us to establish the 'true share' of foreign involvement in each industry, taking into account diversification.

To check the extent of the bias likely to be involved in the traditional approach, we have compared the actual distribution with a 'primary industry distribution' in which all of the matrix firms' productions are classified (erroneously) to their primary industries. For each industry, we have calculated the ratio of actual to erroneous non-EU production, so a value larger/smaller than 1 implies that, by ignoring diversification, we would under/overestimate the size of non-EU production within the industry.

On this basis, we identify the following industries as those in which the traditional approach would have substantially underestimated the scale of production by non-EU firms (in each case, the ratio is shown in brackets): publishing and printing (1.32), metal products (1.27), beverages (1.19), industrial equipment (1.17), toys and sporting goods (1.12), chemicals (1.10), and rubber and plastics (1.10). In these industries there is considerable inward diversification from non-EU companies based in other industries.

On the other hand, the traditional approach would overestimate foreign involvement in the following: pharmaceuticals (0.62), scientific and photographic equipment (0.74), iron and steel (0.83), and electronics (0.84). These are the industries in which there are important outward diversification flows by non-EU companies.

For a number of other industries, foreign production on the matrix is entirely by firms whose primary activities lie in other industries: aerospace, jewellery and watches, textiles, clothing, wood and furniture. In the traditional approach, such industries would be recorded as not having *any* foreign penetration.

Thus, the traditional, aggregated approach, which ignores diversification, can indeed be very misleading.

PART III

The Strategy of EU Firms

9
The Dimensions of Corporate Strategy

9.1 Introduction

This chapter opens the third part of the book, in which the focus switches to the individual firm as the unit of analysis. This has two broad purposes. First, it develops our investigation of the determinants of industry structure and EU integration. So far, we have tended to emphasize deterministic aggregate forces, with individual firms viewed, by implication, as anonymous actors in the grand structural design. This may be a useful first approximation, but ultimately, there is a richer story which acknowledges that industries are not just composed of clones—or 'representative firms'. Rather, firms differ in ways which may have a crucial bearing on the nature of competition. Our aim is to explore these differences and examine some of the implications for the evolving structure of EU industries. So to some extent, we continue the themes of previous chapters, but now at a less aggregate level.

In addition, this part of the book opens up a new subject, less commonly investigated empirically by academic economists—that of the corporate strategies of individual firms. Nearly all of the firms in our matrix are extremely large players on the European stage. Whilst they are all leading producers within individual industries (the criterion for their inclusion in the matrix), many are also highly conglomerate, appearing frequently across industries; similarly, many achieve their dominant European position by producing in a number of member states. Evidently, there is more than one way for a firm to achieve large scale, and the matrix allows us to quantify the differences in considerable detail. Of course, we are not able to observe strategy directly—in general, we have insufficient information on pricing, investment, acquisitions, disposals, marketing, R&D, etc. But we are able to observe the outcome of past decisions in resultant market shares, diversification, and multinational production. In this vein, major questions in this part of the book are: What corporate strategies lead firms to a position of market leadership? Why do strategies differ across firms? And, does nationality make any difference?

As in Part II, a decomposition analysis—but this time at the firm level—provides the starting point, helping to organize our thoughts on the various dimensions of corporate strategy. Two decompositions of a firm's aggregate size are used. In product space, aggregate size depends on the firm's market shares in the industries in which it operates, the sizes of those industries, and its diversification across industries. In geographic space, the firm's size depends on its aggregate shares in the countries in which it operates, the sizes of those countries, and its multinationality across countries. This chapter considers the product decomposition, with particular reference to the trade-off (if any) between market share and diversification. In Chapter 10, we explain econometric-ally the pattern of diversification across firms. In Chapter 11, we explore the geographic decomposition, and present an econometric analysis of the deter-minants of multinationality by firm (to complement the Chapter 7 industry econometrics). Chapter 12 closes Part III by drawing together the spatial and product dimensions of strategy.

In this chapter, Section 9.2 begins by examining the aggregate size distribu-tion, and digresses briefly by exploring the implications for aggregate concen-tration and how the EU compares with the USA and Japan. Section 9.3 derivès the decomposition of firm size in product space, and Section 9.4 describes how its three components vary across the sample of firms. Section 9.5 focuses on the potential trade-off between a large market share and diversification, as altern-ative routes to large firm size. Section 9.6 concludes.

9.2 Aggregate Firm Size

9.2.1 The Size Distribution of Firms

Aggregate firm size is defined as the firm's total production in the EU manu-facturing sector; its distribution across the 313 matrix firms is shown in Figure 9.1. On a logarithmic horizontal scale, it follows a roughly normal shape, sug-gesting that firm size itself has an approximately lognormal distribution. At first sight this is unsurprising: lognormals are frequently reported in empirical studies of corporate size distributions.[1] But, in the present context, this result demands further explanation since we might have expected the matrix to pick up only the very upper tail of the EU size distribution, thereby generating a *truncated* lognormal.

The fact that we do not observe a truncated distribution serves as a timely re-minder of the nature of this particular sample of firms. Recall that it includes all firms who occupy a leading (i.e. top five) position in at least one industry. While this criterion virtually ensures that the matrix will include all of the giants of European industry—it is unlikely that any very large firm will not have a leading market share in at least one industry—it will also include some relatively smaller firms. These may be specialized firms occupying fifth (or even fourth) position in relatively small industries. In other words, our distribution is best thought of as including nearly all of the extreme upper tail of the full EU firm-size distribution, but coupled with a non-random sample of relatively

---

[1] See, for example, Davies *et al.* (1988, ch. 3); Hay And Morris (1991; ch. 15); Curry and George (1983).

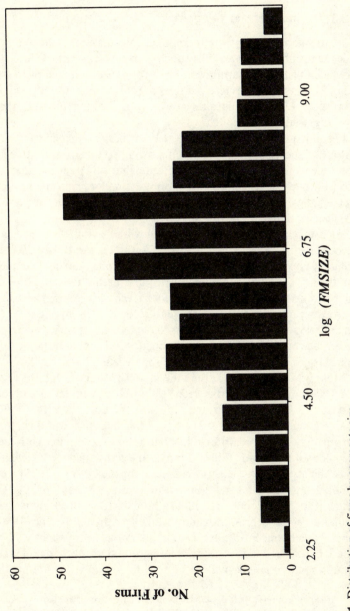

Fig. 9.1 Distribution of firms by aggregate size

smaller firms. Therefore, although perfectly adequate for drawing implications about the upper tail, it should not be viewed as in any way representative of the full EU size distribution.

9.2.2 The Implications for Aggregate Concentration

Since the matrix gives virtually complete information on the upper tail, it provides an insight into a previously uncharted subject at the EU level—the extent to which the manufacturing sector as a whole is dominated by the very largest firms. This is sometimes referred to as overall, or more usually, aggregate, concentration. Although this takes us away from the main thrust of the chapter, a brief digression is warranted.

Recall from Chapter 3 that the 313 matrix firms account for 32.5% of the output of the aggregate EU manufacturing sector. In itself, this is already a crude measure of aggregate concentration, but with a certain amount of noise, precisely because it includes the group of smaller firms mentioned above. In fact, aggregate concentration is traditionally measured by the share of the Top 100 firms and this will be our objective.

. Focusing on the extreme top tail of the distribution, the twenty largest firms account for 14.2%, the top fifty for 21.5% and the top 100 for 26.9%. From the accuracy check reported in Section 3.5 of Chapter 3, we are confident that the top twenty are also the largest twenty EU manufacturers; but, below this, minor adjustments need to be made for a few large firms that are excluded from the matrix because they fail to qualify for the top five in a large industry (mainly cars and basic chemicals[2]). Allowing for these firms adds one half of a percentage point to the share of the top fifty and about one point to the top 100 share. Therefore we estimate Europe's aggregate $C100EU$ as 28%.

Most previous studies at the individual (developed) country level report a Top 100 share somewhere between 30% and 40%, with the UK towards the top end of this range and Germany towards the bottom (Prais (1976), HMSO (1978), Davies *et al.* (1988)). As such, aggregate concentration in the EU seems surprisingly high. But more to the point is how it compares with the two other members of the Triad. Table 9.1 makes the comparison using what we believe to be the most reliable existing estimates for the USA (in 1976) and Japan (in 1988). These estimates should be treated with some caution. The USA figure, which is for sales concentration, is a little dated—unfortunately, more recent figures do not appear to be readily available. Apparently, since 1976, asset and employment concentration for all industry has fallen slightly (White, 1988). The Japanese figure does not take into account very broad and loose business groups, so this might be interpreted as a lower bound estimate, but the evidence

---

[2] As explained in Chapter 3, we have identified three firms, Montedison, Rover, and L'Air Liquide, that were almost certainly amongst the EU's top 100 manufacturers, but are not on the matrix. All three are large firms operating in, but not in the top five of, very large industries. Rover is a car firm, Montedison and L'Air Liquide are chemicals firms.

Table 9.1 International comparison of
aggregate concentration (percentages)

	C50	*C100*
EU	22	28
USA	24	34
Japan	19	n.a.

Notes: *C50* is the fifty firm concentration
ratio, showing the share of the fifty largest
firms in aggregate manufacturing; *C100* is the
100-firm concentration ratio.

Sources: Market share matrix, White (1981),
Doi (1991).

is that such groups exert no real control and often include genuinely competing firms (see Odagiri, 1993). Bearing in mind these caveats then, the EU *CR50* appears to be closely comparable to, and to lie between, that of the other Triad pair; though the share of the next largest fifty firms appears to be significantly smaller than in the USA.

The EU/USA comparison assumes added meaning when contrasted with our earlier result (Table 4.3) that concentration in the typical industry within manufacturing is much lower in the EU than in the USA. Given that we now know that the fifty largest firms account for roughly the same proportion of *total* manufacturing production in both the EU and USA, this implies that the top fifty Europeans must be more diversified than their US counterparts, having smaller market shares of a wider portfolio of industries.

This comparison also raises the speculative thought that, as European integration proceeds, EU industrial structure might move closer to the current US experience. After all, the USA is a mature federal country, of roughly equal size to the EU and with similarly significant geographical dimension. If so, we might observe increasing market dominance but coupled with divestment of non-core activities amongst the very largest EU firms. Equally, major restructuring might occur amongst the firms outside the top fifty, as they bring their aggregate share more into line with that observed in the USA.[3]

9.2.3 A Breakdown by Member States

As already noted in Chapter 3, the national breakdown of the matrix firms is broadly in line with the relative sizes of the member states, although the UK and (to a lesser extent) France have rather more firms than would be expected, whilst the smaller member states (except Benelux) are underrepresented.[4] As

[3] Aggregate concentration is the subject of ongoing research (see Davies, 1995). In future work, we shall investigate the nature of the relationship between aggregate concentration and concentration within individual industries, and between aggregate EU concentration and aggregate concentration within individual member states.

[4] To see this, compare the share of each country in total EU manufacturing production—

The Dimensions of Corporate Strategy

discussed in the previous chapter, there are also thirty-six non-EU 'foreign' multinationals—mainly North American (twenty-eight), and Swiss and Swedish (seven). Table 9.2 explores the country breakdown within four broad size classes in the distribution.

Interestingly, none of the big four member states has a uniform share across the size classes. Germany has particular strength amongst the top fifty firms, as does France to a lesser extent; the UK has proportionately more in the middle two classes; and Italy's representation is heavily bunched towards the smaller end of the distribution. There is also a significant difference between Holland

Table 9.2 The aggregate-size distribution by nationality

Country	*Number of firms in size class, ranked by aggregate size*				
	1–50	51–100	101–200	201–313	TOTAL
Germany	16	10	22	27	75
(28)	(32)	(20)	(22)	(24)	(24)
France	12	3	22	21	58
(18)	(24)	(6)	(22)	(19)	(19)
Italy	4	3	9	33	49
(18)	(8)	(6)	(9)	(30)	(16)
UK	6	16	30	13	65
(15)	(12)	(32)	(30)	(12)	(21)
Holland	4	3	3	1	11
(5)	(8)	(6)	(3)	(1)	(4)
Bel/Lux	1	2	2	7	12
(4)	(2)	(4)	(2)	(6)	(4)
Spain		1	1	3	5
(9)		(2)	(1)	(3)	(2)
Portugal				2	2
(1)				(2)	(1)
USA	5	7	7	6	25
	(10)	(14)	(7)	(5)	(8)
Canada		1	2		3
		(2)	(2)		(1)
Sweden/	2	4	1		7
Switzerland	(4)	(8)	(1)		(2)
Japan			1		1
			(1)		(0)
TOTALS	50	50	100	113	313

Notes: Figures in parentheses denote each country's proportionate share in size class. Figures in parentheses under each country's name show that country's aggregate production as a percentage of the EU total (see Table 2.5).

shown in brackets under the country's name—with the last column, scaled up by a factor of 313/277 = 1.13, to allow for the fact that the thirty-six matrix firms originating from outside the EU cannot be attributed to any member state. Readers with developed skills of mental arithmetic can confirm that the UK and France are overrepresented by 8.5% and 2.9% respectively, whilst Spain is underrepresented by 7%; Denmark, Greece, and Ireland have no matrix firms although they account for 3.3% of total EU manufacturing.

and Belgium, the former being more heavily represented amongst the larger classes. The American and EFTA firms are more likely to appear in the top 100 firms, as might have been predicted from the previous chapter, in which we found firms from EFTA and the USA to be typically larger than average. Some reasons and possible consequences of some of these size differences will emerge in what follows.

9.3 Decomposition of Aggregate Firm Size in Product Space

Because firms differ in how diversified they are and in their market shares, there is clearly a variety of routes for achieving a given large aggregate size; i.e. 'there is more than one way to the top'. For example, the following alternative firm structures each lead to an aggregate size of 1000: (i) a 50% market share in an industry of size 2,000; (ii) a 5% share in an industry of 20,000; (iii) a 1% share in each of ten industries, each of which has size 10,000.

Thus firms may be specialized or diversified; and, because industries differ in size, a moderate share in a very large industry may be equivalent to a very large share in a smaller industry.

9.3.1 Definitions and Derivation

The second key decomposition of the book formalizes this idea. It is derived formally in Appendix 1 as Equation A.32, and the definitions of the various indices are repeated in Table 9.3.

$$FMSIZE = MS * IS * ND \tag{9.1}$$

where:

$FMSIZE$ = the firm's aggregate production in the EU (m. ECUs)
MS = its typical market share in the industries in which it operates
IS = the typical size of industry in which it operates (m. ECUs)
ND = the equivalent number of industries in which it operates

Table 9.3 Indices of firm structure used in the product decomposition

Index	Symbol	Formula
Aggregate firm size	$FMSIZE$	x_i
Typical market share	MS	$\sum_j (MS)_{ij}(x_{ij}/x_i)$
		where $(MS)_{ij} = x_{ij}/x_j$
Diversification		
Number equivalent	ND	$1/(1 - D_i)$
where	D	$1 - \sum_j (x_{ij})^2/(x_i)^2$
Typical size of industry	IS	$\sum_j (w_{ij}.x_j)$
		$w_{ij} = (x_{ij}MS_{ij})/\sum_j (x_{ij}MS_{ij})$

The firm's typical market share is the weighted average market share across industries, where the weight is the proportion of its output in each industry. The equivalent number of industries over which it is diversified is the number-equivalent form of Berry's index of diversification. This is analogous to the number-equivalent form of the Herfindahl concentration index, rising as the firm diversifies into more industries, especially where that diversification entails significant operations in each industry. Its lower bound is unity, for a firm specialized within a single industry; and the upper bound is K, for a firm which has its output spread equally across K different industries. The index of typical industry size, *IS*, is more novel and peculiar to this particular decomposition. For a given firm, it is a weighted average size of all the industries in which the firm operates. The weights depend on both the size of the firm's presence in the industry and its market share, therefore its value is firm-specific.[5] This also means that industry j is given more weight if the firm's operations in that industry are both important to the firm and significant in the industry.

9.3.2 Analysis of means and variances

Evaluated at geometric mean values, as in Table 9.4(*a*), the 'typical' matrix firm has an output of 751m. ECUs. Its diversification is as if the firm spreads that output equally across 1.85 equal-sized industries, each of size 16,432m. ECUs, and in each of which the firm has a market share of 2.47%. On average then, firms are significantly diversified, but typically with only relatively moderate market shares.

However, these are only typical values, and, as we shall see later, they conceal the very much larger values for diversification and market shares of some firms. The analysis of variance, reported in part (*b*) of the table is a device for identifying which of the three component parts accounts for most of the overall variance between firms in *FMSIZE*. It is based on the logarithmic version of the

Table 9.4 The decomposition of aggregate firm size

(*a*) Analysis of Geometric Means

FMSIZE	=	*MS*	*	*IS*	*	*ND*
751	=	2.466	*	16,432	*	1.851

(*b*) Analysis of variances

V(fmsize)	=	V(ms)	+	V(is)	+	V(nd)	+	2C(ms, is)	−	2C(ms, nd)	+	2C(is, nd)
2.577	=	0.782	+	0.987	+	0.366	+	0.175	−	0.083	+	0.350
(100)	=	(30%)	+	(38%)	+	(14%)	+	(7%)	−	(3%)	+	(14%)

[5] Two firms operating in exactly the same set of industries will only record the same value for *IS* if they have an identical configuration of market shares.

decomposition, with lower case symbols denoting logarithms and V and C denoting variances and covariances respectively:

$$V(fmsize) = V(ms) + V(is) + V(nd) + 2C(ms, is) + 2C(ms, nd) + 2C(is, nd) \quad (9.2)$$

In fact, the estimated variances show that each component contributes importantly to variations in aggregate size within this sample, but that industry size is the most important and diversification the least. The covariance terms are far less important numerically. Nevertheless, they reveal two effects which are interesting, if only because they are unexpected: there are moderate tendencies for firms in larger industries to have larger market shares and to be more diversified.[6] Both effects will tend to accentuate the overall variance.

9.4 Different Corporate Strategies?

The decomposition for each of the top 100 firms is given in Table 9.5 (the full list of all 313 firms is presented in Appendix 2.2). A casual inspection will reveal many household names for most readers. It also shows that firms have achieved their positions in a variety of ways: within the top twenty for example, IBM by market share; IRI by diversification; BMW by industry size; and Fiat by all three. In this section we investigate these three components in turn.

Table 9.5 Aggregate firm size and its components in product space: the top 100

Rank	Firm	Country	FMSIZE	MS	ND	IS
1	FIAT	IT	26,451	9.2	2.19	131,479
2	DAIMLER-BENZ	GER	24,883	10.2	1.72	142,436
3	VOLKSWAGEN	GER	24,450	16.2	1.00	151,214
4	SIEMENS	GER	20,362	8.6	5.76	40,873
5	RENAULT	FR	19,625	11.0	1.19	149,875
6	FORD	USA	19,419	9.9	1.41	139,724
7	PSA	FR	17,384	9.6	1.24	146,334
8	PHILIPS	NL	16,256	16.7	4.25	22,974
9	BAYER	GER	15,310	8.2	5.47	33,977
10	BASF	GER	14,017	11.1	4.22	29,985
11	IRI	IT	13,475	4.7	8.10	35,451
12	CGE	FR	13,032	6.3	4.46	46,289
13	IBM	USA	12,994	41.2	1.03	30,616
14	HOECHST	GER	12,406	5.9	4.49	46,510
15	UNILEVER	NL	11,466	6.8	7.60	22,111
16	ICI	UK	10,848	5.5	2.79	70,715
17	BMW	GER	9,979	6.5	1.03	149,449
18	USINOR-SACILOR	FR	9,408	11.5	2.07	39,547
19	THYSSEN	GER	9,309	5.3	4.24	41,105

[6] It might have expected that large industry size would make it less likely that firms would achieve large market shares; and that firms in larger industries would tend to look less frequently to diversification for further expansion. But note that these covariances are not high compared to the variances, and therefore the sample correlations are not very strong.

Table 9.5 (*cont.*)

Rank	Firm	Country	*FMSIZE*	*MS*	*ND*	*IS*
20	THOMSON	FR	9,116	5.2	4.00	43,926
21	ROBERT BOSCH	GER	9,014	8.7	2.52	41,009
22	NESTLE	CH	8,134	6.3	3.22	39,920
23	RHONE-POULENC	FR	7,239	4.2	2.89	60,260
24	BRITISH AEROSPACE	UK	7,006	14.6	1.45	33,168
25	ROYAL DUTCH/SHELL	NL	6,416	4.0	2.04	78,752
26	SAINT-GOBAIN	FR	6,274	11.1	2.98	18,910
27	MANNESMANN	GER	6,214	4.7	6.00	21,939
28	GEC	UK	6,010	3.0	3.99	50,924
29	BRITISH STEEL	UK	5,935	9.8	1.20	50,499
30	ENI	IT	5,875	2.1	3.54	78,107
31	MICHELIN	FR	5,860	24.8	1.00	23,583
32	MAN	GER	5,646	2.0	7.53	38,020
33	ELF AQUITAINE	FR	5,143	1.9	3.52	78,233
34	HANSON	UK	5,127	9.5	1.78	30,164
35	AKZO	NL	5,090	4.8	5.28	20,131
36	BSN	FR	4,895	2.7	7.29	25,280
37	BP	UK	4,744	2.8	1.95	86,365
38	FELDMUHLE NOBEL	GER	4,731	1.4	10.3	33,097
39	SOLVAY	BL	4,725	2.1	3.13	73,211
40	AEROSPATIALE	FR	4,526	13.8	1.00	32,804
41	GALLAHER	USA	4,448	11.9	1.19	31,485
42	FRIED. KRUPP	GER	4,446	1.5	9.87	29,542
43	MESSERSCHMITT	GER	4,174	10.5	1.21	32,844
44	PHILIP MORRIS	USA	4,079	8.5	1.50	31,822
45	PECHINEY	FR	3,809	5.5	2.19	31,659
46	HENKEL KGAA	GER	3,779	2.9	4.23	30,597
47	EI DU PONT	USA	3,690	3.9	4.84	19,614
48	FERRUZZI FINAN.	IT	3,645	6.2	4.12	14,236
49	ASEA BROWN BOVERI	CH/SW	3,640	3.2	3.01	38,227
50	BERTELSMANN	GER	3,628	3.1	1.65	71,586
51	PIRELLI	IT	3,619	6.8	2.41	22,025
52	SEITA	FR	3,614	11.0	1.04	31,749
53	CIBA GEIGY	CH	3,534	2.6	3.01	44,566
54	PROCTER & GAMBLE	USA	3,473	8.7	1.54	25,910
55	OLIVETTI	IT	3,144	6.2	1.67	30,393
56	TABACALERA	SP	3,096	9.8	1.00	31,748
57	COURTAULDS	UK	3,081	2.3	8.07	16,423
58	EFIM	IT	3,071	2.0	5.87	26,435
59	DEGUSSA	GER	2,974	2.3	3.91	33,338
60	BAT INDUSTRIES	UK	2,970	3.1	3.14	29,989
61	ARBED	LUX	2,932	3.8	2.28	34,129
62	HOESCH	GER	2,872	1.4	5.80	35,173
63	DSM	NL	2,851	1.4	3.22	63,370
64	ROLLS ROYCE	UK	2,651	7.0	1.16	32,881
65	SKF	SW	2,564	13.8	1.86	9,988
66	GUINNESS	UK	2,546	6.6	2.66	14,382
67	JACOBS SUCHARD	CH	2,541	6.5	1.97	19,847
68	ELECTROLUX	SW	2,527	7.9	1.95	16,287

69	MARS	USA	2,509	9.4	1.52	17,558
70	SALZGITTER	GER	2,507	2.0	4.52	28,163
71	BEECHAM	UK	2,362	2.8	2.76	30,828
72	GRAND MET.	UK	2,352	2.9	2.95	27,574
73	EASTMAN KODAK	USA	2,247	14.3	2.36	6,639
74	ABF	UK	2,218	3.1	2.21	32,654
75	BOSCH-SIEMENS	GER	2,185	13.7	1.00	15,951
76	METALLGESELLSCHAF	GER	2,176	2.7	2.66	30,476
77	AV. M.DASSAULT	FR	2,169	6.6	1.00	32,804
78	ALLIED LYONS	UK	2,165	3.5	3.76	16,306
79	BTR	UK	2,072	1.1	7.83	23,335
80	TENNECO	USA	2,068	1.7	4.77	25,743
81	SCHNEIDER	FR	2,056	2.4	2.69	31,368
82	HEINEKEN	NL	2,037	6.6	1.60	19,240
83	KLOCKNER-WERKE	GER	2,035	0.8	6.92	37,491
84	3M	USA	2,030	2.2	6.08	14,884
85	REED INT.	UK	1,980	1.2	2.69	59,514
86	HILLSDOWN HLDGS.	UK	1,977	1.3	2.73	55,307
87	ZAHNRADFABRIK FR.	GER	1,962	4.7	1.00	41,522
88	HEWLETT PACKARD	USA	1,961	5.4	1.20	30,400
89	CONTINENTAL GW	GER	1,957	4.3	1.75	25,792
90	UNIGATE	UK	1,898	1.5	2.20	56,131
91	VIAG	GER	1,896	3.3	1.72	33,434
92	DOUWE EGBERTS	NL	1,891	2.5	3.01	25,509
93	RHM	UK	1,880	2.2	3.41	24,975
94	KLOCKNER-H-D.	GER	1,858	1.9	3.77	26,421
95	PILKINGTON	UK	1,855	8.6	1.14	18,910
96	COATS VIYELLA	UK	1,853	1.9	7.29	13,528
97	GOODYEAR	USA	1,851	6.5	1.21	23,658
98	CADBURY SCHWEPPES	UK	1,817	7.2	1.98	12,851
99	ALCAN ALUMINIUM	CAN	1,797	4.6	1.23	31,891
100	ACEC-UNION MIN.	BL	1,786	2.8	2.11	30,734

Notes: Units: *ND* are index numbers; *MS* are percentages; *FIRMSIZE*; thousand ECUs; *IS*: hundred thousand ECUs. Key to countries: BL = Belgium; CAN = Canada; CH = Switzerland; CH/SW = Switzerland/Sweden; FR = France; GER = Germany; IT = Italy; LUX = Luxemburg; NL = Netherlands; SP = Spain; SW = Sweden; UK = United Kingdom; USA = USA.

9.4.1 Typical Industry Size (IS)

The analysis of variance has already shown a dominant role, in purely statistical terms, for *IS*. The reason becomes apparent from further inspection of the top twenty firms. Notwithstanding the fact that some are highly diversified and/or have large market shares, the most striking feature is the very large *IS* values scored by many of these firms: indeed, seven of the top twenty have *IS* > 130b. ECUs, (which is nearly eight times larger than the geometric mean of *IS*). All of these firms (Fiat, Daimler-Benz, Volkswagen, Renault, Ford, PSA, and BMW) are more or less specialized in the car industry, which alone accounts for nearly 7% of total EU manufacturing production. Undoubtedly, there is a strong industry-specific effect at work. This becomes even clearer when firms are ranked in descending order of their *IS* values, the seven largest are the car producers (*IS* > 130bn. ECUs), and the next ten firms (70bn. ECUs < *IS* < 90bn. ECUs) all 'belong' (have at least 50% of their output) in the next two largest industries: basic chemicals or printing and publishing.[7] The industrial locations of firms become more diffuse further down the *IS* ranking, but it remains true that, for many firms, a large aggregate size can be achieved with only moderate market share, if located in a large industry. Returning to Table 9.5, it is not until the forty-eighth ranked firm that we encounter an *IS* value less than the geometric mean; and only nine other firms in the top 100 record *IS* less than the mean. Not surprisingly, therefore, the simple regression (in logged form) of *IS* against *FMSIZE* records a fairly close fit ($R^2 = 0.614$); and the coefficient estimate suggests that *IS* rises almost exactly with the square root of *FMSIZE*—a fact which is used below.

IS is probably the least interesting of the three components to firm size, so far as corporate strategy is concerned. Nevertheless, success in a large industry may require certain specific skills to do with managing large-scale, and this is a point we refer to briefly later on.

9.4.2 Typical Market Share (*MS*)

MS has a more immediate interest value, with possible market power connotations. It also provides a point of contact with our previous analysis of concentration at the industry level. In what follows, it should be remembered that we are discussing 'typical' market share, and it is quite possible for a firm to record a lowish *MS* despite a dominant position in one industry, if it is sufficiently diversified across other industries in which it has a low share.

On the face of it, most matrix firms do not appear to have the sort of market shares usually associated with control over the market, though these figures should be seen in the context of our relatively aggregate 3-digit industry classification. The distribution of *MS* is heavily skewed, with most firms recording fairly modest values: slightly more than half (159) have *MS* < 2.5%, three-quarters (241) have *MS* < 5%, and only seventy-two firms have a typical market share of more than 5%. However, there are eighteen firms, shown in Table 9.6, who record typical market shares in excess of 10%, and they do merit some further attention.

We have already noted that IBM attains a top twenty *FMSIZE* ranking purely on the basis of its very high *MS* value (41%) in a single industry, computers. Similarly, the number 2-ranked firm in this table, Michelin, produces only in the rubber industry, but its share (25%) is sufficiently large to secure it a high ranking in the overall *FMSIZE* distribution. In fact, this is true for most of the firms in this list: only two (Philips and BASF) are genuinely diversified, whilst only one (Piaggio) is not amongst Europe's largest 100 firms. Indeed,

---

[7] Note however that the size of the 'printing and publishing' industry reflects as much on the standard industrial classification as on the scale of any well-defined industry of this name.

Table 9.6 Firms with very large typical market shares (*MS* > 10%)

Rank by *FMSIZE*		Country	*MS*	*ND*	Main industry	Type
13	IBM	USA	41.2	1.03	Computers	2*R*
31	MICHELIN	FR	24.8	1.00	Rubber	2*R*
8	PHILIPS	NL	16.7	4.25	Various electrical	2*AR/R*
3	VOLKSWAGEN	GER	16.2	1.00	Cars	2*AR*
180	PIAGGIO	IT	15.1	1.14	Cycles & m.cycles	2*R*
24	BRITISH AEROSPACE	UK	14.6	1.45	Aerospace	2*R*
73	EASTMAN KODAK	USA	14.3	2.36	Cameras	2*AR*
40	AEROSPATIALE	FR	13.8	1.00	Aerospace	2*R*
66	SKF	SWED	13.8	1.86	Transmission equip.	2*R*
75	BOSCH-SIEMENS	GER	13.7	1.00	Electrical apps.	2*AR*
41	GALLAHER	USA	11.9	1.19	Tobacco	2*A*
18	USINOR-SACILOR	FR	11.5	2.07	Steel	1
26	SAINT-GOBAIN	FR	11.1	2.98	Glass	1
10	BASF	GER	11.1	4.22	Various chemical	2*AR/R*
5	RENAULT	FR	11.0	1.19	Cars	2*R*
52	SEITA	FR	11.0	1.04	Tobacco	2*A*
43	MESSERSCHMITT-B-B	GER	10.5	1.21	Aerospace	2*R*
2	DAIMLER-BENZ	GER	10.2	1.72	Cars	2*AR*

Note: See Table 9.5 for units and key to countries.

thirteen of the eighteen firms are within the top fifty by aggregate size: evidently, a ranking amongst the top fifty by *FMSIZE* is often a sign that the firm concerned has very significant market power in its main industry. BASF and Philips are significant exceptions for two reasons. First, their combinations of high *ND* and *MS* values indicate substantial market power over a range of industries (in the electrical and chemicals sectors respectively). Inevitably, this places them in the forefront of potential anti-trust attention. But, second, they are significant precisely because they are exceptions: no other diversified firm has been able to secure such high market penetration across such a wide range of industries.

The last two columns of the table record, for each firm, the main industry in which it dominates, and the industry type. Significantly, cars and aerospace each account for three 'dominant firms', and tobacco for two. Unsurprisingly, all of the eleven industries listed, except transmission equipment, appear in the twenty most concentrated EU industries shown in Table 4.2. More significantly, all but two of the industries are Type 2—mostly involving high R&D expenditures. This adds an extra dimension to our work in Chapter 6 on the determinants of concentration, since it is suggestive that size inequalities *amongst* the leading firms are an important contributor to concentration in some industries, over and above the symmetric equilibrium lower bound relationships.

Turning to the national identities of the firms, France (six), Germany (five) and the USA (three) are the only countries with more than one firm in the table. Whilst this may not be too surprising for Germany, given its high representation

on the matrix as a whole, both France and the USA are much more than proportionately represented. The tendency for US firms to have higher than average market shares has already been noted in the last chapter. It serves as a
reminder that American multinationals remain a significant force on the
European stage, in spite of the relative decline of recent years in America's role
as a direct investor. The French propensity to high market shares is perhaps
more unexpected. Furthermore, the six French firms tend to be untypical of
this list as a whole, in that they include the only two from Type 1 industries and
one of only two firms from Type 2*A* industries in the table. State ownership/
involvement may provide part of the answer.

9.4.3 Diversification (*ND*)

Ninety-one of the matrix firms are specialized within single industries, and a
further eighty-one record a number-equivalent for diversification of less than
2. Thus nearly 60% of the sample are either not at all, or only moderately, diversified. However, this still leaves 141 firms with clearly diversified operations.
Table 9.7 lists the twenty most diversified (*ND* > 5). Remembering that the
number-equivalent measure does not attach much weight to small scale
operations, *ND* = 5 will typically correspond to a firm operating in many more
than just five industries.

Table 9.7 Firms with high diversification (*ND* > 5)

Rank by *FMSIZE*	Firm	Country	*ND*	*MS*
101	CIR	IT	10.5	1.0
38	FELDMUHLE NOBEL	GER	10.3	1.4
42	F. KRUPP	GER	9.9	1.5
11	IRI	IT	8.1	4.7
57	COURTAULDS	UK	8.1	2.3
79	BTR	UK	7.8	1.1
15	UNILEVER	NL	7.6	6.8
32	MAN	GER	7.5	2.0
113	HERAEUS	GER	7.4	0.9
96	COATS VIYELLA	UK	7.3	1.9
36	BSN	FR	7.3	2.7
83	KLOCKNER-WERKE	GER	6.9	0.8
84	3M	USA	6.1	2.2
27	MANNESMANN	GER	6.0	4.7
182	GROUPE NAV. MIX.	FR	6.0	0.8
58	EFIM	IT	5.9	2.0
62	HOESCH	GER	5.8	1.4
4	SIEMENS	GER	5.7	8.6
9	BAYER	GER	5.5	8.2
35	AKZO	NL	5.3	4.8

Note: See Table 9.4. for units and key to countries.

Only four of these firms rank amongst the very largest, top twenty, matrix firms by *FMSIZE*—IRI, Unilever, Siemens and Bayer. On the other hand, high diversification seems to be almost sufficient for securing a top 100 ranking: only three firms in this table lie outside the top 100 by *FMSIZE*. Beyond this, the most striking feature of the table is that most of these firms have relatively low typical market shares; there are none with *MS* > 10% and only three with *MS* > 5% (Siemens, Bayer and Unilever.) As one suspected from Table 9.5, there are few firms in the EU who have been able to attain significant market power across a very wide range of industries. The national breakdown also makes an interesting contrast with that of the previous table. Here, Germany has nearly half of the firms (nine), followed by the UK and Italy with three each; France has only two and the USA none.

9.5 Market Share versus Diversification

9.5.1 A Graphical Device

Some of the above findings hint at an apparent trade-off between market shares and diversification. Since these are the two dimensions of the decomposition which most obviously relate to corporate strategy, we explore this more fully in the scattergram of *ND* against *MS* shown in Figure 9.2.

To interpret this diagram, it is helpful if we first rewrite the decomposition as:

$$ND = (FMSIZE / IS) * MS^{-1} \qquad (9.3)$$

So, holding a firm's aggregate size and industry size constant, its diversification is inversely related to its typical market share according to a rectangular hyperbola.

Second, recall our earlier finding that *IS* tends to rise roughly with the square root of *FMSIZE*. This allows us to stylize the relationship as:

$$ND = a.(FMSIZE)^{0.5} * MS^{-1} \qquad (9.4)$$

where *a* is a parameter of no particular interest for present purposes. Now, if this equation was exact, for any *FMSIZE*, there would be a perfect inverse relationship between *ND* and *MS*—all firms with a given aggregate size would lie on the same rectangular hyperbola, and this would be the locus of all *ND*, *MS* combinations consistent with that aggregate size. Higher hyperbolas would, indicate higher values of *FMSIZE*. Of course, this is only a stylization since the empirical relationship between *IS* and *FMSIZE*, although close, is by no means exact. Nevertheless, it proves to be helpful when drawing comparisons between firms, or groups of firms.

As an example of how this device can be used, Figure 9.3 shows a family of four curves and selects a few of the observations from the scattergram for illustrative purposes. Referring hereafter to the ratio *FMSIZE/IS* as 'normalized size', the highest curve (curve I) is drawn for normalized size = 0.7; this is

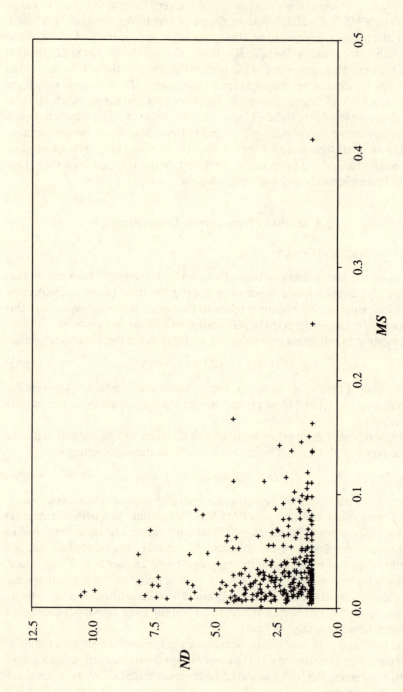

Fig. 9.2 Scattergram of *ND* and *MS*

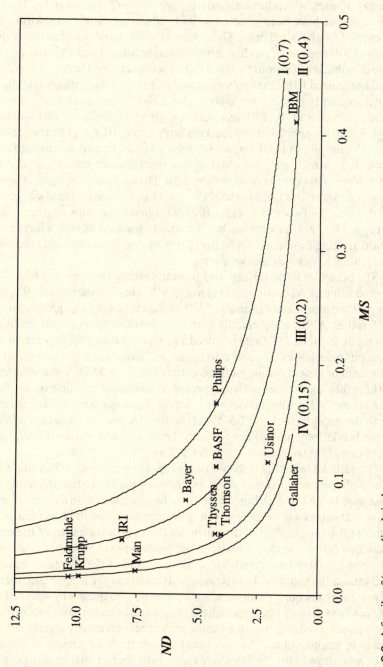

Fig. 9.3 A family of 'normalized size' curves

almost an 'upper bound', which encloses the complete sample, with the exception of Philips, which has a singularly high ND, MS combination. The other three curves have been selected so as to illustrate differences within three groups of similar-sized firms. Thus, curve II relates to normalized size in the region of 0.4, and focuses on four firms ranked between 9 and 13 in the aggregate size distribution. The most marked difference is between the conglomerate IRI and specialized IBM: the former is about eight times more diversified than the latter, but its typical market share is about eight times smaller; the other two firms (Bayer and BASF) have chosen an intermediate route, involving significant diversification and market shares. Curve III moves further down the size distribution to firms ranked between 18 and 21 (with normalized size of about 0.2); here, Usinor has a high typical market share, but only moderate diversification, whilst the reverse is true for Thyssen and Thomson. Curve IV moves down to four firms ranked between 32 and 42 (normalized size of 0.15); in this case, Gallaher (American Brands) is much the same aggregate size as Krupp, Man, and Feldmuhle, but is virtually specialized with a large market share in a single industry, whilst the three German firms are highly diversified, but with much smaller market shares.

The potential trade-off can also be examined by investigating how the expected value of ND varies as we increase MS. This is done in Table 9.8, which records the mean (and variance) of ND within classes of firms grouped by their MS values. Abstracting initially from the fifty-three firms with trivial market shares of less than 1%, there is indeed a general tendency for expected diversification to decline as we move into higher MS size classes. But an exception to this tendency occurs amongst firms in the class $5\% > MS > 2.5\%$, who appear to be rather less diversified than expected. A similar pattern also occurs for the variance of ND within classes—it generally decreases with market share, but with the exception of the 2.5–5% class. Finally, the very smallest MS class records relatively high values for both the mean and variance for ND, but in both cases slightly less than the 1–2.5% class.

Overall, we take this to be weakly supportive evidence of an underlying trade-off between diversification and market shares. Large MS tends to be associated with low ND, but low MS may be associated with a range of alternative ND values. However, the relationship appears not to be particularly robust for this sample. Part of the reason for this may be the nature of the sample. As noted earlier, the matrix really comprises two broad groups of firm. On the one hand, it includes virtually all of the upper tail of the aggregate size distribution, i.e. the giants of European industry; but, on the other hand, there are also some really quite small firms on the matrix, who qualify by virtue of leading positions in very small specialized industries, or minor positions in moderately sized industries. Since the second group includes mostly specialized firms, many of whom will tend to be concentrated in the lower classes of Table 9.8, they may account for the 'blips' in the generally inverse relationship portrayed in the table.

Table 9.8 Mean and variance of diversification by size of market share

Firms with *MS*	Number	Diversification (*ND*)	
		Mean	Variance
> 10%	18	1.76	1.06
7.5 – 10%	19	1.94	1.77
5 – 7.5%	35	2.19	2.06
2.5 – 5%	82	2.05	1.99
1 – 2.5%	106	2.54	3.75
0 – 1%	53	2.42	3.77

In any event, more definitive conclusions would be inappropriate (and are probably unnecessary) at this early stage in our research on the corporate structures of European firms. What is clear is that there is a rich variety of structures. Future research will help in explaining the choice of alternative strategies, and examining the effects those choices have on corporate perform-ance (e.g. growth and profitability). Here, we close this part of our analysis with a brief look at differences between firms with respect to aggregate size and nationality.

9.5.2 The Effect of Firm Size

Table 9.9 shows the (geometric) mean values of the components of the decom-position for each of seven aggregate size classes. With one exception, all three components rise with aggregate size—the exception is a slight dip in mean di-versification amongst the very largest firms, due to the concentration of spe-cialized car manufacturers in the top twenty.

When the class-mean values of *ND* are plotted against *MS*, in Figure 9.4, a distinct pattern emerges. First, there is a general tendency for larger size classes

Table 9.9 The decomposition by firm size class (geometric means)

Firms ranked	*FMSIZE*	*IS*	*MS*	*ND*	Normalized size (*FMSIZE/IS*)
1–20	14,661	59,635	8.98	2.74	0.25
	(12,594)	(37,049)	(8.46)	(4.01)	(0.34)
21–50	5,105	37,049	4.83	2.86	0.14
51–100	2,335	25,925	3.69	2.44	0.09
101–50	1,280	25,848	2.26	2.19	0.05
151–200	677	15,756	2.28	1.89	0.04
201–50	295	12,456	1.65	1.44	0.02
251–313	71	4,661	1.35	1.13	0.02
TOTAL	751	16,432	2.47	1.85	0.05

Note: 1–20 class: numbers in parentheses exclude the seven car manufacturers. See Table 9.5 for units.

The Dimensions of Corporate Strategy

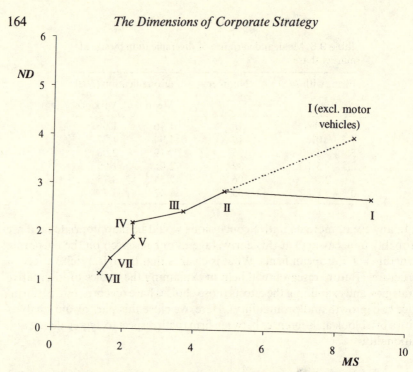

Fig. 9.4 Diversification and market share by aggregate size class
Key to size classes: I top 20; II firms 21–50; III firms 51–100; IV firms 101–150;
V firms 151–200; VI firms 201–250; VII firms 251–313

to lie further away from the origin: this as expected from Equation (9.4)—normalized size is higher for larger size classes. Second, successive points rise very steeply between the four lowest size classes, but the slope becomes much flatter between the four highest. In fact, it actually falls between the largest two classes. As already noted, the last point can be partly explained by the extreme car firm observations; and, if they are excluded (see the dotted line), the upward-sloping relationship re-emerges as quite stable amongst the four largest classes.

Whether or not the car firms are included, the diagram seems to tell a very distinctive story. The relative contribution of diversification to 'growth' in aggregate firm size is much more pronounced amongst smaller and medium sized firms; whilst typical market share takes on relatively more importance amongst the larger and largest firms. It remains for future research to establish whether this cross-firm static description has an analogous counterpart in the evolution of individual firms' structures over time.

9.5.3 The Effect of Firm Nationality

Table 9.10 and Figure 9.5 repeat the analysis, but this time grouping firms by their country of origin. Again, the figure clearly illustrates the main points of

Table 9.10 The decomposition by firm nationality (geometric means)

Country	FMSIZE	IS	MS	ND	Normalized size (FMSIZE/IS)
Germany	864	18,811	2.51	1.83	0.05
France	767	15,117	2.69	1.89	0.05
Italy	287	10,901	1.61	1.63	0.03
UK	983	19,503	2.30	2.19	0.05
Netherlands	1,949	25,926	3.36	2.24	0.08
Bel/Lux	443	14,721	1.91	1.58	0.03
Spain/Portugal	184	9,982	1.84	1.00	0.02
USA/Canada	1,245	16,711	4.32	1.72	0.07
EFTA	3,023	25,668	5.01	2.35	0.12
TOTALS	751	16,432	2.47	1.85	0.05

Note: See Table 9.5. for units.

interest. In terms of normalized size, the EFTA firms are by some way the largest (see Chapter 7); followed by the Dutch and North American;[8] the German, French, and UK firms are next, with virtually identical normalized size; Italian firms are noticeably smaller—more or less on par with the Belgians; and the Spanish and Portugese firms are the smallest by some way.

There are also some revealing differences within these groups. Whilst Dutch and North America are, on average, of broadly equal normalized aggregate size, the American firms attain this with a combination of high market shares and low diversification, but the reverse is true for Dutch firms. Similarly, in spite of the similar average sizes of German, British, and French firms, the British achieve this by higher diversification and lower market shares than do German or French firms.[9]

At this stage, these findings amount to little more than stylized facts. Although there appears to be a significant national dimension, simple bivariate comparisons can never establish causality on their own. In this case, for example, we have not controlled for a firm-size effect. Since the matrix includes many relatively smaller firms from Germany and Italy in particular, this may be important. The next chapter continues the investigation of diversification with a more explicit economic model.

9.6 Conclusion

This part of the book examines the structure of the leading European firms, using the market share database. A brief introduction on the aggregate firm-size distribution, shows that aggregate concentration, measured by the relative

[8] In fact, Dutch firms tend to be larger than Americans in absolute terms, but this is offset by the fact that they tend to operate in larger industries. It should be noted that, throughout the book, Shell and Unilever are counted as Dutch firms.
[9] This is as expected given the identities of the firms in Tables 9.6 and 9.7.

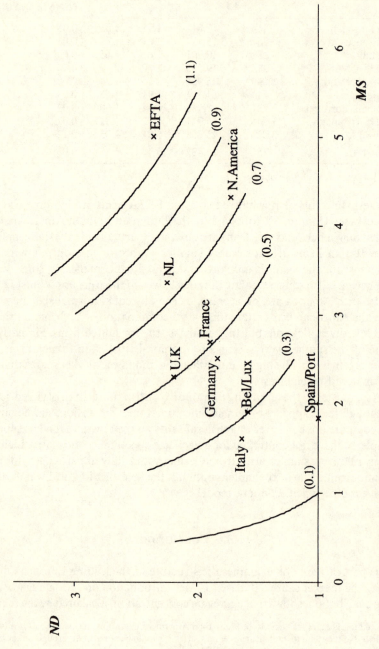

Fig. 9.5 Diversification and market share by nationality

size of the top fifty firms, in the EU is not dissimilar to that in either USA or Japan, although firms ranked 51–100 appear to be relatively smaller than their US counterparts. Aggregate concentration is not a major topic on the current book's agenda, but this result deserves some attention, especially from those concerned about the centralization of economic power in the EU.

This part of the book is devoted to an analysis of the ways in which different firms have achieved their current scales of operation. Aggregate size can be dis-aggregated, both in product space and in geographic space, and the individual components of the two decompositions can each be identified with different aspects of corporate strategy. This chapter has concentrated on the product decomposition. Statistically, the major influence on firms' sizes is the size of industries in which they are located: this is most vividly illustrated by the presence of seven major car firms amongst Europe's largest twenty manufacturing companies. Once this factor is controlled for, however, there is some evidence of a trade-off at work. Large size has been attained either by securing large market shares or with a wide portfolio of diversified operations across a range of industries, but rarely with both. The reasons for, and consequences of, these alternative strategies will have a central role in our future research programme. For now, we have presented some preliminary, largely descriptive, analysis which has provided a starting point. It appears that diversification rises relatively most rapidly with firm size amongst firms outside the top 100, whilst increasing market shares become increasingly important in 'explaining' size differences within the top 100. A number of differences can be observed between firms from the four largest member states: UK firms tend to be more diversified, French firms tend to have larger market shares, and Italian firms are typically smaller and German firms do not stand out as distinctive in any of these dimensions of corporate structure. The relatively few Dutch firms on the matrix are typically much larger—deriving from greater market shares, more diversification, and their location, typically, in larger industries. One of, the most striking results concerns non-EU-owned firms: whether originating from North America, Switzerland, or Sweden, they tend to achieve significantly larger market shares than their EU competitors, and the Swiss and Swedish firms also combine this with high levels of diversification—making them more than four times larger on average, than the typical matrix firm. This serves to remind us that, notwithstanding the EU's healthy balance on foreign direct investment, there is significant production, with market power implications, in many EU industries by 'foreign' multinationals.

STEVE DAVIES and BRUCE LYONS

10

Determinants of Diversification Patterns

10.1 Introduction

For a long time diversified firms have played a major role in both production and distribution activities in almost all industrialized countries. It is hardly surprising then that answers to questions such as why they exist and what effects they have on economic welfare can be traced back to the economic literature of the late 1950s and early 1960s. In the Penrose (1959) tradition, the firm is seen as a collection of specific assets that can be exploited in related activities. In the managerial theory of the firm (Marris, 1964), managers pursue diversification strategies to maximize growth and to reduce risks. More recently, the concept of the multi-product firm has been fully incorporated into neoclassical production theory and the implications of diversified entry, multi-market contacts, tie-in sales, etc. have become important issues in modern industrial organization theory. On the empirical side, the focus has progressively widened from the measurement of the extent of diversification and its general causes, to the study of diversification patterns and directions[1].

This chapter has two main purposes. First, we give a detailed picture of the extent of diversification within the EU's leading firms. This extends the work in Chapter 9 by distinguishing diversification within and across broad industry groups. Second, we undertake an econometric study of the determinants of diversification patterns. In part, this replicates for the EU previous studies which used North American firm/industry data, but we depart from them in two respects: we are able to exploit cross-member state differences to test for alternative behavioural hypotheses; and we use a much richer set of variables measuring specific assets for which we compute the net effect on the likelihood of linkages among industries.

The chapter is organized as follows. The next section defines the main concepts and discusses the characteristics and the limitations of the data. A range of descriptive statistics on the extent of diversification amongst the EU's leading firms are reported, thus widening the initial picture presented in the previous

---

[1] In recent years several authors have tried to explain the determinants of diversification patterns, for example: Lemelin (1982), MacDonald (1985), Schwalbach (1987), Montgomery and Hariharan (1991), Hamilton (1992), and Ingham and Thompson (1992).

chapter. Section 10.3 briefly reviews the seminal contributions and some more recent work on the determinants of diversification patterns, and provides the rationale behind the model estimated in the following section. Section 10.4 explains the technical details of the model and presents the empirical findings. Section 5 concludes.

10.2 Measuring the Extent of Diversification

Throughout the book, independent companies, or groups of affiliated firms, which have production facilities in more than one 3-digit NACE industry are defined as diversified. The analysis is limited to product diversification (geographical diversification is addressed in the next chapter)[2].

10.2.1 Representativeness of the Sample

At the outset, it may be worth recalling a few features of our sample which have a direct bearing on diversification. Remember first that firms are included in this sample because they are one of the five EU leaders in at least one industry. Whilst this produces a sample which includes most of Europe's very largest firms (see Section 3.5), some conglomerate firms ranked among the largest companies in individual countries may not appear because they are insufficiently large in any single industry at the EU level.[3] Conversely, the sample includes some leading firms, in either small or very fragmented industries, who are often specialized with relatively small turnovers. Second, we know that the smaller member states are underrepresented compared to their EU manufacturing share (see Section 9.2); moreover, they are often represented only by single-product firms operating in small industries in which they have a competitive advantage. Equally, different industrial structures, and differences in international specialization lead to a selection of firms which do not always coincide with the national largest firms. Thus our indices are only a rather rough indicator of the average level of diversification in each country.

Two further comments are worth making, relating to the product and geographic extent of diversification. First, no attention is paid to diversification outside the manufacturing sector; all activities concerning agriculture, mining, extraction, the primary transformation of energy sources, and services have not been considered. We are conscious that this represents a limit to our analysis. Leading firms operating in mature industries with increasing competition tend to integrate forward into distribution or high value-added services. For example, Hamilton (1991) found for New Zealand that non-manufacturing industries have in recent years increased their importance as target sectors for diversification, and that these moves represent in some cases the bulk of the

---

[2] As always in this book, diversification is defined broadly to indicate a firm operating in more than one industry. Necessarily therefore, this will include vertical integration.

[3] Two striking examples are Montedison (Italy) and INI (Spain).

diversification process. He shows that, in New Zealand in 1987 and 1988, almost 70% of non-primary employment was in non-manufacturing sectors.

Second, the geographical boundary of the data collection exercise is limited to production within the EU. The activities of both EU and non-EU multinationals are considered, but production facilities located outside the EU are not taken into account. If the purpose of the exercise is to compare the extent of diversification of different types of firms, this is likely to be a major problem in the case of non-EU multinationals, and especially in the case of non-European multinationals. Once again, our results must be interpreted in the context of the extent of diversification within the EU, and not at the global level of diversification[4].

10.2.2 Alternative Indexes of Diversification

In this chapter, three alternative indexes of diversification for each firm *i* have been computed:

- the number of industries in which the firm operates: N_i,
- the diversification ratio: DR_i. This is defined as the share of total production undertaken outside the firm's primary industry.
- Berry's index: Di. This is as used in the previous chapter (see Table 9.3), and is defined more fully in Appendix 1, Section $A1.3.1$.

Note that to calculate the diversification ratio, each of the matrix firms has been assigned to a primary activity, which is simply the industry accounting for the largest share of its total manufacturing production in the EU; all other production is classified as secondary activities.

We have chosen the Berry index instead of other available indices with similar properties (e.g. the entropy index or the Utton index) because it is part of the Chapter 9 decomposition of firm size and it also has the appealing number equivalent interpretation ($ND_i = [1 - D_i]^{-1}$). But our two other indices, Ni and DRi, are appealing for their simplicity and their immediate interpretability. For the sake of expositional clarity, we shall drop the *i* subscripts in the remainder of this chapter.

10.2.3 Descriptive Statistics

Of the 313 matrix firms, 223 are diversified. Table 10.1 reports descriptive statistics for the three indices. Each index has been computed at both the 2- and 3-digit levels, thus allowing us to distinguish, albeit fairly crudely, between related (i.e. within the primary 2-digit sector) and conglomerate (i.e. outside the primary 2-digit sector) diversification[5].

---

[4] For example, the Japanese multinational, Asahi Glass, appears to be a single-industry firm at the EU level but is a very diversified company at the world level.

[5] The ability of the NACE classification to accurately reflect this distinction is, of course, open to debate, given its emphasis on technological relatedness. Incidentally, Utton (1979) refers alternatively, to 'narrow' and 'broad spectrum' diversification.

Table 10.1 Three measures of diversification: summary statistics

	Number of industries N_i		Production outside primary industry(%) DR_i		Berry index % D_i	
	3digit	2-digit	3-digit	2-digit	3-digit	2-digit
Mean	4.9	2.9	28.3	17.1	0.37	0.23
Std. dev.	4.8	2.3	26.0	20.4	0.31	0.25
Max.	33	13	84.8	75.0	0.90	0.83
Min.	1	1	0	0	0	0

As can be seen, by no means all diversification is related within-sector. The average firm operates in 4.9 3-digit industries and in 2.89 2-digit industries; 28% of its total output is produced outside its primary 3- digit industry, and 17% outside its primary 2- digit industry. Comparing the two figures, it follows that as much as 60% of diversified activities is 'unrelated' to the primary activity. The values of the Berry index correspond to number equivalents of 1.6 3-digit industries and 1.3 2-digit sectors.[6]

As reported in the previous chapter, standard deviations are quite high, and for this reason it is important to see the distributions of the three indices. Figures 10.1(b) and 10.1(c) reveal an interesting feature of 3-digit diversification for two of the indices: excluding the non-diversified firms, the shapes of the distribution for both D_i and DR_i are asymmetric, with higher frequencies occurring at above-average levels of diversification. The modal values (0.6–0.7 for the D index and 50-60% for the diversification ratio) are rather higher than their respective means, (0.52 and 39.6% when computed after excluding the non-diversified firms). Thus, if a firm is at all diversified, it will probably be quite significantly so. Although such a pattern is not as clear at the 2-digit level, a significant number of firms display extensive conglomerate diversification.

When the sample is disaggregated by country of origin, results broadly confirm the conventional wisdom (and results of the previous chapter) about the extent of diversification in each member state. According to all our indices, the most diversified countries, at the 3-digit level, are the United Kingdom and the Netherlands; France has a value very close to the EU average, while Italy and Germany are below the average. The EFTA firms are the most highly diversified of all, while the North Americans show a low degree of diversification. If we compute the proportion of diversified activities lying outside the primary

---

[6] The summary statistics for the Berry index differ from those reported in the previous chapter (in Table 9.4 for example) for two reasons. First, here we concentrate on the D index itself, whilst Chapter 9 uses the reciprocal number-equivalent form; and the reciprocal of mean D will not be identical to the mean of the reciprocal of D. Second, here we use arithmetic means while Chapter 9 uses geometric means.

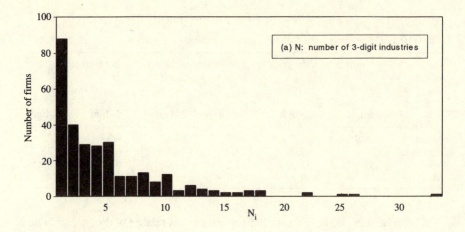

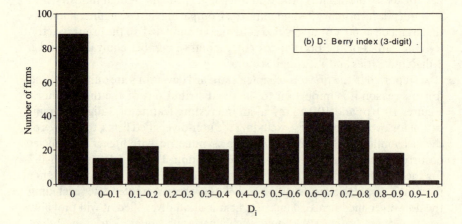

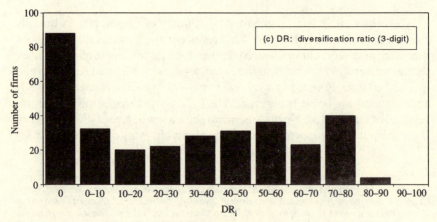

Fig. 10.1 Distribution of firms by related diversification

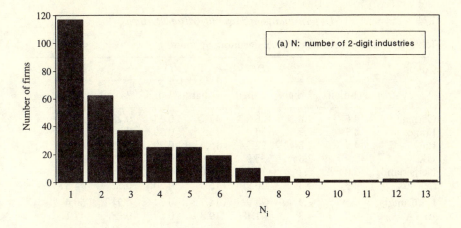

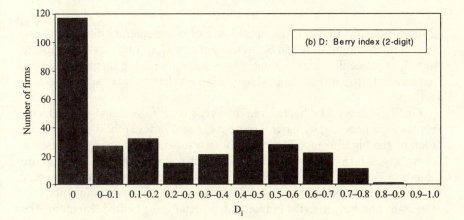

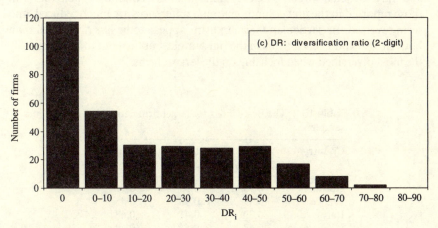

Fig. 10.2 Distribution of firms by conglomerate diversification

Table 10.2 Three measures of diversification: by country

Country	N		DR		D		Ratio of DR 2-digit to 3-digit
	3-digit	2-digit	3-digit	2-digit	3-digit	2-digit	
Germany	4.6	2.8	26.2	17.7	0.33	0.23	62.3
France	4.7	2.9	30.0	16.8	0.39	0.24	57.5
Italy	4.9	2.8	22.5	15.4	0.29	0.21	64.0
UK	5.7	3.3	37.0	20.9	0.48	0.29	55.4
Netherlands	5.0	2.7	35.6	17.6	0.45	0.24	39.0
Bel/Lux	4.3	2.8	20.9	15.0	0.30	0.22	74.8
US/Canada	4.5	2.9	24.9	14.7	0.34	0.21	60.4
EFTA	9.0	4.3	41.1	19.3	0.57	0.28	47.1
TOTALS	4.9	2.9	28.3	17.1	0.37	0.23	60.1

2-digit industry, we get a rough measure of conglomerate diversification. Rather interestingly, Italy and Belgium, i.e. the two EU countries where private as well as public financial holdings play a major role in the shaping of the organizational structure of firms, show the largest share of unrelated secondary activities.

Finally, to check whether this ranking is robust to differences between member states in firm size, we have re-computed the D index at the 3-digit level for each of the big four member states for two sub-samples of large firms: the thirty largest firms and the largest 50% of each country's firms. The results are shown in Table 10.3. As expected, the mean D value increases in each country when we focus only on the larger firms; however, it increases far more for Germany and Italy than for France and, especially, the United Kingdom. The reason lies in the high number of relatively small specialized firms in Germany and Italy. In fact, if we compare the results in the last column of Table 10.3 with those reported in the first column, national differences are much reduced, and seem reversed. In particular, German firms appear to be less diversified than both British and French firms in the full sample, but turn out to be marginally the most diversified when focusing on the largest firms.

Table 10.3 The Berry index for larger firm national samples

Country	Full sample	Largest 30 firms	Largest 50% firms
Germany	0.33	0.59	0.56
France	0.39	0.48	0.48
Italy	0.29	0.41	0.48
UK	0.48	0.54	0.54

10.3 Explaining Patterns of Diversification

10.3.1 Theoretical Background

As recognized in the introduction, a variety of theories would provide a suitable background for empirical research on diversification, although recent studies have mostly focused on hypotheses derived from either the theory of the firm or recent industrial organization theory. We draw on three strands in the existing literature, with particular emphasis on the relatedness of the industries into which firms diversify.

The managerial, growth-oriented motivation, as suggested by Marris (1964), is probably the best-known traditional explanation of why some firms are more likely to diversify than others. A complementary explanation is given by the Coase (1937), Penrose (1959), and Teece (1980, 1982) view of the firm as a collection of specific assets. If such resources, and the services they support, are not exhausted in a firm's current operations, it may be profitable for the firm to use them in new activities (see also Rubin, 1973). Good examples are technological and marketing skills. Provided market transaction costs are not negligible, this may provide an important inducement for a firm to enter new markets. In this respect the firm's decision, or propensity, to diversify will depend on its current stocks of assets—its 'organizational capital' (Prescott and Vischer, 1980). A vector of firm characteristics, reflecting such assets, should accordingly be included in an explanation of outbound diversification, along with variables representing the constraints on further expansion by the firm in its primary industry. However, the lack of available data on firm-specific variables dictates that we shall have to use industry characteristics of the firm's principal activity as proxies.

Stemming from Bain's (1956) analysis of entry conditions, there are a number of hypotheses for why some industries are more likely to attract entry by well-established firms than from small start-up firms. Of most direct relevance here, are the industry-specific characteristics which might reflect the relative attractiveness of investment in an industry. In this respect, profit opportunities and industry growth are generally viewed as measures of *per se* attractiveness of the target industry; high seller concentration within the destination industry might also attract entry, given the prospects of high rates of return, but concentration is also associated with both barriers to entry and the risk of incumbents' retaliation (Lemelin, 1982). However, the role of classical barriers to entry, and especially product differentiation, needs refocusing when the relative advantages of incumbent firms are due to intangible assets that are not industry-specific (Montgomery and Hariharan, 1991). If, for instance, R&D and selling activities are viewed as a collection of assets specific to the firm but transferable across industries, the traditional sources of entry barriers may act as *inducements* for entry by firms well established in other industries where such resources are already available (Yip, 1982).

A third body of research has followed Rumelt's (1974) idea that relationships between different activities will matter in a firm's diversification strategy. Of particular interest to us are the relationships based on (i) markets served and distribution systems; (ii) R&D activities; (iii) similarities in production organizations or techniques. Thus, a firm may have a competitive advantage in, say, R&D, in which case both its primary and secondary activities should be R&D-intensive. Stewart, Harris, and Carleton (1984) give a twist to this idea, by positing that management specialization will affect the choice of the firm to merge with (or the industry to diversify into). From this perspective, relatedness variables—such as advertising or R&D-intensity—are viewed as proxies for the managerial environment, and their significance may be indicative of a preference for mergers with firms that are broadly similar.

The role of inter-industry relatedness is also apparent when transaction cost considerations are applied to suppliers' relations (Williamson, 1979). Where there is the possibility of vertical integration, a firm is more likely to diversify into an industry which is an important supplier or customer. For similar transaction-cost reasons, whenever critical organizational resources, e.g. know-how and brand name, display characteristics of public goods and can be used in different activities, economies of scope fuel diversification, provided transfer via markets is costly relative to internal allocation (Teece, 1980, 1982).

10.3.2 An Econometric Model

We take an 'encompassing' approach, by using information on firm characteristics, primary industry, secondary industry, and relatedness variables to investigate the factors that affect diversification (see Lemelin, 1982 and MacDonald, 1985, for a similar approach). The fact that we have only a snapshot of the pattern of diversification of the leading firms in the EU in 1987 limits us to a static approach, looking at diversity at a point in time rather than flows of diversification or entry decisions over time. Therefore, we shall define a diversified firm simply as one which is engaged in more than one 3-digit manufacturing industry, and attempt to explain instances of diversification into other industries. In that sense, we study the pattern of diversification linkages. In fact, empirical evidence from MacDonald (1985) shows that the results of previous logit analyses of static linkages are quite similar to those from dynamic studies of entry.

Formally our theoretical dependent variable is $P(F, P, S)$, the probability that firm F, with primary activity in industry P, is diversified into secondary industry S. Then a probabilistic model of the pattern of diversification can be written as:

$$P(F,P,S) = f\{ W(F), X(P), Y(S), Z(P,S)\} \qquad (10.1)$$

where $W(F)$ is a vector of characteristics of firm F; $X(P)$ is a vector of characteristics of the firm's primary industry; $Y(S)$ is a vector of characteristics of the potential secondary industry S; and $Z(P, S)$ is a vector of variables describing relatedness between P and S. This specification departs from previous empirical research (Lemelin, 1982, MacDonald, 1985; Montgomery and Hariharan, 1991) in that it includes both a set of firm-specific variables and a list of primary industry characteristics.

Following the Penrose–Marris theory, our vector of firm-specific variables includes firm size ($FMSIZE$), the idea being that large firms have access to more resources than smaller ones. A measure of the firm's home country size ($NATSIZE$), is included to control for domestic market constraints to growth. The 'managerial capitalism' explanation of diversification is proxied by adding a dummy variable for the relative importance of the home country's stock market ($MANAGER$), which reflects the separation between ownership and control.

The vector of primary industry characteristics includes advertising, $ADS(P)$; R&D, $RDS(P)$; and productive skills, $SKILL(P)$. These are used as proxies for the 'organizational capital' which is embodied in the firm's marketing, research, and production organizations. The idea is that, under certain conditions, a collection of specific assets can be profitably applied across industries, thus encouraging diversification. Likewise, the primary industry's capital intensity, $CAPOUT(P)$, is included to capture the idea that a particular know-how develops in managing capital-intensive industries, thus providing a basis for diversified expansion (Montgomery and Hariharan, 1991).

The vector of characteristics of target industries, $Y(S)$ includes variables measuring the degree of attractiveness of investment in an industry, particularly in terms of growth, $GROWTH(S)$, and profit opportunity, $PCM(S)$, (see Lemelin, 1982, Hamilton, 1991 and Montgomery and Hariharan, 1991). Secondary industry R&D, $RDS(S)$, advertising $ADS(S)$, human capital $SKILL(S)$, and capital intensity $CAPOUT(S)$ are traditionally viewed as deterring entry, thus reducing the likelihood of a link through diversification (Hamilton, 1991). However, an alternative perspective suggests that economies of scope may give well-established firms an inducement for diversification if such resources are not industry specific and may thus be transferred across industries.

Four variables representing inter-industry relatedness, $DRDS$, $DADS$, $DSKILL$, and $DCAPOUT$, are included on the grounds that the more closely an industry is related to the primary activity of the firm, the more likely it will be chosen as a target for diversification. These variables are constructed as absolute differences between the primary and secondary industry values (e.g. $DRDS = |\,RDS(P) - RDS(S)\,|$) (see MacDonald, 1985). We expect these variables to enter negatively in the decision to diversify. Following Williamson's arguments on vertical integration, we also include two dichotomous variables proxying forward and backward vertical linkages, FVL and BVL, based on the input-output matrix: both should encourage diversification.

These variables and their sources are summarized in the Appendix to this chapter, and further details can be found in appendix 3 to the book.

10.4 Econometric Results

The operational form of our dependent variable is $D(F, P, S)$, a dummy variable which is equal to 1 for all the cases where a given firm F, from primary industry P, is diversified into industry S. If diversification into S has not occurred, $D = O$. Recalling that the matrix includes 100 industries and 313 firms, since each firm is classified to a single primary industry (i.e. the industry which accounts for the largest share of its total production), it follows that there must be $313 * 99 = 30,987$ possible instances of diversification. In fact, we know from Table 10.1 that firms operate on average in 4.9 industries; therefore, $D = 1$ in 3.9% of all cases.

We also initially split the sample into two subsamples, the former including all the pairs of vertically related industries and the latter including all others. 9.0% of industry pairs have vertical links. The differences between the two subsamples are quite striking. In the sample of vertically related pairs, diversification occurs in 15.9% of cases, whereas in the no-linkage sample the share is far lower, at 2.8%.

Table 10.4 reports the results of logit analyses of diversification, $D(F,P,S)$, both for the full sample (Equation 1) and for the subsample excluding vertically related pairs of industries (Equation 2). The estimates should be interpreted as determining the probability that firm F operating in primary industry P is diversified in secondary industry S.

In both equations almost all the coefficients are significant and those for which we had strong *a priori* hypotheses, are correctly signed. Large firms are more likely to be diversified than small firms, as can be seen from the positive coefficient on *FMSIZE*. The positive coefficient on *MANAGER* suggests that the country of origin matters as far as the functioning of capital markets is concerned: firms originating from countries where the separation between ownership and control is wide-spread are more likely to be diversified.[7] On the other hand, the size of the domestic market (*NATSIZE*) does not appear to have any significant impact on the probability of diversification. This serves to reinforce the view expressed at the end of Section 10.2.3, that nationality matters less once firm size is taken into account.

As far as R&D is concerned, the coefficients on both primary and secondary industries are positively significant and of similar size, whereas the coefficient on the difference in R&D intensities (*DRDS*) is negative and slightly smaller than the others in absolute value. Given the algebraic relation between these three variables, the net influence of R&D on diversification is intriguing, but complex. As an aid to interpretation, Table 10.5 uses the estimated coefficients to show how the likelihood of linkages varies with alternative R&D intensities (assuming representative values for the other variables in the equation). The results can be summarized as follows: reading along the rows tells us that firms

---

[7] This helps to explain the descriptive evidence from Table 10.2 that UK and Dutch firms are amongst the most diversified.

Table 10.4 Logit analysis of diversification

	Equation 1 Full sample	Equation 2 Excl. vert. links	Equation 3 Diversified firms only	Equation 4 Diversified excl. vert. linkages
CONSTANT	−7.43	−6.75	−6.12	−5.77
	(8.15)	(6.18)	(6.58)	(5.22)
FMSIZE	0.047	0.048	0.033	0.035
	(5.79)	(5.54)	(3.52)	(3.55)
MANAGER	0.004	0.005	−0.0003	0.0005
	(4.68)	(4.80)	(0.31)	(0.48)
NATSIZE	−0.010	−0.038	−0.022	−0.042
	(0.32)	(1.08)	(0.71)	(1.19)
RDS(P)	0.148	0.123	0.162	0.132
	(8.49)	(6.39)	(8.49)	(6.45)
ADS(P)	0.278	0.246	0.315	0.277
	(6.88)	(5.41)	(7.70)	(6.00)
CAPOUT(P)	1.001	0.668	0.893	0.558
	(7.54)	(3.73)	(6.47)	(3.03)
SKILL(P)	1.161	1.140	0.014	0.165
	(2.65)	(2.21)	(0.03)	(0.31)
RDS(S)	0.130	0.120	0.138	0.126
	(7.54)	(6.32)	(7.35)	(6.21)
ADS(S)	0.105	0.083	0.115	0.099
	(2.67)	(1.93)	(2.87)	(2.27)
CAPOUT(S)	−0.326	−0.387	−0.377	−0.400
	(2.49)	(2.14)	(2.83)	(2.21)
SKILL(S)	3.256	3.669	3.144	3.666
	(7.94)	(7.40)	(7.59)	(7.36)
GROWTH(S)	0.332	0.384	0.330	0.378
	(2.15)	(2.08)	(2.13)	(2.02)
PCM(S)	1.525	0.948	1.442	1.029
	(1.94)	(1.00)	(1.80)	(1.08)
FVL	1.406	—	1.311	—
	(17.2)	—	(15.95)	—
BVL	0.936	—	1.134	—
	(8.86)	—	(10.5)	—
DRDS	−0.117	−0.097	−0.125	−0.103
	(6.36)	(4.86)	(6.28)	(4.88)
DADS	−0.274	−0.234	−0.299	−0.265
	(6.13)	(4.60)	(6.64)	(5.17)
DCAPOUT	−0.430	−0.580	−0.479	−0.576
	(2.88)	(2.86)	(3.16)	(2.83)
DSKILL	−6.991	−7.804	−6.768	−7.449
	(15.02)	(14.0)	(14.4)	(13.2)
Cases	30,987	28,192	22,077	19,801
Log-Likelihood	−4,399	−3,245	−4,076	−3,017
Restricted L-L	−5,145	−3,556	−4,721	−3,277
X^2	1,492	624	1,289	521

Note: *t*-ratios in parentheses.

Determinants of Diversification Patterns

Table 10.5 Probability of diversification between industry pairs with alternative asset intensities[a]

(a) Research and development (sample mean = 0.6%)

		RDS(S)					
	%	0	1	2	3	4	5
	0	2.19	2.22	2.25	2.27	2.30	2.33
	1	2.26	2.87	2.91	2.94	2.98	3.02
RDS(P)	2	2.33	2.96	3.76	3.81	3.85	3.90
	3	2.40	3.05	3.87	4.91	4.97	5.03
	4	2.47	3.14	3.99	5.05	6.38	6.45
	5	2.55	3.24	4.11	5.20	6.56	8.25

(b) Advertising (sample mean = 1.3%)

		ADS(S)					
	%	0	1	2	3	4	5
	0	2.50	2.12	1.80	1.52	1.29	1.09
	1	2.51	3.62	3.08	2.61	2.22	1.88
ADS(P)	2	2.52	3.64	5.22	4.45	3.79	3.22
	3	2.53	3.65	5.25	7.48	6.40	5.46
	4	2.54	3.67	5.27	7.51	10.60	9.11
	5	2.55	3.69	5.29	7.55	10.65	14.82

(c) Human skills (sample mean = 44.6%)

		SKILL(S)					
	%	0	10	20	30	40	50
	0	0.76	0.53	0.36	0.25	0.17	0.12
	10	0.43	1.18	0.82	0.56	0.39	0.27
SKILL(P)	20	0.24	0.66	1.82	1.26	0.87	0.60
	30	0.13	0.37	1.03	2.81	1.95	1.35
	40	0.07	0.21	0.58	1.59	4.31	3.01
	50	0.04	0.12	0.32	0.89	2.45	6.54

(d) Physical capital (sample mean = 49.7%)

		CAPOUT(S)					
	%	0	10	20	30	40	50
	0	2.00	1.85	1.72	1.60	1.48	1.38
	10	2.11	2.13	1.98	1.84	1.71	1.58
CAPOUT(P)	20	2.23	2.25	2.28	2.12	1.96	1.82
	30	2.36	2.38	2.41	2.43	2.26	2.10
	40	2.50	2.52	2.55	2.57	2.60	2.41
	50	2.64	2.67	2.69	2.72	2.75	2.78

[a] Other variables held at their mean values.

operating in a given primary industry tend to be diversified in secondary industries with the same or higher R&D intensity; second, reading down the columns shows that secondary industries attract diversification from firms operating in primary industries with the same or higher R&D intensity. Putting both points together, R&D is both a push and a pull for diversification. Finally, by reading down the diagonals, we see that firms operating in high R&D-intensity primary industries are more likely to be diversified in high R&D-intensity secondary industries than are firms operating in low R&D-intensity primary industries to be diversified in low R&D-intensity secondary industries.

Now consider the coefficients on advertising intensity. In exactly the same pattern as the R&D case, the coefficients on primary $ADS(P)$ and secondary $ADS(S)$ are both positively significant, whilst that on the difference $(DADS)$ is negatively significant. However, the net effects differ for two reasons: first, the coefficient on primary industry advertising intensity is larger than that on secondary industry intensity, suggesting an asymmetry in behaviour; second, the coefficient measuring relatedness is slightly larger in absolute value than that on the primary industry intensity, and much larger than that on secondary industry intensity. The net effects can be seen from part (b) of Table 10.5. Reading across the rows, firms operating in a given primary industry are more likely to be diversified in secondary industries with the same advertising intensity; reading down the columns, secondary activities only attract diversification from industries with similar or higher advertising; and reading down the diagonals, firms operating in high advertising-intensity primary industries are diversified into high advertising-intensity secondary industries far more often than firms operating in low advertising-intensity primary industries are diversified in low advertising-intensity secondary industries.

The broad signs and significance of labour skills are again similar to advertising and R&D, but again there are some interesting differences. The net effects of human capital intensity are reported in Table 10.5(c). First, as for advertising, firms operating in a given primary industry tend to be diversified in secondary industries with the same human skill intensity; second, unlike for advertising and R&D, secondary industries are also more likely to attract firms from industries with similar skill levels; third, as with the previous two asset intensities, firms operating in primary industries where skilled workers are an important share of the work-force are more likely to be diversified in secondary industries of the same type than firms operating in low human-skilled primary industries are to be diversified in low human-skilled secondary industries.

Summarizing the results obtained so far, specific assets seem to play a major role in explaining firms' diversification strategies. Furthermore, relatedness also matters crucially, since when firms diversify, they tend to enter industries with similar characteristics to those of the primary industry. It follows that for well-established firms, entry barriers seem to be at work only for firms lacking the required specific assets.

Whereas R&D, advertising, and human skill intensity have similar broad effects on the probability of linkages, the coefficients on physical capital intensity tell us a completely different story, in that the coefficient on secondary industry capital intensity *CAPOUT(S)* is negative and significant. This suggests that while the previous characteristics do not act as barriers to diversification, capital intensity does reduce the attractiveness of an industry as a secondary activity. As part (d) of the table shows, however, the quantitative effects are small.

The attraction of secondary industries which are fast growing and profitable is also confirmed by the logit analysis, though the significance of the latter is weak. Finally, trading relations between industries increase the likelihood of ownership linkages, as can be seen from the positive coefficients on *FVL* and *BVL* in Equation 1. Perhaps surprisingly, forward sales seem to be a stronger incentive than input purchases.

Finally, Equations 3 and 4 in Table 10.4 report the results of re-estimation when the ninety non-diversified firms are excluded from the sample. In this case, observations of $D = 1$ rise to 5.5% of the total, and the probability must now be interpreted as conditional on the fact that the firm is diversified. The results are quite similar to those already discussed for the full sample with one important exception: the coefficient on *MANAGER* is now no longer significantly different from zero. Thus, managerial independence affects the initial decision to diversify, but not the subsequent pattern.

10.5 Conclusion

Four main descriptive results emerge from our statistical analysis on the extent of diversification among the EU's leading firms. First, a sizeable number of firms, about 30%, are specialized in only one 3-digit manufacturing industry. Second, if we exclude these non-diversified firms from the sample the share of secondary activities in total production is on average rather large (about 40%). Third, differences in the extent of diversification among countries exist, even if such differences are mainly a consequence of the particular characteristics of our sample.

However, if we restrict our analysis to the big four EU countries, British firms seem to be more diversified and Italian firms less diversified than the average. Fourth, cross-countries differences also emerge in the share of broad, conglomerate diversification. In particular, Italian and Belgian firms show the largest share of non-correlated activities (i.e. share of diversification outside the primary 2-digit industry). It is interesting to note that these two countries also differ from the rest of the EU in terms of corporate control structures. In particular, the important role played by industrial holdings, probably adopting financial portfolio strategies, may at least partly explain the presence of high shares of conglomerate diversification.

Given the nature of our data, the econometric analysis focused on the determinants of the existing pattern of diversification and not on the determinants of entry or exit decisions. To model the probability of linkages among pairs of industries for a given firm's characteristics, we considered simultaneously the effects of the primary industry resource bases, the secondary industry attractiveness/barriers to entry, and the relatedness among pairs of industries. The overall pattern suggests a fascinating story where firms' specific assets not only explain the extent but also the pattern of diversification, in the sense that firms tend to diversify in industries that seem to match the available resources. Traditional barriers to entry still have a role to play, but only for those firms whose pool of resources is not adequate.

LAURA RONDI, ALESSANDRO SEMBENELLI, and ELENA RAGAZZI

APPENDIX to Chapter 10

Variable Definitions and Data Sources

D(F, P, S):   Diversification. D = 1 if firm F, based in primary industry P, produces in secondary industry S; D = 0 otherwise.
FMSIZE: Firm size, 1987 EU production in the primary activity.
NATSIZE: National size of home base, 1987. Gross Domestic Product.
RDS: Simple average of 1987 UK and Italy R&D to sales ratio.
ADS: UK 1987 advertising to sales ratio.
MANAGER: Managerial capitalism. Percentage share of GDP supplied by enterprises quoted on the Stock Exchange (FIBV Statistics, 1992).
SKILL: Share of skilled workers in total employment at two-digit level (Structure of Earnings 1978–9, Eurostat).
CAPOUT: UK 1987 capital–output ratio.
GROWTH: 1984–9 EC apparent consumption growth rate (Eurostat).
PCM: 1987 price–cost margin (Eurostat).
FVL: Forward vertical linkage. Dummy variable = 1 if intermediate input sales from the primary industry to the secondary industry account for more than 5% of total intermediate inputs of the secondary industry; 0 otherwise. (Source: Italian 1984 input–output table).
BVL: Backward vertical linkage. Dummy variable = 1 if the intermediate inputs from the secondary industry to the primary industry account for more than 5% of total intermediate inputs to the primary industry; 0 otherwise. (Source: Italian 1984 input–output table).
*(P):   Value of variable * in the primary industry.
*(S):   Value of variable * in secondary industry.
D*:   Absolute difference in value of * in primary and secondary industries.
Data sources: unless otherwise shown, see Appendix 3.

11

Multinationality at the Firm Level

11.1 Introduction

This chapter moves our examination of corporate strategy from the product to the spatial dimension. Any large firm potentially faces choices on how to arrange its production across the member states within the EU: should it concentrate operations in its home base, or expand into other member states? Just as there may be a trade-off in product space between increasing market shares and diversification, so, in geographic space, increasing spatial dispersion may be an alternative to an increasing share in the home economy[1].

Naturally, this chapter overlaps to some extent with the industry-level analysis of multinationality in Chapter 7: undoubtedly, some firms will be more multinational than others because of the types of industries in which they operate. However, a firm-level analysis widens the perspective. For example, it is possible that a firm may have multinational operations *across* industries, whilst being uninational *within* individual industries. This might happen when a vertically integrated firm locates its production of an intermediate product, *A*, and the finished product, *B*, in different countries. Similarly, a diversified non-EU multinational may choose to locate its production operations in each industry in a different member state. In such cases, firms are multinational, whilst industries may not be. We can also explore multinationality as a two-stage decision: Which factors influence a firm's decision on whether or not to 'go multinational'? And, if it does: What determines the extent of its multinational operations?

The other new angle concerns the role of firm nationality. Are firms from certain member states more likely to be more multinational than others; and, if so, why? It is sometimes argued that firms from some countries are innately more predisposed to international production than others. In its crudest form, this hypothesis points to national stereotypes, perhaps invoking cultural, historical, and sociological differences—this is difficult to test rigorously with the sort of data at our disposal. Rather more amenable to investigation here is the proposition that a firm's corporate strategy, especially concerning growth, is influenced by the characteristics of its home economy. This might affect the

---

[1] The next chapter considers the possibility that the spatial and product decisions may be interdependent.

multinationality choice in a variety of ways. For instance, firms from smaller countries tend to face constraints on growth much earlier than firms from bigger countries; and, although diversification into adjacent industries may be one way of pushing back the domestic constraint to growth, even this may be limited in smaller countries. If so, the multinational option may offer the only real option for sustained growth. Alternatively, a home base of limited scale may prevent the firm from building a strong springboard for overseas success. Especially in industries where international competitiveness demands a specific asset or large production scale, firms from smaller countries may be unable to establish a foothold in the market even in their own countries. In this chapter, we assess how far differences between firms from different member states can be explained by differences in the size of the home market.

Nevertheless, much of the analysis in Chapter 7 remains relevant at the firm level; for instance, we would expect to confirm a strong relationship between multinationality and product differentiation. This present chapter offers an opportunity to test the robustness of the econometric results in Chapter 7 on a larger database (313 firms, as opposed to the 100 industries), whilst now allowing for the possibility of intra- as well as inter- industry differences.

Section 11.2 presents our estimates of multinationality for the 313 matrix firms, and briefly discusses the broad differences between the member states. Section 11.3 introduces the spatial decomposition of *FMSIZE* and assesses the relative contributions of multinationality and country share to aggregate firm size; it also takes the inter-country analysis a little further. Section 11.4 is the main part of the chapter. It tests an econometric model of multinationality at the firm level which recognizes size and industry influences as well as residual inter-country differences. Section 11.5 concludes by answering the question: Are differences between firms explicable purely in terms of size, constraints to growth, and industrial structures, or is there a country-specific effect which remains even after controlling for these other factors?

11.2 Measurement and extent of multinationality within the EU

Multinationality is measured using the index introduced in Chapter 7. For firm i, operating in up to eleven member states, if x_{ik} denotes its output in member state k, then the M index and its number equivalent are:

$$M_i = 1 - \sum_k (x_{ik})^2 / (x_i)^2 \tag{11.1}$$

and

$$NM_i = (1 - M_i)^{-1} \tag{11.2}$$

However, in this chapter, we do *not* distinguish the industries in which the firm operates; instead we focus on its aggregate multinationality across all industries. Note then that, even if a firm is not multinational in any one industry (i.e. $M_{ij} = 0$ for all j), it may yet record a non-zero value for M_i if it produces in different industries in different member states.

Of the matrix firms 176 are multinational by this criterion, and Figure 11.1 shows the distribution of NM across the sample, excluding the 137 firms without multinational production. Even without these uninational firms, the distribution is positively skewed, and a further eighty-four firms record low values ($1 < NM < 1.5$). In other words, only ninety-two firms arrange their EU production with substantial amounts outside their home country.[2]

Table 11.1 lists the top 100 firms by NM values (the last two columns are explained in the next section). Two features of the firms towards the top of the list are immediately apparent. First, although most are amongst the top 100 firms ranked by aggregate size, very few are the real giants: only two of the fifty most multinational firms are from the top ten ranked by aggregate size, and only four are from the top twenty. Second, non-EU firms dominate at the very top: the four most multinational firms are all American, and they are closely followed by two Swiss firms and then a further American. Indeed, within the top twenty, there are only seven EU owned firms—three each from the UK and Holland, and one Belgian firm. Remembering that our data refer only to production *within* the EU, it would be dangerous to draw any comparative conclusions about the *world-wide* multinationality of firms from these figures.[3] Nevertheless, they do refute the hypothesis that the typical non-EU firm chooses a single 'preferred' member state in which to base its entire European activities. For leading non-EU-owned firms operating in the EU, dispersion of operations across the member states is the 'norm'.

Widening attention to the entire size distribution, Table 11.2 reports a breakdown by country of origin. Judged simply by firm numbers, the leading role of non-EU firms is confirmed: all but two of the thirty-six non-EU matrix firms are 'multinational' within the EU. Putting aside these firms, there are 142 EU-owned matrix firms who are multinational; of these, 90% come from the

---

[2] Or, in the case of non-EU firms, outside their main base within the EU.

[3] For non-EU-owned firms in particular, for whom we take no account of home country operations, world-wide multinationality is probably smaller than would be suggested by our NM estimates. For the EU-owned firms, our exclusion of non-EU operations is likely to be less significant and could affect our estimates either upwards or downwards. To see how within-EU 'multinationality' ($NMEU$) compares with world-wide ($NMWW$), consider the following simplified example. Suppose that a given firm produces s % of its output in a single country outside the EU, say the USA, and the remainder within the EU. It can easily be shown that ($NMEU/NMWW$) $= 1 + [s^2(1 + NMEU) - 2s]$. Thus $NMEU$ will tend to be greater than $NMWW$, the larger is s relative to $NMEU$. Taking $NMEU = 3$, a fairly typical value amongst the larger matrix firms, the two indices are, in fact, identical if $s = 0.5$, but for $s > 0.5$, $NMEU$ becomes an overestimate of $NMWW$. Now, if the firm is US owned, s refers to the share of its output produced at home, and this will usually exceed 50%: if so, our estimates will over-record world-wide multinationality. On the other hand, for an EU-owned firm, s refers to the scale of its overseas operations in the USA; and since this is likely to be less than 50%, we would expect $NMEU < NMWW$. Obviously, the picture becomes more confused by introducing third countries, but the main conclusions are qualitatively unchanged.

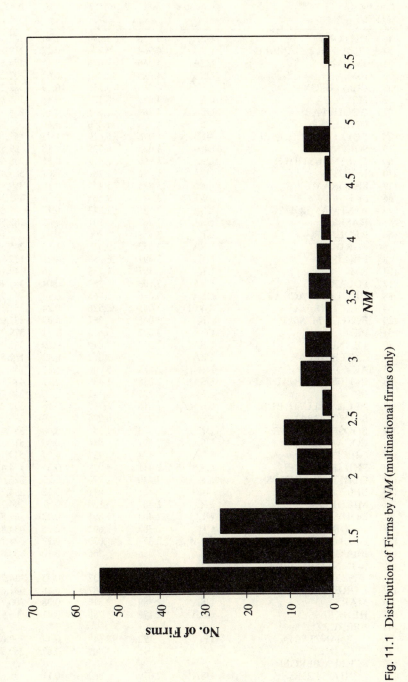

Fig. 11.1 Distribution of Firms by *NM* (multinational firms only)

Table 11.1 The 100 most multinational firms

Rank by FMSIZE		Country	NM	FMSIZE	CS	NATS
47	DU PONT	USA	5.536	3,690	1.94	342,960
54	PROCTER & GAMBLE	USA	4.964	3,474	0.22	319,391
84	3M	USA	4.960	2,036	0.11	374,677
13	IBM	USA	4.925	12,993	0.67	392,218
53	CIBA GEIGY	CH	4.916	3,536	0.19	383,232
22	NESTLE	CH	4.897	8,137	0.46	364,893
97	GOODYEAR	USA	4.769	1,851	0.16	238,928
15	UNILEVER	NL	4.746	11,466	0.69	351,004
25	ROYAL DUTCH/SHELL	NL	4.078	6,419	1.03	152,741
39	SOLVAY	BL	4.035	4,725	1.18	99,535
60	BAT INDUSTRIES	UK	3.960	2,972	0.31	238,688
230	NORTON	USA	3.886	281	0.02	383,872
119	SEAGRAM	CAN	3.835	1,425	0.10	359,098
66	SKF	SWED	3.581	2,565	0.14	495,368
73	EASTMAN KODAK	USA	3.575	2,247	0.17	364,849
265	HASBRO	USA	3.567	141	0.03	142,585
160	REDLAND	UK	3.559	806	0.09	257,448
6	FORD	USA	3.552	19,418	1.85	295,527
8	PHILIPS	NL	3.391	16,255	4.25	112,830
104	RMC	UK	3.107	1,738	0.16	342,142
212	POLAROID	USA	3.103	380	0.04	349,442
88	HEWLETT PACKARD	USA	3.066	1,965	0.14	446,713
64	ELECTROLUX	SWED	3.055	2,526	0.24	351,445
229	FOSECO MINSEP	UK	3.045	282	0.03	335,092
51	PIRELLI	IT	3.027	3,618	0.31	379,951
80	TENNECO	USA	2.972	2,070	0.19	361,969
124	CATERPILLAR	USA	2.917	1,372	0.42	112,519
35	AKZO	NL	2.888	5,090	1.17	150,339
118	INTERNATIONAL PAPER	USA	2.838	1,438	0.12	429,133
37	BP	UK	2.825	4,743	0.70	240,102
99	ALCAN ALUMINIUM	CAN	2.816	1,797	0.16	390,259
26	SAINT-GOBAIN	FR	2.773	6,275	0.59	386,096
299	BOOSEY & HAWKES	UK	2.653	38	0.00	356,430
157	COCA-COLA	USA	2.591	844	0.06	516,922
143	GILLETTE	USA	2.474	937	0.07	549,748
44	PHILIP MORRIS	USA	2.445	4,079	0.37	454,431
102	GLAXO HOLDINGS	UK	2.430	1,770	0.22	323,690
150	BPB	UK	2.425	871	0.12	294,784
31	MICHELIN	FR	2.407	5,859	0.62	394,738
92	DOUWE EGBERTS	NL	2.404	1,891	0.72	109,874
68	JACOBS SUCHARD	CH	2.382	2,542	0.25	434,832
139	GROUPE CARNAUD	FR	2.377	1,023	0.13	328,762
161	BBA GROUP	UK	2.358	806	0.10	350,041
145	KON.NED.PAPIER FABRIEKEN	NL	2.315	932	0.35	114,764
112	L'OREAL	FR	2.268	1,587	0.18	381,891
69	MARS	USA	2.189	2,510	0.38	300,739
46	HENKEL	GER	2.176	3,780	0.31	566,944
48	FERRUZZI FINANZIARIA	IT	2.122	3,648	0.44	392,006
45	PECHINEY	FR	2.095	3,809	0.67	269,914
152	SCHLUMBERGER INDUSTRIES	USA	2.079	862	0.11	388,605

89	CONTINENTAL G-W	GER	2.053	1,958	0.18	521,842
133	VARITY	CAN	2.034	1,138	0.17	329,049
12	CGE	FR	2.019	13,031	1.62	398,393
197	CPC INTERNATIONAL	USA	1.998	522	0.07	392,158
203	FORNARA	IT	1.989	469	0.06	390,756
280	CARBORUNDUM ABRASIVES	UK	1.981	82	0.01	449,344
49	ASEA BROWN BOVERI	CH/SW	1.960	3,641	0.34	550,366
101	CIR	IT	1.949	1,774	0.24	387,250
103	VALEO	FR	1.935	1,744	0.23	389,508
95	PILKINGTON	UK	1.909	1,855	0.26	372,739
82	HEINEKEN	NL	1.805	2,041	1.15	98,072
149	CONTINENTAL CAN	USA	1.798	895	0.12	425,489
251	VAMATEX	IT	1.774	176	0.03	383,195
209	BONDUELLE	FR	1.767	409	0.07	317,500
140	JOHNSON MATTHEY	UK	1.760	1,014	0.18	321,141
186	VILLEROY & BOCH	GER	1.751	591	0.06	564,459
50	BERTELSMANN	GER	1.735	3,627	0.35	591,661
98	CADBURYS SCHWEPPES	UK	1.716	1,817	0.36	294,831
256	GEOBRA BRANDSTAETTER	GER	1.710	170	0.02	408,198
7	PSA HOLDING	FR	1.700	17,383	2.68	381,147
36	BSN	FR	1.686	4,896	0.77	379,458
81	SCHNEIDER	FR	1.675	2,054	0.31	393,869
141	DMC	FR	1.661	1,003	0.14	416,658
14	HOECHST	GER	1.660	12,407	1.25	599,748
16	ICI	UK	1.648	10,850	2.03	323,615
20	THOMSON	FR	1.642	9,118	1.39	400,380
55	OLIVETTI	IT	1.637	3,142	0.49	388,932
67	GUINNESS	UK	1.613	2,546	1.29	122,182
269	BCI HOLDINGS	USA	1.594	125	0.09	85,288
250	SKIS ROSSIGNOL	FR	1.591	179	0.03	392,975
129	ROWNTREE	UK	1.587	1,269	0.28	288,116
4	SIEMENS	GER	1.586	20,359	2.13	601,846
154	SOMMER-ALLIBERT	FR	1.585	853	0.16	343,221
57	COURTAULDS	UK	1.571	3,082	0.62	318,638
63	DSM	NL	1.561	2,856	1.80	101,567
170	TURNER & NEWALL	UK	1.554	749	0.15	323,175
181	VARTA	GER	1.548	642	0.07	602,197
23	RHONE-POULENC	FR	1.548	7,239	1.18	395,304
5	RENAULT	FR	1.519	19,624	3.52	367,181
130	GRUNDIG	GER	1.516	1,220	0.16	496,251
127	LIEBHERR-INTERNATIONAL	CH	1.510	1,338	0.15	594,304
177	HAINDL PAPIER	GER	1.505	680	0.10	456,237
264	ARA SCHUHFABRIKEN	GER	1.492	144	0.04	225,633
71	BEECHAM	UK	1.477	2,362	0.50	318,562
169	SOCIETE BIC	FR	1.434	769	0.14	396,073
148	EPEDA-BERTRAND-FAURE	FR	1.421	910	0.16	399,421
79	BTR	UK	1.407	2,071	0.46	319,913
9	BAYER	GER	1.405	15,309	1.99	547,663
156	PROUVOST	FR	1.395	850	0.16	384,982
125	METALBOX	UK	1.392	1,361	0.32	304,244

Note: *NM* is number-equivalent multinationality; *FMSIZE* is aggregate firm size in m. ECU; *CS* is share of typical country's manufacturing output (%); *NATS* is size of typical country in which firm operates in m. ECU.

Table 11.2 Multinationality by country

Country	Number of firms			Mean[a] *NM*	
	Total	MNE	%	All firms	MNEs only
Germany	75	37	49	1.16	1.32
France	58	33	57	1.33	1.57
Italy	49	16	33	1.16	1.49
UK[c]	65	43	66	1.45	1.67
Netherlands	11	8	73	2.38	2.90
Bel/Lux	12	5	42	1.34	2.01
Spain/Portugal	7	0	0	1.00	1.00
Switzerland	4	4	100	3.43	3.43
Sweden[b]	3	3	100	2.87	2.87
USA	25	23	92	3.00	3.18
Canada	3	3	100	2.90	2.90
Japan	1	1	100	1.28	1.28
TOTALS	317	176	56	1.51	1.90

[a] in this table only, 'mean' refers to the simple arithmetic mean
[b] includes one firm (A.B.B) of joint Swedish/Swiss ownership
[c] Unilever and Shell (both joint UK/Dutch-owned) are counted as Dutch in this and other tables.

four largest member states. This disproportionately high share (the big four only account for 79% of EU manufacturing in aggregate) is largely due to the very high propensity of UK firms to be multinational: there is a two-thirds probability that any UK matrix firm will be multinational, as opposed to only one-third for Italian firms and one-half for German firms; the French propensity is also relatively high, at 57%. Amongst the Benelux countries, the Netherlands has a slightly higher multinational propensity than the UK, whilst Belgium/Luxemburg is closer to the German figure. Turning to the average *extent* of multinational activities, the last two columns show the average value for *NM*—both for all firms and separately for those firms who are multinational. This largely confirms the above picture, although the Dutch firms which are multinational are evidently extensively so (and the same is true, to a lesser extent, for Belgium). Similarly, Italy overtakes Germany because some of Italy's multinational firms are very multinational, whilst this is not true for German firms. Judged on this criterion, German firms are the least multinational amongst the leading member states. Non-EU-owned firms continue to rank as the most multinational on the matrix, although the Dutch MNEs can now be seen to be equally multinational.

11.3 The spatial decomposition of firm size

In Chapter 9, we showed how a firm's aggregate size can be decomposed in product space into diversification, typical market share and typical size of industry. The analogous decomposition in geographic space involves the firm's multinationality, its typical share of country output, and the typical size of country. This can be seen by comparing the following hypothetical symmetric firm structures, each of which leads to an aggregate size of 1,000: (i) a 5% share in a single country of size 20,000; (ii) a 1% share in a single country of 100,000; (iii) a 1% share in each of ten countries, each of which has size 10,000.

11.3.1 Definitions and Derivation

The third key decomposition of the book formalizes this idea. It is derived as Equation A.32 in Appendix 1, using the definitions reproduced in Table 11.3:

$$FMSIZE = CS * NATS * NM \tag{11.3}$$

where

$FMSIZE$ = the firm's aggregate production in the EU (m. ECUs)
CS = its typical share of national output in the member states in which it operates
$NATS$ = the typical size of member state in which it operates (m. ECUs)
NM = the equivalent number of member states in which it operates.

Table 11.3 Indices of firm structure used in the spatial decomposition

Index	Symbol	Formula
Aggregate firm size	$FMSIZE$	x_i
Typical country share	CS	$\sum_k CS_{ik}(x_{ik}/x_i)$
		where $CS_{ik} = x_{ik}/x_k$
Multinationality		
Number equivalent	NM	$1/(1 - M_i)$
where	M	$1 - \sum_k (x_{ik})^2/(x_i)^2$
Typical size of member state	$NATS$	$\sum_k (u_{ik} x_k)$
		$u_{ik} = (x_{ik}CS_{ik})/\sum_k (x_{ik}CS_{ik})$

The typical share of national output, referred to for simplicity as *country share (CS)*, is the firm's weighted average aggregate share across member states, where the weight is the proportion of the firm's output in each member state. The index for the typical size of member state, referred to as *national size (NATS)*, is a weighted average size of all the states in which the firm operates. Since the weights depend on the size of the firm's presence in the country times its share in that country, this index is firm specific.[4] The nature of the

---

[4] Two firms operating in exactly the same set of countries will only record the same value for *NATS* if they have an identical configuration of country shares.

weighting structure is such that country k is given more weight if the firm's operations in that country are both important to the firm and significant in the country.2

11.3.2 Analysis of means and variances

Table 11.1 quantifies this decomposition for the 100 most multinational firms; the full list of all 313 firms is presented in Appendix 2.2. Evaluated at geometric mean values, as in Table 11.4 part (a), the typical firm has an aggregate output of 751m. ECUs, and it is as if the firm spreads this equally across 1.35 equal-sized member states (each of size 353,000), in each of which it has an aggregate share of 0.158% of all manufacturing output.

Table 11.4 The spatial decomposition of aggregate firm size

(a) Analysis of geometric means

FMSIZE	=	NATS	*	CS	*	NM
751	=	353,000	*	0.00158	*	1.350

(b) Analysis of variances

$V(fmsize)$ =	$V(ns)$ +	$V(cs)$ +	$V(nm)$ +	$2C(ns, cs)$ +	$2C(ns, nm)$ +	$2C(cs, nm)$
2.577	= 0.307 +	2.332 +	0.178 −	0.427	− 0.077	+ 0.265
(100)	= (12%) +	(90%) +	(7%) −	(17%)	− (3%)	+ (10%)

Note: definitions as in Table 11.1. Lower case refers to logarithms, with *ns* being log (*NATS*).

Part (b) of the table reports an analysis of variance, based on the logarithmic version of the decomposition, with lower-case symbols denoting logarithms, and *V* and *C* denoting variances and covariances respectively:

$$V(fmsize) = V(ns) + V(cs) + V(nm) + 2C(ns, cs) + 2C(ns, nm) + 2C(cs, nm) \qquad (11.4)$$

The magnitudes of the variances reveal that 90% of the total variation in *FMSIZE* is accounted for by the variance in *CS*, whilst the variances in national size (*NATS*) and multinationality (*NM*) only account for 12% and 7% respectively. Since *NATS* tends to be closely related to the size of a firm's home country, this tells us that the size of nation of origin is far less important than the firm's share in that country; and the extent of the firm's multinational operations is also a *relatively* small contributor to the variance in aggregate size. However, the covariance terms yield additional insights. Apparently, the effect of country share is dampened by its negative correlation with national size: firms in larger countries tend to have smaller shares in those countries. On the other hand, the effects of multinationality are accentuated by its positive correlation with country share: firms with a large share in individual countries tend to be more multinational. Both these results are suggestive of causal influences on corporate strategy and we return to them below.

11.3.3 The Decomposition by Aggregate Size and Nationality

The decomposition also sheds more light on our earlier findings on differences in multinationality between countries, and that it is not necessarily the largest firms who are the most multinational. Table 11.5 shows the decomposition at mean values for each of seven aggregate firm-size classes. As can be seen, mean *NM* rises monotonically, but slowly, as we move up through the aggregate firm-size rankings, until the very largest size class, at which it dips slightly. However, this trend is overshadowed by a much stronger relationship between aggregate size and country share: as was clear from the analysis of variance, it is this component which statistically dominates the explanation of aggregate firm size. It is clear, therefore, that there is only a quantitatively weak positive relationship between a firm's multinationality and its overall size. Finally, the third component, *NATS*, shows no clear tendency across size classes, except that the largest size class records by far the highest value: this is due to the high incidence of German car manufacturers in the largest size class, as described in the previous chapter.

Table 11.5 The spatial decomposition by aggregate firm-size class (geometric means)

Firms ranked	*FMSIZE*	*CS*	*NATS*	*NM*
1–20	14,661	2.054	423,000	1.689
21–50	5,105	0.842	346,000	1.752
51–100	2,335	0.427	326,800	1.675
101–50	1,280	0.242	370,000	1.429
151–200	677	0.154	359,400	1.225
201–50	295	0.072	351,900	1.160
251–313	71	0.019	340,800	1.089
TOTALS	751	0.158	353,000	1.350

Note: *FMSIZE* and *NATS* are measured in m. ECUs; *CS* is expressed as a percentage.

Table 11.6 shows the geometric mean values by nationality of firms. The results for *NM* are similar to those for the arithmetic means already shown in Table 11.2, although geometric means offer a more accurate picture of 'typical' values when, as here, distributions are positively skewed. This table adds to our understanding by setting *NM* alongside the other components of the decomposition. Not surprisingly, *NATS* is closely related to the size of the firm's home country (shown in brackets in the table): it is largest for Germany

Table 11.6 The spatial Decomposition by firm nationality (geometric means)

	FMSIZE	*NATS*	*CS*	*NM*
Germany	864	595 (617)	0.13	1.14
France	767	390 (398)	0.16	1.27
Italy	287	385 (385)	0.07	1.12
UK	983	312 (320)	0.24	1.34
Netherlands	1,949	125 (100)	0.76	2.07
Bel/Lux	443	81 (79)	0.46	1.21
Spain/Portugal	184	102 (102)	0.18	1.00
Sweden/Switzerland	3,023	445	0.23	2.93
USA/Canada	1,245	312	0.15	2.72
TOTALS	751	353	0.16	1.35

Notes: *FMSIZE* is measured in m. ECUs; *NATS* is measured in b. ECUs; *CS* is expressed as a percentage. Figures in parentheses denote the size of each member state's manufacturing sector (b. ECUs)

and smallest for the Benelux countries, and appears to be weakly negatively related to multinationality, at least within EU-owned firms. However, this must be seen against the tendencies for firms from larger countries to record lower country shares; and for larger *NM* values to be associated with higher *CS*.

11.4 Econometric model of the Determinants of Firm Multinationality

This section pursues these results further, but now within a multivariate, behavioural framework. It also introduces some additional industry factors which recall the findings in Chapter 7. Essentially, this has two purposes. First, it enables us to complete our analysis of inter-country differences controlling for the effects of firm size, using the distinction between *NATS* and *CS*, and controlling for differences between firms in their industrial structure. It also provides a test for the robustness of some of the findings in Chapter 7.

We use a two-stage approach which first investigates the factors affecting *whether or not a firm is multinational*, and then explores how these factors affect the *extent* of multinationality after the multinational option has been chosen. We therefore present a double set of increasingly richer models, estimated, first, on the total sample of 313 firms by Probit analysis, and then on the sub-sample of 176 MNEs by Ordinary Least Squares.[5]

---

[5] To control for any sample selection bias arising from the fact that over 40% of the firms are non-multinationals, in the second step we include as a regressor the selection variable (inverse Mills ratio) generated by the Probit model.

11.4.1 Hypotheses

Firm size

We have seen that there is a (weak) tendency for multinationality to increase with aggregate firm size. This is unsurprising if multinationality is activated as a route to growth by firms increasingly confronted by domestic constraints as their size increases. However, there is an obvious problem of two way causality—the decomposition clearly establishes that *NM* is a constituent part of *FMSIZE*, and increases in *NM* will raise *FMSIZE*, *ceteris paribus*. This suggests that the relationship is best investigated by distinguishing different aspects of firm size, and, in this respect, the decomposition offers a simple solution. If increasing firm size provides the impetus for multinationality because the firm becomes 'too large' for its home markets, then we would expect multinationality to become more likely as the firm's home-country share (*CS*) increases, especially if the country (*NATS*) is small. On the other hand, even with a large country share, firms from small countries may not possess the where-withal to 'go multinational' if they have been constrained from fully developing a specific asset which is a necessary condition for successful multinational operations. This suggests that *CS* should have a positive effect on multinationality, whilst *NATS* has an effect which is difficult to sign *a priori*.

Industry-level factors

The econometric results in Chapter 7 confirmed that the multinationality of firms within a given industry is determined, at least in part, by the characteristics of the industry. It follows that some of the inter-firm differences in overall multinationality should also be accounted for by differences in the industrial structures. For example, we should expect that firms located in industries characterized by product differentiation and/or smaller production-scale economies will be more multinational. Therefore we include the vector of explanatory variables used in Chapter 7 to represent the characteristics of the industries in which each firm operates. These are: *MES* (the minimum efficient size of production, relative to industry size), *TRS* (the size of unit transport costs), *ADS* (the advertising to sales ratio), *RDS* (the R&D to sales ratio), *TRADE* (intra-EU trade as a proportion of EU apparent consumption), and *HEU* (EU concentration). The theoretical rationale for these variables is explained more fully in Chapter 7, but very briefly, the expectations are as follows. *ADS* and *RDS* are included to capture the 'intangible asset' story (Caves, 1982), in which large R&D and advertising expenditures are at the root of a firm-specific competitive advantage which is best exploited by local production because of high transaction and agency costs. *MES* and *TRS* are included to allow for the likelihood that the multinational option is less likely to be chosen when production economies of scale are substantial and transport costs are lower (Smith, 1987, and Davies and Lyons, 1991). *HEU* is included to represent the possibility that more concentrated industries offer higher mark-ups, which make it easier to recoup the fixed outlays involved in setting up additional plants in other countries. *TRADE* is used to reflect the extent of EU trade integration in the industry concerned—in Chapter 7, this was found to have an important influence on the above effects. Firm-level data on these characteristics are generally unavailable, so for each firm we have constructed observations on these variables by calculating weighted averages of the levels of the industry characteristics across the different industries in which the firm operates.[6]

Country specific factors

Even after controlling for size and industry factors, there may still be other country differences at work, e.g. distance from relevant market outlets, quality of management and human capital generally, internationalization of the economy and the capital markets, the structure of firms' ownership, the market for corporate control, etc. To capture any such 'residual' effects, we also include a series of country dummy variables.

In summary, therefore, the full model is:

$$NM = f(CS, \ NS, \ MES, \ ADS, \ RDS, \ TRS, \ HEU, \ TRADE,$$
$$COUNTRY \ DUMMIES) \tag{11.5}$$

A similar model also applies for the probability that a firm will be multinational at all.

11.4.2 Econometric results

The results in Table 11.7 refer to Probit analysis of the likelihood that a firm is multinational, and Table 11.8 presents *OLS* estimates of equations designed to explain the extent of multinationality activity amongst the firms who are multinational. There are five pairs of identical equations in the two tables. Equations 1 and 2 are introductory and merely designed to establish the effects of distinguishing the two components of size, *CS* and *NATS*, from *FMSIZE* itself. Equation 3 introduces the vector of industry-level variables, and Equation 4 adds the country dummies. Equation 5 is an alternative to 4, in that it replaces *HEU* with an instrument— the level of concentration in the corresponding US industry, measured by the US four-firm concentration ratio, *C4US*. This allows for the possibility that *HEU* and *NM* are simultaneously

---

[6] The weights are the share of the firm's operations in the industry concerned. So for example, suppose a firm has 75% of its output in industry *A* and 25% in *B*; if the industry values for *RDS* are 1% and 2% respectively, the firm records a composite value of 1.25%.

Table 11.7 Whether or not firms are multinational
Probit analysis, with dependent variable = 1 for multinational firms, 0 otherwise. $n =$ 313

	Estimated coefficients and t values				
	(1)	(2)	(3)	(4)	(5)
Constant	−0.202	0.118	−0.666	1.490	2.913
	(2.18)	(0.54)	(1.90)	(1.49)	(2.56)
FMSIZE	0.213	—	—	—	—
$(*10^{-3})$	(5.36)				
CS	—	0.467	0.522	0.672	0.663
		(3.53)	(2.83)	(3.40)	(3.36)
NATS	—	0.004	0.005	−0.072	−0.090
$(*10^{-4})$		(0.74)	(0.89)	(2.95)	(3.43)
MES	—	—	−1.825	−2.231	−1.193
$(*10^{-3})$			(3.87)	(4.02)	(2.11)
ADS	—	—	0.473	0.453	0.774
			(2.01)	(1.72)	(2.60)
RDS	—	—	0.301	0.416	0.352
			(1.64)	(1.88)	(2.49)
TRS	—	—	0.071	0.071	0.108
			(1.38)	(1.27)	(1.84)
HEU	—	—	18.67	6.536	—
			(1.56)	(0.48)	
C4US	—	—	—	—	−0.049
					(3.02)
TRADE	—	—	0.163	0.019	−0.037
			(1.93)	(2.10)	(2.21)
*MES * TRADE*	—	—	−0.050	−0.065	0.021
$(*10^3)$			(3.45)	(3.66)	(1.11)
*ADS * TRADE*	—	—	−0.019	−0.025	−0.039
			(1.80)	(2.08)	(2.91)
*RDS * TRADE*	—	—	−0.009	−0.127	−0.010
			(1.12)	(1.26)	(2.08)
*HEU * TRADE*	—	—	−0.038	0.187	—
			(0.10)	(0.42)	
*C4US * TRADE*	—	—	—	—	0.033
					(4.13)
Bel/Lux	—	—	—	−2.231	−2.891
				(0.58)	(3.16)
France	—	—	—	0.624	0.579
				(2.28)	(2.08)
Germany	—	—	—	1.950	2.140
				(3.28)	(3.41)
Netherlands	—	—	—	−1.246	−1.582
				(1.64)	(1.99)
UK	—	—	—	0.283	0.159
				(0.90)	(0.49)
Spain/Port	—	—	—	−6.286	−6.919
				(0.14)	(0.16)
Non-EU	—	—	—	2.952	3.195
				(4.54)	(4.60)
Test statistics					
L-L	−191	−206	−183	−155	−145
X^2	46.6	17.3	62.0	118.4	137.4
PCP	72%	69%	71%	76%	77%

Multinationality at the Firm Level

Table 11.8 The extent of firm multinationality
(Ordinary Least Squares, standard errors heteroscedastic consistent) Dependent
Variable: Log NM, multinational firms only ($n = 176$)

	Estimated coefficients and t values				
	(1)	(2)	(3)	(4)	(5)
Constant	1.106 (5.29)	0.775 (1.63)	0.048 (0.11)	0.059 (0.25)	0.309 (1.00)
FMSIZE ($*10^{-3}$)	−0.031 (2.56)	—	—	—	—
CS	—	−0.001 (0.01)	−0.077 (1.02)	−0.022 (0.56)	−0.022 (0.53)
NATS ($*10^{-4}$)	—	−0.011 (4.43)	−0.012 (5.59)	−0.016 (4.31)	−0.015 (3.60)
MES ($*10^{-3}$)	—	—	−0.503 (1.41)	−0.462 (2.42)	−0.038 (0.18)
ADS	—	—	0.122 (1.14)	0.037 (0.55)	0.123 (1.75)
RDS	—	—	0.017 (0.28)	0.055 (1.41)	0.055 (1.95)
TRS	—	—	0.045 (1.45)	0.059 (2.76)	0.059 (2.69)
HEU	—	—	18.63 (3.28)	14.19 (4.62)	—
C4US	—	—	—	—	−0.002 (0.40)
TRADE	—	—	0.015 (2.21)	0.015 (3.56)	0.009 (1.21)
MES * TRADE ($*10^{3}$)	—	—	0.015 (1.41)	0.133 (2.32)	0.000 (0.05)
ADS * TRADE	—	—	−0.002 (0.43)	−0.002 (0.68)	−0.006 (1.73)
RDS * TRADE	—	—	−0.001 (0.20)	−0.001 (0.85)	−0.001 (1.04)
HEU * TRADE	—	—	−0.346 (2.75)	−0.266 (3.09)	—
C4US * TRADE ($*10^{2}$)	—	—	—	—	0.025 (1.07)
Bel/Lux	—	—	—	−0.317 (1.24)	−0.327 (1.31)
France	—	—	—	0.167 (1.73)	0.110 (1.06)
Germany	—	—	—	0.259 (2.12)	0.191 (1.46)
Netherlands	—	—	—	0.379 (2.21)	0.342 (1.79)
UK	—	—	—	0.095 (0.90)	0.034 (0.29)
US/Canada	—	—	—	0.867 (5.62)	0.753 (4.79)
Swed/Switz	—	—	—	1.024 (5.47)	0.928 (4.88)
Japan	—	—	—	−0.693 (3.96)	−0.541 (2.96)
MILLS ratio	−0.76 (2.95)	0.25 (0.38)	0.41 (1.24)	0.31 (2.37)	0.18 (1.31)

Table 11.8 (*cont.*)

	Estimated coefficients and t values				
	(1)	(2)	(3)	(4)	(5)
Test statistics					
R^2	0.053	0.111	0.310	0.603	0.551
Corr. R^2	0.042	0.096	0.254	0.549	0.489
F	4.848	7.178	5.589	11.15	8.987
B-Pagan X^2	11.08	13.63	32.68	37.13	31.45

determined and that *OLS* might generate biased estimates.[7] For the sake of brevity, the discussion is focused on the full form of the model as in 5

The decision to separate *FMSIZE* into its two remaining components, apart from *NM*, is vindicated. Not only is this justified on econometric grounds, but also it reveals some interesting conflicting effects. On the one hand, firms with a large country share (*CS*) are significantly more likely to go multinational, although this variable has no significant effect in explaining the extent of their multinationality in the second stage.[8] On the other hand, firms from larger countries (*NATS*) are significantly less likely to go multinational and, if they are multinational, tend to be significantly less extensively so.[9] We interpret this as confirmation that limits to domestic growth act as an impetus for multinational operations. However, the insignificance of *CS* in the second stage suggests that, although a large home country share may provoke some degree of multinationality, this may not be substantial; perhaps this is because product

[7] At first sight, the inclusion of just a single instrument for *HEU* would not appear to be an ideal solution to the simultaneity problem; but the strong significance of *C4US* in Equation 5 lessens our worries in that respect. In any event, a more developed simultaneous system of equations, including an explanation of *HEU*, would be highly complex, because, for each firm, *HEU* is the (weighted) average level of concentration across all the industries in which the firm operates. Even for the simple case of a single product firm, HEU_i will depend not only on NM_i but also on the multinationality of its rivals in that industry. This implies a complex structure of interdependent disturbance terms. The problem is heightened when the firm is also diversified, since its *HEU* value then depends on the market shares (and indirectly the *NM*) of many firms in different industries. Since an *explanation* of *HEU* (measured in this particular way) is not of interest here, our preference for a single instrument is obvious.

[8] Given that *CS* is measured as the firm's average country share, weighted over all the countries in which it operates, there is a danger that *CS* and *NM* are jointly determined amongst the set of multinational firms. For instance, suppose a firm chooses to go multinational once its home country *CS* exceeds some threshold, say X%. Then, as it expands its foreign operations, its weighted average *CS* will diminish, only to rise again as its share in foreign countries approaches X%. Assuming a firm expands its multinational operations sequentially by moving into ever more countries, one could conceive of a time-path for *CS* which would alternatively decrease and then recover. Thus, *CS* and *NM* will be jointly determined, although not monotonically related. To test for this possibility, all equations were also estimated, replacing *CS* by *OCS* (the 'own country' share). This made virtually no difference to the estimated coefficients of *CS* or any of the other explanatory variables. Since *OCS* is difficult to interpret for non-EU firms or for EU firms with a large proportion of non-home country production (Unilever is a prime example), we prefer to report the results when using *CS*.

[9] Interestingly, the former result only emerges after the inclusion of the country dummy effects in Equations 4 and 5.

diversification at home still offers an alternative to future growth, except when the country is small. The significant negative effect of *NATS* in both stages does not support the hypothesis that small-country firms are at a disadvantage in developing a large home base from which to foster specific assets.

The specification of the equation with respect to the industry-level variables has been dictated by a desire for consistency with the econometrics of Chapter 7, in which we found that the effects of these variables differ, depending on the extent of trade integration (see Table 7.4). Thus, except *TRS*, they are entered separately and interactively with *TRADE* (the extent of intra-EU trade). The estimated coefficients are generally consistent with theoretical expectations, but are not always significant in both stages. *ADS* and *RDS* have similar patterns of coefficient signs and magnitudes in both stages. For advertising, there is a significant effect (at the 5% level in the first stage and at the 10% level in the second), with greater advertising being conducive to multinationality, but in a way which weakens with greater integration, and finally ceases as *TRADE* approaches 20%. The results are similar for R&D, although the coefficient on *RDS * TRADE* is insignificant in the second stage. The magnitudes of the coefficients suggest that the positive influence is sustained to higher levels of *TRADE*. These results are totally consistent with those reported in Chapter 7. *Concentration* is significant in the first stage, but not the second: firms in more concentrated industries are more likely to be multinational, increasingly so, the more trade-integrated is the industry (exactly as implied in Chapter 7), but concentration does not affect the extent of their multinationality. The results for *MES* are similar: as expected, firms operating in industries with large scale economies are less likely to be multinational (as expected), but scale economies have no influence on the extent of their multinationality. *TRS*, is positively significant in both stages (although only at the 10% level in the first stage)—as expected, high transport costs encourage multinationality. Finally, *TRADE* has a complex influence, given its interaction with the other explanatory variables. However, holding other factors constant, it has a significant negative influence in the first (although not the second) stage—firms are less likely to choose multinationality, *ceteris paribus*, where trade is high.

Taken *en bloc*, these industry-level variables add significantly to the overall explanation—as witnessed by the improvement in the test statistics between Equations 2 and 3. Moreover, the signs and magnitudes of coefficients are generally, and reassuringly, consistent with the findings of Chapter 7. On the other hand, the specification of the model makes multicollinearity likely, and the instability of some coefficients between Equations 4 and 5 (which differ only in the measurement of the concentration variable), warns against attaching too much importance to their precise values.

Turning lastly to the country dummies, there are some surprising and interesting findings. First, their inclusion adds importantly to the overall fit in both stages: it seems then that there are significant differences between countries, which cannot be explained by the different industrial structures of their firms, the sizes of the countries, or differences in the shares of the firms in the home economies. To interpret the individual coefficient estimates, it should be noted that the omitted country is Italy, so all coefficients relate to country effects relative to Italy. In the first stage, the firms with the highest probabilities of being multinational are from non-EU, Germany, and France (in that order), and those least likely to be multinational are from Spain, Belgium/Luxemburg, and the Netherlands. Interestingly, UK firms show no significant difference in this respect from the Italians. In the second stage, i.e. amongst the set of firms which are multinational, the extent of multinationality is greatest amongst non-EU firms,[10] followed by the Dutch, but apart from this there are no remaining significant differences. We discuss some of the implications of these results in the final section.

11.5 Conclusion

This chapter has focused on aspects of firms' corporate strategy viewed from a geographic perspective, especially the factors determining the extent of their multinational operations within the EU. By conducting the analysis both econometrically and descriptively we have uncovered a picture which is far more intriguing than is suggested by a first sight.

Superficially, it appears that larger firms tend to be more multinational than smaller firms (although not substantially so), and that firms from certain member states are more likely to be multinational (and to have more extensive multinational operations) than firms from certain other member states. In particular, German and Italian firms are less inclined (whilst UK and Dutch firms are more inclined) to multinational operations. However, once we control for differences between firms in the characteristics of the industries in which they operate, in the sizes of their countries, and in the firms' shares within those countries, some of the international differences disappear. Most strikingly, the lower incidence of multinationality amongst German firms can be explained by the fact that they tend to smaller, *relative to the size of the domestic German market*. Thus, the multinational option is not so compelling as for UK firms which are faced with a typically smaller home market. Indeed, once industrial and size factors are controlled for, we find no evidence for the conventional wisdom that British firms are exceptionally multinational. For the Netherlands, the other member state most usually associated with extensive multinational operations, the results are more mixed. It seems that Dutch firms are no more likely than most to be multinational, but that, if they are, the extent of their multinational operations is significantly higher than average. This result

[10] In the first stage, we represent non-EU firms by a single dummy variable. Since they originate from outside the EU, they are all MNEs by definition; and, with only two exceptions, they are all also multinationals *within* the EU. Thus, it would be pointless to distinguish their exact country of origin. In the second stage, however, we do distinguish North America from EFTA, since they will differ in the extent of their multinationality.

undoubtedly derives from the existence of firms such as Philips, Unilever, and Shell, whose very large size far exceeds anything which could be supported by the limited scale of their home Dutch markets. Some other (rather less-pronounced) effects are discernible for firms from the other member states: for example, French firms are somewhat more likely, and Belgian firms less likely, to be multinational than their country sizes and industrial locations would suggest. But the most persistent results concern firms originating from outside the EU. They tend to record the highest values for NM, and a strong country-specific effect persists, even once size and industry factors are controlled for. While these high values do not necessarily mean that non-EU firms are more multinational worldwide than their EU counterparts (since we ignore production outside the EU), they do reveal substantial geographic dispersion of these firms' production within the EU. This refutes the hypothesis that the typical 'foreign' MNE concentrates its activity in a single preferred member state.

Placing our results in the context of the wider literature on multinational firms, they confirm conventional wisdoms, but also add a new perspective. Thus, we confirm that multinationality is more likely where firms operate in industries characterized by product differentiation, modest scale economies and high transport costs. But beyond this, an intriguing picture has emerged concerning firm size, once we disentangle the different dimensions of scale. Of course, a simple positive correlation between firm size and the extent of multi-nationality does not establish a unique causality—since extensive multi-national operations may be a major reason why firms are large. Once we control for this tautological effect, it becomes clear that what matters is the firm's size *relative* to the scale of its domestic market—only if large, within its own domestic context, is it likely to turn to the multinational option. Needless to say, our findings merit further investigation using future datasets, especially involving a time dimension. But the signs are that a theoretical perspective which embraces both the industry and 'growth of firms' literatures would be the most fruitful.

STEVE DAVIES and LAURA RONDI

12

Alternative Corporate Strategies: Multinationality versus Diversification

12.1 Introduction

Previous chapters have explored two possible trade-offs in corporate strategy. In product space, there is the choice between expanding market share in a primary industry and diversification into other industries. In geographic space, the firm may grow by increasing its operations in its home country or by moving into multinational production. In this chapter, we straddle the two spaces, by asking whether multinationality and diversification are alternative routes to firm growth—are they complementary or substitutes?

At the core of conventional explanations of diversification and multi-nationality is the hypothesis that firm-specific assets are the driving force. The multinational firm is viewed as having some special advantage which it can only properly exploit in foreign markets by actually producing in them. This might be some sort of managerial skill, but it is also frequently associated with product differentiation and/or technological know-how (e.g. Michelin's steel radial tyre, Coca Cola's strong brand image). Similarly, it is argued that firms diversify in order to exploit some technological, marketing or brand loyalty asset in other markets than their original one (e.g. chocolate bars and Mars ice-cream). This will also often involve technological spillovers. But if both di-versification and multinationality require some specific asset, the question arises: is the specific asset a 'public good' within the firm, or is it in finite supply; so if it is used in one direction (e.g. diversification) does this make it less avail-able for the other (multinationality)? Or to change the question slightly: Are some specific assets more or less suited to diversification than to multi-nationality?

In turn, this leads to a number of other questions. Is diversification typically the first (and perhaps easier) stage in corporate growth, which is followed later by multinationality as, and if, the firm successfully builds on its specific asset? Do firms from different member states typically follow different routes, de-pending on comparative institutional factors such as the capital market, social infrastructure (including human capital) etc.? Are different strategies more likely to be successful at different stages in a firm's evolution, and in different types of industries?

These are under-researched topics within industrial organization,[1] and our treatment here is only exploratory. Since our current database refers to only one year and does not include information on firm performance, such as profitability, growth, etc., definitive answers are impossible at this stage. Nevertheless, we are able to compare typical structures between different sizes of firm, and between different countries of origin, and this is a useful first step into relatively uncharted territory. If nothing more, the chapter can be seen as helping to forge a future research agenda.

Section 12.2 plots the relative incidence of diversification and multinationality within the matrix firms and examines whether diversified and multinational firms differ with respect to advertising and research and development. Sections 12.3 and 12.4 examine differences by firm size and country of origin respectively, and Section 12.5 concludes.

12.2 The incidence of multinational and diversified firms and specific assets

A crude indication of whether multinationality and diversification are substitutes is to compare the number of firms which are both multinational and diversified against those who choose only one of the options. Table 12.1, part (a) shows that almost exactly half of the matrix firms (156) are both, while only twenty are specialized multinationals and sixty-eight are exclusively diversified in their home member state. In that sense, the balance is in favour of the complementarity interpretation. The row and column totals of this matrix also show that diversification is more frequent than multinationality: 71% of firms are diversified, whereas only 56% are multinational. No doubt, this partly reflects our definition of diversification,[2] and the fact that exporting will often be a viable alternative to multinationality. But it might also indicate that diversification is an 'easier' route to follow than multinationality.[3]

---

[1] Such questions may be more familiar to readers more conversant with the corporate strategy literature. For instance, the Ansoff matrix (1987) is a well known descriptive device for describing the choice that firms may make between the two types of strategies. But even within that literature, there has been no extensive analysis, statistical or theoretical, either on the relative incidence or causes of diversification and multinationality amongst a sample of leading firms such as is considered here.

[2] Since we define industries using the 3-digit NACE classification, firms may operate in up to 100 different industries, but only across eleven countries. Of course, the NACE classification is necessarily sometimes arbitrary: technologically very close activities are sometimes separated into different industries, whilst some 'industries' are very broadly defined to cover a wide range of heterogeneous activities. This qualifaction applies throughout the book: such problems are unavoidable whatever classification scheme is employed.

[3] It seems likely that entry into a new country is more costly (and risky) than into a new (may be adjacent) industry at home. The former invariably involves a fixed (and largely sunk) cost, whilst the latter may not if the diversification is motivated by a spillover. Similarly, country specificities (due to cultural and institutional differences) may significantly raise entry barriers.

Table 12.1 The incidence of diversified and multinational firms

(a) Simple frequencies

	Number of firms		
	Not diversified	Diversified	Total
Not Multinational	69	68	137
Multinational	20	156	176
TOTALS	89	224	313

(b) Frequencies by high and low

	Number of firms		
	Diversification		
	Low	High	Total
Multinationality			
Low	126	81	207
High	44	62	106
TOTALS	170	143	313

Notes: The critical values for distinguishing 'high' and 'low' multinationality and diversification are $NM = 1.35$ and $ND = 1.85$ respectively.

Of course, simple headcounts are very crude—not least because, as explained in previous chapters, many firms are only marginally multinational and/or diversified. Therefore, in part (b) of the table, we split the sample alternatively into 'high' and 'low' diversification and multinationality groups (where 'high' and 'low' are defined by the geometric mean values for ND and NM [4]). This effectively removes the marginal firms from the 'high' groups.

This does not alter the impression that diversification is the 'easier' option, but it does call complementarity into question. As can be seen, high diversification is more frequent than high multinationality (46% as opposed to 34%); this is because the number of firms combining high diversification with low multinationality (26%) is nearly twice the number who are highly multinational but weakly diversified (14%). On the other hand, the proportion of firms that are both highly multinational and diversified (20%) is now significantly smaller than the proportion only highly multinational or diversified (40%).

We next investigate the incidence of specific assets amongst these four groups, using information on advertising and R&D. We do not have access to individual firm spends on advertising and research, but we are able to compute, for every firm, the weighted average *ADS* (advertising to sales) and *RDS* (R&D

[4] ND and NM are the firms' number-equivalent measures of diversification and multinationality, as defined in Chapters 9 and 11. The geometric means are $ND = 1.85$ and $NM = 1.35$, as reported, respectively in Tables 9.5 and 11.4.

Table 12.2 Specific assets, multinationality, and diversification

(a) Mean values of *ADS*

	Diversification	
	Low	High
Multinationality		
Low	0.54	0.56
High	1.27	0.82

(b) Mean values of *RDS*

	Diversification	
	Low	High
Multinationality		
Low	1.02	1.26
High	1.83	2.27

Notes: See Table 12.2 for definitions of 'high' and 'low'; *ADS* is the industry's advertising to sales ratio; *RDS* is the industry's R&D to sales ratio

to sales) ratios for the industries in which it operates (the weights reflecting the shares of the firm's output in each industry). Parts (a) and (b) of Table 12.2 compare the sample means for *ADS* and *RDS* measured in this way.

Consider first *ADS*, as shown in matrix (a), and compare firms with high and low multinationality, holding diversification constant: higher multinationality is associated with significantly higher advertising than is low multinationality both within the group of specialized firms (1.27 as opposed to 0.54) and within the group of diversified firms (0.82 compared to 0.56[5]). But a rather different picture emerges for diversification. Reading across the rows, higher diversification is associated with significantly *lower* (at the 10% level) advertising than is specialization amongst the high multinationality group (0.82 compared to 1.27); and, amongst the low multinationality group, there is no difference between diversified and specialized firms—for both, *ADS* is low.

For R&D, a similar pattern is apparent for multinationality. Reading down the columns in part (b), higher multinationality is associated with significantly higher R&D than is low multinationality, both within the group of specialized firms (1.83 as opposed to 1.02) and within the group of diversified firms (2.27 compared to 1.26[6]). In this case, diversification *is* also associated with higher R&D— both within the high and low multinational groups—but the differentials are insignificant, and not so pronounced as they are for multinationality.

[5] The former difference is significant at the 5% level, the latter at the 10% level.
[6] The former difference is significant at the 10% level, the latter at the 5% level.

In other words, these simple tests confirm the specific asset story of Chapter 11 for multinationality. But, for diversification, there is no obvious connection with advertising, and even the relationship with R&D seems less pronounced than we might have thought. These results are not necessarily in conflict with those in Chapter 10.[7] Nevertheless, they do pose question marks over conclusions formed on tests of diversification which ignore simultaneous multinationality. For example, a possible explanation is that firm's diversification *in its home country* is inherently different from that in foreign countries—if and when it is multinational. It may be that the latter is driven by a specific asset explanation, whilst the former is less so. This hypothesis is on the agenda for future work.

12.3 Corporate Strategy and Firm Size

We next investigate how the two dimensions of corporate strategy vary across firm-size classes. Figure 12.1 plots geometric mean values of *NM* and *ND*

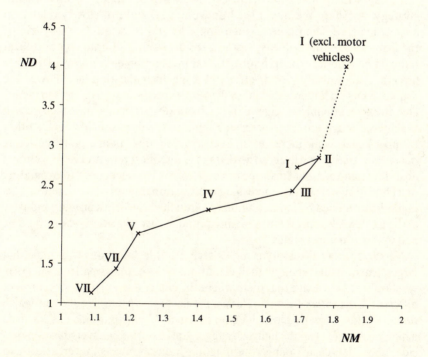

Fig. 12.1 Multinationality and diversification by firm and size class

[7] Here we have merely measured the extent of diversification at the firm level, whereas, in Chapter 10, the focus is on the directional pattern of diversification between industries.

for seven size classes, marked in descending order of size.[8] As can be seen, with the exception of the largest class (I), the continuous line connecting consecutive points is upward sloping, indicating that, *on average*, increases in firm size are accompanied by both increasing multinationality and diversification.

As noted in previous chapters, the largest size class includes the seven very large car firms on the matrix. This is by far the largest single industry in the NACE classification, and all of these firms concentrate most of their operations in that industry—and most tend not to be very multinational. Interestingly, once these firms are excluded, the largest size class also conforms to the general tendency—being both more multinational and diversified than the adjacent smaller class, II.

Putting the car firms to one side, a fascinating feature of the line connecting points is how it varies around the underlying trend. Amongst the smaller classes, VII to V, the rate of increase in *ND* relative to *NM* is especially rapid, but it slackens within the intermediate range, V to III, before again rising very steeply through the largest classes, III to I. This provokes the speculative thought that there may be a 'typical' pattern of firm growth which involves three stages. In the first, growth through diversification appears a 'less difficult' strategy—perhaps mainly in the home country, and not closely related to a specific asset. Then, a first stage upper bound is encountered—perhaps the firm has exploited all easy options for diversification into adjacent local industries—and it turns to multinational production as a source of further growth. Alternatively, perhaps the first-stage diversification has allowed the firm to achieve a larger scale and to develop a specific asset, which then facilitates an expansion into foreign markets. In any event, the second-stage growth is achieved much more by increasing multinational production across other member states, while increases in diversification are kept at a more moderate pace. Eventually however, a third stage is encountered (and here we must abstract from the car firms): resources are diverted once more to expanding diversification, whist only increasing multinationality more moderately. This might be explained by eventual limits to growth in the firm's primary industry at the EU level, leading it into a further round of diversification—both at home and in other member states.

Needless to say, this story is highly stylized. It is dangerous to assume that larger firms are further along their evolutionary paths than smaller firms. Also, we should acknowledge that there will be differences between the structures of different firms *within* each size class: it is easy to find examples of firms which do not fit this stylization: consider, for instance, Michelin, which has achieved a high ranking (31) on the matrix by aggregate size, *without* diversification outside rubber. It is clearly dangerous to ignore industry effects. Nevertheless, as a description of the 'typical' pattern, this embryonic model of firm growth

[8] These are the seven classes used in Table 9.9; i.e. I = firms ranked 1–20, II = 21–50, III = 51–100, IV = 101–50, V = 151–200, VI = 201–50, VII = 251–313.

merits attention in future research, when time-series data on individual firms becomes available.

12.4 Corporate Strategy and Firm Nationality

Figure 12.2 portrays the average diversification/multinationality mix, grouping firms by country of origin. We first consider the pattern ignoring the Netherlands and the non-EU countries.

Except for the Netherlands, all of the member states record average NM values within a fairly narrow range (1 to 1.5), but they differ more significantly with respect to *ND*. The ranking of member states tends to be broadly similar by both *ND* and *NM*, and so the overall effect is a very steep upward relationship between the two (shown by the dotted line). UK firms are the most multinational and diversified, followed in both respects by France, whilst, at the other end, Spanish and Portugese firms are specialized and uninational.[9] One interpretation of this ranking would be that the member states differ in their endowment of specific assets, and that those assets facilitate both diversification and multinationality. However, this would be far too simplistic. For example, the econometric analysis of firm multinationality in Chapter 11 rejected the hypothesis that German firms are less multinational than UK firms, once we control for other factors (notably national size and a firm's country share).

Clearly, a more complex set of factors is at work, and the three-stage growth model of the previous section may have a part to play in this. Abstracting for the moment from differences in specific asset endowment, suppose that, typically, firms from different countries follow the same three-stage growth, but that they switch between stages at different firm sizes, reflecting differences in the sizes of their home country markets. For example, UK firms are more multinational and diversified than German firms because they encounter constraints on primary industry home country growth earlier than German firms; similarly, their home country diversification may be exhausted more easily.

Indeed, if one combines specific assets with constraints on domestic primary growth, allowing also for residual comparative institutional effects, the broad pattern of differences between member states can be at least partly explained as follows.

---

[9] It is important at this stage to qualify conclusions by recalling how this sample of firms has been constructed. Needless to say, the sample is, by definition, biased towards large firms. But having said this, one cannot necessarily equate the matrix firms with the largest firms in each country. As was pointed out in Chapter 3, it is possible for some quite small firms to qualify for inclusion on the matrix, so long as they are leaders in small industries. This tendency is probably most pronounced for Portugal, Spain, Italy, and (to a lesser extent) Germany (in that order), each of which features relatively prominently in some of the smaller industries in the NACE classification. Thus, the comparisons made in this section might not necessarily carry over to population averages.

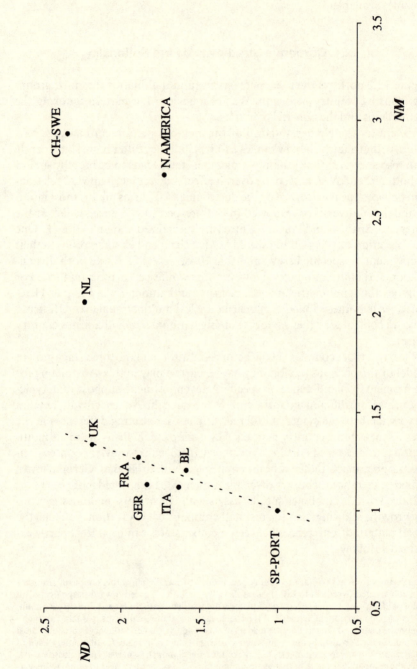

Fig. 12.2 Multinationality and diversification by country

(i) Firms from some member states are typically better endowed than others with specific assets. This partly reflects their stage of development and scientific/human capital infrastructures. This might explain why UK, France, and Germany record the highest ND and NM values, while Spain and Portugal record the lowest, with Italy occupying an intermediate position.

(ii) Against this backcloth, limits to domestic/primary industry growth are encountered at smaller firm sizes for firms from smaller countries. This would explain the UK–France–Germany ranking within the 'developed' top three (reflecting, in reverse order, the relative size of manufacturing in these three countries).

(iii) There are also some other country-specific effects (e.g. differences in a wide range of cultural/political/institutional factors, such as the capital market, patterns of ownership, language, etc.) This might account for the intermediate position of Italy.

Turning to the Netherlands and the non-EU countries, as can be seen, they are clear outliers in the diagram. However, the non-EU firms present special problems of interpretation, especially with respect to 'multinationality'. As was argued in the previous chapter, the exclusion of non-EU production from the database makes it very likely that our figures overestimate the world multinationality of these firms. Similarly, in that we ignore home country diversification, diversification may be underestimated. On the other hand, nearly all of the firms concerned are very large, both on the EU stage, and even more so world-wide. If so, it may be that the 'error' is larger on the multinational side. The Netherlands falls firmly between the two groups in the diagram—achieving similar levels of diversification to the UK and Switzerland/Sweden, but with multinationality between the two. Of course, the limited number of firms involved makes this country particularly sensitive to the structure of individual matrix firms. In this respect, it should be recalled that the convention throughout this book has been to record Unilever and Shell as Dutch-, rather than UK-, owned. If we alternatively count these firms as UK-owned, the location of the UK in the diagram is hardly changed, and while NL moves in a south-westerly direction, it still lies some distance to the right of the dotted line.[10] At this stage, we can only speculate on why the Netherlands appears to be a special case. The three-stage growth model provides part of the answer since, of course, the Dutch firms will typically encounter limits to primary industry domestic growth much earlier than firms from the larger member states. But it is difficult to avoid the conclusion that there is also an important country-specific influence.

---

[10] The mean values with Shell and Unilever counted as Dutch-owned are $NM(UK) = 1.34$, $ND(UK) = 2.19$, $NM(NL) = 2.07$ and $ND(NL) = 2.24$. If they are counted as UK-owned, $NM(UK) = 1.39$, $ND(UK) = 2.23$, $NM(NL) = 1.75$ and $ND(NL) = 1.97$. In other words, both UK figures rise by about 0.05 and both NL figures fall by about = 0.3.

12.5 Conclusion

In bringing multinationality and diversification together, this chapter has generated some new, and fascinating, patterns in our picture of corporate strategy. We have speculated by sketching out a stylized model of firm 'growth' which might account for those patterns, but we must leave more rigorous model building for the future—to be pursued when we are able to add a time dimension to the data, and take explicit account of industry effects. Returning to firmer ground, and taking an overview of this part of the book as a whole, a strong connecting theme has been the specific-asset view of firm behaviour. Empirically, we have associated this with high expenditures on advertising and/or research and development. Our evidence strongly supports the view that much multinational activity can be understood in these terms. The evidence on diversification is not so strong, but, at least for R&D, the specific-asset model appears to account for at least some types of diversification.

This means we have a strong connection between this part and the industry-based Part II of the book: in both, advertising and R&D have important roles to play. However, the theoretical rationale for this differs somewhat. Of course, it is true that, in both parts, advertising and R&D are taken as indicative of product differentiation. But the significance of this for *industrial* structure is that product differentiation often implies *endogenous fixed costs*; while its impact on *firm* structure works through the *specific-asset* model. Needless to say, the two explanations are not mutually exclusive; indeed this appears to be potential fruitful ground for cross-pollination. For instance, if these expenditures are endogenous to the evolution of market structure, then they are also endogenous to the firm's strategy.

This thought suggests that we can neither fully account for industrial structure without reference to the identities and structure of constituent firms, nor can we explain different firm-growth patterns by ignoring the industries in which they are located. At an elementary data level, this returns us to the starting point for this particular project: the construction of a database which integrates firm- and industry-level data. However, at a theoretical level, it underlines the partial nature of most theoretical models. Theoretical explanations of industrial structure tend to focus on industries without a spatial dimension and populated by symmetric firms, whose operations outside the industry are of no significance. Equally, theoretical models of the firm, especially with respect to the role of specific assets, often ignore the importance of strategic behaviour between firms with respect to advertising and R&D. The false impression is sometimes given that specific assets are intrinsic to the firm and reflect some inherent efficiency advantage, rather than being the outcome of oligopolistic rivalry.

STEVE DAVIES, LAURA RONDI and ALESSANDRO SEMBENELLI

PART IV

··

IMPLICATIONS

13

Public Procurement Industries[1]

13.1 Introduction

Purchases by the public sector account for a sizeable part of total demand in
the European Union—somewhere in the range of 15 % to 20 % of total GDP.
The importance of public procurement varies greatly across industries, and in
some cases, government purchasing policy has been highly instrumental in
forming industry structure. Before the Single European Market measures
came into effect, public procurement was still very fragmented with a different
procurement system in place for each member state. This created high (often
prohibitive) barriers for the exports of manufacturers based in other EU member states or outside countries: only 2–3 % of all public procurement contracts
were awarded to enterprises from other member states. Of course, to the extent
that these barriers were only trade-related, 'foreign' manufacturers could
resort to establishing local production units in order to become 'indigenous'
manufacturers. However, other discriminatory measures, or strategic behaviour by national champion firms in collusion with their national governments,
could also sometimes block this kind of market entry.[2] It is probable, therefore,
that measures to eliminate public procurement bias will have a considerable
effect in the reorganization of the industries concerned.

The opening up of public procurement in the single market can therefore be
expected to have a particularly profound impact on the structure of some
industries. This will involve not only closure and relocation of production
units in general, but also changes in ownership structure through various kinds
of mergers and acquisitions across the borders of member states. It follows
that Foreign Direct Investment (FDI) flows within public procurement industries merit close examination.

The rest of this chapter is organized in four sections. Section 13.2 briefly
characterizes the nature of a public procurement industry; and Section 13.3
discusses some theoretical issues relating to FDI into these industries. Section
13.4 takes an empirical perspective—describing the state of these industries

[1] We should like to acknowledge DG3 for providing some of the data for this chapter, and
R. Morsink, of the Netherlands Economic Research Institute for research assistance.
[2] Barriers to the supply of goods by subsidiaries of foreign companies were most likely when
goods had a strategic defence dimension.

prior to the Single Market legislation, and tracing some trends in the following years. Section 13.5 concludes.

13.2 The Characteristics of Public Procurement Industries

Public procurement markets will often differ considerably from markets in which customers are mainly from the private sector. Private sector markets are structured by competitive pressures originating from underlying cost and demand conditions (see Chapter 6); demand generally comes from a multitude of buyers with a variety of specific needs; and the number of suppliers depends on economies of scale, the size of the market and the type of competitive weapon. For example, although Type 1 products may sometimes be horizontally differentiated, they are mostly standardized for all customers, using known technology. Type 2 products actively compete in quality using R&D and advertising.

Public procurement markets tend to be organized differently. Generally, there is only one institution which typically demands a very specific, custom-made product. The institution belongs to the public sector, and operates under budget mechanisms rather than price mechanisms. The supply of the product comes from one firm, or a limited set of firms, which have close ties with the public institution for reasons of national strategic importance. The firm could even be state-owned. Procurement terms, including volume, quality, and price of projects, goods or the provision of services are generally negotiated or subjected to tendering systems. As many of the projects involve the acquisition of new technologies and/or infrastructure, products tend to be highly innovative and technically advanced. They also involve high value contracts.

13.3 Foreign Direct Investment and Public Procurement: theoretical perspectives

Because of the particular nature of public procurement transactions, national governments or agencies often used their buying power to favour local firms, even if a foreign supplier could offer better terms. However, if the foreign firm's better terms derived from a firm-specific advantage, then it might be able to circumvent this discrimination by establishing a production unit in the purchasing country. The resulting foreign direct investment (FDI) is then trade-substituting.

13.3.1 The ownership–localization–internalization framework

This type of FDI can be integrated into the encompassing theoretical framework developed by Dunning (1980). A firm will engage in FDI only if the following three conditions are simultaneously satisfied:

1. The firm must possess *ownership specific advantages* such as private knowledge of a technology or product design, which local firms in foreign countries do not possess or to which they cannot gain easy access. These advantages are necessary for a multinational firm to compete with local firms which have the advantage of knowing the local business conditions better and do not face the high international co-ordination cost of a multinational.

2. *Locational advantages* in foreign countries explain why firms find it more profitable to locate part of their production facilities in these countries instead of exporting from the home country. These advantages may be either on the cost side (e.g. transport costs, tariffs, cheap local labour) or on the marketing side (e.g. easy access to customers).

3. *Internalization advantages* are necessary to explain why a firm possessing an ownership-specific advantage, which is best exploited by foreign production, also prefers to produce the product itself and does not want to sell/license the advantage to local firms in foreign countries. The key problem is that it is often very difficult to sell ideas to foreign firms at an appropriate price, particularly because of the uncertainties associated with controlling and disseminating information. The costs of dealing with these uncertainties (e.g. writing, monitoring, and enforcing contracts, or adapting to changing circumstances) are known as transaction costs.

If a firm has ownership-specific advantages which are profitably exploitable by foreign production, and if the transaction costs are lower when the firm uses these advantages itself, then the company will engage in foreign direct investment. If the firm does not see locational advantages, it will prefer to establish trade relations with the foreign market. If there are no transaction cost advantages from internalization, but locational advantages exist in the foreign country, the company may license its ownership-specific advantages to a local firm in the country.

Within this general framework, Dunning has classified multinationals into several broad types based on the nature of the ownership, location and internalization advantages that motivate their internationalization. Of particular relevance here are what he calls *export platform* and *import substituting* MNEs. The motivation behind an export platform MNE is to achieve lower production costs, and use the low-cost country as a platform from which to supply third markets. In contrast, the motivation for an import-substituting MNE is as an alternative to exports as a means of supplying a local market. These two types differ importantly with respect to 'access to the market'. Export platform multinationals enjoy that access as an ownership advantage, conferred by, for example, a successful product design or international marketing network. For import-substituting multinationals, especially those in public procurement industries, access is more of a locational advantage and, to an extent, in the gift of national governments. This difference changes the nature of intervention by *dirigiste* governments concerned to promote local employment. Ownership advantages for export platforms have to be courted by governments, often with grants and tax incentives, while the courting for locational advantages must be done by the firm. In the import-substitution case, governments can strategically discriminate against imports in order to raise the relative locational advantage. Import substitution is the context of many MNEs in public procurement industries.[3]

13.3.2 Strategic issues

The locational advantages in import-substituting MNEs extend beyond simple market access. There are often strategic competitive advantages in local production, even when exporting to the local market might look the cheaper option. Apart from avoiding discrimination against imports, these strategic advantages arise from the avoidance of marginal transport and other trading costs, protection from other foreign competition, and a highly credible commitment to the market as a result of making investments in sunk production set-up costs. A full analysis of such strategic advantages soon becomes complex, and is sensitive to factors such as economies of scale and the degree to which indigenous firms are already locked into the market (see Smith, 1987, Horstmann and Markusen, 1987, Davies and Lyons, 1989). However, the essence of the strategic advantage can be given in the following simplified analysis.

Suppose there is one indigenous, local firm which we may call the 'national champion', and one foreign firm which could either export from its own home market or produce also in the local market (in the EU case, another member state). Thus, we assume that internalization advantages are such that licensing is unattractive. Further suppose that the nature of competition is such that each firm would respond to a higher output level by its rival by reducing its own output. This is known as strategic substitution: it is better to (partially) accommodate than to fight a credibly more aggressive competitive stance by a rival.[4] The best responses for both firms are drawn in Figure 13.1. RL is the best response by the local national champion for any given supply to the market by the foreign firm. RF_X is the best response of a foreign exporter (importer into the local market) to any given supply by the local firm. RF_M is the foreign firm's best response if it decides to produce locally (i.e. to become a multinational). The intersection of the relevant curves gives the equilibrium outputs for each firm.

---

[3] Governments also influence the decision to go multinational through internalization/transaction costs. Most importantly, they create a legal system which determines property rights and supports contractual relations. This influence is pervasive and it affects the general congeniality of a particular country for inward investment. Although contractual safeguards may also be more important for particular industries (e.g. intellectual property rights are more relevant in Type 2R industries than in Type 1), we do not pursue this here.

[4] The classic oligopoly model that generates such behaviour is due to Cournot. Buigues and Jacquemin (1994) use a similar reaction curve exposition to the following, albeit in a slightly different context.

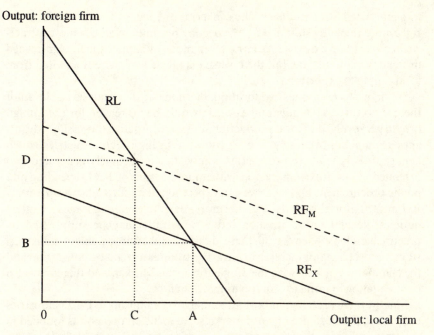

Fig. 13.1 Strategic interaction between a local and a foreign firm in a public procurement market

What determines the position of these curves? A firm with lower marginal costs of production or with a product which is preferred by customers (either because it is higher quality or there is procurement bias) will have a best response curve further from the origin. Because the multinational option avoids both trading costs and some kinds of procurement bias, the RF_M curve is drawn further to the right than the RF_X curve. Thus, the multinational option has the strategic attraction of gaining market share at the expense of the local firm.

Overhead costs (e.g. production set-up costs) do not in themselves affect the position of these curves, because they do not affect marginal output decisions.[5] However, they do affect overall profitability, and if sufficiently high, such overheads influence the entry/exit decision. Put another way, the strategic advantage of local production must outweigh the extra costs of multinational location. Sometimes, a local national champion may be able to commit to the market either by 'over-investment' or by influencing the political process, in order to keep out the foreign firm. Similarly, the local firm must cover its (non-sunk) overheads to survive. Therefore, in certain circumstances, it may be possible for multinational entry to be used to force the exit of a local competitor.

The elimination of public procurement bias normally reduces the disadvantage of exporting more than any possible disadvantage of being a

[5] Of course, overheads which raise quality (e.g. R&D) do shift out the best response function.

foreign-owned local producer. Thus, in terms of Figure 13.1, RF_X shifts to the right more than any shift in RF_M. Exporting becomes relatively more attractive in order to save overheads. For a given mode of supply, the foreign-owned firm gains market share, but the reverse may be true if there is a switch from local supply to exporting.[6]

So far, we have emphasized location, but none of this analysis is relevant if there is no ownership advantage—there would be no reason for the foreign firm to get involved in local production. In fact, distinctive ownership advantages are much more likely to be substantial in high-tech industries which engage in R&D, where proprietary knowledge is regularly generated and exploited. Thus, it is in industries with an interaction of R&D spending and public procurement bias, that we can expect to see import substituting intra-EU multinational activity. Furthermore, despite the advantages of international specialization in such industries, trade may be suppressed by procurement bias. Therefore, in these high-tech public procurement industries, we can expect a major increase in intra-EU trade as a result of integration and the elimination of bias with the Single European Market, and there may also be a reduction in intra-EU multinational activity.[7]

Finally, there are some important strategic mechanisms in R&D industries because of the existence of third markets. We focus on two points founded in the same basic idea that the larger are a firm's sales, the greater is its incentive to engage in R&D. First, a large, protected, home market can encourage R&D spending, and this makes the protected firm's product more competitive in its own export markets, which, in turn, further raises the attractions of R&D, etc.: there can be a virtuous circle based on protection (Krugman, 1987). If all countries attempt to exploit this idea, of course, they will fail as those potential export markets disappear; but this does not gainsay the temptation to protect high-tech industries. Second, the competitive escalation of R&D (in a process described in Chapter 6) can be expected to have a major impact on previously protected public procurement industries. The Single Market should see significant rationalizations and higher per firm R&D spends, as the national champions fight it out for leadership across the EU (and often in the global market).

13.3.3. Corporate Reorganisation

We have argued that the opening up of public procurement is likely to result in more intense competition in a wider market and as a consequence lead to important industry restructuring.

---

[6] The situation for export platform MNEs following the reduction of non-tariff barriers to trade is likely to be quite different, as lower trading costs make such MNEs more viable for supplying the various member states of the EU.
[7] Public procurement should have less influence on more standardized Type 1 industries, because of reduced ownership advantages and less trade even without the bias.

If scale economies are important and competition increases, an efficient European industry structure will support fewer firms operating at fuller capacity. Also, within their reorganization process, the structure of firms is changing and adapting to strategies designed for the new market environment. Within the new strategies, two factors remain essential: the need for integration of activities to save on overheads and more efficiently develop products; and the need to cater for local demands. Combining these two factors, Prahalad and Doz (1987) formulate what they call the integration-responsiveness grid.

The vertical axis shows the extent of integration of activities. As markets become integrated, a multinational firm may see opportunities to combine certain activities into one larger unit serving the integrated markets (e.g. concentration of manufacturing or marketing) instead of separate units for each sub-market. The horizontal axis represents the extent of responsiveness to local market conditions. If a market continues to show very specific requirements, it is more likely that a firm will try to meet these requirements by establishing local subsidiaries in each foreign market, in spite of some efficiency losses.

In the past, many of the advantages offered to locally operating firms in public procurement markets have also attracted firms to invest in these countries. Most of the advantages related to the better conditions offered to locally established firms, and their ability to better meet local requirements. Before the opening up of the Single Market, the typical organizational choice was therefore low on integration and high on responsiveness, including the replication of

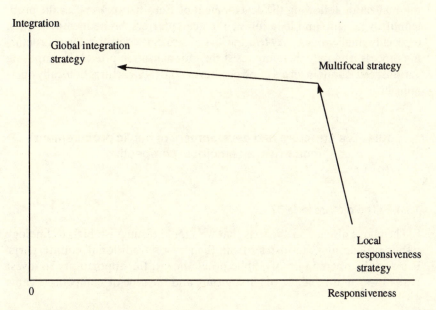

Fig. 13.2 Integration–responsiveness grid

all major functions (production, R&D, etc.) in each country. The ongoing realization of the Single Market for public procurement is forcing firms to revise those strategies and to build up Euro-network organizations which combine local responsiveness with a high degree of centralization and co-ordination of major supporting activities. Prahalad and Doz would label the underlying strategy as a multifocal strategy. However, as time passes, and public authorities further harmonize and co-ordinate their procurement policies, more firms will be able to develop global integration strategies which may lead to further efficiency gains and more intense competition in a wider market.

The adoption of multi-focal or global integration strategies needs to be implemented through the creation of pan-European network organizations (including joint ventures). The spatial organization of such pan-European networks may involve a major shift in the location pattern of key functions within the firm. The old decentralized multinational organization, which duplicated major functions in each country, needs to transform into an integrated system in which the key elements show a different degree of regional concentration.[8]

As a consequence of the new organizational structure, different types of international transactions are expected to occur. Specialization and concentration of activities in certain regions will lead to more trade among member states. Because of the network system, trade will increasingly develop into intra-firm trade and intra-industry trade, with a greater exchange of intermediate goods among the elements of the network. Also, the structure of foreign investment transactions will change and follow more closely the locational characteristics of the Euro-network system. The organizational rationalization following the development of Euro-networks poses the problem of ownership and location of the headquarters. Some member states, especially smaller ones, may fear the loss of strategic control in the restructuring process, and may therefore resist the rationalization process by imposing various restrictions in terms of ownership or control structures of locally operating firms.

13.4 The structure and development of public procurement industries: an empirical perspective

13.4.1 The picture in 1987

The above discussion suggests that we should distinguish high-technology public procurement industries from their more 'traditional' counterparts. Prior to the opening up of public procurement, the opportunity to invest abroad was more real for the first group, and the type of competitive game

---

[8] Vandermerwe (1992) suggests how this might happen.

tended to be very different from that in the traditional industries. For the latter group, the ownership or internalization advantages were often not strong enough to overcome the entry barriers imposed by national governments. Table 13.1 shows some basic characteristics for the list of ten industries usually identified as 'public procurement' (see *European Economy*, 1990). They are split into two groups—high-tech and traditional—and the data refer to the period 1985–7, i.e. before the measures to open up public procurement came into effect.

Table 13.1 Basic characteristics of public procurement industries in 1985–1987

	% share in:		imports as share of demand		Dispersion of prices net of taxes
	value added	employ- ment	intra- EU	extra- EU	
'High Tech'					
257 Pharmaceuticals	2.5	1.6	10.6	6.4	32.7
330 Computers & office machinery	2.5	1.3	30.9	36.3	7.4
341 Insulated wires & cables	1.4	1.5	11.2	8.8	8.9
342 Electrical machinery	3.4	3.7	17.9	13.0	n.a.
344 Telecom equip.	4.3	4.3	22.4	28.8	8.9
364 Aerospace	2.2	2.1	18.1	24.3	17.1
372 Medical instruments	0.4	0.5	32.0	31.4	21.1
'Traditional'					
315 Boilers & containers	n.a.	n.a.	n.a.	n.a.	n.a.
361 Shipbuilding	0.8	1.2	7.8	21.7	n.a.
362 Rail stock	0.4	0.4	5.0	3.5	21.7

Source: *European Economy*, 1990.

High-tech public procurement industries are associated with strong technological developments. Invariably, they belong to what we refer to as Type 2*R*, e.g. computers and office equipment, telecommunications equipment, and medical equipment. These industries were, and still are, characterized by high cross-investment between countries, with an important presence of Japanese and American multinational companies in Europe. There was a substantial openness to trade; both intra-EU and extra-EU imports accounted for a very significant share of apparent consumption in the member states (though often a little less than the overall Type 2*R* average 22%). Because of this trade and foreign investment exposure, competitive pressures were important, and this may explain why the dispersion of prices across the member states was already small in 1985.[9]

The group of traditional public procurement industries includes boiler-making, railway equipment, and shipbuilding: these are more likely to display

[9] The exception is pharmaceuticals, which have very large regulatory barriers to trade.

the characteristics of our Type 1. Most of these industries were protected through limited access to public procurement by 'outside firms' and strict regulations. There was little foreign investment between countries and the share of imports as a percentage of apparent consumption in the member states was typically below the overall Type 1 average 11%.

One consequence of this domestic protection, shown in Table 13.2, was that the level of capacity utilization in traditional industries was typically around or below 60%, and the number of producers was significantly higher than in the USA, in spite of the substantial scale economies characterizing these industries. In contrast, the high-tech industries had better capacity utilization, and the numbers of producers were more comparable to those for the USA.[10]

Table 13.2 Capacity utilization and economies of scale

	Capacity utilization(%)	Number of producers		Economies of scale (%)[a]
		EU	US	
Mainframe computers	80	5	9	5%
Telephone exchanges	70	11	4	20%
Telephone handsets	90	12	17	n.a.
Turbine generators	60	10	2	12%
Boiler-making	20	12	6	20%
Locomotives	50–80	16	2	20%

[a] % unit cost reductions resulting from a doubling of output.

Source: *European Economy*, 'The Economics of 1992', no.35, 1988.

More detail on the industrial structure of public procurement industries, based on the decomposition of Chapter 4, is given in Table 13.3. Recall that *NM* is a number-equivalent measure of intra-EU multinationality of operations by firms in the industry, *SPEC* is a measure of the specialization of production in a few member states, *TRADESPEC* is a measure of intra-EU trade specialization (see Chapter 5), and *HEU* and *HNAT* are Herfindahl indices of industrial concentration at the EU and typical member state levels.

Again, there is a marked difference between high-tech and more traditional industries. In part, this is only to be expected given the nature of R&D competition, so more meaningful comparisons are with the overall averages for Type 2*R* industries (for high-tech sectors) and Type 1 (for traditional industries). *The effect of public procurement on intra-EU multinationality is striking: it raises the incidence of multinationals in high-tech sectors, where local production is necessary to avoid the bias,*[11] *and completely eliminates multinationality in traditional industries, where the ownership advantages are too small to*

---

[10] This is a general result for high-tech industries. In Chapter 6, we show that EU concentration levels are closer to the USA in Type 2*R* industries than in Type 1.

[11] The exception is aerospace, which is closely tied to defence and so has a unique degree of bias in favour of domestically owned firms.

Table 13.3 Industrial structure in public procurement industries

NACE	Industry	*NM*	*SPEC*	*TRADE-SPEC*	*HEU*	*HNAT*
High-tech						
257	Pharmaceuticals	1.92	0.17	0.012	0.02	0.06
330	Computers	3.62	0.22	0.071	0.20	0.26
341	Insulated cables	1.89	0.30	0.015	0.01	0.03
342	Electrical machinery	2.03	0.25	0.059	0.01	0.02
344	Telecom/measuring equip.	1.88	0.29	0.027	0.03	0.05
364	Aerospace	1.02	0.30	0.009	0.09	0.29
372	Medical inst.	1.61	0.32	0.042	0.03	0.06
Type 2*R* overall average		1.49	0.26	0.049	0.03	0.08
Traditional						
315	Boilers, containers	1.00	0.26	0.017	0.002	0.01
361	Shipbuilding	1.00	0.15	0.024	0.01	0.09
362	Rail stock	1.00	0.23	0.025	0.04	0.19
Type 1 overall average		1.24	0.20	0.031	0.006	0.023

overcome any bias against foreign ownership. Furthermore, although there is no apparent distortion in the international specialization of production, *SPEC*, this turns out to be largely due to consumption patterns. The specialization of trade, *TRADESPEC*, is generally less in public procurement industries, a tendency that is particularly clear in the traditional sectors. Differences in economies of scale cloud the comparison of concentration, but the relative sizes of national and EU concentration summarize the combined effect of bias against foreign ownership and foreign production. For high-tech industries, multinational operations largely compensate for any trade bias, so the ratio of *HNAT* to *HEU* is around 2 or 3, like in other Type 2*R* industries. However, for traditional industries, public procurement bias keeps EU concentration very low compared with national concentration.

Overall, high-tech public procurement firms tend to produce in several national public procurement markets and thus have a large share of European production. Hence the relatively high levels of EU concentration observed for this group of industries. In contrast, firms in traditional industries tend to produce in only one national market, often dominated by a national champion.[12]

13.4.2 Developments since 1987

Most of the measures to open up public procurement were decided and came gradually into effect after 1987, the year the Single European Act was made law. It is therefore interesting to see what has happened in these industries since

[12] Abravanel and Ernst (1992) operationalize the idea of a national champion by defining one as a company that earns more than a third of total revenues and profits in its home country and has long enjoyed formal or informal government protection. This would appear to be a rather loose definition in the case of traditional industries.

Table 13.4 Changes in country specialization in production
and trade, 1987–1992

	Change in:	
	SPEC	*TRADE*
High-tech		
Pharmaceuticals	–0.01	+4
Computers & office machinery	+0.01	n.a.
Insulated wires & cables	n.a.	n.a.
Electrical machinery	+0.02	+2
Telecom & measuring equipment	+0.02	n.a.
Aerospace	–0.02	+33
Medical instruments	–0.01	+3
Traditional		
Boilers & containers	+0.01	+3
Shipbuilding	–0.01	+8
Rail stock	–0.01	+16

1987. Table 13.4 shows how country specialization, *SPEC*, and intra-EU trade
flows relative to total demand changed between 1987 and 1992.

The specialization of country shares in production has not significantly
changed after 1987. This suggests that the allocation of production capacities
across the countries has typically remained roughly the same. On the other
hand, intra-European trade has increased in all public procurement industries,
with the most significant increases for the traditional public procurement
industries. The implication is that the prime effect of the Single Market in these
industries has been to raise intra-industry trade (as suggested by the theory in
Section 13.3).

Table 13.5 investigates developments within three member states, Germany,
Spain, and France, for which we have been able to collect appropriate data. The
first columns show the development of 'revealed comparative advantage'. This
is a measure of relative specialization, measured by production or exports, in a
particular industry by a particular country: numbers less than one suggest a
comparative disadvantage, while numbers greater than one suggest comparative advantage.

A very clear pattern emerges for Germany, with both advantages (e.g. in
electrical machinery and telecoms) and disadvantages (e.g. in pharmaceuticals, computers, and aerospace) being reinforced as public procurement bias is
reduced. This pattern is also shown by the higher and increasing import penetration in disadvantage industries, and low and stable import penetration in
industries with a comparative advantage. There is a similar, though less clear
pattern with exports. One interesting twist is provided by aerospace, which is
the only industry in which intra-EU imports are growing much faster than
extra-EU import penetration. While it seems that the reduction of public procurement bias is having a fairly even-handed effect with respect to member and

Table 13.5(a) Changes in specialization and international trade of German public procurement industries

NACE Industry		Revealed comparative advantage				Import penetration (%)				Export share (%)	
		Production		Exports		Intra-EU		Extra-EU			
		1987	1992	1987	1992	1987	1992	1987	1992	1987	1992
High-tech											
257	Pharmaceuticals	0.76	0.60	0.74	0.71	11	13	9	11	29	32
330	Computers	1.00	0.85	0.66	0.59	30	30	31	37	57	51
342	Electrical machinery	2.11	4.08	1.61	1.74	5	6	6	7	15	21
344	Telecoms	1.65	2.44	1.31	1.46	5	5	7	9	22	21
364	Aerospace	0.45	0.42	0.62	0.51	59	79	26	29	82	100
372	Medical instruments	1.63	1.95	1.37	1.33	14	17	21	27	51	50
Traditional											
315	Boilers & containers	1.12	1.25	1.37	1.32	2	5	2	3	16	17
361	Shipbuilding	0.77	0.62	0.89	0.78	9	6	4	10	41	47
362	Rail stock	0.53	0.49	0.98	2.82	10	10	12	11	56	55

Notes: (1) Comparative advantage index: $\{X_{jk}/X_{jEU}\}/\{\{X_k/X_{EU}\}$ where X_{jk} is production (or export) of industry j in (or from) country k; X_k is total manufacturing output in (or exports from) country k.
(2) Import penetration is imports divided by demand = production – exports + imports
(3) Export share equals exports divided by total production.

Table 13.5(b) Changes in specialization and international trade of Spanish public procurement industries

NACE	Industry	Revealed comparative advantage				Import penetration (%)				Export share (%)	
		Production		Exports		Intra-EU		Extra EU			
		1987	1992	1987	1992	1987	1992	1987	1992	1987	1992
High-tech											
257	Pharmaceuticals	0.92	1.30	1.11	0.86	87	65	60	34	16	12
330	Computers	0.28	0.16	0.72	0.68	75	70	28	33	93	169
342	Electrical machinery	0.52	0.49	0.52	0.67	61	68	87	91	15	25
344	Telecoms equipment	0.37	0.39	0.27	0.53	23	48	48	62	11	23
364	Aerospace	0.17	0.30	0.31	0.40	99	99	63	63	47	76
372	Medical instruments	0.21	0.19	0.46	0.48	33	34	64	48	71	93
Traditional											
315	Boilers & containers	0.53	0.56	0.52	0.81	26	37	53	22	7	13
361	Shipbuilding	1.24	1.25	1.80	2.72	89	95	8	29	24	50
362	Rail stock	1.74	2.30	0.43	0.97	58	30	98	21	4	13

Note: See notes to Table 13.5(a).

Table 13.5(c) Changes in specialization and international trade of French public procurement industries

NACE	Industry	Revealed comparative advantage				Import penetration (%)				Export share (%)	
		Production		Exports		Intra-EU		Extra-EU			
		1987	1992	1987	1992	1987	1992	1987	1992	1987	1992
High-tech											
257	Pharmaceuticals	1.36	1.36	1.23	1.05	6	10	3	6	18	22
330	Computers	1.17	1.14	1.06	0.87	36	37	22	23	50	50
342	Electrical machinery	0.98	0.75	1.35	1.22	16	20	6	8	28	35
344	Telecoms	0.58	0.56	1.04	0.99	20	21	13	19	37	42
364	Aerospace	2.38	2.33	1.50	4.44	7	90	7	54	28	100
372	Medical instruments	0.80	0.98	0.81	0.81	32	32	25	23	47	49
Traditional											
315	Boilers & containers	2.45	2.04	1.31	1.25	3	3	0	0	7	10
361	Shipbuilding	0.37	0.48*	0.97	1.63*	18	58*	15*	24*	56	85*
362	Rail stock	1.03	0.88	5.02	1.20	7	18	9	13	67	56

* Data are for 1991.

Note: See notes to Table 13.5(a).

non-member states, there have been more purchasing and intra-EU alliances in defence-dominated aerospace.

Spain has had a different experience, reflecting a lower relative production base in the high-tech sectors. In some of these (e.g. aerospace and telecoms) a prior disadvantage is disappearing, presumably as work is being contracted out to this lower-cost member state. Spain seems to be similarly benefiting from the reduction of procurement bias in the traditional industries.

In France however, there has been a remarkable stability in specialization and trade, which by 1992 was still showing few signs of change due to the Single Market (but aerospace and shipbuilding are noticeable exceptions).

The trends in three further measures of industrial organization are presented in Table 13.6. We start again with Germany. As we have already found in Chapter 5, there is greater intra-industry trade in the high-tech sectors; and this appears to be an increasing trend. This is in line with our earlier prediction that the first effect of reducing procurement bias might be to create Euro-networks, mergers, joint-ventures, and other alliances, and the exchange of intermediate goods, possibly prior to greater rationalization at a later date. However, given that intra-industry trade has been increasing in general (see Table 2.6), on this evidence we cannot claim to have identified a clear public procurement effect. Nevertheless, the trend in intra-industry trade in components[13] in some

Table 13.6(a) Changes in intra-industry trade, vertical integration, and foreign ownership of German public procurement industries

NACE	Industry	Intra-industry trade				Vertical integration		Foreign ownership	
		Total		Components					
		1987	1992	1987	1992	1987	1992	1987	1992
High-tech									
257	Pharmaceuticals	0.74	0.80	0.89	0.85	0.49	0.49	0.02	0.03
330	Computers	0.92	0.67	0.89	0.76	0.45	0.42	0.69	0.57
342	Electrical mach.	0.65	0.71	0.48	0.52	0.48	0.45	0.37	0.20
344	Telecoms	0.65	0.76	0.91	0.92	0.58	0.56	0.29	0.37
364	Aerospace	0.90	0.97	0.85	0.43	0.52	0.47	n.a.	n.a.
372	Medical insts.	0.69	0.88	0.40	0.67	0.59	0.59	0.10	0.04
Traditional									
315	Boilers etc.	0.41	0.60	0.57	0.77	0.45	0.46	0.07	0.03
361	Shipbuilding	0.37	0.39	0.37	0.10	0.33	0.29	n.a.	n.a.
362	Rail stock	0.36	0.29	0.34	0.54	0.50	0.48	n.a.	n.a.

Notes: Intra-industry trade is measured by the Grubel–Lloyd index (see Table 2.6). Vertical integration is measured as the ratio of value added to sales. Foreign ownership is measured as the share of output accounted for by foreign firms. Components are defined in footnote 13.

[13] Components are subsectors (SITC codes) within the NACE group which cover mainly spare parts and intermediate goods belonging to that NACE industry. We are grateful to D. Mardas for providing us with data on this variable. See also Mardas (1993).

Table 13.6(b) Changes in intra-industry trade, vertical integration, and foreign ownership of Spanish public procurement industries

NACE	Industry	Intra-industry trade				Vertical integration		Foreign owneship	
		Total		Components					
		1987	1992	1987	1992	1987	1992	1987	1992
High-tech									
257	Pharmaceuticals	0.86	0.86	0.35	0.35	0.40	0.39	0.90	0.84
330	Computers	0.57	0.55	0.48	0.47	n.a.	n.a.	0.84	0.94
342	Electrical mach.	0.70	0.75	0.59	0.51	—	—	0.35	0.64
344	Telecoms	0.35	0.54	0.32	0.64	—	—	0.77	0.63
364	Aerospace	0.77	0.77	0.92	0.76	—	—	n.a.	n.a.
372	Medical insts.	0.48	0.41	0.79	0.73	—	—	0.31	0.30
Traditional									
315	Boilers etc.	0.73	0.77	0.86	0.35	n.a.	n.a.	n.a.	n.a.
361	Shipbuilding	0.26	0.41	0.37	0.22	—	—	—	—
362	Rail stock	0.81	0.81	0.94	0.45	—	—	0.26	0.30

Note: See notes to Table 13.6(a).

Table 13.6(c) Changes in intra-industry trade, vertical integration, and foreign ownership of French public procurement industries

NACE	Industry	Intra-industry trade				Vertical integration		Foreign ownership	
		Total		Components					
		1987	1992	1987	1992	1987	1992	1987	1992
High-tech									
257	Pharmaceuticals	0.61	0.79	0.67	0.77	0.33	0.34	0.45	0.55
330	Computers	0.83	0.79	0.99	0.88	0.53	0.42	0.67	0.74
342	Electrical mach.	0.84	0.83	0.88	0.62	0.52	0.42	0.27	0.25
344	Telecoms	0.92	0.96	0.64	1.00	0.56	0.43	0.27	0.31
364	Aerospace	0.60	0.90	0.41	0.60	0.46	0.31	0.05	0.05
372	Medical insts.	0.83	0.87	0.36	0.88	0.60	0.50	0.84	0.83
Traditional									
315	Boilers etc.	0.60	0.55	0.84	0.86	0.53	0.42	0.03	0.07
361	Shipbuilding	0.56	0.84	0.20	0.57	0.34	0.33	—	—
362	Rail stock	0.20	0.53	0.41	0.72	0.42	0.36	0.23	0.10

Note: See notes to Table 13.6(a).

industries lends some support to our interpretation of intra-group specialization, as does the fairly systematic decline in our measure of vertical integration. Finally, there has been a general decline in foreign ownership, a finding which complements the increasing imports result found in Table 13.5(a). This suggests an unravelling of foreign-owned multinationals which had been motivated by the need to avoid public procurement bias.

232   *Public Procurement Industries*

A very similar picture emerges for France (see Table 13.6(c)), with a strong reduction in measured vertical integration, but a weaker trend in foreign ownership. The latter ties in with the stability in French import penetration and generally slow structural response to the Single Market. Finally, there has been much less change in the Table 13.6(b) variables in Spain. Consistent with the increasing use of Spain as a subcontractor location, we find a reduction in the proportion of intra-industry trade (i.e. increasing share of 'comparative advantage' trade) in components in traditional industries.

13.5 Conclusion

Public procurement bias has been one of the most significant barriers to free trade within the EU. It affects high-tech and more traditional industries in different ways. Economies of scale in R&D give an incentive for high-tech firms to try to get round the bias by locating production in the purchasing member state. This strategic incentive is not present in traditional industries, which typically have fewer specific ownership advantages worth applying internationally. Thus, while public procurement bias always suppresses trade integration, it can actually stimulate the international integration of corporate strategy.[14]

Looking in detail at the structure of public procurement industries in 1987, we find that they did have lower import penetration, and high-tech industries did compensate by multinational operations. Five years later, when some important parts of the Single Market programme had been implemented, we could already observe some unwinding of these multinational operations. The geographical specialization of the EU had not yet changed significantly, but there were signs of change in trade and ownership. For example, Germany was consolidating according to its apparent comparative advantage, French public procurement industries were becoming less vertically integrated, and Spain was able to increase its share of components for the previously protected industries.

LEO SLEUWAEGEN and BRUCE LYONS

[14] Our results in this chapter on the effects of public procurement on multinationality help to explain the lack of statistical significance of the *PUB* variable in the econometric analysis of multinationality in Chapter 7. It is now apparent that 'PUB' has a positive influence for Type 2R industries, but a negative influence for Type 1.

14

Conclusions and Applications

14.1 Introduction

We opened this book with a statement of our main research objectives concerning the structure of manufacturing in the European Union. Factually, we wanted to widen the scope, and deepen the detail, of what was already known about individual firms and industries in this key sector. We also argued that the definition of 'structure' should be sufficiently wide to include dimensions of international trade and corporate strategy, as well as industrial organization. This is necessary if one is to rigorously pursue the underlying theoretical thesis of our work, namely, that by observing different elements of structure, we can learn much about the competitive processes which have helped to form that structure. Coming from this perspective, our third aim was to contribute to the current debate about the integration of European industry.

The purpose of this chapter is neither to extensively summarize our results, which would be repetitive, nor to evaluate our success in meeting our objectives—the reader will form her/his own judgement on this. Instead, in Section 14.2 we give a brief overview, and Section 14.3 emphasizes the importance of our industry typology. This leads into a longer discussion of some applications of our results, with particular reference to the significance of economics of scale; EU integration and the Single Market; Competition policy; and the role of nationality. We conclude in Section 14.5 with some directions for future research.

14.2 An Overview

With the hindsight engendered by finally writing up a research project in book form, there are three essential distinctive features to our work: the market share matrix, the core decompositions, and the development of the theoretical Type 1/Type 2 typology.

We believe that the market share matrix is a remarkably efficient means for distilling the essence of industrial and firm structure into a compact and easy to use database. With information on little more than 300 firms, it can generate a stream of information, much of which was previously unknown. Thus we now know that Europe's largest 100 firms account for just under 30% of total manufacturing output; and, in the typical industry, the top five firms are responsible for about one-quarter of total output—although, in some cases, it is much more. We have found that individual firms may achieve large aggregate size in a variety of ways—sometimes 'simply' by virtue of securing a large market share in a large industry, sometimes by wide diversification across industries, and, in both cases, sometimes by arranging production across a number of different member states. Neither diversification nor multinationality has been previously plotted in such detail, and our findings open up a range of possibilities.[1] A regularly updated matrix would provide a rich resource for those engaged in research and interested in policy issues concerning the European Union, especially if supplemented with other data sources such as input–output tables, world trade statistics, and financial company databases.

On a more conceptual level, the matrix leads fairly naturally to the decomposition analysis which we have used extensively throughout the book. Undoubtedly, this provides an overall presentational framework. But, more important, it highlights the relatedness of the various elements of structure at EU and national, and at industry and firm levels. From a theoretical angle, this helps us to draw together the related subjects of industrial organization, international trade and corporate strategy. Empirically, it emphasizes the scope for cross-pollination in statistical results.

The third distinctive feature is the typology of Type 1 and Type 2 industries, and its ramifications. On this, it is worth reiterating our intellectual debt to Sutton (1991). Unlike the matrix and the decompositions, the full implications of industry type only really became apparent as the project progressed. If the matrix forms the factual core, and the decompositions the methodological core, then the Type 1/Type 2 distinction emerges strongly as the theoretical core to our work. The next section develops this claim.

14.3 Industry Types

A major theme in this book has been the importance of distinguishing the type of industry according to its prevalent form of competitive weapon and the way that product differentiation is created. Our typology had its roots in three sub-disciplines of economics: international trade, industrial organization, and international business. Product differentiation is a major motive for international trade as products are exchanged to cater for consumers with differing tastes or incomes. The escalation of advertising and R&D spending, as firms attempt to gain the competitive edge of higher perceived quality than rivals, is limited only by the size of the market and this has a profound effect on the structure of the industry. Such spending, and the talent behind it, creates firm specific advantages that are often best exploited, not by exports or licensing,

---

[1] For example, the estimates of multinationality at the individual level offer a real alternative to FDI statistics, which are typically over-aggregate and often subject to a large margin of error.

but by international production. Thus, the consequences of the different types of competition affect the country, the industry, and the firm.

We operationalized our typology by focusing on these two most visible sources of product differentiation, sources which are under the control of firms and which are overhead costs creating economies of scale. We distinguished Type 1 industries, which engage in little advertising or R&D, from Type 2 industries. We further distinguished Type 2 according to whether an industry engages in only advertising, only R&D, or both (Type 2A, Type 2R, or Type 2AR respectively). Just over half of manufacturing industries are classified as Type 1, and these are mainly associated with the processing of material such as iron and steel, cement, foundries, grain-milling, and the textile and wood-processing industries. Type 2A, accounting for about an eighth of manufacturing, mostly come from food, drink, and tobacco. Type 2R, about a quarter of manufacturing, include some chemicals, but mainly come from the engineering sectors of machinery, instruments, and transport equipment. The overlap of advertising and R&D comes in just nine large industries which account for 14% of manufacturing output, and these Type 2AR industries include a relatively broad range of consumer durables (e.g. cars, domestic electrical appliances) and non-durables (e.g. pharmaceuticals, soaps and detergents).

It is possible to characterize some of the most noticeable differences in the industrial organization of the four types. In terms of the global context of the EU relative to the USA and Japan, we showed in Chapter 2 that the EU has a weak production and export performance in R&D intensive sectors, but does well in sectors associated with advertising. The Type 2R industries are most open to trade, especially outside the EU, while Type 2A industries trade relatively little, and then mainly between member states. As shown in Chapter 5, a large share of the Type 2R trade is intra-industry. Looking at the size and international spread of firms operating within the industry types, Type 2AR are much the most concentrated and also the most multinational within the EU. Even allowing for other factors such as production economies of scale, Type 1 are the least concentrated and least multinational (Chapters 6 and 7). However, there are some interesting differences within the Type 2 groups, where Type 2R are more concentrated and less multinational than Type 2A.[2] The association between advertising, R&D, and multinationality is reinforced by the pattern of ownership by non-EU multinationals (Chapter 8).

Putting together the evidence on trade and multinationality, we find that only around one-third of Type 1 industries are integrated across the EU, compared with over a half of Type 2A and well over three-quarters of R&D intensive industries. The predominant form of integration for Type 1 industries is by trade, Type 2R are integrated equally by trade and by multinational operation, and nearly all integrated advertising-intensive industries are integrated by

[2] Recent trends in mergers and foreign direct investment look to be reinforcing this characterization of the different industrial structures by industry type (see Chapter 2).

multinational operations. The strength of this characterization is reinforced by the fact that some Type $2R$ industries have been forced into a multinational strategy when trade has been suppressed by public procurement bias, and a more balanced form of integration seems to be emerging with the reduction in this bias (see Chapter 13). This picture is developed further in Part III of the book, where R&D and advertising are shown to be crucial sources of specific assets which result in the corporate strategies of multinational operation and diversification. Furthermore, firms tend to diversify across industries of a similar type.

The explanation of these observed patterns is to be found in the individual chapters of this book, and there is no space to repeat them here. However, we do draw on our earlier behavioural analysis, as well as the industry typology, to develop some policy-relevant applications in the following section.

14.4 Applications

In this section, we apply the theoretical framework and results found in this book to see what light can be shed on four important questions of immediate policy relevance. What are the most important sources of economies of scale in manufacturing industry and how does competition help to achieve such cost savings? How integrated was the EU market in the late 1980s and how will the 1992 Single Market reforms have changed that? Which particular industries are the greatest concern for competition policy and does a clear pattern emerge to aid in formulating rules of intervention? Does nationality matter either in the location of production or in the ownership of firms and, if so, are there discernible patterns of national dominance? We do not claim to provide definitive answers to these questions, but focus on what can be learned from the results in this book and at this stage of our research.

14.4.1 Economies of Scale

It has long been appreciated that economies of scale are important in determining the structure of industry. However, until recently, much less was understood about the mechanisms which relate different types of economy of scale to the different elements of structure. It was only with the work of Sutton (1991) that a clear empirical distinction was made between the effect of production economies of scale and overheads such as advertising and R&D.

While it is approximately true to claim that production economies of scale are exogenous,[3] this cannot be claimed for advertising or R&D. For example,

---

[3] This is only approximately true because new technological developments tend to incorporate economies of scale relevant to the size of the market. For example, although there is nothing fundamentally different about the science of making cars or tractors, the mass market for cars has led car technology in the direction of larger economies of scale.

R&D is not an exogenous overhead, but it is actively used by firms as a competitive weapon. There is no upper limit to R&D as long as extra spending enhances the possibility of generating an innovation. Furthermore, R&D is heavily dependent on the size of the market: the larger the market over which new products can be marketed and cost savings applied, the greater the incentive to engage in R&D. Similar considerations apply to marketing expenditures such as advertising, with one important difference. Whereas the fruits of R&D spending can often be internationally applied, mass advertising is normally aimed at national markets, if only because of language differences.

Throughout this book, these simple differences in the types of economy of scale have been shown to have profoundly different effects on the central elements of industrial structure: trade, concentration, and multinationality. In the following paragraphs, we tie together some of the results from Chapters 5, 6, 7, and 11, in order to draw out the inter-relatedness of industrial structure and the different sources of economies of scale.

Although economies of scale in production are insufficiently large systematically to affect the international distribution of production and trade, they are a major influence on individual firms. This can be seen in our econometric work on the determinants of concentration and multinationality. Production economies are by far the most important influence on concentration in Type 1 industries. However, this effect is diluted in Type 2 industries, and production economies cease to have any influence on concentration when firms compete in both advertising and R&D.

There is another twist. Although production economies do not affect the international location of production, they do affect the pattern of international ownership. With large economies of scale, individual firms find it less profitable to spread their production internationally. Thus, large production economies of scale raise EU concentration at the same time as reducing international ownership, and without any discernible effect on intra-EU trade. Just what this implies for European integration is taken up in the next section.

R&D and advertising both act to raise consumer willingness to pay for a product—in short, its perceived quality. This results in the competitive escalation of these overhead costs, the ultimate size of which is limited only by the size of the market. Thus, unlike with production economies, it makes no sense to talk about the achievement of economies of scale in advertising or R&D as long as a little more spending can give your product a little more competitive edge. It is this that blunts the effect of production economies on concentration, particularly with that potent mix of advertising alongside R&D competition. These two endogenous fixed costs also create a strong incentive for firms to exploit their proprietary knowledge internationally. Although this is a well-known finding for R&D, we find an even stronger intra-EU multinationality effect associated with advertising. Finally, along with this quality effect, there is often also an increase in horizontal differentiation between products which compete in this way. Since it is not possible for each country to supply all varieties, because of production economies of scale, this results in increased intra-industry trade in Type 2 industries, with consumers from different countries buying the product that most closely matches their particular tastes.

The aim of this book is to understand the organization of EU industry, and we have largely avoided the important implications for competition policy. One reason for this self-imposed restraint is that the most important anti-competitive effects are likely to be observed at a more disaggregated level than the 3-digit industries we have worked with here. Nevertheless, we believe that the central mechanisms we have highlighted here are also working at the 4- or 5-digit level of industry definition— the finer level at which most anti-trust enforcement rightly operates. Because of this, some lessons on the achievement of economies of scale can still be drawn.

At the heart of most competition policy investigations is a trade-off between potential cost savings versus price raising due to a proposed merger, an existing dominant position, or restrictive practice between firms. Our findings reinforce the view that trans-boundary mergers in the EU might be an important mechanism for firms to exploit their knowledge base due to R&D or marketing skills. However, in the absence of international rationalization, such mergers are not going to achieve lower production costs.[4] This suggests that, judged on production costs alone, there should be greater competition policy vigilance for EU mergers in Type 1 as opposed to Type 2 industries. Some further reflections on competition policy are developed below, following a discussion of European integration.

14.4.2 Integration and the Single European Market (SEM)

As soon as the Single European Act was signed in 1986, the European Commission commissioned a series of wide-ranging studies into the potential impact of the 300 or so detailed measures that together were expected to create a single market in the EU by the end of 1992. These measures included the abolition of all remaining tariffs and quotas, but they were mainly aimed at the non-tariff barriers of: frontier controls; national differences in technical regulations; public procurement bias in favour of domestic producers; and so-called fiscal frontiers created by differences in national tax levels and regimes. The commissioned studies were collected under the title 'The Costs of Non-Europe', though this is often referred to as the Cecchini Report after the chairman of the project steering committee.

---

[4] Of course, a takeover by a better managed firm may achieve cost savings, but this has no necessary link with economies of scale. It is also questionable whether management techniques can successfully be transferred in such a way.

Based on these studies, Emerson (1988) brings together the overall framework and mechanisms through which the SEM was expected to affect EU industry.[5] Four principal mechanisms were identified:

(1) direct cost savings due to the elimination of non-tariff barriers (e.g. fewer customs delays and costs of multiple certification);

(2) cost savings derived from the change in volume and location of production, including the achievement of economies of scale, learning economies, and better exploitation of comparative advantage;

(3) increased competitive pressure reducing prices and inefficiency due to more firms from different member states competing across the EU; and

(4) the same increased competitive pressure generating speedier innovation.

Some brave attempts were made to evaluate the potential contribution of these mechanisms, but inevitably these were hampered by the lack of a relevant database on the structure of EU industry at the time, as well as a fragmented view of the way that structure was likely to evolve, and the usual problems of forecasting in an uncertain world. Nevertheless, it was argued that the direct cost savings would be beneficial, but these were expected to be small in comparison with the potential savings and dynamism that might be generated by the other mechanisms.

As a snapshot of 1987, this book cannot in itself evaluate the 1992 Single Market programme, but it does give an important perspective. We have generated a comprehensive, compact, base-year database from which changes in the various dimensions of industrial structure can be measured.[6] Moreover, this has enabled us to gain greater insight into the nature of economic integration in the EU at the time, and so we have a clearer view of how it is likely to change in response to the SEM. In particular, we identify two types of integration: trade integration and the integration of corporate strategy. Only the first of these was measured for a wide range of industries in the Cecchini report, and consequently trade received much the most emphasis, even though the corporate location of production was found to be important in some of the industry studies (e.g. pharmaceuticals).

In this book, we have been able to examine both dimensions of integration across the entire range of manufacturing, and this gives a clearer view of the likely changes that the SEM might bring. For example, in the simple classification of industries in Table 7.5, only 29% were trade-integrated in 1987, but this figure rises to 49% once the intra-EU multinational operations of firms in those industries are taken into account. Although the definitions

---

[5] Emerson (1988) was first published as a special issue of the journal *European Economy*. The background studies were written by independent academics and consultants, and the final report was pulled together as a collaborative work by economists mostly from DGII (Directorate-General for Economic and Financial Affairs).

[6] A retrospective analysis of the effects of the SEM is currently the subject of our ongoing research.

used are fairly arbitrary, these figures strongly suggest that trade alone gives only a very partial picture of EU integration.

Furthermore, our Chapter 6 results on the determinants of industrial structure allow an evaluation of the role of trade integration by industry type. As a group, Type $2AR$ industries were already substantially integrated by 1987. The prime form of integration for Type $2A$ industries was by multinational operation, and apart from some rationalization in industries where production economies of scale are large, this pattern is likely to continue. Only in Type 1 and Type $2R$ industries was there evidence that the extent of existing trade integration was having a major influence on the pattern of competition. For these industry types, the reduction of non-tariff barriers is likely to raise intra-EU trade and the intensity of EU competition. Inasmuch as this happens, we can expect to observe an increase in EU industrial concentration. This need not imply a move towards monopoly because the change in the geographic level at which competition operates will have brought it about. For example, in the extreme case where competition shifts entirely from national markets to the EU level, then if we want to understand the changing pressure on price competition, we should compare pre-SEM national concentration with post-SEM EU concentration. Of course, it is unlikely that any industry will experience such a drastic change, but this example serves to focus on one of the complexities in interpreting structure and competition in the context of the SEM.

These observations are obviously most relevant to the third of Emerson's SEM transmission mechanisms, i.e. relating to the effects on competitive pressure. As to the other three mechanisms, we have nothing new to add to what has already been said about the direct-cost savings. The savings attributable to higher volumes of production have been discussed in the previous section, where we stressed the importance of production economies of scale to Type 1 industries, but their much reduced role in Type 2 industries. In the context of the SEM, this means that the most significant reductions in production costs are likely to be in low-trade type 1, and possibly in low-trade type 2R industries which have experienced substantial national protection. For type 2A industries, the expectations are less clear, but there may be some substitution of trade integration for multinational operation in some industries.

We can be a little more confident in what will happen to innovation (the fourth mechanism), since most R&D-intensive industries are already integrated in one form or the other. Thus, they are already likely to be setting their R&D budgets at a level appropriate to the European, or even global, market. Apart from some important direct-cost savings (e.g. in avoiding multiple certification), for many industries the SEM is unlikely to add greatly to the pace of technical progress and innovation. Once again, some highly protected Type $2R$ industries, particularly those selling to the public sector, are an exception to this conclusion, and we return to these shortly.

Only two Chapters in this book begin to look directly at what has happened since 1987. In chapter 2, we examine recent trends in mergers, foreign direct investment flows (FDI), and trade. There was a large surge in mergers beginning in 1987, though this should be seen as part of a global phenomenon. Interestingly, the sectors most affected by mergers were chemicals followed by food, drink, and tobacco. These sectors include most of the advertising-intensive industries. There was also considerable activity in some other R&D-intensive sectors. Consistent with our analysis in Section 14.2, the declared motive for these mergers shifted towards reasons to do with the strengthening of market position, and away from reasons related to economies of scale. FDI displayed a similar pattern of activity. However, there was less growth in intra-EU trade in the late 1980s than there had been in earlier years. Alongside an increase in the share of intra-industry trade, this suggests there was no significant increase in international specialization after 1987.

It is against this background that the public procurement industries should be compared. This is a group that was protected by some of the strongest non-tariff barriers pre-SEM, and so gives a strong indicator of the extent to which the SEM may have a significant effect. In 1987, the distortions created by public procurement bias had encouraged high-tech firms to become more multinational in their production strategies in order to gain a national identity. Such a strategy also required significant local content of inputs, one consequence of which was excessive national vertical integration. By 1992, however, there were already signs of this biased structure unravelling, with trade increasing and multinationality declining. To the extent that this is the only consequence of the SEM in these industries, and there is no extra widening of the market horizons of individual firms, it would add little to the incentive to engage in R&D. However, given our finding that low-trade Type $2R$ industries are less concentrated than those with similar production scale economies relative to the EU market size, the opening of public procurement is likely to raise concentration in these industries. The competitive process by which this will be achieved may involve greater price competition, but the crucial process will be an increase in R&D spending to gain the competitive edge. Taken together, these two dimensions of competition will leave less room for lower spending firms, who will have to exit the market, form joint ventures, or merge in order to survive.

Thus, it is only by looking at both the trade and corporate strategy dimensions of integration, *and* at sensitive industry groups in comparison with the general trends, that a true picture of the impact of the SEM can be observed.[7]

14.4.3 Competition Policy

The theoretical analysis in Chapter 6 showed how important it is to understand why an observed industrial structure is as it is. Given a certain level of production economies of scale, more competition results in greater industrial

---

[7] In as much as many of the SEM measures will benefit all industries, such comparisons underestimate the true impact.

concentration, as lower prices leave less room for a large number of profitable firms. Similarly, successful collusion can lead to excessive entry of firms at the sacrifice of scale economies. Thus, once industrial structure is appreciated as endogenous, the classic causal link between high concentration and low competition is reversed. This is *not* to say that high concentration does not increase the ability to exploit monopoly power. It does. The point is that we cannot simply say that high concentration is bad. Unfortunately for those who like simple policy rules, the general results in this book do not translate into general rules. On the contrary, we can only support the *ad hoc* approach to competition policy.

Nevertheless, it remains important that those charged with administering competition policy have some suggestive indicators of the industries in which the lack of competition is most likely to be a problem. In this section, we identify three broad groups of potential problem industries, based on simple indicators of their potential for the abuse of monopoly power and their degree of international integration. The indicator of potential abuse is, as is usual for competition policy, the level of concentration, but here we are able to use EU concentration to supplement the typical national measures. Table 14.1 contains the set of industries for which either *EUC5* exceeds 25% (roughly a third of all manufacturing industries) or the weighted average national four-firm concentration ratio for Germany, Italy, and the UK exceeds 45% (again, roughly a third of all industries).[8] The two criteria substantially overlap, so high national concentration adds only seven industries to the thirty-four with high EU concentration. We suggest that this list of forty-one industries includes most of those that can be identified at the 3-digit level as having a potential anti-competitive problem.

The qualification 'at the 3-digit level' is important. Practical competition operates in much more narrowly defined markets. This means that competition authorities cannot safely ignore all industries that are not on this list, because they may include important monopolized market segments. For example, pharmaceuticals is not on the list even though one or two patented drugs often

Table 14.1 High concentration and trade integration

NACE	Industry	Type	Comment[4]
Group 1: Global industries[1]			
373	Optical instruments	*2AR*	Multinational
330	Computers & office machinery	*2R*	Public procurement; multinational
259	Domestic/office chemicals	*2R*	
260	Man-made fibres	*2R*	Economies of scale
343	Electrical equipment	*2R*	Multinational
222	Steel tubes	1	
326	Transmission equipment	*2R*	Multinational
224	Non-ferrous metals	1	Economies of scale; multinational

[8] The national concentration ratios are taken from Lyons and Matraves (1995).

364	Aerospace	2R	Public procurement; Economies of scale
345	Radio & TV	2AR	Multinational
347	Electric lighting	2R	Multinational
351	Motor vehicles	2AR	Economies of scale
372	Medical instruments	2R	Public procurement; multinational
353	Motor vehicle parts	2R	Multinational
256	Ind. & agric. chemicals	2R	
246	Abrasives	1	Multinational
346	Domestic elec. appliances	2AR	Multinational
221	Iron & steel	1	Economies of scale

Group 2: Local industries[2]

242	Cement	1	National concentration
427	Beer	2A	Regulated
428	Soft drinks	2A	Regulated; multinational
420	Sugar	1	
362	Rail stock	2R	Public procurement
429	Tobacco	2A	Economies of scale
341	Insulated wires & cables	2R	Regulated; multinational; national concentration
361	Shipbuilding	1	Regulated; national concentration
411	Oils & fats	2A	Multinational; national concentration
258	Soap & detergents	2AR	Multinational
418	Starch	1	National concentration
255	Paint & ink	2AR	
421	Choc. & sugar confect.	2A	Multinational

Group 3: Intermediate trade integration[3]

247	Glass	1	Multinational
481	Rubber	2R	Multinational
344	Telecom/measuring equipment	2R	Regulated; multinational
321	Tractors/agricultural mach.	2AR	Economies of scale; multinational
251	Basic chemicals	2R	Economies of scale; multinational
244	Asbestos	1	National concentration
424	Distilling	2A	
415	Fish products	1	National concentration
363	Cycle & motor cycle	2R	
223	Steel-forming cold	1	

Notes: All industries in this table are highly concentrated, either at the EU level ($EUC5 > 25\%$) or at the national level ($AVNATC4 > 45\%$), or both.

1. Group 1 industries have extra-EU imports plus exports relative to apparent consumption > 80%. They are ranked here by extra-EU trade intensity, with the *highest* first.

2. Group 2 industries have intra-EU imports relative to apparent EU consumption < 15% and extra-EU trade intensity < 50%. (Only telecom & measuring equipment and distilling are excluded from Group 2 under the latter criterion.) They are ranked here by intra-EU trade, with the lowest first.

3. Group 3 includes all remaining high concentration industries. They are ranked here by intra-EU multinationally, with the highest first.

4. 'Comment' indicates a distinctive feature which partly accounts for the high concentration. 'Multinational' is defined as intra-EU $NM > 1.4$. 'Regulated' and 'public procurement' industries are identified as such in European Economy (1990). 'Economies of scale' is defined as $MES > 500$ (see Appendix 3). 'National concentration' identifies industries with $EUC5 < 25\%$ but average national concentration > 45%.

dominate certain therapeutic segments. The key issue here is that, in such industries, there are very few substitution possibilities between individual products, either for consumers or producers. Nevertheless, we believe that our list provides a meaningful guide to policy, as long as it is sensitively interpreted in the light of individual market conditions.

We have divided the list of high concentration industries into three groups according to two definitions of trade integration. So far in this book, we have focused exclusively on intra-EU trade integration, since this is a central element of the conceptual framework developed in Part II. However, in order to gain a wider perspective on global competition, it is necessary also to look at extra-EU trade integration. Our two measures of integration, based on 1987 data, are: the intensity of extra-EU trade, as an indicator of globalization; and the intensity of intra-EU trade, as an indicator of EU trade integration.

Group 1, the 'global industries', includes only those with a very high level of extra-EU trade[9]. Group 2, the 'local industries', includes only those with both a very low level of intra-EU trade and low extra-EU trade. Group 3 includes all the remaining high concentration industries, which have intermediate levels of trade integration.

All but four of the eighteen Group 1 global industries are R&D intensive. In such industries, the R&D budgets of leading firms will be set according to global considerations, and it would be inappropriate to investigate competition issues at the EU level alone. Most of these industries are highly multinational within Europe and, though we have no direct measures, many of the leading firms have significant operations outside the EU as well. Three of the four Type 1 industries are in metals, and the fourth is the small abrasives sector. These industries are characterized by relatively standardized products and traditionally relatively large economies of scale. They have also attracted significant national government intervention to resist the enormous international market pressures to restructure.

The profile of the Group 2 local industries is quite different. Over half of this group of thirteen are advertising intensive. A further two are R&D intensive, but both are protected by regulation or public procurement. Three of the four Type 1 industries are on the list only because of national concentration, not high EU concentration, but it is significant that most of these industries have a history of competition policy investigations. Shipbuilding is another industry which has faced major international competitive pressure to restructure. Overall, this group is a warning list of potential candidates for competition policy intervention. It also highlights the important role played by advertising

---

[9] Extra-EU trade intensity differs conceptually from intra-EU trade in that it can be unbalanced. However, it turns out that trade is substantially balanced for most of the industries under consideration. For example, to define Group 1, we use a cut-off of 80% for the sum of extra-EU imports and exports relative to apparent consumption. As it happens, none of the industries in this group has either an import or export intensity less than 35%. Similarly, none in Group 2 has either ratio greater than 35% and only three in Group 3 meet this criterion.

in securing dominant positions in markets where international trade does not provide a competitive constraint.

While Group 1 is readily identified with R&D competition, and Group 2 with advertising competition, the ten industries in Group 3 are more mixed. Three of the group only narrowly miss out on our criterion for inclusion as a global industry, and this may alleviate the potential problem of low competition. Rubber and cycles and motor cycles have extra-EU trade in excess of 70%, and fish products have extra-EU imports of 40%. However, rubber is also amongst the five industries in Group 3 which have high intra-EU multinationality. Inasmuch as multinationality may be associated with the leading firms controlling the flows of international trade, this suggests that competition may be blunted, so once again there is a competition policy warning signal. Notice, however, that four of these five highly multinational industries are strongly associated with R&D, and the multinational activity may be necessary to gain the widest possible market to maximize incentives to develop new technology. This may be especially true for telecommunication and measuring equipment, where national regulations have suppressed intra-EU trade. Of the other industries in this group, distilling raises an additional issue. In spite of a high advertising intensity, trade in this industry is quite high. In part, this reflects horizontal differentiation, based originally on national taste differences and comparative advantages (e.g. Scotch whisky and French brandy). Whether one reads this as a case for potential anti-trust concern depends, to some extent, on how widely the market is defined: is whisky a substitute for brandy?

14.4.4 Nationality

A number of popular debates and policy issues revolve around nationality, either in terms of the location of production or the ownership of firms. Does Germany dominate EU industry? Are important industries drawn to the core of the EU or to larger countries, at the expense of the periphery or smaller member states? Are there national characteristics in corporate strategy? Do non-EU multinationals control important sectors of EU industry?

Some measures of industrial dominance are summarized in Table 14.2. Certainly, the Big 4 member states (Germany, France, Italy, and the UK) dominate the location of production, accounting for 79% of total manufacturing production in the EU. Germany alone accounts for 28%. It is rather less straightforward to identify the core of the EU, but a geographical grouping of Germany, France, the Netherlands, and Belgium/Luxemburg is probably not too controversial. Together, these countries supply 55% of EU manufacturing. Although these two statistics are reasonably interesting, it is probably more important to examine the type of industries in which these countries dominate. For example, Germany accounts for over one-third of production in the dynamic R&D-intensive industries. A similar, if slightly diluted, picture emerges when comparing the shares of the Big 4 and Core 4 in R&D-intensive

Table 14.2 Dominance by Core 4, Big 4, and Germany
(percentage shares)

	Core 4	Big 4	Germany
All manufacturing	55	79	28
Type 1	49.5	77.3	23.8
Type 2A	51.7	70.1	23.0
Type 2R	61.9	84.4	36.5
Type 2AR	62.5	82.0	33.3
Production of matrix firms by:			
Location	65	87	36
Origin*	69	88	36

* excluding firms of non-EU origin.

Notes: The 'Core 4' are defined as Germany, France, Netherlands,
and Belgium/Luxemburg. The 'Big 4' are defined as Germany,
France, Italy, and the UK.

Source: Tables 2.9 and 3.4.

relative to the other industry types. The Core 4 show a slightly greater relative
dominance in Type 2R and 2AR industries than do the Big 4 because of Italy's
weakness in these sectors. Putting these results another way, the smaller countries, but especially the periphery member states, tend to be more specialized in
the less dynamic Type 1 and Type 2A industries.

A conceptually quite different, and even more striking, picture of dominance is revealed by the nationality of the EU market leaders, i.e. the 313 firms
on the market shares matrix. Whether measured by the location of their production or by their ownership irrespective of where the production is located,
the share of Germany and the Core 4 in the production by market leaders is
about 25% higher than their overall share by all firms. As before, this picture is
diluted by Italy's presence in the Big 4. On closer inspection, Germany shows a
particular leadership dominance in mechanical engineering and vehicles, as
well as in metals (see Davies, 1995). The French and non-EU multinationals
enjoy a disproportionate number of leadership positions in electrical engineering, as do UK firms in food and drink. In contrast, but reflecting the overall EU
strength in global terms, leadership positions in the chemical industries are
well distributed across the prominent member states.

Of course, the dominance of particular types of EU industry, or of market
leadership, by certain member states need not have strong economic implications for consumers in a fully integrated market. However, more dynamic
industries tend to create more productive and better-paid jobs. They also grow
faster and are less under challenge by the emerging economies. Moreover,
it would be naïve to ignore the political strength that goes with industrial
muscle. This is also an important issue in relation to the role of non-EU multinationals, which are naturally attracted by their firm-specific assets into the
R&D-intensive, as well as advertising-intensive, industries.

The second thread of nationality issues, complementing the analysis of dominance, relates to corporate strategy. In this book, we have measured firm size only by the scale of production in the EU, and this should be borne in mind as a context for our conclusions. With that qualification, we find that, on average, the largest firms are non-EU owned, particularly EFTA-based, followed by the Dutch and with the UK, Germany, and France some way behind (Chapter 9). However, this masks some strong differences in how firms achieve their aggregate size. The non-EU firms typically have the largest market shares, though this is at least partly to do with a selection bias—only the globally successful tend to produce in the EU, and in any case they disproportionately enter the Type 2 industries which are more concentrated. Among the member states, the Dutch have the largest market shares, followed by the French and Germans. Another reason why the Dutch and EFTA firms are particularly large is that they operate in some of the larger industries, and this also explains part of the large size of UK and German firms.

The results in this book cast most light on two other aspects of strategy: diversification and intra-EU multinationality. At a descriptive level, the UK, Dutch, and EFTA firms are the most diversified, and the Italians, Germans, and Americans are more specialized. However, most of this pattern can be accounted for by the overall size of the firms involved, with bigger firms being naturally more diversified. For example, looking only at the largest firms, the Germans are the most diversified member state, and UK firms are no more diversified than other nationalities. Nevertheless, there remain some important national institutional differences, such as the importance of stock market capital and the existence of publicly owned industrial holding companies, that do contribute a national element to the explanation of diversification (Chapter 10).

This lesson—that purely *descriptive* statistics relating to nationality can be misleading—is repeated when we consider intra-EU multinationality. Among the member states, firms originating from the Netherlands are most multinational, followed by the UK, then Belgium and France. Germany is very low. However, taking account of country size, firm size, and industrial structure, the residual national contribution to multinational production is greatest in Germany, followed by France. We conclude that, although different nationality firms do look superficially different in terms of their corporate strategies, nationality itself is much less important than characteristics such as firm size and the industries in which a firm operates.

14.5 The Future

We started this research project in the hope that it would be only the first stage in an ongoing and organic research programme; but we harboured some doubts. We were uncertain about the logistics. Would the sheer magnitude of the data collection, and the difficulties of co-ordinating research teams working in different countries brush aside the more analytical side to our work? And, even if it did not, would our catholic conceptualization of structure lead to a jumble of disconnected separate studies of the different dimensions, resulting in an incoherent whole? In the event, data collection *was* more demanding than we hoped, but we were able to constrain it to manageable proportions. Methodologically, the core decompositions of concentration and firm size proved to be the key to imposing an overall coherence to the analytical work.

Nevertheless, at the moment, all we have is a static picture for 1987—and one which is largely confined to structure. Our aims for the future include an immediate update to 1993[10] (and the hope that the database can be regularly updated thereafter), in order to study the dynamics of structural change. We are also making efforts to marry the matrix to a commercially produced company-level financial database. Unlike with census type sources, the market share matrix is founded on information on specific named firms, and this will allow us to widen our investigations to matters of profitability, productivity, and growth. Given the richness we have found in our simple snapshot of industrial structure, we are encouraged to believe that these developments will prove particularly fertile in providing new insights into competition and competitiveness in European industry.

STEVE DAVIES and BRUCE LYONS

[10] We anticipate that updates will be considerably less time-consuming because so many of the fixed costs will have already been incurred. We also anticipate that the updating process will reveal some errors in our estimates for 1987. We do not expect these to be substantial, but, for reasons of historical accuracy and for inter-temporal comparisons, it may be necessary to produce a slightly corrected Mark II version of the 1987 matrix at some appropriate time in the future.

Appendix 1

Indices of Industry and Firm Structure and the Three Core Decompositions

This appendix introduces the algebraic notation and formally defines the indices of structure used throughout the book. It then shows how they can be used to derive the three key decompositions which underpin Parts II and III.

We focus on four key elements of structure: at the industry level, concentration and the specialization of EU production across the member states; and, at the firm level, diversification and multinationality. Since the EU manufacturing sector is an aggregation, both in product space (across individual industries) and in geographical space (across member states), these elements of structure are measured at various levels of aggregation. Table A1.1 provides a summary which should be helpful for quick reference.

From the wide range of candidate index numbers which might be used to measure each of these concepts, we have opted for the Herfindahl family of indices. The literature on the relative merits of alternative concentration indices is sufficiently well known and documented not to require repetition here; we have chosen the Herfindahl partly for its reasonably convenient decomposition properties, and partly because it is widely used in the literature.[1] We define each dimension of structure in a Herfindahl form, or some derivative thereof; and we also employ the *number-equivalent* version.

A1.1 Basic Notation

Suppose that the EU comprises:[2]

$i = 1 \ldots n$ firms
$j = 1 \ldots 100$ industries
$k = 1 \ldots 11$ countries (member states)

where

---

[1] Ease of decomposition makes the Herfindahl far more convenient for our purposes than, say, the familiar concentration ratio; but many other indices score just as well on that count (e.g. Entropy). Our preference over these measures is mainly on the grounds of the Herfindahl's more common usage in previous studies. The literature on choosing between concentration indices is well summarized in a number of places; for example, Curry and George, 1983; Davies and Lyons, 1988, ch. 6; Hannah and Kay, 1977.

[2] Here, 'EU' is used as shorthand for the manufacturing sector of the EU. Belgium and Luxemburg are counted as one country.

Table A 1.1 Definitions of variables used in the decompositions

Definition	Variable*	Equation
EU concentration in industry j	HEU_j	A.1
Typical national concentration in j	$HNAT_j$	A.2
Specialization of EU in j	$SPEC_j$	A.6
Diversification of firm i	D_i	A.8
Typical firm diversification	D	A.10
Multinationality of firm i	M_i	A.12
Multinationality of firm i in j	M_{ij}	A.13
Typical multinationality in j	Mj	A.14
Aggregate EU firm size	$FMSIZE_i$	A.25/A.32
Typical market share of firm i	MS_i	A.20
Typical size of industry for firm i	IS_i	A.23
Typical country share of firm i	CS_i	A.27
Typical size of country for firm i	$NATS_i$	A.30
Weights:		
industry j	w_j	
country k	uk	
firm i	v_j	

* Number equivalent forms are denoted by an N prefix.

x_{ijk} = firm i's production in industry j in country k
x_i = firm i's total production in all industries in the EU
x_j = total EU production in industry j
x_k = total production in country k
x = total production in the EU

A1.2 Summary Indices of Industry Structure

A1.2.1 Concentration

The Herfindahl index of concentration in any industry involves summing the squared production shares of all firms in that industry. In effect, this amounts to calculating a weighted average market share for the firms in the industry, in which the weights are the firms' market shares. Given n firms, it has a lower bound of $1/n$, when all firms are equal-sized, and it will increase in value as more of the industry's production is concentrated in the leading firms. The upper bound is unity, corresponding to monopoly.

Concentration must be defined at both the EU and national levels:

EU concentration   in industry j:

$$HEU_j = \sum_j (x_{ij})^2/(x_j)^2 \tag{A.1}$$

Typical national concentration   for industry j.
This is the (weighted) average of industry concentration across the eleven member states:

$$HNAT_j = \sum_k u_{jk}\, H_{jk} \qquad\qquad (\text{A}.2)$$

where

$$u_{jk} = (x_{jk})^2 / \sum_j (x_{jk})^2 \qquad\qquad (\text{A}.3)$$

and

$$H_{jk} = \sum_i (x_{ijk})^2 / (x_{jk})^2 \qquad\qquad (\text{A}.4)$$

Note that the weight is the individual member state's squared production in the industry, as a proportion of the sum of all member states' squared EU production in that industry: thus the weights sum to unity. This rather unusual weighting structure, which attaches increasingly greater importance to larger member states, is dictated by the decomposition properties of the H index. It is also typical of the weighting structures used below in defining other 'typical' values.

Number-equivalent concentration   Any Herfindahl index can be defined in its number-equivalent form (see Adelman, 1969). Numerically, this is the reciprocal of the H value. Conceptually, it identifies the number of hypothetical equal-sized firms which would be required to generate that H value. For example, if a given industry records $H = 0.01$, it is said to have a number equivalent of 100, since this is the number of equal-sized firms needed to record that H value. It is often argued that number equivalents are easier to interpret, and we sometimes employ them in the text. Notationally, the number equivalents to all indices are indicated by replacing H with N. So, for example,

$$NEU_j = 1/HEU_j \qquad\qquad (\text{A}.5)$$

A1.2.2 International Specialization

The specialization of EU production is a measure of the extent to which it is concentrated in the largest producing member states. This is also a Herfindahl type index, but in this case each state is taken as the individual entity, and the index entails summing the countries' squared shares of the EU aggregate. This rises from a lower value of 1/11, when all countries are equal-sized in the industry concerned, to unity, when the entire EU production is produced in just one member state. Thus for industry j,

$$SPEC_j = \sum_k (x_{jk})^2 / x_j^2 \qquad\qquad (\text{A}.6)$$

The number equivalent is:

$$NSPEC_j = 1/SPEC_j \qquad\qquad (\text{A}.7)$$

A1.3 Summary Indices of firm Structure

Given that firms need not necessarily confine their production activities to either a single industry or a single member state, we require measures of diversification across products (i.e. industries) and multinationality across member states.[3] Both are defined using an index which is the complement of a Herfindahl index. For diversification, this follows a long tradition established first by Berry (1975); for multinationality, this is the first known use of this index, but it is also perfectly appropriate.

A1.3.1 Firm Diversification

We measure the extent to which an individual firm diversifies its production across different industries as:

$$D_i = 1 - \sum_j (x_{ij})^2 / (x_i)^2 \qquad (A.8)$$

Thus a firm which is specialized in a single industry records $D_i = 1 - 1 = 0$, while one spreading its output in equal amounts across k industries records $D_i = 1 - \sum 1/(k)^2 = 1 - (1/k)$, which tends to unity as k becomes large. In effect, $1 - D_i$ is the sum of shares weighted by themselves (exactly as in the H index); and it can therefore usefully be interpreted as a measure of the share of a firm's output in a 'typical' industry. For example, a firm with 40% of its output in its primary industry, 24% in its secondary industry, and 9% in each of four other industries will record $1 - D_i = 0.25$: the same as if it shared its output equally across just four industries. Alternatively, the *number equivalent* is:

$$ND_i = (1 - D_i)^{-1} \qquad (A.9)$$

where ND interprets diversification as if the firm is operating equally across industries: in the above example, four industries.

When aggregating diversification across firms, we use the concept of *typical firm diversification*,[4] defined as:

$$D = \sum_i v_i D_i \qquad (A.10)$$

where

$$v_i = (x_i)^2 / \sum_i (x_i)^2 \qquad (A.11)$$

As before, the weighting structure is dictated by the nature of the index.

---

[3] It should be emphasized that diversification is broadly defined to include firms producing across vertically related industries—thus vertical integration will be part of our measure of diversification. Multinationality is defined as producing in more than one EU member state. A more precise definition is *intra-EU multinational production* within manufacturing. Note, for example, that we take no account of production outside the EU or outside manufacturing. For our purposes, therefore, a firm would not be defined as 'multinational' if its only foreign production activities were in, say, the USA, or in retailing, either outside or inside the EU.

[4] This concept is not used directly in any of the three core decompositions used in this book. However, it is part of another, related, decomposition which links aggregate concentration to industry concentration, (see Section 9.2.2, and Davies (1995)).

A1.3.2 Firm Multinationality

The degree of a firm's multinationality is defined in an exactly equivalent way to diversification, with member states replacing industries. Thus for firm i, operating across up to eleven member states, its aggregate multinationality is:

$$M_i = 1 - \sum_k (x_{ik})^2 / (x_i)^2 \qquad (A.12)$$

In this case, we must also distinguish between a firm's aggregate multinationality and its multinationality within a given industry, j:

$$M_{ij} = 1 - \sum_k (x_{ijk})^2 / (x_{ij})^2 \qquad (A.13)$$

It is important to note that a given firm may be multinational in the aggregate sense, without necessarily being multinational within given industries. This would be true, for example, if the firm produced its entire output of industry I in country A, and its entire output of industry II in country B.

We also employ the concept of *typical multinationality* within a given industry. This is defined as the weighted average of the M_{ij} for constituent firms in industry j:

$$M_j = \sum_i v_{ij} M_{ij} \qquad (A.14)$$

where

$$v_{ij} = (x_{ij})^2 / \sum_i (x_{ij})^2 \qquad (A.15)$$

The number equivalent measure of multinationality is

$$NM_i = (1 - M_i)^{-1} \qquad (A.16)$$

where NM interprets multinationality as if the firm is operating equally across member states.

A1.4 Decompositions and the Market Share Matrix[5]

The market share matrix is three-dimensional, recording firm output by industry and by country of production. Not only does this enable us to calculate the indices just described, but also it provides the scope for a large number of decompositions of those indices. In this book, we only use three decompositions, but a number of others are possible, especially involving the relationship between aggregate concentration and industry concentration (see Section 9.2.2, and Davies, 1995).

---

[5] An earlier forerunner to this work was provided by Clarke and Davies (1983, 1984).

A1.4.1 A spatial decomposition of EU industry concentration (Chapter 4)

The relationship, between concentration, for a given industry, at the EU level and concentration in the constituent member states provides the backbone of the five chapters in Part II of the book. It is derived as follows.

first, sum (A4) across k and (A13) across i:

$$\sum_k H_{jk}(x_{jk})^2 = \sum\sum_{ki}(x_{ijk})^2$$

$$\sum\sum_{ki}(x_{ijk})^2 = \sum_i(x_{ij})^2 - \sum M_{ij}(x_{ij})^2$$

Then equate the two expressions and divide by x_j^2:

$$\sum_k H_{jk}(x_{jk})^2/(x_j)^2 = \sum_i(x_{ij})^2/(x_j)^2 - \sum M_{ij}(x_{ij})^2/(x_j)^2$$

Substituting in the expressions for HEU_j from (A.1), $HNAT_j$ from (A.2), $SPEC_j$ from (A.6), and M_j from (A.14) gives:

$$HNAT_j * SPEC_j = HEU_j * (1 - M_j)$$

and thus:

$$HEU_j = HNAT_j * SPEC_j * (1 - M_j)^{-1} \qquad (A.17)$$

In words, EU concentration in industry *j* is the product of typical national concentration and the specialization across countries, divided by the complement of firms' multinationality in that industry. In number-equivalent form this is:

$$NEU_j = NNAT_j * NSPEC_j / NM_j \qquad (A.18)$$

These two expressions are used, as Equations (4.2) and (4.3) in Chapter 4.

A1.4.2 A decomposition of EU firm size in product space (Chapter 9)

Part III of the book uses two decompositions of aggregate firm size. This will be denoted for firm *i* by $x_i = FMSIZE_i$. We first derive the decomposition in product space.

Notationally, it is now convenient to switch to market shares,[6] denoted for firm *i* in industry *j* by

$$MS_{ij} = x_{ij}/x_j \qquad (A.19)$$

Weighting market shares by the share of the firm's production in each industry and summing over $j = 1...100$ industries, the firm's typical market share is:

$$MS_i = \sum_j MS_{ij}(x_{ij}/x_i) \qquad (A.20)$$

Next, rewrite the index of diversification (A.8) as

$$D_i = 1 - \sum_j (MS_{ij})^2(x_j)^2/(x_i)^2 \qquad (A.21)$$

---

[6] Strictly speaking, our data refer to production shares.

Combining the two indices gives:

$$MS_i(1 - D_i)^{-1} = x_i [\sum_j MS_{ij} x_{ij}] / [\sum_j MS_{ij} (x_{ij}) (x_j)] \quad \text{(A.22)}$$

Next define an index of the typical size of industry for firm i:

$$IS_i = \sum_j (w_{ij}.x_j) \quad \text{(A.23)}$$

where

$$w_{ij} = (x_{ij} MS_{ij}) / \sum (x_{ij} MS_{ij}) \quad \text{(A.24)}$$

Then (A.22) can be rewritten to give the following expression for the firm's aggregate size:

$$FMSIZE_i = x_i = MS_i * IS_i * (1 - D_i)^{-1}$$

This can be rewritten, using the number-equivalent form for diversification, as:

$$FMSIZE_i = x_i = MS_i * IS_i * ND_i \quad \text{(A.25)}$$

In words, the firm's aggregate EU size is the product of its typical market share, the typical size of industry in which it operates, and the equivalent number of industries in which it is diversified.

Some comment is needed in interpreting the *IS* index. As can be seen, for firm i, it is a weighted average size of all the industries in which the firm operates. Since the weights depend on the size of the firm's presence in the industry times its market share, this index is firm-specific. This means that industry j is given more weight in the index if the firm's operations in that industry are both important to the firm and significant in the industry.

Expression (A.25) is introduced as Equation (9.1) in Chapter 9.

A1.4.3 A decomposition of EU firm size in geographic space (Chapter 11)

The equivalent decomposition in geographic space is derived as follows. first define firm i's share of country k's aggregate production as:

$$CS_{ik} = x_{ik} / x_k \quad \text{(A.26)}$$

Weighting this by the share of the firm's sales in each country and summing over $k = 1...11$ countries, the index of typical country share is:

$$CS_i = \sum_k CS_{ik} (x_{ik} / x_i) \quad \text{(A.27)}$$

Next, rewrite the index of multinationality (A.12) as:

$$M_i = 1 - \sum_k CS_{ik}^2 (x_k)^2 / (x_i)^2 \quad \text{(A.28)}$$

Combining the two indices gives:

$$CS_i (1 - M_i)^{-1} = x_i [\sum_k CS_{ik} x_{ik}] / [\sum_k CS_{ik} (x_{ik}) (x_k)] \quad \text{(A.29)}$$

Next define an index of the typical size of country for firm i:

$$NATS_i = \sum_k (u_{ik} x_k) \tag{A.30}$$

where

$$u_{ij} = (x_{ik} CS_{ik}) / \sum (x_{ik} CS_{ik}) \tag{A31}$$

Then (A.29) can be rewritten to give the following expression for the firm's aggregate size:

$$FMSIZE_i = x_i = CS_i * NATS_i * (1-M_i)^{-1}$$

This can also be rewritten, using the number-equivalent form for multi-nationality, as:

$$FMSIZE_i = x_i = CS_i * NATS_i * NM_i \tag{A32}$$

In words, the firm's aggregate EU size is the product of its typical country share, the typical size of country in which it operates, and the equivalent number of countries in which it produces. Similar comments apply to the interpretation of the *NATS* index as for *IS*, as explained in the previous sub-section. Expression (A.32) is introduced as Equation (11.3) in Chapter 11.

STEVE DAVIES

Appendix 2

The Matrix Industries and Firms

Table A2.1 The industries

Nace	Industry	HEU	HNAT	SPEC	M	CSEU	TYPE	CONSPEC	SIZEADJ	TRADESPEC	TRADE	INTRA	HTRADE
221	Iron & Steel	0.041	0.198	0.183	0.108	40	1	0.185	-0.004	0.046	0.501	0.773	0.160
222	Steel tubes	0.044	0.216	0.196	0.036	41	1	0.176	0.018	0.047	0.422	0.719	0.160
223	Steel forming cold	0.037	0.172	0.207	0.032	34	1	0.199	0.006	0.041	0.416	0.764	0.174
224	Non-ferrous metals	0.021	0.078	0.184	0.321	25	1	0.192	-0.010	0.043	0.693	0.845	0.160
241	Clay products	0.005	0.028	0.163	0.071	12	1	0.163	-0.001	0.023	0.101	0.404	0.146
242	Cement	0.017	0.098	0.160	0.049	24	1	0.159	0.001	0.017	0.067	0.422	0.200
243	Concrete	0.006	0.017	0.169	0.515	12	1	0.169	0.000	0.007	0.040	0.566	0.163
244	Asbestos	0.013	0.036	0.262	0.273	20	1	0.243	0.018	0.029	0.297	0.812	0.262
245	Stone products	0.003	0.012	0.208	0.027	8	1	0.202	0.004	0.037	0.199	0.529	0.159
246	Abrasives	0.036	0.110	0.204	0.379	36	1	0.184	0.018	0.054	0.517	0.745	0.168
247	Glass	0.048	0.097	0.181	0.636	37	1	0.179	0.001.	0.036	0.410	0.775	0.154
248	Ceramics	0.006	0.024	0.216	0.150	12	1	0.197	0.016	0.054	0.398	0.670	0.171
251	Basic chemicals	0.021	0.072	0.208	0.291	25	2R	n.a.	n.a.	n.a.	n.a.	n.a.	n.a.
255	Paint & ink	0.038	0.212	0.157	0.128	36	2AR	0.153	0.002	0.036	0.265	0.657	0.159
256	Ind. & Agri.chemicals	0.023	0.111	0.161	0.236	26	2R	0.157	0.001	0.049	0.513	0.755	0.153
257	Pharmaceuticals	0.019	0.069	0.173	0.386	24	2AR	0.171	0.002	0.012	0.230	0.855	0.134
258	Soaps & detergents	0.034	0.058	0.187	0.681	35	2AR	0.180	0.006	0.025	0.210	0.699	0.159
259	Domestic & office chems.	0.118	0.401	0.237	0.194	63	2R	0.240	-0.006	0.062	0.820	0.806	0.152
260	Man-made fibres	0.105	0.466	0.199	0.116	63	2R	0.184	-0.001	0.124	0.836	0.628	0.159
311	Foundries	0.011	0.038	0.219	0.217	18	1	0.214	0.005	0.008	0.127	0.844	0.162
312	Forging	0.002	0.011	0.191	0.000	8	1	0.188	0.003	0.008	0.054	0.647	0.171
313	Metal treatment	0.001	0.004	0.220	0.030	4	1	0.216	0.004	0.015	0.100	0.631	0.173
314	Metal structures	0.002	0.009	0.179	0.000	6	1	0.177	0.002	0.011	0.131	0.792	0.171
315	Boilers & containers	0.002	0.009	0.259	0.000	7	1	0.248	0.010	0.017	0.109	0.611	0.155
316	Tools & cans	0.002	0.006	0.214	0.287	6	1	0.197	0.016	0.039	0.309	0.674	0.152
321	Tractors & agri. mach.	0.017	0.050	0.212	0.364	25	2AR	0.190	0.018	0.067	0.391	0.550	0.146
322	Machine tools	0.006	0.017	0.312	0.083	13	2R	0.275	0.034	0.051	0.376	0.678	0.179
323	Textile machinery	0.012	0.039	0.301	0.020	19	2R	0.228	0.061	0.110	0.505	0.477	0.172
324	Food & chemical machinery	0.006	0.025	0.244	0.000	11	1	0.199	0.038	0.083	0.458	0.538	0.155
325	Mining/construction mach.	0.009	0.031	0.230	0.225	15	1	0.208	0.020	0.049	0.365	0.661	0.154
326	Transmission equipment	0.045	0.054	0.301	0.642	33	2R	0.247	0.048	0.079	0.579	0.686	0.189
327	Paper, wood, etc. machinery	0.013	0.033	0.359	0.099	20	2R	0.253	0.087	0.137	0.589	0.445	0.175
328	Other machinery	0.012	0.049	0.227	0.054	17	2R	0.198	0.026	0.061	0.496	0.691	0.159
330	Computers & office mach.	0.203	0.266	0.217	0.716	71	2R	0.203	0.009	0.071	1.159	0.843	0.151
341	Insulated wires & cables	0.015	0.029	0.303	0.410	21	2R	0.301	0.002	0.015	0.161	0.763	0.146

Code	Industry												
342	Electrical machinery	0.010	0.022	0.251	0.424	17	2R	0.218	0.029	0.059	0.438	0.679	0.178
343	Electrical equipment	0.030	0.100	0.205	0.306	31	2R	0.190	0.011	0.060	0.588	0.746	0.160
344	Telecom & measurg. equip.	0.027	0.053	0.294	0.432	32	2R	0.277	0.016	0.027	0.239	0.722	0.163
345	Radio & television	0.045	0.064	0.233	0.665	37	2AR	0.246	-0.016	0.048	0.607	0.808	0.169
346	Domestic elec. appliances	0.060	0.177	0.200	0.408	46	2AR	0.173	0.017	0.104	0.559	0.536	0.162
347	Electric lights	0.189	0.468	0.185	0.543	65	2R	0.184	-0.004	0.073	0.524	0.650	0.157
351	Motor vehicles	0.104	0.325	0.250	0.216	63	2AR	0.212	0.032	0.082	0.597	0.665	0.169
353	Motor vehicle parts	0.031	0.084	0.252	0.322	31	2R	0.230	0.017	0.072	0.550	0.694	0.184
361	Shipbuilding	0.013	0.087	0.151	0.000	21	1	0.139	0.011	0.024	0.147	0.603	0.163
362	Railway stock	0.043	0.188	0.227	0.000	40	2R	0.225	0.001	0.025	0.098	0.419	0.199
363	Cycles & motor cycles	0.046	0.163	0.231	0.180	39	2R	0.194	0.033	0.067	0.454	0.626	0.158
364	Aerospace	0.087	0.286	0.295	0.026	57	2R	0.292	0.004	0.009	0.345	0.953	0.339
371	Measuring instruments	0.005	0.010	0.289	0.399	10	2R	0.259	0.028	0.044	0.364	0.696	0.160
372	Medical instruments	0.029	0.059	0.316	0.359	27	2R	0.299	0.015	0.042	0.428	0.736	0.141
373	Optical instruments	0.135	0.276	0.243	0.501	73	2AR	0.208	0.013	0.149	1.373	0.737	0.171
374	Clocks & watches	0.011	0.025	0.317	0.267	19	2AR	0.242	0.056	0.136	0.643	0.522	0.197
411	Oils & fats	0.019	0.043	0.168	0.617	23	2A	0.165	0.001	0.046	0.235	0.506	0.160
412	Meat products	0.002	0.008	0.154	0.321	6	1	0.174	-0.024	0.068	0.353	0.467	0.130
413	Dairy products	0.009	0.027	0.158	0.529	14	2A	0.155	0.002	0.040	0.282	0.646	0.159
414	Fruit & vegetable prod.	0.007	0.024	0.154	0.472	14	2A	0.181	-0.037	0.102	0.557	0.514	0.141
415	Fish products	0.014	0.079	0.141	0.188	19	1	0.153	-0.020	0.091	0.401	0.360	0.127
416	Grain milling	0.006	0.032	0.193	0.000	13	1	0.190	0.003	0.014	0.095	0.615	0.140
417	Pasta	0.021	0.069	0.267	0.128	24	1	0.234	0.030	0.054	0.140	0.149	0.204
418	Starch	0.013	0.065	0.170	0.159	22	1	0.203	-0.037	0.060	0.329	0.539	0.156
419	Bread & biscuits	0.005	0.031	0.154	0.085	12	1	0.155	-0.001	0.009	0.069	0.679	0.155
420	Sugar	0.033	0.151	0.165	0.247	32	1	0.160	0.005	0.026	0.109	0.374	0.141
421	Confectionary	0.050	0.122	0.193	0.529	44	2A	0.199	-0.007	0.032	0.287	0.705	0.145
422	Animal foods	0.005	0.028	0.148	0.100	10	2A	0.145	0.002	0.015	0.099	0.598	0.144
423	Other foods	0.010	0.029	0.182	0.495	17	2A	0.187	-0.005	0.021	0.208	0.734	0.142
424	Distilling	0.032	0.140	0.174	0.246	33	2A	0.161	0.010	0.047	0.215	0.496	0.187
425/6	Wine & cider	0.007	0.025	0.238	0.176	16	2A	0.217	0.017	0.065	0.211	0.221	0.156
427	Beer	0.022	0.076	0.209	0.269	27	2A	0.212	-0.003	0.012	0.078	0.571	0.139
428	Soft drinks	0.024	0.081	0.162	0.449	29	2A	0.163	-0.001	0.009	0.082	0.758	0.186
429	Tobacco	0.074	0.345	0.202	0.061	56	2A	0.198	0.003	0.034	0.122	0.346	0.180
431	Wool	0.003	0.013	0.225	0.015	7	1	n.a.	n.a.	n.a.	n.a.	n.a.	n.a.
432	Cotton	0.003	0.012	0.171	0.223	8	1	n.a.	n.a.	n.a.	n.a.	n.a.	n.a.
433	Silk	0.001	0.006	0.208	0.098	5	1	n.a.	n.a.	n.a.	n.a.	n.a.	n.a.
434	Flax & hemp	0.007	0.032	0.220	0.000	15	1	n.a.	n.a.	n.a.	n.a.	n.a.	n.a.
436	Knitting	0.002	0.007	0.244	0.063	6	1	0.201	0.018	0.159	0.649	0.381	0.157
437	Textile finishing	0.004	0.015	0.207	0.209	10	1	n.a.	n.a.	n.a.	n.a.	n.a.	n.a.

Table A2.1 (*cont.*)

Nace	Industry	HEU	HNAT	SPEC	M	C5EU	TYPE	CONSPEC	SIZEADJ	TRADESPEC	TRADE	INTRA	HTRADE
438	Carpets	0.011	0.048	0.160	0.265	16	1	0.186	-0.053	0.164	0.785	0.488	0.166
439	Miscellaneous textiles	0.010	0.054	0.164	0.150	19	1	0.165	-0.002	0.035	0.589	0.844	0.149
441	Leather tanning	0.002	0.007	0.298	0.058	7	1	0.250	0.043	0.076	0.338	0.475	0.183
442	Leather products	0.004	0.012	0.277	0.116	9	1	0.252	0.020	0.072	0.339	0.480	0.168
451	Footwear	0.002	0.007	0.255	0.020	6	1	0.188	0.027	0.202	0.616	0.208	0.172
453	Clothing	0.001	0.004	0.223	0.000	4	1	0.206	0.016	0.039	0.309	0.665	0.146
455	Household textiles	0.004	0.016	0.224	0.041	10	1	0.218	0.004	0.051	0.356	0.597	0.126
456	Fur	0.002	0.009	0.183	0.000	6	1	n.a.	n.a.	n.a.	n.a.	n.a.	n.a.
461	Wood sawing	0.004	0.022	0.174	0.000	9	1	0.169	0.004	0.033	0.217	0.598	0.145
462	Wood boards	0.004	0.022	0.185	0.000	11	1	0.177	0.005	0.058	0.351	0.561	0.144
463	Wooden structures	0.002	0.009	0.183	0.035	5	1	0.184	-0.001	0.008	0.056	0.625	0.140
464	Wooden containers	0.001	0.006	0.182	0.000	4	1	0.182	0.001	0.003	0.041	0.787	0.137
465	Other wood products	0.001	0.003	0.286	0.000	3	1	0.278	0.008	0.032	0.201	0.585	0.146
466	Cork & brushes	0.005	0.033	0.164	0.000	13	1	0.175	-0.020	0.092	0.423	0.421	0.142
467	Wooden furniture	0.001	0.004	0.193	0.115	3	1	0.187	0.004	0.046	0.211	0.455	0.158
471	Paper & pulp	0.010	0.034	0.178	0.357	16	1	0.174	0.003	0.041	0.484	0.788	0.157
472	Processed paper	0.004	0.020	0.177	0.182	10	1	0.174	0.002	0.032	0.301	0.730	0.160
473/4	Printing & publishing	0.004	0.018	0.158	0.232	9	1	0.159	-0.001	0.011	0.086	0.673	0.148
481/2	Rubber	0.080	0.164	0.196	0.598	49	2R	0.192	0.004	0.018	0.473	0.908	0.167
483	Plastics	0.002	0.010	0.185	0.130	6	1	0.178	0.006	0.038	0.359	0.729	0.154
491	Jewellery	0.004	0.013	0.290	0.050	8	1	n.a.	n.a.	n.a.	n.a.	n.a.	n.a.
492	Musical instruments	0.009	0.027	0.304	0.094	17	2A	0.264	0.036	0.063	0.469	0.666	0.162
493	Photographic labs.	0.007	0.035	0.175	0.150	15	1	0.175	0.000	0.019	0.131	0.647	0.170
494	Toys & Sports	0.013	0.064	0.179	0.148	18	2A	0.208	-0.036	0.087	0.700	0.676	0.146
495	Miscellaneous manuf.	0.010	0.029	0.198	0.403	16	1	n.a.	n.a.	n.a.	n.a.	n.a.	n.a.

Variable definitions: Appendix 1 for: HEU, HNAT, SPEC, M; Appendix 3 for C5EU, and TYPE; Appendix to Chapter 5 for CONSPEC, SIZEADJ, TRADESPEC, TRADE, INTRA and HTRADE. Units: all variables are index numbers, except C5EU which is reported as a percentage.

Table A2.2 The firms

Firm	Country	FMSIZE	MS	ND	IS	CS	NM	NATS
1 FIAT	IT	26,451	9.17	2.19	1,315	5.49	1.25	3,856
2 DAIMLER-BENZ	GER	24,883	10.18	1.72	1,424	3.72	1.09	6,150
3 VOLKSWAGEN	GER	24,450	16.17	1.00	1,512	3.64	1.11	6,039
4 SIEMENS	GER	20,362	8.65	5.76	409	2.13	1.59	6,018
5 RENAULT	FR	19,625	11.04	1.19	1499	3.52	1.52	3672
6 FORD	USA	19,419	9.89	1.41	1,397	1.85	3.55	2,955
7 PSA	FR	17,384	9.56	1.24	1,463	2.68	1.70	3,811
8 PHILIPS	NL	16,256	16.66	4.25	230	4.25	3.39	1,128
9 BAYER	GER	15,310	8.24	5.47	340	1.99	1.40	5,477
10 BASF	GER	14,017	11.07	4.22	300	1.91	1.24	5,930
11 IRI	IT	13,475	4.69	8.10	355	3.50	1.00	3,855
12 CGE	FR	13,032	6.31	4.46	463	1.62	2.02	3,984
13 IBM	USA	12,994	41.22	1.03	306	0.67	4.93	3,922
14 HOECHST	GER	12,406	5.94	4.49	465	1.25	1.66	5,997
15 UNILEVER	NL	11,466	6.82	7.60	221	0.69	4.75	3,510
16 ICI	UK	10,848	5.49	2.79	707	2.03	1.65	3,236
17 BMW	GER	9,979	6.45	1.03	1,494	1.62	1.00	6,172
18 USINOR-SACILOR	FR	9,408	11.48	2.07	395	1.88	1.25	4,005
19 THYSSEN	GER	9,309	5.34	4.24	411	1.45	1.04	6,164
20 THOMSON	FR	9,116	5.19	4.00	439	1.39	1.64	4,004
21 BOSCH	GER	9,014	8.73	2.52	410	1.12	1.32	6,098
22 NESTLE	CH	8,134	6.33	3.22	399	0.46	4.90	3,649
23 RHONE-POULENC	FR	7,239	4.15	2.89	603	1.18	1.55	3,953
24 BRITISH AEROSPACE	UK	7,006	14.56	1.45	332	2.19	1.00	3,204
25 ROYAL DUTCH/SHELL	NL	6,416	3.99	2.04	788	1.03	4.08	1,527
26 SAINT-GOBAIN	FR	6,274	11.14	2.98	189	0.59	2.77	3,861
27 MANNESMANN	GER	6,214	4.72	6.00	219	0.79	1.28	6,142
28 GEC	UK	6,010	2.95	3.99	509	1.62	1.16	3,201
29 BRITISH STEEL	UK	5,935	9.78	1.20	505	1.85	1.00	3,204

Table A2.2 (*cont.*)

Firm	Country	FMSIZE	MS	ND	IS	CS	NM	NATS
30 ENI	IT	5,875	2.13	3.54	781	1.46	1.04	3,855
31 MICHELIN	FR	5,860	24.85	1.00	236	0.62	2.41	3,947
32 MAN	GER	5,646	1.97	7.53	380	0.87	1.09	5,994
33 ELF AQUITAINE	FR	5,143	1.87	3.52	782	0.95	1.36	3,960
34 HANSON	UK	5,127	9.54	1.78	302	1.60	1.00	3,204
35 AKZO	NL	5,090	4.79	5.28	201	1.17	2.89	1,503
36 BSN	FR	4,895	2.66	7.29	253	0.77	1.69	3,795
37 BP	UK	4,744	2.81	1.95	864	0.70	2.82	2,401
38 FELDMUHLE NOBEL	GER	4,731	1.39	10.30	331	0.71	1.09	6,134
39 SOLVAY	BL	4,725	2.06	3.13	732	1.18	4.03	995
40 AEROSPATIALE	FR	4,526	13.80	1.00	328	1.14	1.00	3,982
41 AMERICAN BRANDS GALLAHER	USA	4,448	11.86	1.19	315	1.39	1.00	3,204
42 FRIED. KRUPP	GER	4,446	1.52	9.87	295	0.70	1.03	6,171
43 MBB	GER	4,174	10.52	1.21	328	0.58	1.17	6,148
44 PHILIP MORRIS	USA	4,079	8.54	1.50	318	0.37	2.45	4,544
45 PECHINEY	FR	3,809	5.50	2.19	317	0.67	2.09	2,699
46 HENKEL	GER	3,779	2.92	4.23	306	0.31	2.18	5,669
47 DU PONT	USA	3,690	3.89	4.84	196	1.94	5.54	343
48 FERRUZZI FINANZIARIA	IT	3,645	6.22	4.12	142	0.44	2.12	3,920
49 ASEA BROWN BOVERI	CH/SW	3,640	3.16	3.01	382	0.34	1.96	5,504
50 BERTELSMANN	GER	3,628	3.07	1.65	716	0.35	1.74	5,917
51 PIRELLI	IT	3,619	6.83	2.41	220	0.31	3.03	3,800
52 SEITA	FR	3,614	10.98	1.04	317	0.91	1.00	3,982
53 CIBA GEIGY	CH	3,534	2.63	3.01	446	0.19	4.92	3,832
54 PROCTER & GAMBLE	USA	3,473	8.73	1.54	259	0.22	4.96	3,194
55 OLIVETTI	IT	3,144	6.19	1.67	304	0.49	1.64	3,889
56 TABACALERA	SP	3,096	9.75	1.00	317	1.65	1.00	1,872
57 COURTAULDS	UK	3,081	2.33	8.07	164	0.62	1.57	3,186
58 EFIM	IT	3,071	1.98	5.87	264	0.78	1.02	3,855

59	DEGUSSA	GER	2,974	2.28	3.91	333	0.40	1.25	6,025
60	BAT	UK	2,970	3.15	3.14	300	0.31	3.96	2,387
61	ARBED	LUX	2,932	3.76	2.28	341	3.69	1.01	787
62	HOESCH	GER	2,872	1.41	5.80	352	0.44	1.06	6,169
63	DSM	NL	2,851	1.40	3.22	634	1.80	1.56	1,016
64	ROLLS ROYCE	UK	2,651	6.98	1.16	329	0.83	1.00	3,204
65	SKF	SW	2,564	13.78	1.86	100	0.14	3.58	4,954
66	GUINNESS	UK	2,546	6.65	2.66	144	1.29	1.61	1,222
67	JACOBS SUCHARD	CH	2,541	6.51	1.97	198	0.25	2.38	4,348
68	ELECTROLUX	SW	2,527	7.95	1.95	163	0.24	3.05	3,514
69	MARS	USA	2,509	9.41	1.52	176	0.38	2.19	3,007
70	SALZGITTER	GER	2,507	1.97	4.52	282	0.41	1.00	6,172
71	BEECHAM	UK	23,62	2.77	2.76	308	0.50	1.48	3,186
72	GRAND METROPOLITAN	UK	2,352	2.89	2.95	276	0.66	1.24	2,871
73	EASTMAN KODAK	USA	2,247	14.33	2.36	66	0.17	3.57	3,648
74	ABF	UK	2,218	3.08	2.21	327	0.68	1.01	3,205
75	BOSCH-SIEMENS HAUSGERATE	GER	2,185	13.70	1.00	160	0.35	1.00	6,172
76	METALLGESELLSCHAFT	GER	2,176	2.68	2.66	305	0.33	1.07	6,169
77	AVIONS MARCEL DASSAULT	FR	2,169	6.61	1.00	328	0.54	1.00	3,982
78	ALLIED LYONS	UK	2,165	3.53	3.76	163	0.57	1.21	3,150
79	BTR	UK	2,072	1.13	7.83	233	0.46	1.41	3,199
80	TENNECO	USA	2,068	1.68	4.77	257	0.19	2.97	3,620
81	SCHNEIDER	FR	2,056	2.44	2.69	314	0.31	1.67	3,939
82	HEINEKEN	NL	2,037	6.61	1.60	192	1.15	1.81	981
83	KLOCKNER-WERKE	GER	2,035	0.78	6.92	375	0.32	1.04	6,171
84	3M	USA	2,030	2.24	6.08	149	0.11	4.96	3,747
85	REED INTERNATIONAL	UK	1,980	1.24	2.69	595	0.53	1.20	3,143
86	HILLSDOWN	UK	1,977	1.31	2.73	553	0.51	1.22	3,189
87	ZAHNRADFABRIK	GER	1,962	4.72	1.00	415	0.29	1.10	6,166
88	HEWLETT PACKARD	USA	1,961	5.38	1.20	304	0.14	3.07	4,467
89	CONTINENTAL GUMMI	GER	1,957	4.33	1.75	258	0.18	2.05	5,218
90	UNIGATE	UK	1,898	1.54	2.20	561	0.59	1.00	3,204

Table A2.2 (cont.)

Firm	Country	FMSIZE	MS	ND	IS	CS	NM	NATS
91 VIAG	GER	1,896	3.29	1.72	334	0.31	1.00	6,172
92 DOUWE EGBERTS	NL	1,891	2.46	3.01	255	0.72	2.40	1,099
93 RHM	UK	1,880	2.20	3.41	250	0.57	1.04	3,205
94 KLOCKNER-HUMBOLDT-DEUTZ	GER	1,858	1.87	3.77	264	0.24	1.25	6,109
95 PILKINGTON	UK	1,855	8.62	1.14	189	0.26	1.91	3,727
96 COATS VIYELLA	UK	1,853	1.88	7.29	135	0.44	1.39	3,033
97 GOODYEAR	USA	1,851	6.49	1.21	237	0.16	4.77	2,389
98 CADBURYS SCHWEPPES	UK	1,817	7.16	1.98	129	0.36	1.72	2,948
99 ALCAN ALUMINIUM	CAN	1,797	4.58	1.23	319	0.16	2.82	3,903
100 ACEC-UNION MINIERE	BL	1,786	2.75	2.11	307	2.27	1.00	787
101 CIR	IT	1,775	0.96	10.48	176	0.24	1.95	3,873
102 GLAXO	UK	1,770	4.25	1.00	416	0.22	2.43	3,237
103 VALEO	FR	1,744	3.30	2.15	246	0.23	1.93	3,895
104 RMC	UK	1,738	5.34	1.19	273	0.16	3.11	3,421
105 THORN EMI	UK	1,715	2.34	4.67	157	0.38	1.39	3,232
106 MARLIS (HACHETTE)	FR	1,091	2.02	1.05	793	0.39	1.08	3,978
107 SAINT-LOUIS	FR	1,675	4.11	2.65	154	0.35	1.22	3,950
108 DEUTSCHE BABCOCK	GER	1,655	1.85	1.90	471	0.27	1.00	6,172
109 RHEINISCH-WESTFALISCHES	GER	1,618	5.39	1.88	160	0.23	1.16	6,151
110 CARL-ZEISS-STIFTUNG	GER	1,606	7.77	2.15	96	0.25	1.04	6,171
111 LAFARGE-COPPEE	FR	1,588	2.97	3.20	167	0.35	1.14	3,983
112 L'OREAL	FR	1,587	3.94	1.54	263	0.18	2.27	3,819
113 HERAEUS	GER	1,531	0.92	7.36	227	0.25	1.00	6,172
114 DALGETY	UK	1,505	1.69	3.14	284	0.44	1.07	3,196
115 BULL	FR	1,503	4.91	1.00	306	0.38	1.00	3,982
116 LVMH	FR	1,466	3.04	3.90	124	0.37	1.00	3,982
117 UNITED BISCUITS	UK	1,447	1.98	2.32	315	0.39	1.15	3,184
118 INTERNATIONAL PAPER	USA	1,436	4.24	1.33	255	0.12	2.84	4,291
119 SEAGRAM	CAN	1,425	7.87	1.48	122	0.10	3.83	3,591

120	BASS	UK	1,413	5.14	1.44	191	0.44	1.00	3,204
121	RHEINMETALL BERLIN	GER	1,411	0.86	4.34	378	0.21	1.11	6,134
122	SOURCE PERRIER	FR	1,379	3.80	2.71	134	0.28	1.25	3,954
123	FREUDENBERG	GER	13,73	2.84	3.59	134	0.16	1.37	6,089
124	CATERPILLAR	USA	1,371	3.64	1.15	327	0.42	2.92	1,125
125	METALBOX	UK	1,363	1.17	2.19	532	0.32	1.39	3,042
126	NORTHERN FOODS	UK	1,346	0.78	3.09	556	0.42	1.00	3,204
127	LIEBHERR	CH	1,338	2.11	1.89	335	0.15	1.51	5,943
128	FAG KUGELFISCHER	GER	1,298	5.51	2.60	91	0.19	1.14	6,137
129	ROWNTREE	UK	1,269	6.07	1.22	172	0.28	1.59	2,881
130	GRUNDIG	GER	1,220	3.18	1.05	365	0.16	1.52	4,963
131	AXEL SPRINGER	GER	1,203	1.52	1.00	794	0.19	1.00	6,172
132	PWA	GER	1,179	2.16	1.52	359	0.19	1.00	6,172
133	VARITY	CAN	1,138	2.47	2.51	184	0.17	2.03	3,290
134	BARILLA	IT	1,093	6.37	2.17	79	0.27	1.05	3,853
135	COOP MELKPRODUKT NOORD	NL	1,092	1.87	1.00	583	1.09	1.00	1,003
136	ITALMOBILIARE	IT	1,082	3.86	2.08	134	0.28	1.00	3,855
137	PERNOD RICARD	FR	1,079	4.07	2.15	124	0.26	1.04	3,982
138	COCKERILL SAMBRE	BL	1,077	0.62	3.86	449	1.01	1.33	,802
139	GROUPE CARNAUD	FR	1,024	1.06	1.77	546	0.13	2.38	3,288
140	JOHNSON MATTHEY	UK	1,013	0.84	2.94	409	0.18	1.76	3,211
141	DMC	FR	1,004	2.41	3.33	125	0.14	1.66	4,167
142	CARTIERE BURGO	IT	959	1.56	1.76	348	0.25	1.00	3,855
143	GILLETTE	USA	937	2.34	2.54	158	0.07	2.47	5,497
144	NEI	UK	933	0.57	4.20	387	0.29	1.00	3,204
145	KON NEDERLANDSE PAPIER	NL	931	2.51	1.00	372	0.35	2.31	1,148
146	DIEHL	GER	922	1.22	4.89	155	0.13	1.12	6,165
147	NEWS INTERNATIONAL	UK	915	0.98	1.20	777	0.29	1.00	3,204
148	EPEDA-BERTRAND-FAURE	FR	909	0.52	4.47	392	0.16	1.42	3,994
149	CONTINENTAL CAN	USA	895	1.04	1.59	540	0.12	1.80	4,255
150	BPB	UK	871	1.09	3.28	244	0.12	2.43	2,948
151	BRITISH SUGAR	UK	866	5.12	1.28	132	0.27	1.00	3,204

Table A2.2 (cont.)

Firm	Country	FMSIZE	MS	ND	IS	CS	NM	NATS
152 SCHLUMBERGER	USA	862	2.71	2.48	129	0.11	2.08	3,886
153 TRAFALGAR HOUSE	UK	857	0.80	3.98	269	0.22	1.20	3,210
154 SOMMER-ALLIBERT	FR	854	1.54	2.18	255	0.16	1.58	3,432
155 BICC	UK	853	1.40	3.09	197	0.27	1.00	3,204
156 PROUVOST	FR	849	1.08	4.18	188	0.16	1.40	3,850
157 COCA-COLA	USA	844	7.40	1.00	114	0.06	2.59	5,169
158 BLUE CIRCLE	UK	830	4.51	1.48	125	0.26	1.00	3,204
159 TATE & LYLE	UK	816	4.27	1.68	114	0.24	1.21	2,800
160 REDLAND	UK	806	1.56	2.15	240	0.09	3.56	2,574
161 BBA	UK	805	2.31	1.75	199	0.10	2.36	3,500
162 BENETTON	IT	804	1.81	1.72	259	0.19	1.11	3,853
163 CIMENTS FRANCAIS	FR	789	3.06	1.98	130	0.17	1.18	3,948
164 VDO ADOLF SCHINDLING	GER	787	1.32	1.58	378	0.11	1.12	6,159
165 GROUPE VALLOUREC	FR	784	5.35	1.40	105	0.20	1.00	3,982
166 BEKAERT	BL	771	4.36	1.21	146	0.75	1.30	793
167 TARMAC	UK	770	2.50	2.29	135	0.24	1.00	3,204
168 BOEHRINGER MANNHEIM	GER	769	3.19	2.53	95	0.12	1.00	6,172
169 SOCIETE BIC	FR	768	3.38	3.25	70	0.14	1.43	3,961
170 TURNER & NEWALL	UK	748	1.54	4.27	114	0.15	1.55	3,232
171 GUYOMARC'H	FR	730	1.24	1.77	333	0.18	1.00	3,982
172 BOC	UK	715	1.48	2.29	211	0.17	1.28	3,188
173 BREMER VULKAN	GER	710	2.61	1.73	157	0.12	1.00	6,172
174 COOP VERENIGING SUIKER	NL	709	4.14	1.30	131	0.71	1.00	1,003
175 MOD	UK	708	4.60	1.00	154	0.22	1.00	3,204
176 VOITH	GER	707	1.32	3.73	143	0.11	1.00	6,172
177 HAINDL PAPIER	GER	680	2.69	1.00	252	0.10	1.50	4,562
178 ARJOMARI PRIOUX	FR	659	1.89	1.37	255	0.17	1.00	3,982
179 BSC/GKN	UK	659	3.13	1.45	145	0.21	1.00	3,204
180 PIAGGIO	IT	651	15.09	1.14	38	0.14	1.23	3,800

181	VARTA	GER	642	3.54	1.16	156	0.07	1.55	6,022
182	GROUPE NAVIGATION MIXTE	FR	611	0.84	5.96	122	0.15	1.00	3,982
183	RADICI FIL SAS	IT	607	1.98	4.16	74	0.13	1.28	3,791
184	GROUPE ORTIZ	FR	596	1.24	3.44	139	0.15	1.00	3,982
185	GRANDS MOULINS DE PARIS	FR	591	1.44	2.14	192	0.15	1.00	3,982
186	VILLEROY & BOCH	GER	590	3.21	1.31	141	0.06	1.75	5,645
187	KLAUS STEILMANN	GER	589	1.11	1.00	531	0.10	1.00	6,172
188	GFT	IT	587	1.11	1.00	531	0.14	1.11	3,856
189	MARLEY	UK	580	0.72	3.08	261	0.13	1.36	3,220
190	MANIF MARZOTTO E FIGLI	IT	567	1.56	3.72	98	0.15	1.00	3,855
191	BOOTS	UK	564	1.11	2.92	173	0.17	1.01	3,205
192	W SCHLAFHORST	GER	540	6.52	1.00	83	0.09	1.00	6,172
193	VSEL	UK	538	3.06	1.14	154	0.17	1.00	3,204
194	BAHLSEN	GER	534	1.49	1.00	358	0.09	1.00	6,172
195	ASAHI GLASS	JAP	529	2.79	1.00	190	0.52	1.28	790
196	CIA IND DE ABASTECIMIEN	SP	523	2.97	1.00	176	0.28	1.00	1,872
197	CPC	USA	521	1.92	2.81	96	0.07	2.00	3,922
198	HEPWORTH	UK	504	1.22	3.78	110	0.13	1.28	3,093
199	MEYER	UK	499	4.03	1.74	71	0.15	1.01	3,204
200	DYCKERHOFF	GER	487	2.35	1.58	131	0.08	1.00	6,172
201	PETER ECKES	GER	486	3.92	1.00	124	0.08	1.00	6,172
202	POLIET	FR	476	1.53	1.86	167	0.10	1.17	3,973
203	FORNARA	IT	469	2.28	1.13	182	0.06	1.99	3,908
204	PINAULT	FR	458	1.42	3.06	105	0.11	1.00	3,982
205	CA-FIN CASTELVETRO FIN	IT	443	0.68	1.00	647	0.11	1.00	3,855
206	BRITISH RAIL ENGINEERING	UK	433	8.16	1.00	53	0.14	1.00	3,204
207	OELMUHLE HAMBURG	GER	417	2.43	1.00	171	0.07	1.00	6,172
208	MARCEGAGLIA	IT	413	0.69	3.46	174	0.11	1.00	3,855
209	BONDUELLE	FR	409	2.75	1.00	149	0.07	1.77	3,175
210	ESSILOR	FR	408	7.76	1.07	49	0.09	1.09	3,983
211	WESTERN UNITED	UK	382	0.54	1.10	645	0.12	1.00	3,204
212	POLAROID	USA	380	7.75	1.00	49	0.04	3.10	3,494

Table A2.2 (*cont.*)

Firm	Country	FMSIZE	MS	ND	IS	CS	NM	NATS
213 RUGBY GROUP	UK	370	1.04	2.53	140	0.11	1.08	3,205
214 DLW	GER	367	1.86	2.51	79	0.06	1.00	6,172
215 WELLE	GER	353	0.89	1.00	395	0.05	1.21	6,134
216 CHARGEURS	FR	347	0.77	4.02	113	0.08	1.14	3,982
217 PAUL HARTMANN	GER	341	4.06	1.10	76	0.04	1.29	6,100
218 ETERNIT	FR	339	0.85	2.54	158	0.06	1.34	3,978
219 VEREINIGTE KUNSTMUHLEN	GER	336	1.91	1.00	176	0.05	1.00	6,172
220 SALAMANDER	GER	329	1.94	1.00	170	0.05	1.00	6,172
221 FINMAR	IT	320	0.60	1.00	531	0.08	1.00	3,855
222 ROCA RADIADORES	SP	309	1.76	1.00	175	0.17	1.00	1,872
223 HENKELL & SOHNLEIN	GER	302	2.97	1.00	102	0.05	1.00	6,172
224 MAGNET & SOUTHERN	UK	301	0.94	2.02	159	0.08	1.13	3,173
225 PFLEIDERER HOLZWERK	GER	300	2.30	1.80	73	0.05	1.00	6,172
226 REMY & ASSOCIES	FR	297	1.27	2.06	113	0.07	1.00	3,982
227 C & J CLARK	UK	291	1.16	1.44	173	0.09	1.10	3,095
228 VANDEMOORTELE	BL	286	1.67	1.00	171	0.36	1.00	787
229 FOSECO MINSEP	UK	284	3.08	1.92	48	0.03	3.04	3,351
230 NORTON	USA	281	6.85	2.43	17	0.02	3.89	3,839
231 CHARTER CONSOLIDATED	UK	273	0.98	2.86	97	0.09	1.00	3,204
232 IND ZIGNAGO S MARG	IT	264	0.59	2.67	168	0.07	1.00	3,855
233 UCO	BL	262	0.74	2.51	141	0.33	1.00	787
234 AMYLUM	BL	256	7.41	1.00	35	0.33	1.00	787
235 ADOLPH WURTH	GER	250	0.93	1.00	270	0.04	1.00	6,172
236 SALOMON	FR	238	4.88	1.00	49	0.05	1.13	3,987
237 FONTANA LUIGI	IT	238	0.88	1.00	270	0.06	1.00	3,855
238 FININVEST	IT	233	0.97	1.80	133	0.06	1.01	3,855
239 PICANOL	BL	222	2.68	1.00	83	0.28	1.00	787
240 ALNO MOBELWERKE	GER	221	0.56	1.00	395	0.04	1.00	6,172
241 GROUPE ANDRE	FR	216	0.55	2.08	189	0.05	1.00	3,982

	Firm	Country							
242	CAGIVA MOTOR ITALIA	IT	214	3.31	1.64	39	0.06	1.00	3,855
243	ETS LOUIS DE POORTERE	BL	212	2.70	1.22	64	0.19	1.37	809
244	CONCERIE COGOLO	IT	208	2.31	1.00	90	0.05	1.00	3,855
245	IRIS CERAMICA	IT	204	1.46	1.00	140	0.05	1.00	3,855
246	GUCCI GUCCIO	IT	191	0.73	3.72	70	0.05	1.00	3,855
247	CLN-COILS LAMIERE	IT	190	1.38	1.00	138	0.05	1.00	3,855
248	PITTARD GARNAR	UK	189	1.67	1.27	89	0.05	1.27	3,076
249	POGGENPOHL	GER	180	0.46	1.00	395	0.03	1.00	6,172
250	SKIS ROSSIGNOL	FR	179	3.35	1.09	49	0.03	1.59	3,930
251	AMATEX	IT	176	2.12	1.00	83	0.03	1.77	3,832
252	LEGLER IND TESSILE	IT	174	0.91	1.00	192	0.05	1.00	3,855
253	VINCENZO ZUCCHI	IT	173	1.74	1.44	69	0.04	1.00	3,855
254	SFIM	FR	170	1.37	1.44	87	0.04	1.00	3,982
255	MATTEL	USA	170	3.49	1.00	49	0.03	1.00	6,172
256	GEOBRA BRANDSTAETTER	GER	170	3.49	1.00	49	0.02	1.71	4,082
257	WELLMAN-KUCHEN	GER	169	0.43	1.00	395	0.03	1.00	6,172
258	TRINITY ALIMENTAIRE IT	IT	161	1.46	1.47	75	0.04	1.00	3,855
259	ARMSTRONG WORLD IND	USA	154	0.14	3.08	353	0.02	1.26	5,937
260	MARTINI E ROSSI	IT	152	1.37	1.09	102	0.04	1.00	3,855
261	ROSY BLUE	BL	151	1.63	1.00	93	0.19	1.00	787
262	UNDAERRE	IT	147	1.58	1.00	93	0.04	1.00	3,855
263	MARIOVILLA	IT	145	1.56	1.00	93	0.04	1.00	3,855
264	ARA SCHUHFABRIKEN	GER	144	0.85	1.00	170	0.04	1.49	2,256
265	HASBRO	USA	142	2.92	1.00	49	0.03	3.57	1,426
266	B & J GABOR	GER	141	0.83	1.00	170	0.02	1.00	6,172
267	ROYAL MINT	UK	134	1.44	1.00	93	0.04	1.00	3,204
268	RANK ORGANISATION	UK	133	0.75	4.11	43	0.04	1.00	3,204
269	BCI	USA	126	2.49	1.00	50	0.09	1.59	853
270	ROTRING	GER	125	3.07	1.00	41	0.02	1.00	6,172
271	IMETAL	FR	112	0.74	2.08	72	0.03	1.00	3,982
272	OSTERMANN	GER	110	1.50	1.00	73	0.02	1.00	6,172
273	HERMES	FR	106	2.10	1.00	50	0.03	1.00	3,982

Table A2.2 (cont.)

	Firm	Country	FMSIZE	MS	ND	IS	CS	NM	NATS
274	RDB	IT	106	0.56	2.00	94	0.03	1.00	3,855
275	STEIGER & DESCHLER	GER	97	1.16	1.00	83	0.02	1.00	6,172
276	P A LUCKENHAUS	GER	97	1.16	1.00	83	0.02	1.00	6,172
277	RATTI	IT	94	1.12	1.00	83	0.02	1.26	3,857
278	NORDDEUTSCH SCHLEIFMITTEL	GER	92	6.04	1.00	15	0.01	1.00	6,172
279	FINANCIERA MADERERA	SP	86	1.17	1.00	73	0.05	1.00	1,872
280	CARBORUNDUM ABRASIVES	UK	82	5.41	1.00	15	0.01	1.98	4,493
281	FRATELLI FELTRINELLI	IT	82	0.99	1.19	69	0.02	1.00	3,855
282	CONCERIE VAL D'ALPONE	IT	82	0.91	1.00	90	0.02	1.00	3,855
283	NAK STOFFE	GER	78	0.92	1.00	85	0.01	1.00	6,172
284	AMORIM & IRMAOS	PORT	73	3.30	1.00	22	0.33	1.00	222
285	FRATELLI DELECCO	IT	71	1.46	1.10	44	0.02	1.00	3,855
286	HORLOGERE	FR	71	4.24	1.00	17	0.02	1.00	3,982
287	LA BROSSE ET DUPONT	FR	66	3.01	1.00	22	0.02	1.00	3,982
288	BECKER & HACH	GER	65	1.30	1.00	50	0.01	1.00	6,172
289	COLOMER	SP	65	0.72	1.00	90	0.03	1.00	1,872
290	AGNESI	IT	65	1.31	1.11	45	0.02	1.00	3,855
291	STRITMATER	FR	62	2.62	1.00	23	0.02	1.00	3,982
292	COMUS	IT	61	1.06	1.99	29	0.02	1.00	3,855
293	ADDIS	UK	57	0.67	2.00	43	0.02	1.00	3,204
294	MATY	FR	56	3.38	1.00	17	0.01	1.00	3,982
295	MICHELE SOLBIAITI SASIL	IT	54	3.80	1.00	14	0.01	1.00	3,855
296	MIELI WALTER	IT	52	0.63	1.00	83	0.01	1.00	3,855
297	MATH HOHNER	GER	48	5.02	1.00	10	0.01	1.00	6,172
298	SCIAGES ET GRUMES	FR	39	0.56	1.00	69	0.01	1.00	3,982
299	BOOSEY & HAWKES	UK	38	2.67	1.42	10	0.01	2.65	3,564
300	STEINWAY & SONS	GER	36	3.76	1.00	10	0.00	1.00	6,172
301	PIERO DELLA VALENTINA	IT	36	1.03	1.08	32	0.01	1.00	3,855
302	JOMAR	PORT	35	0.50	1.00	69	0.16	1.00	222

303	DE VEZELPERS	NL	32	0.64	1.00	50	0.03	1.00	1,003
304	SOFECOME	FR	28	0.88	1.00	32	0.01	1.00	3,982
305	WILHELM SCHIMMEL	GER	27	2.82	1.00	10	0.00	1.00	6,172
306	RICARDENS	FR	24	1.55	1.00	16	0.01	1.00	3,982
307	SPRUNG FRERES (ETS)	FR	22	1.37	1.00	16	0.01	1.00	3,982
308	RENITEX HOLZ.	GER	21	0.66	1.00	32	0.00	1.00	6,172
309	TRAVHYDRO ECHAFAUDAGES	BL	21	0.37	1.12	50	0.03	1.00	787
310	ARPEL MAN PELLICCE ART	IT	17	1.10	1.00	16	0.00	1.00	3,855
311	TEXAPEL	IT	16	1.02	1.00	16	0.00	1.00	3,855
312	BERGAMIN	IT	16	0.50	1.00	32	0.00	1.00	3,855
313	BANCHI DORIANO	IT	14	0.91	1.00	16	0.00	1.00	3,855

Variable definitions: see Appendix 1. Units: NM and ND are index numbers; MS and CS are percentages; FIRMSIZE: million ecus; IS and NATS: hundred million ecus Key to countries: BL = Belgium CAN = Canada CH = Switzerland CH/SW = Switzerland/Sweden FR = France GER = Germany IT = Italy JAP = Japan NL = Netherlands PORT = Portugal SP = Spain SW = Sweden UK = UK USA = USA

Appendix 3

Data Sources for Explanatory Variables

This appendix lists most of the explanatory variables and reports their data sources. Where appropriate, it explains any non-trivial manipulations we have made on the data. To avoid repetition, it excludes some variables which only appear in a single chapter; in those cases, details are provided at the end of the chapter concerned. It also excludes all variables which are derived directly from the data in the market share matrix. These are defined in Appendix 1.

(a) Industry Types

TYPE2A   = 1 if the industry is advertising-intensive, but not R&D-intensive

             = 0 otherwise

TYPE2R   = 1 if the industry is R&D-intensive, but not advertising intensive

             = 0 otherwise

TYPE2AR = 1 if the industry is both R&D- and advertising-intensive

             = 0 otherwise

Appropriately comprehensive advertising data in the EU are only available for the UK: we have aggregated advertising agency data provided by MEAL to the 3-digit industry level. These figures are expressed relative to UK apparent consumption: national industry size (see below) minus exports plus imports (Source: 'Overseas Trade Analysed in Terms of Industry', 4th quarter 1987: *Business Monitor* MQ10, BSO). Denoting this ratio by *ADSUK*, advertising intensive industries are those for which $ADSUK > 1\%$. The results in the text are not sensitive to small changes in this cut-off point.

R&D data are available for both the UK and Italy. For the UK, the variable is defined as *RDSUK*—the source is the *Business Monitor*, MO14, CSO 1989. Some observations are at the 2-digit level, in which case they were disaggregated to the 3-digit NACE level assuming the same R&D intensity among constituent industries. For Italy, the variable is defined as *RDSIT*; the source is CERIS. These data are at a slightly more aggregate level than the UK data, and are disaggregated in the same way. In order to use both sets of available data, and to make as much use of overlapping detail as possible, we defined industries as R&D intensive if $RDSUK > 1\%$ and $RDSIT > 0.25\%$, or if $RDSUK > 0.25\%$ and $RDSIT > 1\%$. As for advertising, our main results are not sensitive to this cut-off.

(b) Industry size and minimum efficient size

EU Industry Size (EUSIZE)

Published 3-digit EUROSTAT data (*Structure and Activity of Industry*, 1987) are available for 'sales of products manufactured by the Kind of Activity Unit and revenue from industrial services rendered to others' (EUROSTAT code 19 by KAU) expressed in m. ECUs for our base year of 1987. We have made extensive use of the footnotes to make good the numerous gaps in the data. However, these data still only refer to sales by firms employing at least twenty persons (*SALES20+*).

Consequently, we have grossed up these figures to take account of production by smaller firms (which can be a very significant proportion in some industries). No small firm EU data were collected for 1987, but in 1988 data were published at the 2-digit level for sales by smaller firms (*Enterprises in Europe, Second Report*, EUROSTAT, 1992). Further data, disaggregated to the 3-digit level, were kindly supplied by Directorate *D* of EUROSTAT. Unfortunately, this was very incomplete, though coverage of most of our 100 manufacturing industries was available for Belgium, France, Italy, and Portugal. These four countries were assumed to be representative of the EU share of output supplied by small firms *within* each 2-digit NACE industry, and the four-country figures were used to disaggregate the EU figures as follows. Writing:

SMSH2eu = share of industry output supplied by small firms in the EU at the 2-digit level

SMSH2bfip = share of industry output supplied by small firms in the four countries at the 2-digit level

SMSHbfip = share of industry output supplied by small firms in the four countries at the 3-digit level

SMSHeu = share of industry output supplied by small firms in the EU at the 3-digit level

Then:

$$SMSHeu = SMSH2eu * (SMSHbfip / SMSH2bfip)$$

Finally, EU production (*EUSIZE*) is given by the 1987 figure for larger firms, grossed up by *SMSHeu* (for 1988):

$$EUSIZE = SALES20+ / (1-SMSHeu)$$

Minimum efficient size (MES)

MES is expressed in m. ECUs. The basic source for these engineering estimates of minimum efficient size is Pratten, *The Costs of Non-Europe* ii (1987). Unfortunately, many estimates in that survey derive from studies dating back to the 1960s and 1970s. As far as is possible, our estimates refer to technological production economies, and exclude economies of R&D, marketing, etc. Although Pratten's is a comprehensive review of such estimates, there are numerous gaps: some 3-digit industries are not covered; some estimates are not representative of the 3-digit NACE industry; and often the information is not provided as a sales value. Sometimes, for the last problem, we made use of additional data on unit values from, for example, the *UK Annual Abstract of Statistics*, or case studies. (All ECU exchange rates come from Eurostat.) Industries were placed in eleven size classes for *MES* reflecting the 'typical' minimum efficient size. This was felt to be as fine a categorization as the data would allow.

Very often, industries were classified on the assumption that they would have a similar technology to another industry for which a direct estimate was available (e.g. various types of industrial machinery). Some products (e.g. tobacco, cars) have such high demand that they are able to use a distinct level of mass production technology compared with other products of similar composition and complexity (e.g. processed paper, tractors). Such high-demand industries have a higher *MES*. Other product groups (e.g. instruments) tend to be so differentiated that engineering estimates are small relative to apparently similar products (e.g. computers). This suggests a warning that engineering estimates are not as exogenous as is sometimes claimed, and in the long run they must be sensitive to demand conditions.

(c) Concentration

HEU

HEU is estimated using the market-share matrix, supplemented by additional assumptions concerning the sizes of non-matrix firms. This entails the following five step procedure for each industry:

(i) The contribution (i.e. sum of squared shares) from the top five firms, H5, is identified directly from the matrix.

(ii) The contribution of all other known firms is calculated and denoted by *HA*. These firms are either other matrix firms which hold non-leading positions in the industry concerned, or firms for which data were collected at an earlier stage as they were potential candidates for a top five position. This procedure gives an arbitrary number of firms in each Herfindahl, depending on the pattern of diversification and the depth of our quest for firms in each industry. The next stage was designed to standardize on the use of twenty firms for each industry.

(iii) The sizes of firms ranked 6 to 20 were estimated on the basis of a simple size distribution: the Pareto curve with a fixed parameter $\alpha = 1$. We had intended to vary α according to industry, but the following exercise led us back to the simplified distribution. EUROSTAT business-size distribution tables were used to estimate Pareto curves in order to predict the sizes of firms outside the top five. Nearly all estimates of $\log(RANK) = \text{Log}(K) - \alpha \, \text{Log}(SIZE)$ yielded estimates of α insignificantly different from unity (only four industries had $\alpha > 2$). For simplicity, and given the substantial problems of the Eurostat definition of a firm for our purposes, we assumed $\alpha = 1$ to calculate the predicted market shares for the 6th- through 20th-ranked firms. Defining S_i as the market share of the *i*th largest firm, and *CR20* as the 20-firm concentration ratio, then firm shares were calibrated on the share of the 5th largest firm, *S5*; i.e. $S_i = S5 * (5/i)$. In order to avoid double counting with stage (ii), the number and closest sizes of the stage (ii) firms were excluded prior to squaring and summing the market shares calculated in this stage. This sum is denoted by *HB*. Our estimate of the minimum Herfindahl is given by:

$$Hmin = H5 + HA + HB$$

(iv) Hmin would be our best estimate if all shares beyond *S20* were trivial. The maximum extent to which this is an underestimate is given by $HC = [(100 - CR20)/S20] * S20^2$. The term in square brackets is the maximum number of firms possible in the industry if all the remainder were of size equal to the 20th ranked. The maximum possible adjustment is then given by multiplying this number of firms by their squared maximum market shares. *HC* never exceeded 0.005 for any industry. Nevertheless, it gives:

$$Hmax = H5 + HA + HB + HC$$

(v) Our final estimate is given by the average of *Hmin* and *Hmax*:

$$HEU = 0.5 * (Hmin + Hmax)$$

Concentration ratios, C4NAT

C5EU and *C4EU* are derived directly from the matrix.

USA   US four-firm concentration ratios are published only at the 4-digit level (Census of Manufactures), and the aggregation problems are well known. The principal problem is that the extent of diversification by market leaders across constituent 4-digit industries within a 3-digit industry is unknown. A standard response is the 'average' method of aggregation. The maximum level of 3-digit concentration, C_{3d}^X, is given by assuming that the four market leaders are the same firms in each constituent industry, and taking the shipments weighted average of the 4-firm ratios, C_{4d}^V. The minimum, C_{3d}^{N1}, is given by assuming that the top four firms in each constituent industry are the same size and that they are not diversified; so the single 4-digit industry with the largest top four provides the numerator for the 3-digit industry. This can be modified to allow for a distribution of firm sizes within the top four of each industry. We assumed a similar distribution to that within the EU top four in the relevant 3-digit industry to estimate the sizes of all 4-digit leaders; and again assuming no diversification, we could isolate the four largest firms to provide the numerator to C_{3d}^{N2}. The simple average of C_{3d}^X and one of the two 'minimum' estimates give C_{3d}^{V1} and C_{3d}^{V2} respectively. In practice, the allowance for an unequal size distribution within the top four raises the average estimates only slightly (on average, by 0.7% points); though the gap between the maximum and minimum is large (on average, 13.2% points for C_{3d}^{V2}). A problem with this simple average method is that it implicitly assumes (approximately) 50% diversification within all 3-digit industries, independent of the number of constituent 4-digit industries; whereas it seems likely there will be less complete diversification if there are many constituent industries than if there are few.

This thought underlies our second method of adjustment. Although there is no comprehensive set of industry-specific diversification data, Ravenscraft and Scherer (1985) characterize 'typical' 4-digit diversification as a firm with eleven lines contributing 41, 20, 12, 9, 5, 4, 3, 2, 2, 1, and 1% to its domestic manufactured product sales. We approximate this distribution as 50%, 25%, 12.5%, etc. Our diversification 'adjusted' method makes the assumptions that this distribution of activities holds for all market leaders in all industries, and that firms first diversify across constituent 4-digit industries before diversifying more widely. Because of the poor decomposition properties of the concentration ratio, we use an indirect method of adjustment using the Herfindahl index of concentration, H, the Berry numbers equivalent measure of diversification, ND, and a numbers equivalent index of constituent industries (the reciprocal of the Herfindahl of industry sizes). It can be shown that $H_{3d} = H_{4d}^X * ND/NI$, where H_{4d}^X is the weighted average of 4-digit Herfindahls. ND can be calculated using our diversification assumptions (e.g. for $NI = 2$, leaders are assumed to have a half their total output in their primary industry and a quarter in the next, so within the 3-digit industry, $ND = 1/[0.67^2 + 0.33^2] = 1.8$), with interpolations for intermediate values. Next, we assumed that the average (log-linear regression) relationship between the EU 3-digit Herfindahl of concentration and the EU concentration ratio, $ln(HEU) = -9 + 1.7 \, ln(EU \, CR4)$, holds at both the 3- and 4-digit levels in the USA. Then our diversification adjusted measure of 3-digit concentration is $ln(C_{3d}^J) = ln(C_{3d}^X) + ln(ND/NI)/1.7$. In general, $C_{3d}^J > C_{3d}^X$ if there are few constituent 4-digit industries, and the reverse if there are many. In practice, the weighted average of C_{3d}^J is 1.3% points higher than C_{3d}^V, and the smallness of this difference adds a little confidence to our comparisons between the EU and USA. In the text, we have used C_{3d}^{V2}, since it is most easily understood. Full details of these comparisons are available in Lyons (in preparation).

Germany   Where necessary, concentration data were aggregated from 4-digit *SYPRO* to 3-digit *NACE* using a weighted average of the constituent industries using the same average method as for the USA. In fact, the German SYPRO is at the 3-digit level for most industries. Data was for *CR3* and *CR6* only. Pareto's Law was used to interpolate *CR4* (see Italy below). If only *CR6* and/or *CR10* were available, *CR4* could still be extrapolated but there was obviously a greater margin of error. Additional industry-size data were derived from *Statistisches Bundesamt, 1987/88*, converted from SYPRO/WZ1979 (German code) into NACE.

UK Adjustments to the *Census of Production (1986)* 5-firm sales concentration ratios were made using detailed estimates of market shares within the top five (using a similar methodology to the EU market share estimates). Additional industry size data from *Census of Production, 1986: PA1002*.

Italy Derived from the ISTAT size distribution tables using employment (as information was unavailable by sales). Typically, there were more than four firms in the largest size class. Interpolations were then made by assuming a Pareto distribution of firm sizes within the top class, and applying Van der Vijk's Law. Pareto's Law states that the number of firms of size greater than s is given by $N(s) = \beta s^{-\alpha}$ for $s > s^0$ and $\alpha > 0$. Van der Vijk's Law states that within the largest size class of firms, $s' = s_L (\alpha/\alpha-1)$ where s' is the average size of these leading firms and s_L is the class lower bound. This provides an estimate of α to substitute into the equation of Pareto's Law, and thus provide an estimate of *CR4*. The 1987 *CR4s* correlated closely with 1983 *CR4s* estimated using more detailed information by the CERIS institute, Turin. Additional industry-size data were taken from ISTAT size-distribution tables, 1987.

(d) Other industry variables

TRS: Total transport costs relative to sales. Such data are rarely collected in a systematic manner. An exception was the UK 1968 Census of Production, which collected details of wages, salaries, fuel, tyres, spare parts for vehicles, payments to other organizations for transport (road, rail, and other except postal), and costs of operating road goods vehicles (insurance, licences, depreciation, and maintenance). These costs were expressed relative to 1968 production, and reclassified from the SIC (1968) to the NACE.

NTB: The level of non-tariff barriers: low = 1, moderate = 2, and high = 3. Source: *European Economy, 1990*, table 2.1, supplemented by Buigues and Ilkovitch, 'The Sectoral Impact of the Internal Market' (CEC document II/335/88-EN).

REG: A dummy variable indicating whether or not government regulation is important in the industry concerned. Source: *European Economy, 1990*, table 2.1, supplemented by Buigues and Ilkovitch, 'The Sectoral Impact of the Internal Market' (CEC document II/335/88-EN).

PUB: A dummy variable indicating whether or not public procurement is important in the industry concerned. Source: *European Economy, 1990*, table 2.1, supplemented by Buigues and Ilkovitch, 'The Sectoral Impact of the Internal Market' (CEC document II/335/88-EN).

HET: A measure of the heterogeneity of the industry. This is the (log) count of the number of different activities listed in each 3-digit industry.

TRADE: Intra-EU trade relative to apparent EU consumption (i.e. production plus imports minus exports). Trade data provided by Eurostat. In all chapters except chapter 5, we work with the average of measured intra-EU imports and intra-EU exports. These should be the same, but differ slightly due to measurement error. The actual difference is, for our purposes, relatively minor. Chapter 5 is an exception because the decomposition we develop suggests the use of total imports plus exports in the numerator (i.e. twice the figure used elsewhere).

Extra-EU trade data were derived from the same source. Note that there are some classification problems with the trade data. NACE 373 (optical instruments), 456 (fur), and 491 (jewellery) have both import and export ratios >100%. Data for 251 (basic chemicals) is taken as trade categories 252 and 253. Trade categories 431 and 432 (also known as 43A and 43B) include NACE 431 and 432, plus 433 (silk), 434 (flax and hemp), and 437 (textile finishing). Thus, where used, textile figures are aggregated and then disaggregated according to production. Also 495 (miscellaneous manuf.) appears to have been used as a dustbin for odd categories and records massive trade, so it has been treated as not available. Whenever precise estimates are required in the book (e.g. for econometric estimation), we have tried to exclude these industries with the most dubious trade statistics.

INV, *INT* and *GOV*: Percentage of industry supply sold to other firms as investment goods (*INV*), to other firms as intermediate inputs (*INT*) and to government agencies (*GOV*). The basic data sources were the UK *Input–Output Tables for 1984* and the Italian *Input–Output Tables for 1985*. In both cases, the domestic and import use matrices were combined, and exports were subtracted (on the implicit assumption that the share going to consumers is the same in other countries). Thus, we have estimates of the percentage industry supply (production – exports + imports) sold to various categories of purchaser for the UK and Italy. The UK data were less aggregated (seventy-nine I–O industries covering NACE 2–5, compared with fifty-two for Italy), so the UK figures formed the base, which was adjusted to take account of additional information in the Italian figures. In general, the constituent NACE industries were assumed to have the same customer sales ratio as the more aggregate *I–O* industry, but a small number of *ad hoc* adjustments were made to some of the most aggregated figures where this seemed appropriate on the basis of the range of products made by individual industries.

Bibliography

Abravanel, R. and Ernst, D. (1992), 'Alliance and Acquisition Strategies for European National Champions', *The McKinsey Quarterly*, no. 2: 45–62.

Adelman, M. (1969), 'Comment on the "H" Concentration Measure as a Numbers Equivalent', *Review of Economics and Statistics*, 51: 99–101.

Agarwal, J. P. (1980), 'Determinants of Foreign Direct Investment: A Survey', *Weltwirtschaftliches Archiv*, 116: 739–73.

Ansoff, I. (1987), *Corporate Strategy*, New York: McGraw-Hill.

Berry, C. (1975), *Corporate Growth and Diversification*, Princeton: Princeton University Press.

Buckley, P. J. and Casson, M. (1976), *The Future of Multinational Enterprise*, London: Macmillan Press.

—— —— (1985), *The Economic Theory of the Multinational Enterprise*, London: Macmillan Press.

Buigues, P., Ilzkovitz, F. and Lebrun, J.-F. (1990), *Social Europe*, 'The Impact of the Internal Market by Industrial Sector: The Challenge for the Member States', special edition of *European Economy*.

Buigues, P. and Jacquemin, A. (1994), 'Foreign Direct Investment and Exports to the European Community', in M. Mason and D. Encornation (eds), *Does Ownership matter?*, Oxford: Clarendon Press.

Caves, R. (1974), 'Multinational Firms, Competition and Productivity in Host Country Industries', *Economica*, 41: 176–93.

—— (1982), *Multinational Enterprise and Economic Analysis*, Cambridge: Cambridge University Press.

Clarke, R. (1987), *Industrial Economics*, Oxford: Blackwell.

—— and Davies, S. W. (1983), 'Aggregate Concentration, Market Concentration, and Diversification', *Economic Journal*, 93. 182–92.

—— —— (1984), 'On Measuring Diversification and Concentration', *Economic Letters*, 15: 145–52.

Coase, R. H. (1937), 'The Nature of the Firm', *Economica*, 4: 386–405.

Commission of the European Communities (1993), *XXIInd Report on Competition Policy 1992*, Luxemburg.

Curry, B. and George, K. (1983), 'Industrial Concentration: A Survey', *Journal of Industrial Economics*, 31: 203–55.

Dasgupta, P. and Stiglitz, J. (1980), 'Industrial Structure and the Nature of Innovative Activity', *Economic Journal*, 90: 266–93.

Davies, S. W. (1979*a*), *Diffusion of Process Innovations*, Cambridge: Cambridge University Press.

—— (1979*b*), 'Choosing Between Concentration Indices: The Iso-Concentration Curve', *Economica*, 46: 67–75.

—— (1992), *European Community Direct Investment 1984–1989*, Luxemburg: Office for Official Publications of the European Communities.

—— (1995), 'Aggregate Concentration in the European Union', UEA Working Paper.

Davies, S. W. and Lyons, B. R. (1988), *Economics of Industrial Organisation*, London: Longman Group UK.

—— —— (1980), 'Theories of Horizontal MNEs', mimeo, University of East Anglia.

—— —— (1991), 'Characterizing Relative Performance: The Productivity Advantage of Foreign-Owned Firms in the UK', *Oxford Economic Papers*, 43: 584–95.

—— and Morris, C. (1991), 'A Market Share Matrix: UK Manufacturing, 1986', University of East Anglia Discussion Paper No. 9105.

—— Geroski, P., Lund, M., and Vlassopoulos, A. (1991), *The Dynamics of Market Leadership in the UK Manufacturing Industry, 1979–1986*, Centre for Business Strategy, London Business School.

Demsetz, H. (1973), 'Industry Structure, Market Rivalry and Public Policy', *Journal of Law and Economics*, 16: 24–37.

Dixit, A. and Stiglitz, J. (1977), 'Monopolistic Competition and Optimum Product Differentiation', *American Economic Review*, 67: 297–308.

Doi, N. (1991), 'Aggregate Export Concentration in Japan', *Journal of Industrial Economics*, 39: 433–38.

Dunning, J. H. (1979), 'Explaining Changing Patterns of International Production: In Defence of the Eclectic Theory', *Oxford Bulletin of Economics and Statistics*, 41/4: 269–95.

—— (1981), 'Explaining the International Direct Investment Position of Countries: Towards a Dynamic or Developmental Approach', *Weltwirtschaftliches Archiv*, Heft 1: 30–64.

—— (1982), 'Multinational Enterprises in the 1970's', in H. Kopt (ed.), *European Merger contract*, Berlin: De fruyter.

—— (1988), 'The Eclectic Paradigm of International Production: A Restatement and some Possible Extensions', *Journal of International Business Studies*, 19/1: 1–31.

—— (1993), *The Globalisation of Business: The Challenge of the 1990s*, London and New York: Routledge.

Dun's Europa, (1991), Dun & Bradstreet Europe.

Emerson, M., Aujean, M., Catinat, M., Goybet, P., and Jacquemin, A. (1988), *The Economics of 1992*, Oxford: Oxford University Press.

Eurostat NACE: General Industrial Classification of Economic Activities within the European Communities (1985), Luxemburg: Office for Official Publications of the European Community.

Europe's 15000 Largest Companies (1989), London: ELC International.

Eurostat (1990), *Structure and Activity of Industry: 1986–1988*, Luxemburg: Office for Official Publications of the European Community.

—— (1993), *Basic Statistics of the Community, 1993*, 30th edn., Luxemburg.

France 30000 (1991), Paris: Dun & Bradstreet International.

Gabszewicz, J. and Thisse, J. F. (1980), 'Entry (and Exit) in a Differentiated Industry', *Journal of Economic Theory*, 22: 327–38.

George, K. and Ward, T. (1975), *The Structure of Industry in the EEC*, Cambridge: Cambridge University Press.

Golbe, D. L. and White L. J. (1988), 'A Time-Series Analysis of Mergers and Acquisitions in the US Economy', in A. Auerbach (ed.), *Corporate Take-Overs: Causes and Consequences*, London: University of Chicago Press.

Greenaway, D. and Milner, C. R. (1989), 'The Growth and Significance of

Intra-industry Trade' in J. Black and A. MacBean (eds.), *Causes of Changes in the Structure of International Trade*, London: Macmillan Press.

Grossman, G. (1981), 'The Theory of Domestic Content Protection and Content Preference', *Quarterly Journal of Economics*, 21: 583–603.

—— and Shapiro, C. (1984), 'Informative Advertising with Differentiated Products', *Review of Economic Studies*, 51: 33–52.

HMSO (1978), *A Review of Monopolies and Mergers Policy* (Green Paper), Cmnd. 7198, London: HMSO.

—— (1981), *Indexes to the Standard Industrial Classification*, rev. 1980, London: CSO.

Hamilton, R. T. (1992), 'Diversification and Concentration Changes in a Liberalised Environment: The Case of New Zealand Manufacturing Industries', *International Journal of Industrial Organisation*, 10: 15–25.

Hannah, L. and Kay, J. A. (1977), *Concentration in Modern Industry: Theory, Measurement and the UK experience*, London: Macmillan Press.

Hay, D. and Morris, D. (1991), *Industrial Economics and Organization: Theory and evidence*, Oxford: Oxford University Press.

Helpman, E. and Krugman, P. R. (1985), *Market Structure and Foreign Trade*, Cambridge, Mass.: MIT Press.

Hirsch, S. (1976), 'An International Trade and Investment Theory of the Firm', *Oxford Economic Papers*, 28: 258–71.

Hollander, A. (1987), 'Content Protection and Transnational Monopoly', *Journal of International Economics*, 23: 283–97.

Hymer, S. (1976), *The International Operation of National Firms: A Study of Foreign Direct Investment*, Cambridge Mass.: MIT Press.

Ingham, I. and Thomson, S. (1992), 'Deregulation, Firm Capabilities and Diversifying Entry Decisions: The Case of Financial Services', mimeo.

Jacquemin, A. and Sapir, A. (1988), 'International trade and integration of the European Community', *European Economic Review*, 32: 1439–50.

Key British Enterprises (1987), London: Dun & Bradstreet, Business Marketing Division.

Kompass, *United Kingdom (1987)*, East Grinstead: Kompass Publishers Ltd.

Krugman, P. R. (1979), 'Increasing Returns, Monopolistic Competition, and International Trade', *Journal of International Economics*, 9: 469–79.

—— (1980), 'Scale Economies, Product Differentiation and the Patterns from Trade', *American Economic Review*, 70: 950–59.

—— (1981), 'Intra-Industry Specialisation and the Gains from Trade', *Journal of Political Economy*, 89: 959–73.

—— (1991), *Geography and Trade*, Cambridge, Mass.: MIT Press.

—— and Venables, A. (1990), 'Integration and the Competitiveness of Peripheral Industry', in C. Bliss and J. Braga, *Unity with Diversity in the European Community*, Cambridge: Cambridge University Press.

Lemelin, A. (1982), 'Relatedness in the Patterns of Inter-Industry Diversification', *Review of Economics and Statistics*, 64: 646–57.

Linder, S. B. (1961), *An Essay on Trade and Transformation*, New York: Wiley.

Loertscher, O. and Wolter, F. (1980), 'Determinants of Intra-Industry Trade Among Countries and Across Industries', *Weltwirtschlafiches Archiv*, 8: 280–93.

Lyons, B. R. (1984), 'The Pattern of International Trade in Differentiated Products: An Incentive for the Existence of Multinational Firms', in H. Kierzkowski (ed.), *Monopolistic Competition and International Trade*, Oxford: Clarendon Press.

Lyons, B. R. and Matraves, C. (1995), 'Industrial Concentration and Endogenous Sunk Costs in the European Union', University of East Anglia Discussion Paper No. 9505.

MacDonald, J. M. (1985), 'R&D and the Direction of Diversification', *Review of Economics and Statistics*, 67: 583–90.

McLachlan, D. L. (1985), 'Discriminatory Public Procurement, Economic Integration and the Role of Bureaucracy', *Journal of Common Market Studies*, 23/4: 357–72.

Marris, R. (1964), *The Economic Theory of Managerial Capitalism*, New York: Free Press.

Martin, S. (1991), 'Direct Foreign Investment in the United States', *Journal of Economic Behaviour and Organisation*, 19: 283–93.

Montgomery, C. A. and Hariharan, S. (1991), 'Diversified Expansion by Large Established Firms', *Journal of Economic Behaviour and Organisation* , 15: 71–89.

NEI, *New Location Factors for Mobile Investment in Europe* (1993), Luxemburg, Netherlands Economic Institute in co-operation with Ernst & Young, Commission of the European Communities, DG for Regional Policies, Regional Development Studies, No. 6.

Neven, D. and Roller, L. H. (1991), 'European Integration and Trade Flows', *European Economic Review*, 35: 1295–1309.

Owen, R. (1982), 'Inter-Industry Determinants of Foreign Direct Investments: A Canadian perspective', in A. Rugman (ed), *New Theories of the Multinational Enterprise*, London: Croom-Helm.

Panorama of EC Industry, (1990, 1994), Luxemburg: Commission of the European Communities.

Penrose, E. (1959), *The Theory of the Growth of the Firm*, London: Oxford University Press.

Porter, M. E. (1990), *The Competitive Advantage of Nations*, London: Macmillan Press.

Prahalad, C. K. and Doz, Y. (1987), *The Multinational Mission, Balancing Local Demands and Global Vision*, New York: Free Press.

Prais, S. (1976), *The Evolution of Giant Firms in Britain*, Cambridge: Cambridge University Press.

Pratten, C. (1987), *A Survey of Economies of Scale*, Report prepared for the European Commission, Brussels.

Prescott, E. and Visscher, M (1980), 'Organisation Capital', *Journal of Political Economy*, 88: 48–61.

Ravenscraft, D. and Scherer, F. M. (1985), *Mergers, Sell-offs and Economic Efficiency*, Washington, DC: Brookings Institution.

Richardson, M. (1991), 'The Effects of a Content Requirement on a Foreign Duopsonist', *Journal of International Economics*, 31: 143–55.

Rubin, P. H. (1973), 'The Expansion of Firms', *Journal of Political Economy*, 81: 936–49.

Rumelt, R. P. (1974), *Strategy, Structure and Economic Performance*, Cambridge, Mass.: Harvard University Press.

Saunders, R. (1982), 'The Determinants of Inter-Industry Variation of Foreign-Ownership in Canadian Manufacturing', *Canadian Journal of Economics*, 25: 77–84.

Scherer, F. M. (1980), *Industrial Market Structure and Economic Performance*, 2nd edn., Chicago: Rand-McNally.

Schmalensee, R. (1992), 'Sunk Costs and Market Structure: A Review Article', *Journal of Industrial Economics*, 40/2: 125–34.

Schwalbach, J. (1987), 'Entry by Diversified Firms into German Industry', *International Journal of Industrial Organisation*, 5: 43–9.

Shaked, A. and Sutton, J. (1983), 'Natural Oligopolies', *Econometrica*, 51: 1469–84.

Sleuwaegen, L., Goedhuys M., Plaetinck H., and de Backer, K. (1992), 'De Toekomst van de Belgische Defensie-industrie: Industrieel-strategische aspecten', Leuven, Belg.: Katholieke Universiteit.

Smith, A. (1987), 'Strategic Investment, Multinational Corporations and Trade Policy', *European Economic Review*, 31: 89–96.

Stafford, D. and Purkis, R. (1989), *Macmillan Directory of Multinationals*, i and ii, London: Macmillan Publishers Ltd.

Stewart, J., Harris R., and Carleton, W. (1984), 'The Role of Market Structure in Merger Behaviour', *Journal of Industrial Economics*, 32: 293–312.

Sutton, J. (1991) *Sunk Costs and Market Structure: Price Competition, Advertising, and the Evolution of Concentration*, Cambridge, Mass.: MIT Press.

—— (1995*a*), 'One Smart Agent', LSE Working Paper.

—— (1995*b*), 'The Size Distribution of Businesses, part 1: A "bounds" approach', LSE Working Paper.

Teece, D. (1980), 'Economies of Scope and the Scope of the Enterprise', *Journal of Economic Behaviour and Organisation*, 1: 223–47.

—— (1982), 'Towards an Economic Theory of the Multiproduct Firm', *Journal of Economic Behaviour and Organisation*, 3: 39–63.

Thomsen, S. and Nicolaides, P. (1991), *The Evolution of Japanese Direct Investment in Europe: Death of a Salesman*, London: Royal Institute of International Affairs.

Tirole, J. (1988), *The Theory of Industrial Organization*, Cambridge, Mass.: MIT Press.

Truman, E. M. (1975), 'The Effect of European Economic Integration on the Production and Trade of Manufactured Products', in B. Balassa (ed), *European Economic Integration*, Amsterdam: North Holland.

United Nations (1991), *Handbook of International Trade and Development Statistics*.

Utton, M. A. (1979), *Diversification and Competition*, Cambridge: Cambridge University Press.

Vandermerwe, S., 'A Framework for Constructing Euro-Networks', *European Management Journal*, 11: 55–61.

Veugelers, R. (1994), 'Alliances and the Pattern of Comparative Advantages: A Sectoral Analysis', in *International Business Review* (forthcoming).

Vousden, N. (1987), 'Content Protection and Tariffs Under Monopoly and Competition', *Journal of International Economics*, 23: 263–82.

White, L. J. (1981), 'What Has Been Happening to Aggregate Concentration in the US?', *Journal of Industrial Economics*, 29: 223–30.

Who Owns Whom 1990: Continental Europe, (1990), i & ii, Dun & Bradstreet International.

Williamson, O. (1975), *Markets and Hierarchies, Analysis and Antitrust Implications*, New York: Free Press.

—— (1981), 'The Modern Corporation, Origins, Evolution, Attributes', *Journal of Economic Literature*, 19: 1537–68.

—— (1985), *The Economic Institution of Capitalism: Firms, Markets and Relational Contracting*, New York: Free Press.

Yip, G. (1982), *Barriers to Entry: A Corporate Strategy Perspective*, Lexington: Lexington Books.

Index